W9-AYM-985

MOTOROLA

MC68020

32–BIT MICROPROCESSOR
USER'S MANUAL

Second Edition

PRENTICE-HALL, Inc., Englewood Cliffs, N.J. 07632

ISBN: 0-13-566860-3 (Prentice-Hall edition)

ISBN: 0-13-566878-6 (Motorola edition)

Printed in the United States of America

10 9 8 7 6 5 4

ISBN 0-13-566860-3 01 {PRENTICE-HALL ED.}

ISBN 0-13-566878-6 01 {MOTOROLA ED.}

Prentice-Hall International (UK) Limited, *London*
Prentice-Hall of Australia Pty. Limited, *Sydney*
Prentice-Hall Canada Inc., *Toronto*
Prentice-Hall Hispanoamericana, S.A., *Mexico*
Prentice-Hall of India Private Limited, *New Delhi*
Prentice-Hall of Japan, Inc., *Tokyo*
Prentice-Hall Southeast Asia Pte. Ltd., *Singapore*
Editora Prentice-Hall do Brasil, Ltda., *Rio de Janeiro*
Whitehall Books Limited, *Wellington, New Zealand*

TABLE OF CONTENTS

TABLE OF CONTENTS
(Continued)

Section 3
Instruction Set Summary

Section 4
Signal Description

TABLE OF CONTENTS
(Continued)

TABLE OF CONTENTS
(Continued)

TABLE OF CONTENTS
(Continued)

TABLE OF CONTENTS
(Continued)

TABLE OF CONTENTS
(Continued)

TABLE OF CONTENTS
(Continued)

Section 9
Instruction Execution Timing

TABLE OF CONTENTS
(Concluded)

Section 10
Electrical Specifications

Section 11
Ordering Information and Mechanical Data

APPENDICES

LIST OF ILLUSTRATIONS

LIST OF ILLUSTRATIONS
(Continued)

LIST OF ILLUSTRATIONS
(Continued)

LIST OF ILLUSTRATIONS
(Concluded)

LIST OF TABLES

LIST OF TABLES
(Concluded)

SECTION 1
INTRODUCTION

The MC68020 is the first full 32-bit implementation of the M68000 Family of micro-processors from Motorola. Using VLSI technology, the MC68020 is implemented with 32-bit registers and data paths, 32-bit addresses, a rich instruction set, and versatile addressing modes.

The MC68020 is object code compatible with the earlier members of the M68000 Family and has the added features of new addressing modes in support of high level languages, an on-chip instruction cache, and a flexible coprocessor interface with full IEEE floating-point support (the MC68881). Also, the internal operations of this microprocessor are designed to operate in parallel, allowing multiple instructions to be executed concurrently. The execution time of an instruction can be completely absorbed by the execution time of surrounding instructions for a net execution time of zero clock periods.

The asynchronous bus structure of the MC68020 utilizes a non-multiplexed bus with 32 bits of address and 32 bits of data. The processor supports a dynamic bus sizing mechanism that allows the processor to transfer operands to or from external devices while automatically determining device port size on a cycle-by-cycle basis. The dynamic bus interface allows for simple, highly efficient access to devices of differing data bus widths, in addition to eliminating all data alignment restrictions.

The resources available to the MC68020 user consist of the following:
- Virtual Memory/Machine Support
- Sixteen 32-Bit General-Purpose Data and Address Registers
- Two 32-Bit Supervisor Stack Pointers
- 32-Bit Program Counter
- Five Special Purpose Control Registers
- 4 Gigabyte Direct Addressing Range
- Two Processor Speeds: 12 and 16 MHz
- 18 Addressing Modes
- Memory Mapped I/O
- Coprocessor Interface
- High Performance On-Chip Instruction Cache
- 32-Bit Upgraded and New Instructions
- Operations on Seven Data Types
- Complete Floating-Point Support via the MC68881 Coprocessor

A block diagram of the MC68020 is shown in Figure 1-1. The major blocks depicted operate in a highly independent fashion that maximizes concurrency of operation while managing the essential synchronization of instruction execution and bus operation.

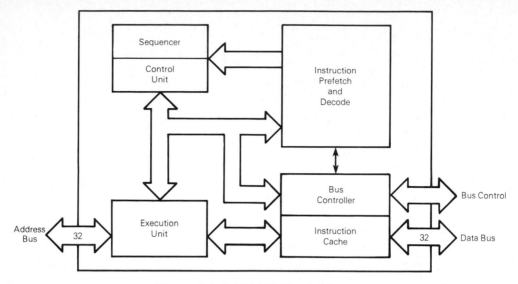

Figure 1-1. MC68020 Block Diagram

The bus controller loads instructions from the data bus into the decode unit and the on-chip cache. The sequencer and control unit provide overall chip control, managing the internal buses, registers, and functions of the execution unit.

As shown in the programming models (Figures 1-2 and 1-3), the MC68020 has 16 32-bit general-purpose registers, a 32-bit program counter, a 16-bit status register, a 32-bit vector base register, two 3-bit alternate function code registers, and two 32-bit cache handling (address and control) registers. Registers D0-D7 are used as data registers for bit and bit field (1 to 32 bits), byte (8-bit), word (16-bit), long word (32-bit), and quad word (64-bit) operations. Registers A0-A6 and the user, interrupt, and master stack pointers are address registers that may be used as software stack pointers or base address registers. In addition, the address registers may be used for word and long word operations. All of the 16 (D0-D7, A0-A7) registers may be used as index registers.

The vector base register is used to determine the location of the exception vector table in memory to support multiple vector tables. The alternate function code registers allow the supervisor to access any address space.

The cache registers (control — CACR; address — CAAR) allow software manipulation of the on-chip instruction cache. Control and status accesses to the instruction cache are provided by the cache control register (CACR), while the cache address register (CAAR) holds the address for cache control functions when required.

The status register (Figure 1-4) contains the interrupt priority mask (three bits) as well as the condition codes: extend (X), negative (N), zero (Z), overflow (V), and carry (C). Additional control bits indicate that the processor is in the trace mode (T1 and T0), supervisor/user state (S), and master/interrupt state (M).

1

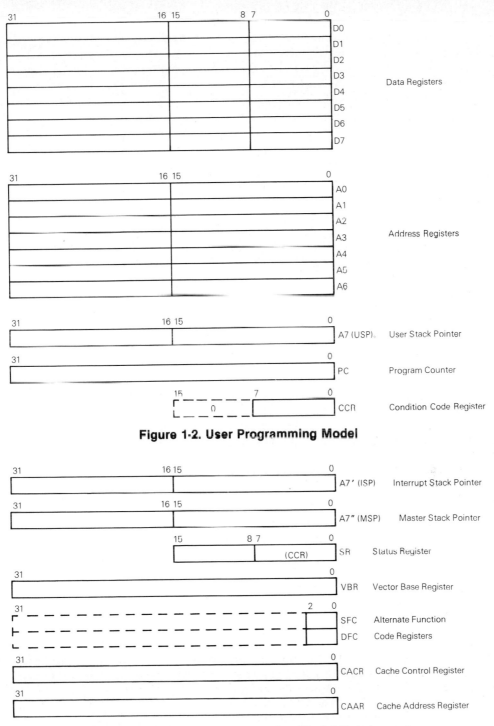

Figure 1-2. User Programming Model

Figure 1-3. Supervisor Programming Model Supplement

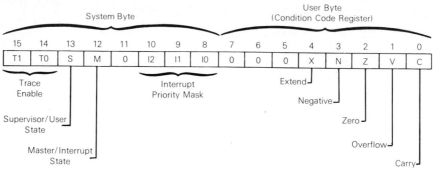

Figure 1-4. Status Register

1.1 DATA TYPES AND ADDRESSING MODES

Seven basic data types are supported. These data types are:

- Bits
- Bit Fields (Field of consecutive bits, 1-32 bits long)
- BCD Digits (Packed: 2 digits/byte, Unpacked: 1 digit/byte)
- Byte Integers (8 bits)
- Word Integers (16 bits)
- Long Word Integers (32 bits)
- Quad Word Integers (64 bits)

In addition, operations on other data types such as memory addresses, status word data, etc., are supported in the instruction set. The coprocessor mechanism allows direct support of floating-point operations with the MC68881 floating-point coprocessor, as well as specialized user-defined data types and functions.

The 18 addressing modes, shown in Table 1-1, include nine basic types:

- Register Direct
- Register Indirect
- Register Indirect with Index
- Memory Indirect
- Program Counter Indirect with Displacement
- Program Counter Indirect with Index
- Program Counter Memory Indirect
- Absolute
- Immediate

Included in the register indirect addressing modes are the capabilities to postincrement, predecrement, offset, and index. The program counter relative mode also has index and offset capabilities. Both modes are extended in the MC68020 to provide indirect reference through memory. In addition to these addressing modes, many instructions implicitly specify the use of the condition code register, stack pointer, and/or program counter.

Table 1-1. Addressing Modes

Addressing Modes	Syntax
Register Direct	
Data Register Direct	Dn
Address Register Direct	An
Register Indirect	
Address Register Indirect	(An)
Address Register Indirect with Postincrement	(An) +
Address Register Indirect with Predecrement	− (An)
Address Register Indirect with Displacement	(d_{16},An)
Register Indirect with Index	
Address Register Indirect with Index (8-Bit Displacement)	(d_8,An,Xn)
Address Register Indirect with Index (Base Displacement)	(bd,An,Xn)
Memory Indirect	
Memory Indirect Post-Indexed	([bd,An],Xn,od)
Memory Indirect Pre-Indexed	([bd,An,Xn],od)
Program Counter Indirect with Displacement	(d_{16},PC)
Program Counter Indirect with Index	
PC Indirect with Index (8-Bit Displacement)	(d_8,PC,Xn)
PC Indirect with Index (Base Displacement)	(bd,PC,Xn)
Program Counter Memory Indirect	
PC Memory Indirect Post-Indexed	([bd,PC],Xn,od)
PC Memory Indirect Pre-Indexed	([bd,PC,Xn],od)
Absolute	
Absolute Short	(xxx).W
Absolute Long	(xxx).L
Immediate	#<data>

NOTES:

  Dn = Data Register, D0-D7

  An = Address Register, A0-A7

d_8, d_{16} = A twos-complement, or sign-extended displacement, added as part of the effective address calculation, size is 8 or 16 bits (d_{16} and d_8 are 16- and 8-bit displacements); when omitted, assemblers use a value of zero.

  Xn = Address or data register used as an index register, form is Xn.SIZE*SCALE, where SIZE is .W or .L (indicates index register size) and SCALE is 1, 2, 4, or 8 (index register is multiplied by SCALE); use of SIZE and/or SCALE is optional.

  bd = A twos-complement base displacement; when present, size can be 16 or 32 bits.

  od = Outer displacement, added as part of effective address calculation after any memory indirection; use is optional with a size of 16 or 32 bits.

  PC = Program Counter

<data> = Immediate value of 8, 16, or 32 bits

  ( ) = Effective address

  [ ] = Use as indirect address to long word address.

1.2 INSTRUCTION SET OVERVIEW

The MC68020 instruction set is shown in Table 1-2. Special emphasis has been placed on the instruction support of structured high-level languages and sophisticated operating systems. Each instruction, with few exceptions, operates on bytes, words, and long words and most instructions can use any of the 18 addressing modes.

Table 1-2. Instruction Set Summary

Mnemonic	Description	Mnemonic	Description
ABCD	Add Decimal with Extend	MULS	Signed Multiply
ADD	Add	MULU	Unsigned Multiply
ADDA	Add Address	NBCD	Negate Decimal with Extend
ADDI	Add Immediate	NEG	Negate
ADDQ	Add Quick	NEGX	Negate with Extend
ADDX	Add with Extend	NOP	No Operation
AND	Logical AND	NOT	Logical Complement
ANDI	Logical AND Immediate	OR	Logical Inclusive OR
ASL, ASR	Arithmetic Shift Left and Right	ORI	Logical Inclusive OR Immediate
Bcc	Branch Conditionally	PACK	Pack BCD
BCHG	Test Bit and Change	PEA	Push Effective Address
BCLR	Test Bit and Clear	RESET	Reset External Devices
BFCHG	Test Bit Field and Change	ROL, ROR	Rotate Left and Right
BFCLR	Test Bit Field and Clear	ROXL, ROXR	Rotate with Extend Left and Right
BFEXTS	Signed Bit Field Extract	RTD	Return and Deallocate
BFEXTU	Unsigned Bit Field Extract	RTE	Return from Exception
BFFFO	Bit Field Find First One	RTM	Return from Module
BFINS	Bit Field Insert	RTR	Return and Restore Codes
BFSET	Test Bit Field and Set	RTS	Return from Subroutine
BFTST	Test Bit Field	SBCD	Subtract Decimal with Extend
BKPT	Breakpoint	Scc	Set Conditionally
BRA	Branch	STOP	Stop
BSET	Test Bit and Set	SUB	Subtract
BSR	Branch to Subroutine	SUBA	Subtract Address
BTST	Test Bit	SUBI	Subtract Immediate
CALLM	Call Module	SUBQ	Subtract Quick
CAS	Compare and Swap Operands	SUBX	Subtract with Extend
CAS2	Compare and Swap Dual Operands	SWAP	Swap Register Words
CHK	Check Register Against Bound	TAS	Test Operand and Set
CHK2	Check Register Against Upper and Lower Bounds	TRAP	Trap
		TRAPcc	Trap Conditionally
CLR	Clear	TRAPV	Trap on Overflow
CMP	Compare	TST	Test Operand
CMPA	Compare Address	UNLK	Unlink
CMPI	Compare Immediate	UNPK	Unpack BCD
CMPM	Compare Memory to Memory		
CMP2	Compare Register Against Upper and Lower Bounds	**COPROCESSOR INSTRUCTIONS**	
DBcc	Test Condition, Decrement and Branch	cpBcc	Branch Conditionally
DIVS, DIVSL	Signed Divide	cpDBcc	Test Coprocessor Condition, Decrement, and Branch
DIVU, DIVUL	Unsigned Divide	cpGEN	Coprocessor General Instruction
EOR	Logical Exclusive OR	cpRESTORE	Restore Internal State of Coprocessor
EORI	Logical Exclusive OR Immediate	cpSAVE	Save Internal State of Coprocessor
EXG	Exchange Registers	cpScc	Set Conditionally
EXT, EXTB	Sign Extend	cpTRAPcc	Trap Conditionally
ILLEGAL	Take Illegal Instruction Trap		
JMP	Jump		
JSR	Jump to Subroutine		
LEA	Load Effective Address		
LINK	Link and Allocate		
LSL, LSR	Logical Shift Left and Right		
MOVE	Move		
MOVEA	Move Address		
MOVE CCR	Move Condition Code Register		
MOVE SR	Move Status Register		
MOVE USP	Move User Stack Pointer		
MOVEC	Move Control Register		
MOVEM	Move Multiple Registers		
MOVEP	Move Peripheral		
MOVEQ	Move Quick		
MOVES	Move Alternate Address Space		

1.3 VIRTUAL MEMORY/MACHINE CONCEPTS

The full addressing range of the MC68020 is 4 gigabytes (4,294,967,296). However, most MC68020 systems implement a smaller physical memory. Nonetheless, by using virtual memory techniques, the system can be made to appear to have a full 4 gigabytes of physical memory available to each user program. These techniques have been used for many years in large mainframe computers and more recently in minicomputers. With the MC68020 (as with the MC68010 and MC68012), virtual memory can be fully supported in microprocessor-based systems.

In a virtual memory system, a user program can be written as though it has a large amount of memory available to it when actually, only a smaller amount of memory is physically present in the system. In a similar fashion, a system can be designed in such a manner as to allow user programs to access other types of devices that are not physically present in the system such as tape drives, disk drives, printers, or terminals. With proper software emulation, a physical system can be made to appear to a user program as any other M68000 computer system and the program may be given full access to all of the resources of that emulated system. Such an emulated system is called a virtual machine.

1.3.1 Virtual Memory

The basic mechanism for supporting virtual memory is to provide a limited amount of high-speed physical memory that can be accessed directly by the processor while maintaining an image of a much larger "virtual" memory on secondary storage devices such as large capacity disk drives. When the processor attempts to access a location in the virtual memory map that is not resident in physical memory (referred to as a page fault), the access to that location is temporarily suspended while the necessary data is fetched from secondary storage and placed in physical memory; the suspended access is then either restarted or continued.

The MC68020 uses instruction continuation to support virtual memory. In order for the MC68020 to use instruction continuation, it stores its internal state on the supervisor stack when a bus cycle is terminated with a bus error signal. It then loads the program counter with the address of the virtual memory bus error handler from the exception vector table (entry number two) and resumes program execution at that new address. When the bus error exception handler routine has completed execution, an RTE instruction is executed which reloads the MC68020 with the internal state stored on the stack, re-runs the faulted bus cycle (when required), and continues the suspended instruction.

Instruction continuation is crucial to the support of virtual I/O devices in memory-mapped input/output systems. Since virtual registers may be simulated in the memory map, an access to such a register will cause a fault and the function of the register can be emulated by software.

1.3.2 Virtual Machine

A typical use for a virtual machine system is the development of software, such as an operating system, for a new machine also under development and not yet available for programming use. In such a system, a governing operating system emulates the hardware of the prototyped system and allows the new operating system to be executed and debugged as though it were running on the new hardware. Since the new operating system is controlled by the governing operating system, it is executed at a lower privilege level than the governing operating system. Thus, any attempts by the new operating system to use virtual resources that are not physically present (and should be emulated) are trapped to the governing operating system and handled by its software. In the MC68020, a virtual machine is fully supported by running the new operating system in the user mode. The governing operating system executes in the supervisor mode and any attempt by the new operating system to access supervisor resources or execute privileged instructions will cause a trap to the governing operating system.

In order to fully support a virtual machine, the MC68020 must protect the supervisor resources from access by user programs. The only supervisor resource that is not fully protected on the MC68000 and MC68008 is the system byte of the status register. On the MC68000 and MC68008, the MOVE from SR instruction allows user programs to test the S bit in the status register (in addition to the T bits and interrupt mask) and thus determine that they are running in the user mode. For full virtual machine support, an operating system must not be aware of the fact that it is running in the less privileged user mode and thus should not be allowed direct access to the S bit. For this reason, the MOVE from SR instruction on the MC68010, MC68012, and MC68020 is a privileged instruction and the MOVE from CCR (condition code register) instruction is available to allow user programs direct access to the condition codes. By making the MOVE from SR instruction privileged, when the new operating system attempts to access the system byte of the status register, a trap to the governing operating system will occur, where the operation can be emulated.

1.4 PIPELINED ARCHITECTURE

The MC68020 uses a three stage instruction pipe, as shown in Figure 1-5, to implement a pipelined internal architecture. The pipeline is completely internal to the microprocessor. The benefit of the pipeline is to allow concurrent operations to occur for up to three words of a single instruction or for up to three consecutive instructions.

Instructions are loaded from the on-chip cache or from external memory during instruction prefetch into stage B. The instructions are sequenced from stage B through stage C to D. Stage D presents a fully decoded and validated instruction to the control unit for execution. Instructions with immediate data and extension words find these words already loaded in stage C and ready for use by the control and execution units.

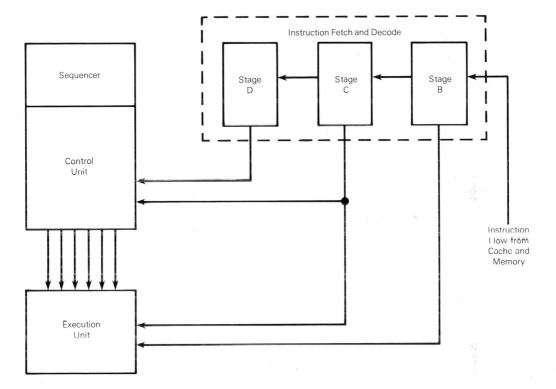

Figure 1-5. MC68020 Pipeline

SECTION 2
DATA ORGANIZATION AND ADDRESSING CAPABILITIES

This section contains a description of the registers and the data organization of the MC68020.

2.1 OPERAND SIZE

Operand sizes are defined as follows: a byte equals 8 bits, a word equals 16 bits, a long word equals 32 bits, and a quad word equals 64 bits. The operand size for each instruction is either explicitly encoded in the instruction or implicitly defined by the instruction operation. The coprocessor interface allows the support of any operand size from a bit to 256 bytes.

2.2 DATA ORGANIZATION IN REGISTERS

The eight data registers support data operands of 1, 8, 16, 32, and 64 bits, addresses of 16 or 32 bits, and bit fields of 1 to 32 bits. The seven address registers and the stack pointers support address operands of 16 or 32 bits. The six control registers (SR, VBR, SFC, DFC, CACR, and CAAR) support various data sizes depending on the register specified. Coprocessors may define unique operand sizes, and support them with on-chip registers accordingly.

2.2.1 Data Registers

Each data register is 32 bits wide. Byte operands occupy the low order 8 bits, word operands the low order 16 bits, and the long word operands the entire 32 bits. The least significant bit of an integer is addressed as bit zero and the most significant bit is addressed as bit 31. For bit fields, the most significant bit is addressed as bit zero and the least significant bit is addressed as the width of the field minus one.

The quad word data type is two long words and is used only for 32-bit multiply and divide (signed and unsigned) instructions. Quad words may be organized in any two data registers without restrictions on order or pairing. There are no explicit instructions for the management of this data type, although the MOVEM instruction can be used to move a quad word into or out of the registers.

When a data register is used as either a source or destination operand, only the appropriate low order byte or word (in byte or word operations, respectively) is used or changed; the remaining high order portion is neither used nor changed.

2.2.2 Address Registers

Each address register and stack pointer is 32 bits wide and holds a full 32-bit address. Address registers can not be used for byte-sized operands. Therefore, when an address register is used as a source operand, either the low order word or the entire long word operand is used, depending upon the operation size. When an address register is used as the destination operand, the entire register is affected regardless of the operation size. If the operation size is word, operands are sign extended to 32 bits before the operation is performed. Address registers may also be used to support some simple data operations.

2.2.3 Control Registers

The status register (SR) is 16 bits wide with the lower byte accessed as the condition code register (CCR). Not all 16 bits of the status register are defined, and undefined bits are read as zeros and ignored when written. Operations to the condition code register are word operations; however, the upper byte is read as all zeroes and ignored when written.

The cache control register (CACR) provides control and status access to the on-chip instruction cache. The cache address register (CAAR) holds the necessary address for those cache control functions that require one. The vector base register (VBR) provides the starting address of the exception vector table. All operations involving the CACR, CAAR, and VBR are long word operations regardless of whether these registers are used as the source or destination operand.

The alternate function code registers (SFC and DFC) are three bits wide and contain the address space values placed on FC0-FC2 during the operand read or write of a MOVES instruction. Transfers to and from the alternate function code registers are accomplished using the MOVEC instruction and are long word, although the upper 29 bits are read as zeroes and ignored when written.

Accesses to the control registers are privileged operations and are available only in the supervisor mode.

2.3 DATA ORGANIZATION IN MEMORY

Memory is organized on a byte-addressable basis where lower addresses correspond to higher-order bytes. The address, N, of a long word datum corresponds to the address of the most significant byte of the higher-order word. The lower-order word is located at address N+2, leaving the least significant byte at address N+3 (see Figure 2-1). Notice that the MC68020 does not require data to be aligned on even byte boundaries (see Figure 2-22) but the most efficient data transfers occur when data is aligned on the same byte boundary as its operand size. However, **instruction** words must be aligned on even byte boundaries.

The data types supported in memory by the MC68020 are: bit and bit field data; integer data of 8, 16, or 32 bits; 32-bit addresses; and binary coded decimal data (packed and unpacked). These data types are organized in memory as shown in Figure 2-2. (The quad word is only an operand when located in the data registers.) Note that all of these data types can be accessed at any byte address.

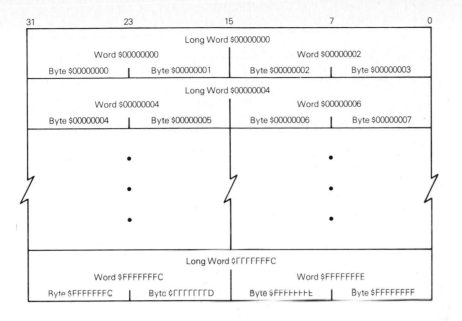

Figure 2-1. Memory Operand Addressing

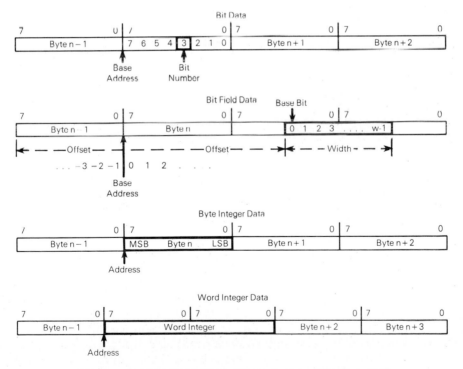

Figure 2-2. Memory Data Organization (Sheet 1 of 2)

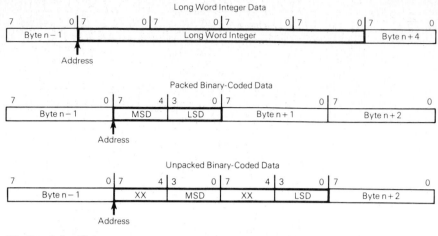

Figure 2-2. Memory Data Organization (Sheet 2 of 2)

Coprocessors may implement any data types and lengths. For example, the MC68881 Floating-Point Coprocessor supports memory accesses for quad-word sized items (double-precision floating-point values).

A bit datum is specified by a base address that selects one byte in memory (base byte) and a bit number that selects the one bit in this byte. The most significant bit of the byte is bit number seven.

A bit field datum is specified by:
1) a base address that selects one byte in memory,
2) a bit field offset that indicates the leftmost (base) bit of the bit field in relation to the most significant bit of the base byte, and
3) a bit field width that determines how many bits to the right of the base bit are in the bit field.

The most significant bit of the base byte is bit offset 0, the least significant bit of the base byte is bit offset 7, and the least significant bit of the previous byte in memory is bit offset -1. Bit field offsets may have values in the range of -2^{31} to $2^{31} - 1$ and bit field widths may range between 1 and 32.

2.4 INSTRUCTION FORMAT

All instructions are at least one word and up to 11 words in length as shown in Figure 2-3. The length of the instruction and the operation to be performed is determined by the first word of the instruction, the operation word. The remaining words, called extension words, further specify the instruction and operands. These words may be immediate operands, extensions to the effective address mode specified in the operation word, branch displacements, bit number or bit field specifications, special register specifications, trap operands, pack/unpack constants, argument counts, or coprocessor condition codes.

· Operation Word (One Word, Specifies Operation and Modes)
Special Operand Specifiers (If Any, One or Two Words)
Immediate Operand or Source Effective Address Extension (If Any, One to Five Words)
Destination Effective Address Extension (If Any, One to Five Words)

Figure 2-3. Instruction Word General Format

2.5 PROGRAM/DATA REFERENCES

The MC68020 separates memory references into two classes: program references and data references. Program references, as the name implies, are references to that section of memory that contains the program instructions. Data references refer to that section of memory that contains the program data. Generally, operand reads are from the data space. All operand writes are to the data space, except when caused by the MOVES instruction.

2.6 ADDRESSING

Instructions for the MC68020 contain two kinds of information: the function to be performed and the location of the operand(s) on which that function is performed. The methods used to locate (or address) the operand(s) are explained in the following paragraphs.

Instructions specify an operand location in one of three ways:

Register Specification — The number of the register is given in the register field of the instruction.

Effective Address — Use of the various effective addressing modes.

Implicit Reference — The definition of certain instructions implies the use of specific registers.

2.7 REGISTERS: NOTATION CONVENTIONS

Registers are identified by the following mnemonic description:

An — Address register n (e.g., A3 is address register 3)

Dn — Data register n (e.g., D5 is data register 5)

Rn — Address or Data Register n

Xn — Denotes index register n (data or address)

PC — The program counter

SR — The status register

CCR — The condition code register; part of the status register

SP — The active stack pointer; SP and A7 are equivalent names.

USP — The user stack pointer (A7)

ISP — The interrupt stack pointer (A7')

MSP — The master stack pointer (A7″)
SSP — The supervisor stack pointer, either the master (MSP) or interrupt (ISP) stack pointer
SFC — The source function code register
DFC — The destination function code register
VBR — The vector base register
CACR — The cache control register
CAAR — The cache address register

The register field within an instruction specifies the register to be used. Other fields within the instruction specify whether the register selected is an address or data register and how the register is to be used.

2.8 EFFECTIVE ADDRESS

Most instructions specify the location of an operand by using the effective address field (EA) in the operation word. For example, Figure 2-4 shows the general format of the single effective address instruction operation word. The effective address is composed of two 3-bit fields; the mode field and the register field. The value in the mode field selects one of the addressing modes. The register field contains the number of a register. The instruction operand word for each instruction is located in **APPENDIX C.**

15	14	13	12	11	10	9	8	7	6	5	4	3	2	1	0
										\multicolumn{6}{c	}{Effective Address}
X	X	X	X	X	X	X	X	X	X	\multicolumn{3}{c	}{Mode}	\multicolumn{3}{c	}{Register}

Figure 2-4. Single-Effective-Address Instruction Operation Word

The effective address field may require additional information to fully specify the operand address. This additional information, called the effective address extension, is contained in following word or words and is considered part of the instruction, as shown in Figure 2-3. Details describing the format of the extension words can be found in **2.9 EFFECTIVE ADDRESS ENCODING SUMMARY.**

2.8.1 Register Direct Modes

These effective addressing (EA) modes specify that the operand is in one of sixteen general purpose registers or one of six control registers (SR, VBR, SFC, DFC, CACR, and CAAR).

2.8.1.1 DATA REGISTER DIRECT. The operand is in the data register specified by the effective address register field.

Generation: EA = Dn
Assembler Syntax: Dn
Mode: 000
Register: n
Data Register: Dn

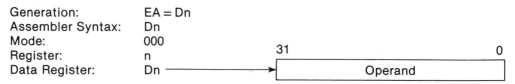

2.8.1.2 ADDRESS REGISTER DIRECT. The operand is in the address register specified by the effective address register field.

Generation: EA = An
Assembler Syntax: An
Mode: 001
Register: n
Address Register: An

```
31                                          0
┌──────────────────────────────────────────┐
│                 Operand                    │
└──────────────────────────────────────────┘
```

2.8.2 Register Indirect Modes

These effective addressing modes specify that the operand is in memory and the contents of a register is used to calculate the address of the operand.

2.8.2.1 ADDRESS REGISTER INDIRECT. The address of the operand is in the address register specified by the register field.

Generation: EA = (An)
Assembler Syntax: (An)
Mode: 010
Register: n
Address Register: An

```
31                                          0
┌──────────────────────────────────────────┐
│              Memory Address                │
└──────────────────────────────────────────┘
31                                          0
```

Memory Address:

```
┌──────────────────────────────────────────┐
│                 Operand                    │
└──────────────────────────────────────────┘
```

2.8.2.2 ADDRESS REGISTER INDIRECT WITH POSTINCREMENT. The address of the operand is in the address register specified by the register field. After the operand address is used, it is incremented by one, two, or four depending upon whether the size of the operand is byte, word, or long word. Coprocessors may support incrementing for any size, up to 256 bytes, of operand. If the address register is the stack pointer and the operand size is byte, the address is incremented by two rather than one to keep the stack pointer on a word boundary.

Generation: EA = (An)
                 An = An + SIZE
Assembler Syntax: (An) +
Mode: 011
Register: n
Address Register: An

Operand Length (1, 2, or 4):

Memory Address:

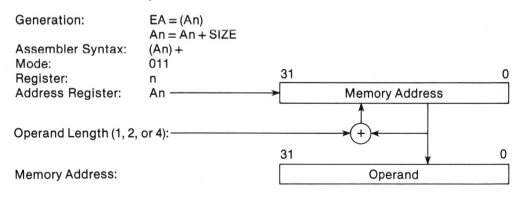

2.8.2.3 ADDRESS REGISTER INDIRECT WITH PREDECREMENT. The address of the operand is in the address register specified by the register field. Before the operand address is used, it is decremented by one, two, or four depending upon whether the operand size is byte, word, or long word. Coprocessors may support decrementing for any size, up to 256 bytes, of operand. If the address register is the stack pointer and the operand size is byte, the address is decremented by two rather than one to keep the stack pointer on a word bounary.

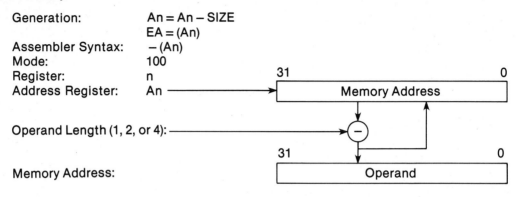

Generation: An = An − SIZE
                      EA = (An)
Assembler Syntax: − (An)
Mode: 100
Register: n
Address Register: An

Operand Length (1, 2, or 4):

Memory Address:

2.8.2.4 ADDRESS REGISTER INDIRECT WITH DISPLACEMENT. This addressing mode requires one word of extension. The address of the operand is the sum of the address in the address register and the sign-extended 16-bit displacement integer in the extension word. Displacements are always sign extended to 32 bits prior to being used in effective address calculations.

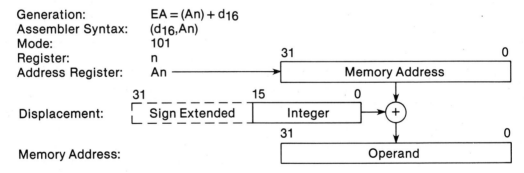

Generation: EA = (An) + d$_{16}$
Assembler Syntax: (d$_{16}$,An)
Mode: 101
Register: n
Address Register: An

Displacement:

Memory Address:

2.8.3 Register Indirect with Index Modes

These effective addressing modes specify that the contents of an address register are used in calculating the final effective address of the operand. In addition, an index register and a displacement are also used in calculating the final address (the values are both sign extended to 32 bits before the calculation). The variations available for adjusting the index register cause the index to be considered an "index operand".

The format of the index operand is "Xn.SIZE*SCALE". "Xn" selects any data or address register as the index register. "SIZE" specifies the index size and may be "W" for word size or "L" for long word size. "SCALE" allows the index register value to be multiplied by a value of one (no scaling), two, four, or eight.

Displacements and index operands are always sign extended to 32 bits prior to being used in effective address calculations.

2.8.3.1 ADDRESS REGISTER INDIRECT WITH INDEX (8-BIT DISPLACEMENT). This addressing mode requires one word of extension that contains the index register indicator (with its size selector and scaling mode), and an 8-bit displacement. In this mode, the address of the operand is the sum of the address register, the sign extended displacement value in the low order eight bits of the extension word, and the sign extended contents of the index register (possibly scaled). The user must specify the displacement, the address register, **and** the index register in this mode.

Generation: $EA = (An) + (Xn) + d_8$
Assembler Syntax: $(d_8,An,Xn.SIZE*SCALE)$
Mode: 110
Register: n

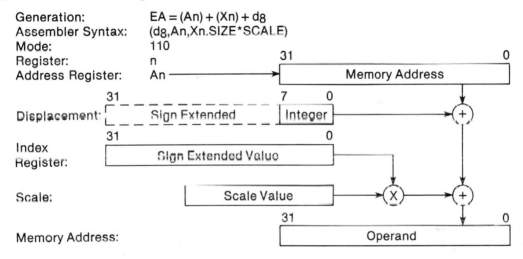

2.8.3.2 ADDRESS REGISTER INDIRECT WITH INDEX (BASE DISPLACEMENT). This form of address register indirect with index requires one, two, or three extension words that contain index register indication and an optional 16- or 32-bit base displacement (which is sign extended before it is used in the effective address calculation). The address of the operand is the sum of the contents of the address register, the scaled contents of the sign-extended index register and the base displacement.

In this mode, specification of all three addends is optional. If none are specified, the processor creates an effective address of zero.

Note that if an index register is specified, but not the address register, and a data register (Dn) is used as the index register, then a "data register indirect" access can be generated.

Generation: $EA = (An) + (Xn) + bd$
Assembler Syntax: (bd,An,Xn.SIZE*SCALE)
Mode: 110
Register: n
Address Register: An

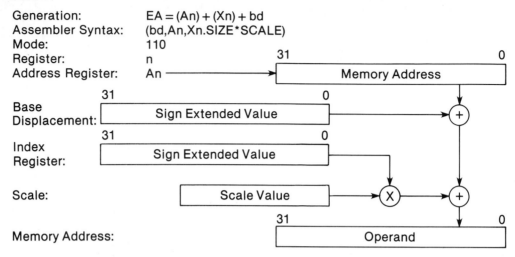

2.8.4 Memory Indirect

This addressing mode requires one to five words of extension, as detailed in **2.9 EFFEC-TIVE ADDRESS ENCODING SUMMARY.** Memory indirect is distinguished from address register indirect by use of square brackets ([ ]) in the assembler notation. The assembler generates the appropriate indicators in the extension words when this addressing mode is selected.

In this case, four user-specified values are used in the generation of the final address of the operand. An address register is used as a base register and its value can be adjusted by adding an optional base displacement. An index register specifies an index operand and finally, an outer displacement can be added to the address operand, yielding the effective address.

The location of the square brackets determines the user-specified values to be used in calculating an intermediate memory address. An address operand is then fetched from that intermediate memory address and it is used in calculating the effective address. The index operand may be added in after the intermediate memory access (post-indexed) or before the intermediate memory access (pre-indexed).

All four user-specified values are optional. Both the base and outer displacements may be null, word, or long word. When a displacement is null, or an element is suppressed, its value is taken as zero in the effective address calculation.

2.8.4.1 MEMORY INDIRECT POST-INDEXED. In this case, an intermediate indirect memory address is calculated using the base register (An) and base displacement (bd). This address is used for an indirect memory access of a long word, followed by adding the index operand (Xn.SIZE*SCALE) to the fetched address. Finally, the optional outer displacement (od) is added to yield the effective address.

Generation: $\quad$ EA = (bd + An) + Xn.SIZE*SCALE + od
Assembler Syntax: $\quad$ ([bd,An],Xn.SIZE*SCALE,od)
Mode: $\quad$ 110
Address Register: $\quad$ An

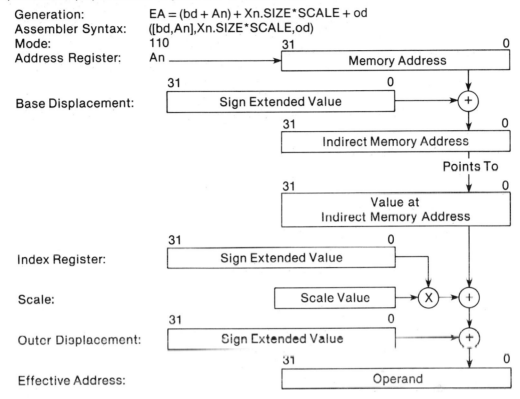

2.8.4.2 MEMORY INDIRECT PRE-INDEXED. In this case, the index operand (Xn.SIZE*SCALE) is added to the base register (An) and base displacement (bd). This intermediate sum is then used as an indirect address into the data space. Following the long word fetch of the operand address, the optional outer displacement (od) may be added to yield the effective address.

Generation: $EA = (bd + An + Xn.SIZE*SCALE) + od$
Assembler Syntax: ([bd,An,Xn.SIZE*SCALE],od)
Mode: 110

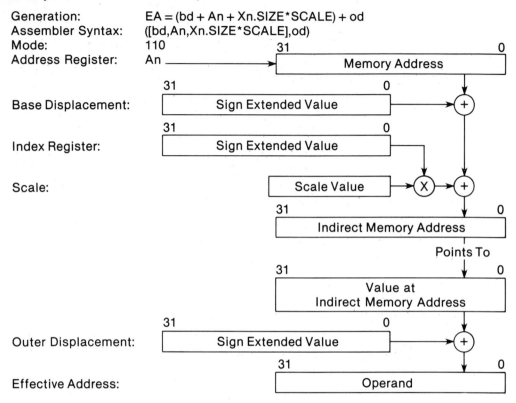

2.8.5 Program Counter Indirect With Displacement Mode

This addressing mode requires one word of extension. The address of the operand is the sum of the address in the program counter and the sign extended 16-bit displacement integer in the extension word. The value in the program counter is the address of the extension word. The reference is classified as a program reference.

Generation: $EA = (PC) + d_{16}$
Assembler Syntax: (d_{16}, PC)
Mode: 111
Register: 010

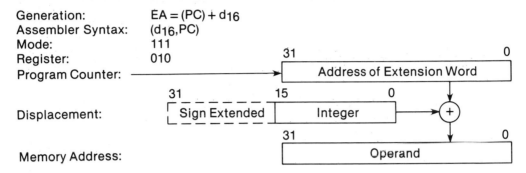

2.8.6 Program Counter Indirect with Index Modes

These addressing modes are analogous to the register indirect with index modes described in 2.8.3, but the PC is used as the base register. As before, the index operand (sized and scaled) and a displacement are used in the calculation of the effective address also. Displacements and index operands are always sign extended to 32 bits prior to being used in effective address calculations.

PC relative accesses are always classified as program space references.

2.8.6.1 PC INDIRECT WITH INDEX (8-BIT DISPLACEMENT). The address of the operand is the sum of the address in the program counter, the sign extended displacement integer in the lower eight bits of the extension word, and the sized and scaled sign-extended index operand. The value in the PC is the address of the extension word. This reference is classified as a program space reference. The user must include the displacement, the PC, **and** the index register when specifying this address mode.

Generation: $EA = (PC) + (Xn) + d_8$
Assembler Syntax: (d8,PC,Xn.SIZE*SCALE)
Mode: 111
Register: 011

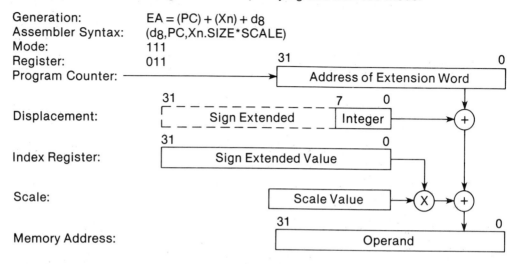

2.8.6.2 PC INDIRECT WITH INDEX (BASE DISPLACEMENT). This address mode requires additional extension words that contain the index register indication and an optional 16-or 32-bit base displacement (which is sign extended to 32 bits before being used). The address of the operand is the sum of the contents of the PC, the scaled contents of the sign-extended index register, and the base displacement.

In this mode, specification of all three addends is optional. However, in order to distinguish this mode from address register indirect with index (base displacement), when the user wishes to specify no PC, the assembler notation "ZPC" (zero value is taken for the PC) must be used. This allows the user to access the program space, without necessarily using the PC in calculating the effective address. Note that if ZPC and an index register are specified, and a data register (Dn) is used, then a "data register indirect" access can be made to the program space, without using the PC.

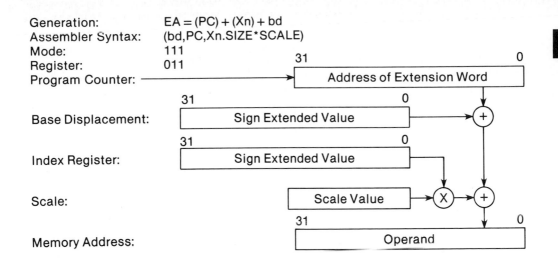

Generation: $EA = (PC) + (Xn) + bd$
Assembler Syntax: (bd,PC,Xn.SIZE*SCALE)
Mode: 111
Register: 011

2.8.7 Program Counter Memory Indirect Modes

As in the memory indirect modes (refer to **2.8.4 Memory Indirect**) the square brackets ([ ]) indicate that an intermediate access to memory is made as part of the final effective address calculation.

In this case, the PC is used as a base register and its value can be adjusted by adding an optional base displacement. An index register specifies an index operand and finally, an outer displacement can be added to the address operand, yielding the effective address.

The location of the square brackets determines the user-specified values to be used in calculating an intermediate memory address. An address operand is then fetched from that intermediate address and it is used in the final calculation. The index operand may be added in after the intermediate memory access (post-indexed) or before that access (pre-indexed).

All four user-specified values are optional. Both the base and outer displacements may be null, word, or long word. When using null displacements, the value of zero is used in the effective address calculation. In order to specify no PC but still make program space references, the notation "ZPC" should be used in its place.

2.8.7.1 PROGRAM COUNTER MEMORY INDIRECT POST-INDEXED. An intermediate indirect memory address is calculated by adding the PC, used as a base register, and a base displacement (bd). This address is used for an indirect memory access into program space of a long word, followed by adding the index operand (Xn.SIZE*SCALE) with the fetched address. Finally, the optional outer displacement (od) is added to yield the effective address.

Generation: EA = (bd + PC) + Xn.SIZE*SCALE + od
Assembler Syntax: ([bd,PC],Xn.SIZE*SCALE,od)
Mode: 111
Register Field: 011

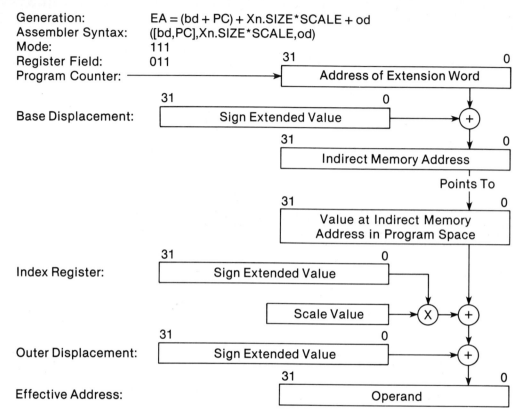

2.8.7.2 PROGRAM COUNTER MEMORY INDIRECT PRE-INDEXED. In this case, the index operand (Xn.SIZE*SCALE) is added to the program counter and base displacement (bd). This intermediate sum is then used as an indirect address into the program space. Following the long word fetch of the new effective address, the optional outer displacement may be added to yield the effective address.

Generation: $EA = (bd + PC + Xn.SIZE*SCALE) + od$
Assembler Syntax: ([bd,PC,Xn.SIZE*SCALE],od)
Mode: 111
Register Field: 011

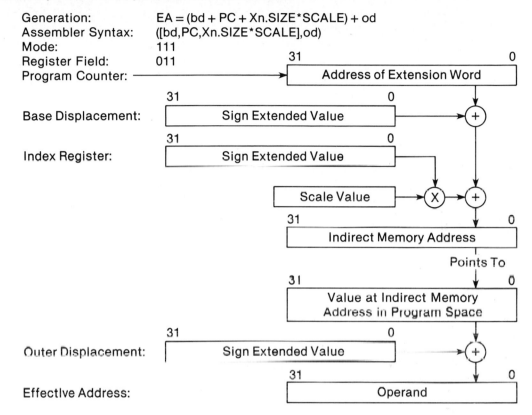

2.8.8 Absolute Address Modes

Absolute address modes have the address of the operand in the extension word(s).

2.8.8.1 ABSOLUTE SHORT ADDRESS. This addressing mode requires one word of extension. The address of the operand is in the extension word. The 16-bit address is sign extended to 32 bits before it is used.

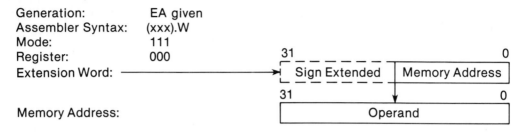

Generation: EA given
Assembler Syntax: (xxx).W
Mode: 111
Register: 000
Extension Word:
Memory Address:

2.8.8.2 ABSOLUTE LONG ADDRESS. This addressing mode requires two words of extension. The address of the operand is developed by the concatenation of the extension words. The high order part of the address is the first extension word; the low order part of the address is the second extension word.

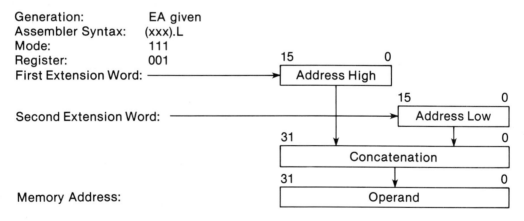

Generation: EA given
Assembler Syntax: (xxx).L
Mode: 111
Register: 001
First Extension Word:
Second Extension Word:
Memory Address:

2.8.9 Immediate Data

This addressing mode requires one or two words of extension, depending on the size of the operation.

Byte Operation	— Operand is in the low order byte of the extension word
Word Operation	— Operand is in the extension word
Long Word Operation	— Operand is in two extension words; high order 16 bits are in the first extension word; low order 16 bits are in the second extension word. Coprocessors may provide support for immediate data of any size with the instruction portion taking at least one word.

Generation:	Operand given
Assembler Syntax:	#xxx
Mode:	111
Register:	100

2.9 EFFECTIVE ADDRESS ENCODING SUMMARY

Table 2-1 details effective address word formats. The instruction operand extension words fall into three categories: single-effective-address instruction, indexed/indirect (brief format), and indexed/indirect (full format). The longest instruction for the MC68020 contains ten extension words. They consist of both source and destination effective addresses using the full format extension word, with both base displacements and outer displacements being 32 bits.

Table 2-1. Effective Address Specification Formats

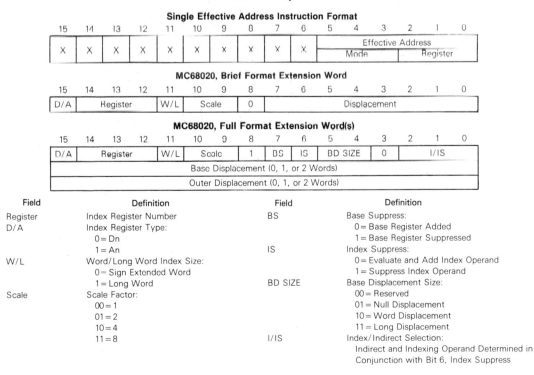

Field	Definition	Field	Definition
Register	Index Register Number	BS	Base Suppress:
D/A	Index Register Type:		0 = Base Register Added
	0 = Dn		1 = Base Register Suppressed
	1 = An	IS	Index Suppress:
W/L	Word/Long Word Index Size:		0 = Evaluate and Add Index Operand
	0 = Sign Extended Word		1 = Suppress Index Operand
	1 = Long Word	BD SIZE	Base Displacement Size:
Scale	Scale Factor:		00 = Reserved
	00 = 1		01 = Null Displacement
	01 = 2		10 = Word Displacement
	10 = 4		11 = Long Displacement
	11 = 8	I/IS	Index/Indirect Selection:
			Indirect and Indexing Operand Determined in Conjunction with Bit 6, Index Suppress

The index suppress (IS) and index/indirect selection (I/IS) fields are combined to determine the type of indirection to be performed using the index/indirect full format addressing mode. The encodings and subsequent operations are described in Table 2-2.

Table 2-2. IS-I/IS Memory Indirection Encodings

IS	Index/ Indirect	Operation
0	000	No Memory Indirection
0	001	Indirect Pre-Indexed with Null Displacement
0	010	Indirect Pre-Indexed with Word Displacement
0	011	Indirect Pre-Indexed with Long Displacement
0	100	Reserved
0	101	Indirect Post-Indexed with Null Displacement
0	110	Indirect Post-Indexed with Word Displacement
0	111	Indirect Post-Indexed with Long Displacement
1	000	No Memory Indirection
1	001	Memory Indirect with Null Displacement
1	010	Memory Indirect with Word Displacement
1	011	Memory Indirect with Long Displacement
1	100-111	Reserved

Table 2-3 is the encoding of the effective addressing modes discussed in the previous paragraphs.

Table 2-3. Effective Address Encoding Summary

Addressing Mode	Mode	Register
Data Register Direct	000	Reg #
Address Register Direct	001	Reg #
Address Register Indirect	010	Reg #
Address Register Indirect with Postincrement	011	Reg #
Address Register Indirect with Predecrement	100	Reg #
Address Register Indirect with Displacement	101	Reg #
Address Register and Memory Indirect with Index	110	Reg #
Absolute Short	111	000
Absolute Long	111	001
Program Counter Indirect with Displacement	111	010
Program Counter and Memory Indirect with Index	111	011
Immediate Data	111	100
Reserved for Future Motorola Use	111	101
Reserved for Future Motorola Use	111	110
Reserved for Future Motorola Use	111	111

2.10 SYSTEM STACK

Address register seven (A7) is used as the system stack pointer (SP) where any one of three system stack registers is active at any one time. The M and S bits of the status register determine which stack pointer is used. If S = 0, the user stack pointer (USP) is the active system stack pointer and the master and interrupt stack pointers cannot be referenced. If S = 1 and M = 1, the master stack pointer (MSP) is the active system stack pointer and the user and interrupt stack pointers cannot be referenced as address registers. If S = 1 and M = 0, the interrupt stack pointer (ISP) is the active system stack pointer and the user and master stack pointers cannot be referenced as address registers. (This corresponds to the MC68000, MC68008, MC68010, and MC68012 supervisor mode.) The term supervisor stack pointer (SSP) refers to the master or interrupt stack pointers, depending on the state of the M bit. Each system stack fills from high to low memory.

The active system stack pointer is implicitly referenced by all instructions that use the system stack for linkage or storage allocation.

The program counter is saved on the active system stack on subroutine calls and restored from the active system stack on returns. During the processing of traps and interrupts, both the program counter and the status register are saved on the supervisor stack (either master or interrupt). Thus, the execution of supervisor state code is not dependent on the behavior of user code or condition of the user stack, and user programs may use the user stack pointer independent of supervisor stack requirements.

In order to keep data on the system stack aligned for maximum efficiency when byte data is pushed on to or pulled from the system stack, the stack pointer is decremented or incremented by two as appropriate.

The efficiency of the MC68020 system stacking operations (e.g., stacking of exception frames, subroutine calls, etc.) is significantly increased in long word organized memory when the stack pointer is long word aligned.

2.11 USER PROGRAM STACKS

Additional user program stacks can be implemented by employing the address register indirect with postincrement and predecrement addressing modes. Using an address register (A0 through A6), the user may implement stacks which are filled either from high memory to low memory, or vice versa. The important considerations are:
- using predecrement, the register is decremented before its contents are used as the pointer to the stack;
- using postincrement, the register is incremented after its contents are used as the pointer to the stack.

Care must be exercised when mixing byte, word, and long word items in these stacks.

Stack growth from high to low memory is implemented with
     − (An) to push data on the stack,
     (An) + to pull data from the stack.

After either a push or a pull operation, register An points to the top item on the stack. This is illustrated as:

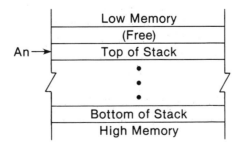

Stack growth from low to high memory is implemented with
(An) + to push data on the stack,
– (An) to pull data from the stack.

After either a push or pull operation, register An points to the next available space on the stack. This is illustrated as:

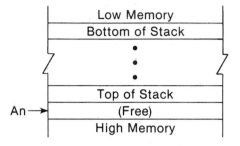

2.12 QUEUES

User queues can also be implemented with the address register indirect with postincrement or predecrement addressing modes. Using a pair of address registers (two of A0 through A6), the user may implement queues which are filled either from high memory to low memory, or vice versa. Because queues are pushed from one end and pulled from the other, two registers are used: the 'put' and 'get' pointers.

Queue growth from low to high memory is implemented with
(An) + to put data into the queue,
(Am) + to get data from the queue.

After a put operation, the 'put' address register points to the next available space in the queue and the unchanged 'get' address register points to the next item to be removed from the queue. After a 'get' operation, the 'get' address register points to the next item to be removed from the queue and the unchanged 'put' address register points to the next available space in the queue. This is illustrated as:

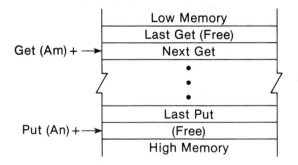

If the queue is to be implemented as a circular buffer, the relevant address register should be checked and, if necessary, adjusted before the 'put' or 'get' operation is performed. The address register is adjusted by subtracting the buffer length (in bytes), producing a "wrap-around."

Queue growth from high to low memory is implemented with
  – (An) to put data into the queue,
  – (Am) to get data from the queue.

After a 'put' operation, the 'put' address register points to the last item put in the queue and the unchanged get address register points to the last item removed from the queue. After a 'get' operation, the 'get' address register points to the last item removed from the queue and the unchanged 'put' address register points to the last item put in the queue. This is illustrated as:

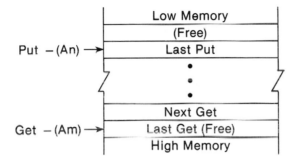

If the queue is to be implemented as a circular buffer, the 'get' or 'put' operation should be performed first, and then the relevant address register should be checked and, if necessary, adjusted. The address register is adjusted by adding the buffer length (in bytes).

SECTION 3
INSTRUCTION SET SUMMARY

This section contains an overview of the MC68020 instruction set. The instructions form a set of tools to perform the following operations:

Data Movement	Bit Field Manipulation
Integer Arithmetic	Binary Coded Decimal Arithmetic
Logical	Program Control
Shift and Rotate	System Control
Bit Manipulation	Multiprocessor Communications

The complete range of instruction capabilities combined with the flexible addressing modes described previously provide a very flexible base for program development.

The following notations will be used throughout this section.

$$An = \text{any address register, A0-A7}$$
$$Dn = \text{any data register, D0-D7}$$
$$Rn = \text{any address or data register}$$
$$CCR = \text{condition code register (lower byte of status register)}$$
$$cc = \text{condition codes from CCR}$$
$$SP = \text{active stack pointer}$$
$$USP = \text{user stack pointer}$$
$$SSP = \text{supervisor stack pointer}$$
$$DFC = \text{destination function code register}$$
$$SFC = \text{source function code register}$$
$$Rc = \text{control register (VBR, SFC, DFC, CACR, CAAR, USP, MSP, ISP)}$$
$$d = \text{displacement; } d_{16} \text{ is a 16-bit displacement}$$
$$<ea> = \text{effective address}$$
$$list = \text{list of registers, e.g., D0-D3}$$
$$\#<data> = \text{immediate data; a literal integer}$$
$$\{offset{:}width\} = \text{bit field selection}$$
$$label = \text{assembly program label}$$
$$[7] = \text{bit 7 of respective operand}$$
$$[31{:}24] = \text{bits 31 through 24 of operand; i.e., high order byte of a register}$$
$$X = \text{extend (X) bit in CCR}$$
$$N = \text{negative (N) bit in CCR}$$
$$Z = \text{zero (Z) bit in CCR}$$
$$\sim = \text{invert; operand is logically complemented}$$
$$\Lambda = \text{logical AND}$$
$$V = \text{logical OR}$$
$$\oplus = \text{logical exclusive OR}$$

Dc = data register, D0-D7 used during compare
Du = data register, D0-D7 used during update
Dr, Dq = data register, remainder or quotient of divide
Dh,Dl = data register, high or low order 32 bits of multiply result

3.1 DATA MOVEMENT

The basic means of address and data manipulation (transfer and storage) is accomplished by the move (MOVE) instruction and its associated effective addressing modes. Data movement instructions allow byte, word, and long word operands to be transferred from memory to memory, memory to register, register to memory, and register to register. Address movement instructions (MOVE or MOVEA) allow word and long word operand transfers to ensure that only legal address manipulations are executed. In addition to the general MOVE instruction there are several special data movement instructions: move multiple registers (MOVEM), move peripheral data (MOVEP), move quick (MOVEQ), exchange registers (EXG), load effective address (LEA), push effective address (PEA), link stack (LINK), unlink stack (UNLK). Table 3-1 is a summary of the data movement operations.

Table 3-1. Data Movement Operations

Instruction	Operand Syntax	Operand Size	Operation
EXG	Rn, Rn	32	Rn ↔ Rn
LEA	<ea>,An	32	<ea> → An
LINK	An,#<d>	16, 32	SP−4 → SP; An → (SP); SP → An; SP + d → SP
MOVE MOVEA	<ea>, <ea> <ea>, An	8, 16, 32 16, 32 → 32	source → destination
MOVEM	list, <ea> <ea>, list	16, 32 16, 32 → 32	listed registers → destination source → listed registers
MOVEP	Dn, (d$_{16}$,An) (d$_{16}$,An),Dn	16, 32	Dn[31:24] → (An+d); Dn[23:16] → (An+d+2); Dn[15:8] → (An+d+4); Dn[7:0] → (An+d+6) (An+d) → Dn[31:24]; (An+d+2) → Dn[23:16]; (An+d+4) → Dn[15:8]; (An+d+6) → Dn[7:0]
MOVEQ	#<data>,Dn	8 → 32	immediate data → destination
PEA	<ea>	32	SP−4 → SP; <ea> → (SP)
UNLK	An	32	An → SP; (SP) → An; SP+4 → SP

3.2 INTEGER ARITHMETIC OPERATIONS

The arithmetic operations include the four basic operations of add (ADD), subtract (SUB), multiply (MUL), and divide (DIV) as well as arithmetic compare (CMP, CMPM, CMP2), clear (CLR), and negate (NEG). The ADD, CMP, and SUB instructions are available for both address and data operations, with data operations accepting all operand sizes. Address operations are limited to legal address size operands (16 or 32 bits). The clear and negate instructions may be used on all sizes of data operands.

The MUL and DIV operations are available for signed and unsigned operands using word multiply to produce a long word product, long word multiply to produce a long word or quad word product; a long word dividend with word divisor to produce a word quotient with a word remainder; and a long word or quad word dividend with long word divisor to produce long word quotient and long word remainder.

Multiprecision and mixed size arithmetic can be accomplished using a set of extended instructions. These instructions are: add extended (ADDX), subtract extended (SUBX), sign extend (EXT), and negate binary with extend (NEGX).

Refer to Table 3-2 for a summary of the integer arithmetic operations.

Table 3-2. Integer Arithmetic Operations

Instruction	Operand Syntax	Operand Size	Operation
ADD	Dn, <ea>	8, 16, 32	source + destination → destination
	<ea>, Dn	8, 16, 32	
ADDA	<ea>, An	16, 32	
ADDI	#<data>, <ea>	8, 16, 32	immediate data + destination → destination
ADDQ	#<data>, <ea>	8, 16, 32	
ADDX	Dn, Dn	8, 16, 32	source + destination + X → destination
	−(An), −(An)	8, 16, 32	
CLR	<ea>	8, 16, 32	0 → destination
CMP	<ea>, Dn	8, 16, 32	destination − source
CMPA	<ea>, An	16, 32	
CMPI	#<data>, <ea>	8, 16, 32	destination − immediate data
CMPM	(An)+, (An)+	8, 16, 32	destination − source
CMP2	<ea>, Rn	8, 16, 32	lower bound <= Rn <= upper bound
DIVS/DIVU	<ea>, Dn	32/16 → 16:16	destination/source → destination (signed or unsigned)
	<ea>, Dr:Dq	64/32 → 32:32	
	<ea>, Dq	32/32 → 32	
DIVSL/DIVUL	<ea>, Dr:Dq	32/32 → 32:32	
EXT	Dn	8 → 16	sign extended destination → destination
	Dn	16 → 32	
EXTB	Dn	8 → 32	
MULS/MULU	<ea>, Dn	16 × 16 → 32	source*destination → destination (signed or unsigned)
	<ea>, Dl	32 × 32 → 32	
	<ea>, Dh:Dl	32 × 32 → 64	
NEG	<ea>	8, 16, 32	0 − destination → destination
NEGX	<ea>	8, 16, 32	0 − destination − X → destination
SUB	<ea>, Dn	8, 16, 32	destination − source → destination
	Dn, <ea>	8, 16, 32	
SUBA	<ea>, An	16, 32	
SUBI	#<data>, <ea>	8, 16, 32	destination − immediate data → destination
SUBQ	#<data>, <ea>	8, 16, 32	
SUBX	Dn, Dn	8, 16, 32	destination − source − X → destination
	−(An), −(An)	8, 16, 32	

3.3 LOGICAL OPERATIONS

Logical operation instructions AND, OR, EOR, and NOT are available for all sizes of integer data operands. A similar set of immediate instructions (ANDI, ORI, and EORI) provide these logical operations with all sizes of immediate data. TST is an arithmetic comparison of the operand with zero which is then reflected in the condition codes. Table 3-3 is a summary of the logical operations.

Table 3-3. Logical Operations

Instruction	Operand Syntax	Operand Size	Operation
AND	<ea>, Dn Dn, <ea>	8, 16, 32 8, 16, 32	source Λ destination → destination
ANDI	#<data>,<ea>	8, 16, 32	immediate data Λ destination → destination
EOR	Dn, <ea>	8, 16, 32	source ⊕ destination → destination
EORI	#<data>,<ea>	8, 16, 32	immediate data ⊕ destination → destination
NOT	<ea>	8, 16, 32	~ destination → destination
OR	<ea>, Dn Dn, <ea>	8, 16, 32 8, 16, 32	source V destination → destination
ORI	#<data>,<ea>	8, 16, 32	immediate data V destination → destination
TST	<ea>	8, 16, 32	source − 0 to set condition codes

3.4 SHIFT AND ROTATE OPERATIONS

Shift operations in both directions are provided by the arithmetic shift instructions ASR and ASL, and logical shift instructions LSR and LSL. The rotate instructions (with and without extend) available are ROR, ROL, ROXR, and ROXL.

All shift and rotate operations can be performed on either registers or memory.

Register shifts and rotates support all operand sizes and allow a shift count (from one to eight) to be specified in the instruction operation word or a shift count (modulo 64) to be specified in a register.

Memory shifts and rotates are for word operands only and allow only single-bit shifts or rotates. The SWAP instruction exchanges the 16-bit halves of a register. Performance of shift/rotate instructions is enhanced so that use of the ROR or ROL instructions with a shift count of eight allows fast byte swapping.

Table 3-4 is a summary of the shift and rotate operations.

Table 3-4. Shift and Rotate Operations

Instruction	Operand Syntax	Operand Size	Operation
ASL	Dn, Dn #<data>, Dn <ea>	8, 16, 32 8, 16, 32 16	
ASR	Dn, Dn #<data>, Dn <ea>	8, 16, 32 8, 16, 32 16	
LSL	Dn, Dn #<data>, Dn <ea>	8, 16, 32 8, 16, 32 16	
LSR	Dn, Dn #<data>, Dn <ea>	8, 16, 32 8, 16, 32 16	
ROL	Dn, Dn #<data>, Dn <ea>	8, 16, 32 8, 16, 32 16	
ROR	Dn, Dn #<data>, Dn <ea>	8, 16, 32 8, 16, 32 16	
ROXL	Dn, Dn #<data>, Dn <ea>	8, 16, 32 8, 16, 32 16	
ROXR	Dn, Dn #<data>, Dn <ea>	8, 16, 32 8, 16, 32 16	
SWAP	Dn	32	

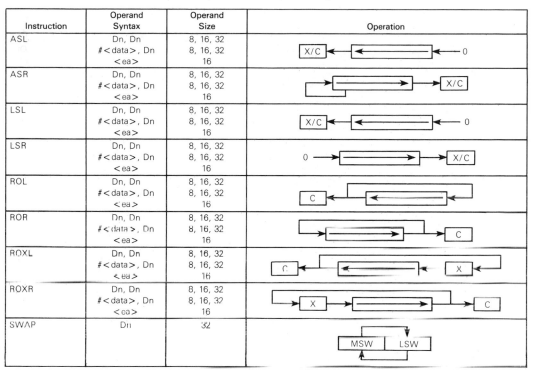

3.5 BIT MANIPULATION OPERATIONS

Bit manipulation operations are accomplished using the following instructions: bit test (BTST), bit test and set (BSET), bit test and clear (BCLR), and bit test and change (BCHG). All bit manipulation operations can be performed on either registers or memory, with the bit number specified as immediate data or by the contents of a data register. Register operands are always 32 bits, while memory operands are always 8 bits. Table 3-5 is a summary of the bit manipulation operations. (Z is bit 2, the "zero" bit, of the status register.)

Table 3-5. Bit Manipulation Operations

Instruction	Operand Syntax	Operand Size	Operation
BCHG	Dn, <ea> #<data>,<ea>	8, 32 8, 32	~ (<bit number> of destination) → Z → bit of destination
BCLR	Dn, <ea> #<data>,<ea>	8, 32 8, 32	~ (<bit number> of destination) → Z; 0 → bit of destination
BSET	Dn, <ea> #<data>,<ea>	8, 32 8, 32	~ (<bit number> of destination) → Z; 1 → bit of destination
BTST	Dn, <ea> #<data>,<ea>	8, 32 8, 32	~ (<bit number> of destination) → Z

3.6 BIT FIELD OPERATIONS

The MC68020 supports variable length bit field operations on fields of up to 32 bits. The bit field insert (BFINS) inserts a value into a bit field. Bit field extract unsigned (BFEXTU) and bit field extract signed (BFEXTS) extracts a value from the field. Bit field find first one (BFFFO) finds the first bit that is set in a bit field. Also included are instructions that are analagous to the bit manipulation operations; bit field test (BFTST), bit field test and set (BFSET), bit field test and clear (BFCLR), and bit field test and change (BFCHG).

Table 3-6 is a summary of the bit field operations.

Table 3-6. Bit Field Operations

Instruction	Operand Syntax	Operand Size	Operation
BFCHG	<ea> {offset:width}	1-32	~ Field → Field
BFCLR	<ea> {offset:width}	1-32	0's → Field
BFEXTS	<ea> {offset:width},Dn	1-32	Field → Dn; Sign Extended
BFEXTU	<ea> {offset:width},Dn	1-32	Field → Dn; Zero Extended
BFFFO	<ea> {offset:width},Dn	1-32	Scan for first bit set in Field; offset → Dn
BFINS	Dn,<ea> {offset:width}	1-32	Dn → Field
BFSET	<ea> {offset:width}	1-32	1's → Field
BFTST	<ea> {offset:width}	1-32	Field MSB → N; ~ (OR of all bits in field) → Z

NOTE: All bit field instructions set the N and Z bits as shown for BFTST before performing the specified operation.

3.7 BINARY CODED DECIMAL OPERATIONS

Multiprecision arithmetic operations on binary coded decimal numbers are accomplished using the following instructions: add decimal with extend (ABCD), subtract decimal with extend (SBCD), and negate decimal with extend (NBCD). PACK and UNPACK allow conversion of byte encoded numeric data, such as ASCII or EBCDIC strings, to BCD data and vice versa. Table 3-7 is a summary of the binary coded decimal operations.

Table 3-7. Binary Coded Decimal Operations

Instruction	Operand Syntax	Operand Size	Operation
ABCD	Dn, Dn – (An), – (An)	8 8	$source_{10} + destination_{10} + X \rightarrow destination$
NBCD	<ea>	8	$0 - destination_{10} - X \rightarrow destination$
PACK	– (An), – (An), #<data> Dn, Dn, #<data>	16→8 16→8	unpacked source + immediate data → packed destination
SBCD	Dn, Dn – (An), – (An)	8 8	$destination_{10} - source_{10} - X \rightarrow destination$
UNPK	– (An), – (An), #<data> Dn, Dn,#<data>	8→16 8→16	packed source → unpacked source unpacked source + immediate data → unpacked destination

3.8 PROGRAM CONTROL OPERATIONS

Program control operations are accomplished using a set of conditional and unconditional branch instructions and return instructions. These instructions are summarized in Table 3-8.

Table 3-8. Program Control Operations

Instruction	Operand Syntax	Operand Size	Operation
Conditional			
Bcc	\<label\>	8, 16, 32	if condition true, then PC + d → PC
DBcc	Dn, \<label\>	16	if condition false, then Dn − 1 → Dn if Dn ≠ − 1, then PC + d → PC
Scc	\<ea\>	8	if condition true, then 1's → destination; else 0's → destination
Unconditional			
BRA	\<label\>	8, 16, 32	PC + d → PC
BSR	\<label\>	8, 16, 32	SP − 4 → SP, PC → (SP); PC + d → PC
CALLM	#\<data\>,\<ea\>	none	Save module state in stack frame; load new module state from destination
JMP	\<ea\>	none	destination → PC
JSR	\<ea\>	none	SP − 4 → SP; PC → (SP); destination → PC
NOP	none	none	PC + 2 → PC
Returns			
RTD	#\<d\>	16	(SP) → PC; SP + 4 + d → SP
RTM	Rn	none	Reload saved module state from stack frame; place module data area pointer in Rn
RTR	none	none	(SP) → CCR; SP + 2 → SP; (SP) → PC; SP + 4 → SP
RTS	none	none	(SP) → PC; SP + 4 → SP

The conditional instructions provide testing and branching for the following conditions:

CC — carry clear   LS — low or same
CS — carry set   LT — less than
EQ — equal   MI — minus
F — never true*   NE — not equal
GE — greater or equal PL — plus
GT — greater than   T — always true*
HI — high   VC — overflow clear
LE — less or equal   VS — overflow set

*Not available for the Bcc or cpBcc instructions.

3.9 SYSTEM CONTROL OPERATIONS

System control operations are accomplished by using privileged instructions, trap generating instructions, and instructions that use or modify the condition code register. These instructions are summarized in Table 3-9.

Table 3-9. System Control Operations

Instruction	Operand Syntax	Operand Size	Operation
		Privileged	
ANDI	#<data>, SR	16	immediate data $\wedge$ SR $\rightarrow$ SR
EORI	#<data>, SR	16	immediate data $\oplus$ SR $\rightarrow$ SR
MOVE	<ea>, SR SR, <ea>	16 16	source $\rightarrow$ SR SR $\rightarrow$ destination
MOVE	USP, An An, USP	32 32	USP $\rightarrow$ An An $\rightarrow$ USP
MOVEC	Rc, Rn Rn, Rc	32 32	Rc $\rightarrow$ Rn Rn $\rightarrow$ Rc
MOVES	Rn, <ea> <ea>, Rn	8, 16, 32	Rn $\rightarrow$ destination using DFC source using SFC $\rightarrow$ Rn
ORI	#<data>, SR	16	immediate data V SR $\rightarrow$ SR
RESET	none	none	assert $\overline{\text{RESET}}$ line
RTE	none	none	(SP) $\rightarrow$ SR; SP + 2 $\rightarrow$ SP; (SP) $\rightarrow$ PC; SP + 4 $\rightarrow$ SP; Restore stack according to format
STOP	#<data>	16	immediate data $\rightarrow$ SR; STOP
		Trap Generating	
BKPT	#<data>	none	if breakpoint cycle acknowledged, then execute returned operation word, else trap as illegal instruction
CHK	<ea>, Dn	16, 32	if Dn<0 or Dn>(ea), then CHK exception
CHK2	<ea>, Rn	8, 16, 32	if Rn<lower bound or Rn>upper bound, then CHK exception

ILLEGAL	none	none	SSP $-$ 2 $\rightarrow$ SSP; Vector Offset $\rightarrow$ (SSP);
			    SSP $-$ 4 $\rightarrow$ SSP; PC $\rightarrow$ (SSP);
			    SSP $-$ 2 $\rightarrow$ SSP; SR $\rightarrow$ (SSP);
			    Illegal Instruction Vector Address $\rightarrow$ PC

TRAP	#<data>	none	SSP $-$ 2 $\rightarrow$ SSP; Format and Vector Offset $\rightarrow$ (SSP);
			    SSP $-$ 4 $\rightarrow$ SSP; PC $\rightarrow$ (SSP); SSP $-$ 2 $\rightarrow$ SSP;
			    SR $\rightarrow$ (SSP); Vector Address $\rightarrow$ PC

TRAPcc	none #<data>	none 16, 32	if cc true, then TRAP exception
TRAPV	none	none	if V then take overflow TRAP exception
		Condition Code Register	
ANDI	#<data>, CCR	8	immediate data $\wedge$ CCR $\rightarrow$ CCR
EORI	#<data>, CCR	8	immediate data $\oplus$ CCR $\rightarrow$ CCR
MOVE	<ea>, CCR CCR, <ea>	16 16	source $\rightarrow$ CCR CCR $\rightarrow$ destination
ORI	#<data>, CCR	8	immediate data V CCR $\rightarrow$ CCR

3.10 MULTIPROCESSOR OPERATIONS

Communication between the MC68020 and other processors in the system is accomplished by using the TAS, CAS, CAS2 instructions (which execute indivisible read-modify-write bus cycles), and coprocessor instructions. These instructions are summarized in Table 3-10.

Table 3-10. Multiprocessor Operations

Instruction	Operand Syntax	Operand Size	Operation
		Read-Modify-Write	
CAS	Dc, Du, <ea>	8, 16, 32	destination − Dc → CC; if Z then Du → destination else destination → Dc
CAS2	Dc1:Dc2, Du1:Du2, (Rn):(Rn)	16, 32	dual operand CAS
TAS	<ea>	8	destination − 0; set condition codes; 1 → destination [7]
		Coprocessor	
cpBcc	<label>	16, 32	if cpcc true then PC + d → PC
cpDBcc	<label>, Dn	16	if cpcc false then Dn − 1 → Dn If Dn ≠ − 1, then PC + d → PC
cpGEN	User Defined	User Defined	operand → coprocessor
cpRESTORE	<ea>	none	restore coprocessor state from <ea>
cpSAVE	<ea>	none	save coprocessor state at <ea>
cpScc	<ea>	8	if cpcc true, then 1's → destination; else 0's → destination
cpTRAPcc	none # <data>	none 16, 32	if cpcc true then TRAPcc exception

SECTION 4
SIGNAL DESCRIPTION

This section contains a brief desciption of the input and output signals by their functional groups, as shown in Figure 4-1. Each signal is explained in a brief paragraph with reference (if applicable) to other sections that contain more detail about the function being performed.

NOTE

The terms assertion and negation are used extensively. This is done to avoid confusion when dealing with a mixture of "active-low" and "active-high" signals. The term **assert** or **assertion** is used to indicate that a signal is active or **true,** independent of whether that level is represented by a high or low voltage. The term **negate** or **negation** is used to indicate that a signal is inactive or **false.**

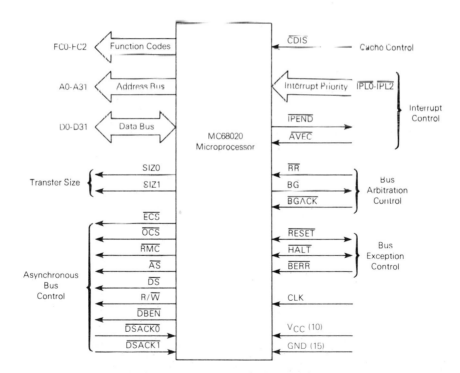

Figure 4-1. Functional Signal Groups

4.1 FUNCTION CODE SIGNALS (FC0 through FC2)

These three-state outputs identify the processor state (supervisor or user) and the address space of the bus cycle currently being executed as defined in Table 4.1.

Table 4-1. Function Code Assignments

FC2	FC1	FC0	Cycle Type
0	0	0	(Undefined, Reserved) *
0	0	1	User Data Space
0	1	0	User Program Space
0	1	1	(Undefined, Reserved) *
1	0	0	(Undefined, Reserved) *
1	0	1	Supervisor Data Space
1	1	0	Supervisor Program Space
1	1	1	CPU Space

* Address space 3 is reserved for user definition, while 0 and 4 are reserved for future use by Motorola.

By decoding the function codes, a memory system can utilize the full 4 gigabyte address range for several address spaces.

4.2 ADDRESS BUS (A0 through A31)

These three-state outputs provide the address for a bus transfer during all currently defined cycles except CPU-space references. During CPU-space references the address bus provides CPU related information. The address bus is capable of addressing 4 gigabytes (2^{32}) of data.

4.3 DATA BUS (D0 through D31)

These three-state, bidirectional signals provide the general purpose data path between the MC68020 and all other devices. The data bus can transmit and accept data using the dynamic bus sizing capabilities of the MC68020. Refer to **4.4 TRANSFER SIZE (SIZ0, SIZ1)** for additional information.

4.4 TRANSFER SIZE (SIZ0, SIZ1)

These three-state outputs are used in conjunction with the dynamic bus sizing capabilities of the MC68020. The SIZ0 and SIZ1 outputs indicate the number of bytes of an operand remaining to be transferred during a given bus cycle.

4.5 ASYNCHRONOUS BUS CONTROL SIGNALS

The asynchronous bus control signals for the MC68020 are described in the following paragraphs.

4.5.1 External Cycle Start (ECS)

This output is asserted during the first one-half clock of every bus cycle to provide the earliest indication that the MC68020 may be starting a bus cycle. The use of this signal must be validated later with address strobe, since the MC68020 may start an instruction fetch cycle and then abort it if the instruction word is found in the cache. The MC68020 drives only the address, size, and function code outputs (not address strobe) when it aborts a bus cycle due to cache hit.

4.5.2 Operand Cycle Start (OCS)

This output signal has the same timing as $\overline{ECS}$, except that it is asserted only during the first bus cycle of an operand transfer or instruction prefetch.

4.5.3 Read-Modify-Write Cycle (RMC)

This three-state output signal provides an indication that the current bus operation is an indivisible read-modify-write cycle. This signal is asserted for the duration of the read-modify-write sequence. $\overline{RMC}$ should be used as a bus lock to insure integrity of instructions which use the read-modify-write operation.

4.5.4 Address Strobe (AS)

This three-state output signal indicates that valid function code, address, size, and R/W state information is on the bus.

4.5.5 Data Strobe (DS)

In a read cycle, this three-state output indicates that the slave device should drive the data bus. In a write cycle, it indicates that the MC68020 has placed valid data on the data bus.

4.5.6 Read/Write (R/W)

This three-state output signal defines the direction of a data transfer. A high level indicates a read from an external device, a low level indicates a write to an external device.

4.5.7 Data Buffer Enable (DBEN)

This three-state output provides an enable to external data buffers. This signal allows the R/W signal to change without possible external buffer contention.

This pin is not necessary in all systems.

4.5.8 Data Transfer and Size Acknowledge (DSACK0, DSACK1)

These inputs indicate that a data transfer is complete and the port size of the external device (8-, 16-, or 32-bits). During a read cycle, when the processor recognizes $\overline{DSACKx}$, it latches the data and then terminates the bus cycle; during a write cycle, when the processor recognizes $\overline{DSACKx}$, the bus cycle is terminated. See **5.1.1 Dynamic Bus Sizing** for further information on $\overline{DSACKx}$ encodings.

The processor will synchronize the $\overline{DSACKx}$ inputs and allow skew between the two inputs. See **10.6 AC ELECTRICAL SPECIFICATIONS—READ AND WRITE CYCLES** for further information.

4.6 CACHE DISABLE ($\overline{\text{CDIS}}$)

This input signal dynamically disables the on-chip cache. The cache is disabled internally after the cache disable input is asserted and synchronized internally. The cache will be reenabled internally after the input negation has been synchronized internally. See **SECTION 7 ON-CHIP CACHE MEMORY** for further information.

4.7 INTERRUPT CONTROL SIGNALS

The following paragraphs describe the interrupt control signals for the MC68020. Refer to **5.2.4.1 INTERRUPT OPERATION** for additional information.

4.7.1 Interrupt Priority Level ($\overline{\text{IPL0}}$, $\overline{\text{IPL1}}$, $\overline{\text{IPL2}}$)

These inputs indicate the encoded priority level of the device requesting an interrupt. Level seven is the highest priority and cannot be masked; level zero indicates that no interrupts are requested. The least significant bit is $\overline{\text{IPL0}}$ and the most significant bit is $\overline{\text{IPL2}}$.

4.7.2 Interrupt Pending ($\overline{\text{IPEND}}$)

This output indicates that the encoded interrupt priority level active on the $\overline{\text{IPL0}}$-$\overline{\text{IPL2}}$ inputs is higher than the current level of the interrupt mask in the status register or that a non-maskable interrupt has been recognized.

4.7.3 Autovector ($\overline{\text{AVEC}}$)

The $\overline{\text{AVEC}}$ input is used to request internal generation of the vector number during an interrupt acknowledge cycle.

4.8 BUS ARBITRATION SIGNALS

The following paragraphs describe the three-wire bus arbitration pins used to determine which device in a system will be the bus master. Refer to **5.2.7 BUS ARBITRATION** for additional information.

4.8.1 Bus Request ($\overline{\text{BR}}$)

This input is wire-ORed with all request signals from all potential bus masters and indicates that some device other than the MC68020 requires bus mastership.

4.8.2 Bus Grant ($\overline{\text{BG}}$)

This output signal indicates to potential bus masters that the MC68020 will release ownership of the bus when the current bus cycle is completed.

4.8.3 Bus Grant Acknowledge ($\overline{BGACK}$)

This input indicates that some other device has become the bus master. This signal should not be asserted until the following conditions are met:

1) $\overline{BG}$ (bus grant) has been received through the bus arbitration process,
2) $\overline{AS}$ is negated, indicating that the MC68020 is not using the bus,
3) $\overline{DSACK0}$ and $\overline{DSACK1}$ are negated indicating that the previous external device is not using the bus, and
4) $\overline{BGACK}$ is negated, which indicates that no other device is still claiming bus mastership.

$\overline{BGACK}$ must remain asserted as long as any other device is bus master.

4.9 BUS EXCEPTION CONTROL SIGNALS

The following paragraphs describe the bus exception control signals for the MC68020.

4.9.1 Reset ($\overline{RESET}$)

This bidirectional open-drain signal is used as the systems reset signal. If $\overline{RESET}$ is asserted as an input, the processor will enter reset exception processing. As an output, the processor asserts $\overline{RESET}$ to reset external devices, but is not affected internally. Refer to **6.3.1 Reset** for more information.

4.9.2 Halt ($\overline{HALT}$)

The assertion of this bidirectional, open-drain signal stops all processor bus activity at the completion of the current bus cycle. When the processor has been halted using this input, all control signals will be placed in their inactive state, the $R/\overline{W}$, function code, and size signals, and the address bus remain driven with the previous bus cycle information. The $\overline{RMC}$ signal will be driven inactive, if asserted. The data bus is three-stated.

When the processor has stopped executing instructions, due to a double bus fault condition, the $\overline{HALT}$ line is driven by the processor to indicate to external devices that the processor has stopped.

4.9.3 Bus Error ($\overline{BERR}$)

This input signal informs the processor that there has been a problem with the bus cycle currently being executed. These problems may be the result of:

1) Non-responding devices,
2) Interrupt vector number acquisition failure,
3) Illegal accesses as determined by a memory management unit, or
4) Various other application dependent errors.

The bus error signal interacts with the halt signal to determine if the current bus cycle should be re-run or aborted with a bus error. Refer to **SECTION 5 BUS OPERATION** for additional information.

4.10 CLOCK (CLK)

The MC68020 clock input is a TTL-compatible signal that is internally buffered to develop internal clocks needed by the processor. The clock should not be gated off at any time and must conform to minimum and maximum period and pulse width times.

4.11 SIGNAL SUMMARY

Table 4-2 provides a summary of the electrical characteristics of the signals discussed in the previous paragraphs.

Table 4-2. Signal Summary

Signal Function	Signal Name	Input/Output	Active State	Three-State
Function Codes	FC0-FC2	Output	High	Yes
Address Bus	A0-A31	Output	High	Yes
Data Bus	D0-D31	Input/Output	High	Yes
Size	SIZ0-SIZ1	Output	High	Yes
External Cycle Start	ECS	Output	Low	No
Operand Cycle Start	OCS	Output	Low	No
Read-Modify-Write Cycle	RMC	Output	Low	Yes
Address Strobe	AS	Output	Low	Yes
Data Strobe	DS	Output	Low	Yes
Read/Write	R/W	Output	High/Low	Yes
Data Buffer Enable	DBEN	Output	Low	Yes
Data Transfer and Size Acknowledge	DSACK0-DSACK1	Input	Low	—
Cache Disable	CDIS	Input	Low	—
Interrupt Priority Level	IPL0-IPL2	Input	Low	—
Interrupt Pending	IPEND	Output	Low	No
Autovector	AVEC	Input	Low	—
Bus Request	BR	Input	Low	—
Bus Grant	BG	Output	Low	No
Bus Grant Acknowledge	BGACK	Input	Low	—
Reset	RESET	Input/Output	Low	No*
Halt	HALT	Input/Output	Low	No*
Bus Error	BERR	Input	Low	—
Clock	CLK	Input	—	—
Power Supply	V_{CC}	Input	—	—
Ground	GND	Input	—	—

*Open Drain

SECTION 5
BUS OPERATION

This section describes the control signal and bus operation during data transfer operations, bus arbitration, bus error and halt conditions, and reset operation.

NOTE

In the paragraphs dealing with bus transfers, a "port" refers to the external data bus width at the slave device (memory, peripheral, etc.).

During a write cycle, the MC68020 always drives all sections of the data bus.

The term "synchronization" is used repeatedly when discussing bus operation. This delay is the time period required for the MC68020 to sample an external asynchronous input signal, determine whether it is high or low, and synchronize the input to the internal clocks of the processor. Figure 5-1 shows the relationship between the clock signal, an external input, and its associated internal signal that is typical for all of the asynchronous inputs.

Furthermore, for all inputs, there is a sample window during which the processor latches the level of the input. This window is illustrated in Figure 5-2. In order to guarantee the recognition of a certain level on a specific falling edge of the clock, that level must be held stable on the input through the sample window. If an input makes a transition during the sample window, the level recognized by the processor is not predictable; however, the processor will always resolve the latched level to a logic high or low before taking action on it. One exception to this rule is for the late assertion of $\overline{BERR}$ (see **5.2.5.1 BUS ERROR OPERATION**), where the signal **must** be stable through the window or the processor may exhibit erratic behavior. In addition to meeting input setup and hold times, all input signals must obey the protocols described later in this section (e.g., when $\overline{DSACKx}$ is asserted, it must remain asserted until $\overline{AS}$ is negated).

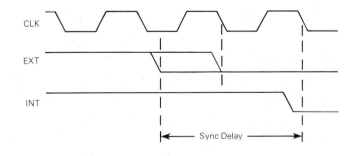

**Figure 5-1. Relationship Between External
and Internal Signals**

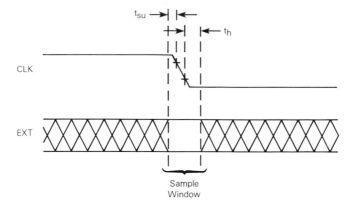

Figure 5-2. Sample Window

5.1 OPERAND TRANSFER MECHANISM

The MC68020 architecture supports byte, word, and long word operands allowing access to 8-, 16-, and 32-bit data ports through the use of the data transfer and size acknowledge inputs ($\overline{\text{DSACK0}}$ and $\overline{\text{DSACK1}}$). The $\overline{\text{DSACKx}}$ inputs are controlled by the slave device currently being accessed and are discussed further in **5.1.1 Dynamic Bus Sizing.**

The MC68020 places no restrictions on the alignment of operands in memory, that is, word and long word operands may be located at any byte boundary. However, instruction alignment on word (even byte) boundaries is enforced for maximum efficiency and in order to maintain compatibility with earlier members of the M68000 Family. The user should be aware that misalignment of word or long word operands may cause the MC68020 to perform multiple bus cycles for the operand transfer and therefore, processor performance is optimized if word and long word memory operands are aligned on word or long word boundaries, respectively. Refer to **5.1.3 Effects of Dynamic Bus Sizing and Operand Misalignment** for a discussion of the impact of dynamic bus sizing and operand alignment.

5.1.1 Dynamic Bus Sizing

The MC68020 allows operand transfers to or from 8-, 16-, and 32-bit ports by dynamically determining the port size during each bus cycle. During an operand transfer cycle, the slave device signals its port size (byte, word, or long-word) and transfer status (complete or not complete) to the processor through the use of the $\overline{\text{DSACKx}}$ inputs. The $\overline{\text{DSACKx}}$ inputs perform the same transfer acknowledge function as does the $\overline{\text{DTACK}}$ input of other processors in the M68000 Family as well as informing the MC68020 of the current port width. See Table 5-4 for $\overline{\text{DSACKx}}$ encodings and assertion results.

For example, if the processor is executing an instruction that requires a read of a long word operand it will attempt to read 32 bits during the first bus cycle (refer to **5.1.2 Misalignment of Bus Transfers**). If the port responds that it is 32 bits wide, the MC68020 latches all 32 bits of data and continues with the next operation. If the port responds that it is 16 bits wide, the MC68020 latches the 16 bits of valid data and runs another cycle to obtain the other 16 bits. An 8-bit port is handled similarly, but with four read cycles.

It is important to realize that the assertion of $\overline{\text{DSACK}}$, in addition to signalling completion of the bus cycle, indicates the device port size **not** the transfer size. For example, a 32-bit device **always** returns $\overline{\text{DSACK}}$ for a 32-bit port regardless of whether the bus cycle is a byte, word, or long word operation.

Each port is fixed in assignment to particular sections of the data bus. A 32-bit port is located on data bus bits 31 through 0, a 16-bit port is located on data bus bits 31 through 16, and an 8-bit port is located on data bus bits 31 through 24. The MC68020 makes these assumptions in order to locate valid data. This scheme minimizes the number of bus cycles needed to transfer data to the 8- and 16-bit ports. The MC68020 will always attempt to transfer the maximum amount of data on all bus cycles; i.e. for a long word operation, it always assumes that the port is 32 bits wide when beginning the bus cycle.

Figure 5-3 shows the required organization of data ports on the MC68020 bus for 8-, 16-, and 32-bit devices. The "OPn" labels in Figure 5-3 define the various operand bytes, with OP0 being the most significant. Figure 5-4 shows the internal organization of byte, word, and long word operands. The four bytes shown in Figure 5-3 are routed to the external data bus via the data multiplex and duplication hardware which is also shown. This hardware provides the basic mechanism through which the MC68020 supports dynamic bus sizing and operand misalignment.

The multiplexor operation, as detailed in Figure 5-3, shows the multiplexor connections for different combinations of address and data sizes. The multiplexor takes the four bytes of the 32-bit bus and routes them to their required positions. For example, OP0 can be routed to D31-D24, as would be the normal case, or it can be routed to any other byte position in order to support a misaligned transfer. The same is true for any of the operand bytes. The positioning of bytes is determined by the size (SIZ1 and SIZ0) and address (A0 and A1) outputs.

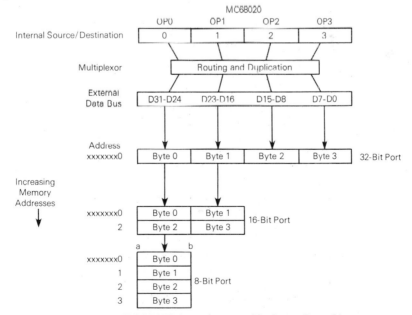

Figure 5-3. MC68020 Interface to Various Port Sizes

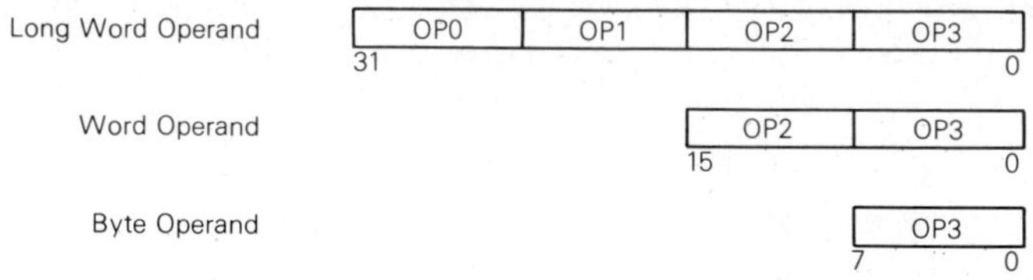

Long Word Operand	OP0	OP1	OP2	OP3

31   0

Word Operand	OP2	OP3

15   0

Byte Operand	OP3

7   0

Figure 5-4. Internal Operand Representation

The multiplexor routes and/or duplicates the bytes of the bus to allow for any combination of aligned or misaligned transfers to take place. The SIZ0 and SIZ1 outputs indicate the remaining number of bytes to be transferred during the next bus cycle.

The number of bytes transferred during a bus cycle will be equal to or less than the operand size indicated by the SIZ0 and SIZ1 outputs, depending on port width and operand alignment. For example, during the first bus cycle of a long word transfer to a word port, the size outputs will indicate four bytes are to be transferred although only two bytes will be moved on that cycle. Table 5-1 shows the encodings of SIZ1 and SIZ0.

Table 5-1. SIZE Output Encodings

SIZ1	SIZ0	Size
0	1	Byte
1	0	Word
1	1	3 Byte
0	0	Long Word

The address lines A0 and A1 also effect operation of the data multiplexor. During an operand transfer (instruction or data), A2-A31 indicate the long word base address of that portion of the operand to be accessed, while A0 and A1 give the byte offset from the base. For example, consider a word write to a long word address with an offset of one byte (A1/A0 = 01). The MC68020 will initiate the transfer (SIZ1/SIZ0 = 10, A1/A0 = 01) and the data multiplexor will place OP2 and OP3 (see Figure 5-3 and 5-4) on D16-D23 and D8-D15 respectively. Table 5-2 shows the encodings of A1 and A0 and the corresponding byte offsets from the long word base.

Table 5-2. Address Offset Encodings

A1	A0	Offset
0	0	+ 0 Bytes
0	1	+ 1 Byte
1	0	+ 2 Bytes
1	1	+ 3 Bytes

Table 5-3 describes the use of SIZ1, SIZ0, A1, and A0 in defining the transfer pattern from the MC68020's internal multiplexor to the external data bus.

Table 5-3. MC68020 Internal to External Data Bus Multiplexor

Transfer Size	Size		Address		Source/Destination External Data Bus Connection			
	SIZ1	SIZ0	A1	A0	D31:D24	D23:D16	D15:D8	D7:D0
Byte	0	1	x	x	OP3	OP3	OP3	OP3
Word	1	0	x	0	OP2	OP3	OP2	OP3
	1	0	x	1	OP2	OP2	OP3	OP2
3 Byte	1	1	0	0	OP1	OP2	OP3	OP0
	1	1	0	1	OP1	OP1	OP2	OP3
	1	1	1	0	OP1	OP2	OP1	OP2
	1	1	1	1	OP1	OP1	OP2	OP1
Long Word	0	0	0	0	OP0	OP1	OP2	OP3
	0	0	0	1	OP0	OP0	OP1	OP2
	0	0	1	0	OP0	OP1	OP0	OP1
	0	0	1	1	OP0	OP0	OP1*	OP0

* On write cycles this byte is output, on read cycles this byte is ignored.

x = don't care.

NOTE: The OP labels on the external data bus refer to a particular byte of the operand that will be read or written on that section of the data bus (see Figure 5-4).

Table 5-4 describes the encodings of the $\overline{\text{DSACKx}}$ pins to signal current port size.

Table 5-4. $\overline{\text{DSACK}}$ Codes and Results

$\overline{\text{DSACK1}}$	$\overline{\text{DSACK0}}$	Result
H	H	Insert Wait States in Current Bus Cycle
H	L	Complete Cycle — Data Bus Port Size is 8 Bits
L	H	Complete Cycle — Data Bus Port Size is 16 Bits
L	L	Complete Cycle — Data Bus Port Size is 32 Bits

Figure 5-5 shows the basic control flow associated with an aligned long word transfer to a 16-bit port. Refer to Figure 5-6 for timing relationships. The high order word of the long word (OP0 and OP1) will be transferred to the port located on D16-D31 during the first bus operation. The size outputs will indicate a long word operand and the lower address bits will show a zero offset from the long word base (SIZ1/SIZ0/A1/A0 = 0000). The port responds to the processor by asserting the $\overline{\text{DSACK}}$ inputs to indicate completion of a 16-bit transfer ($\overline{\text{DSACK1}}/\overline{\text{DSACK0}}$ = LH). The MC68020 terminates this cycle and begins a second cycle to complete the transfer. For the second cycle, the size and address outputs will indicate that a word transfer is to occur on the upper data bus D16-D31 (SIZ1/SIZ0/A1/A0 = 1010). The base offset has been incremented by two in order to access the next highest word location. The processor also multiplexes the lower word of the operand to D31-D16 and the port again responds by asserting the $\overline{\text{DSACKx}}$ inputs ($\overline{\text{DSACK1}}/\overline{\text{DSACK0}}$ = LH).

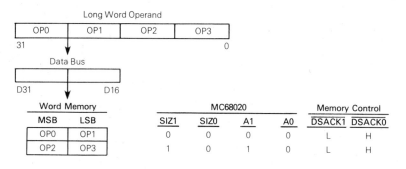

Figure 5-5. Example of Long Word Transfer to Word Bus

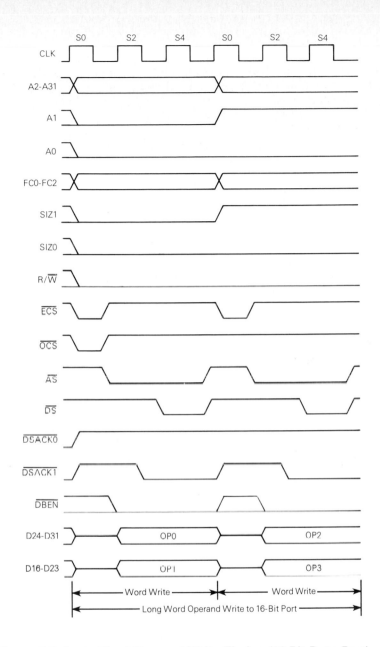

Figure 5-6. Long Word Operand Write Timing (16-Bit Data Port)

5

The control flow for an aligned long word transfer to an 8-bit port is shown in Figure 5-7. Four bus cycles will be required to transfer this operand, moving one byte per cycle. Similar to the previous example, the size outputs indicate a long word transfer during the first cycle, three byte during the second, word during the third, and byte during the final cycle. See Table 5-3 for processor multiplexor operation during this transfer. Figure 5-8 shows timing relationships for these transfers.

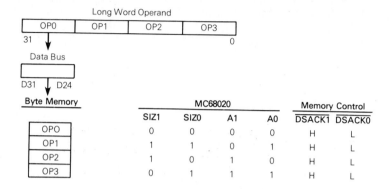

	SIZ1	SIZ0	A1	A0	$\overline{\text{DSACK1}}$	$\overline{\text{DSACK0}}$
OPO	0	0	0	0	H	L
OP1	1	1	0	1	H	L
OP2	1	0	1	0	H	L
OP3	0	1	1	1	H	L

Figure 5-7. Example of Long Word Transfer to Byte Bus

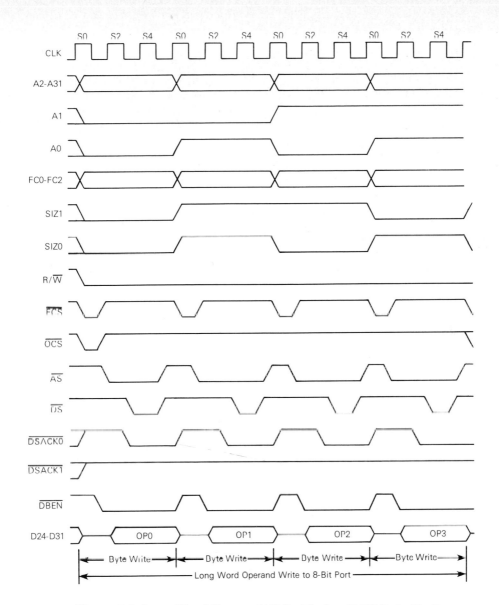

Figure 5-8. Long Word Operand Write Timing (8-Bit Data Port)

5

5.1.2 Misalignment of Bus Transfers

In the 32-bit architecture of the MC68020, it is possible to execute an operand transfer on a memory address boundary that may not fall on an equivalent operand size boundary. Examples are words transferred to odd addresses and long words transferred to addresses other than long word boundaries. The MC68000, MC68008, and MC68010 implementations allow long word transfers on odd word boundaries but force an exception if word or long word operand transfers are attempted at odd byte addresses.

The MC68020 does not enforce any data alignment restrictions. Some performance degradation can occur due to the multiple bus accesses that the MC68020 must make when long word (word) operand accesses do not fall on long word (word) boundaries.

Note that instructions, and their associated (if any) extension words, are required to fall on word address boundaries, but this is not required for program space operand references. The MC68020 forces an address error exception if an instruction prefetch is attempted at an odd address. This occurs when an instruction (e.g., a branch with an odd offset) leaves the program counter set to an odd address.

Dynamic bus sizing also affects the transfer position of misalignment operands.

NOTE

In the following examples for misaligned transfers, xxx in a byte denotes that the value is left unchanged.

Figure 5-9 shows the control associated with transferring a long word operand to an odd address in word organized memory. Figure 5-10 shows the timing relationship for this operation. This transfer requires that the MC68020 place a long word in memory starting at the least significant byte of long word 0. This transfer crosses two word boundaries and requires three bus cycles to complete. The first cycle executes with A2/A1/A0 = 001) and the size outputs indicating a long word transfer (SIZ1/SIZ0 = 00). The word addressed during this transfer contains only one byte of the destination and will respond with DSACK1/DSACK0 = LH (port width = 16 bits). The system designer must ensure that the unused byte of the word accessed during this cycle does not receive an enable (refer to **5.1.4 Address, Size, and Data Bus Relationships**). The processor executes

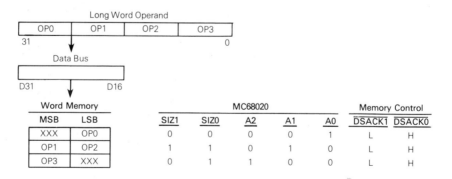

Word Memory		MC68020					Memory Control	
MSB	LSB	SIZ1	SIZ0	A2	A1	A0	DSACK1	DSACK0
XXX	OP0	0	0	0	0	1	L	H
OP1	OP2	1	1	0	1	0	L	H
OP3	XXX	0	1	1	0	0	L	H

Figure 5-9. Misaligned Long Word Transfer to Word Bus Example

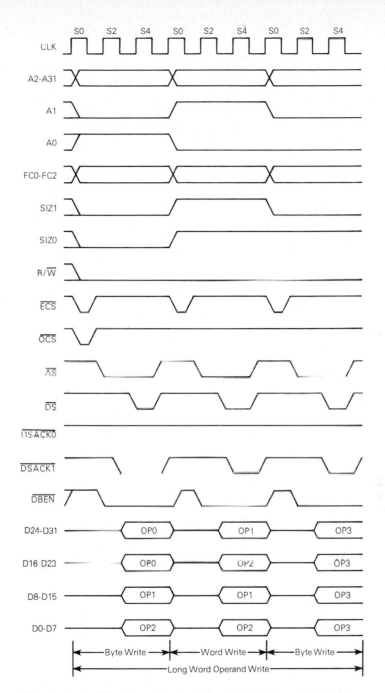

Figure 5-10. Misaligned Long Word Transfer to Word Bus

5-11

the next transfer with A2/A1/A0 = 010 and SIZ1/SIZ0 = 11 (three bytes remaining). The memory accepts two bytes on this transfer and again asserts $\overline{\text{DSACK1}}/\overline{\text{DSACK0}}$ = LH. The final cycle is executed with the transfer of a single byte (SIZ1/SIZ0 = 01) to address A2/A1/A0 = 100.

Figure 5-11 shows an example of a word transfer to an odd address in word organized memory. This example is similar to the one shown in Figure 5-9 except that the operand is of word size and requires only two bus cycles. Figure 5-12 shows the signal timing associated with this example.

Word Memory				MC68020				Memory Control	
MSB	LSB	SIZ1	SIZ0	A2	A1	A0		DSACK1	DSACK0
XXX	OP2	1	0	0	0	1		L	H
OP3	XXX	0	1	0	1	0		L	H

Figure 5-11. Example of Misaligned Word Transfer to Word Bus

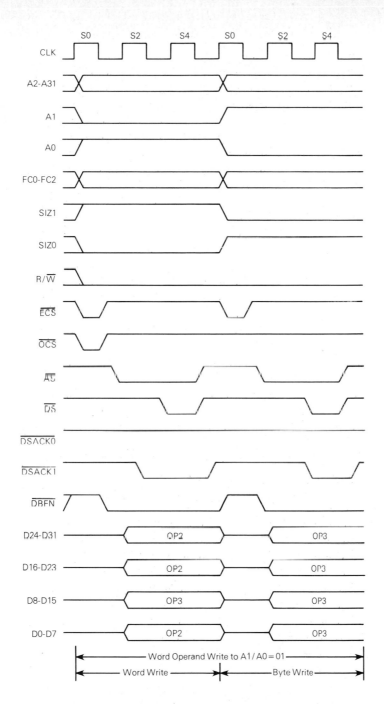

Figure 5-12. Misaligned Word Transfer to Word Bus

Figure 5-13 shows an example of a long word transfer to an odd address in long-word-organized memory. In this example, a long word access is attempted beginning at the least significant byte of a long-word-organized memory. Thus, only one byte is transferred in the first bus cycle. The second bus cycle then consists of a three byte access to a long word boundary. Since the memory is long word organized, no further bus cycles are necessary. Figure 5-14 shows the signal timing associated with this example.

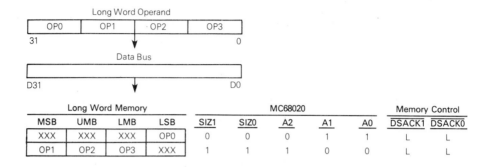

Long Word Memory				MC68020					Memory Control	
MSB	UMB	LMB	LSB	SIZ1	SIZ0	A2	A1	A0	DSACK1	DSACK0
XXX	XXX	XXX	OP0	0	0	0	1	1	L	L
OP1	OP2	OP3	XXX	1	1	1	0	0	L	L

Figure 5-13. Misaligned Long Word Transfer to Long Word Bus

5.1.3 Effects of Dynamic Bus Sizing and Operand Misalignment

The combination of operand size, operand alignment, and port size affect the operation of the MC68020 operand transfer mechanism by dictating the number of bus cycles required to perform a particular memory access. Table 5-5 shows the number of bus cycles that are required for different operand sizes through different port sizes based on the alignment of that operand.

Table 5-5. Memory Alignment and Port Size Influence on Bus Cycles

	A1/A0	Number of Bus Cycles			
		00	01	10	11
Instruction*		1:2:4	N/A	N/A	N/A
Byte Operand		1:1:1	1:1:1	1:1:1	1:1:1
Word Operand		1:1:2	1:2:2	1:1:2	2:2:2
Long-Word Operand		1:2:4	2:3:4	2:2:4	2:3:4

Data Port Size 32-Bits: 16-Bits: 8-Bits
*Instruction prefetches are always two words from a long word boundary.

As can be seen in this table, the MC68020 bus throughput can be significantly affected by port size and alignment. The MC68020 system designer should be aware of and account for these effects, particularly in time critical applications.

Table 5-5 shows that the processor always prefetches instructions by reading two words from a long word boundary. When the MC68020 prefetches from the instruction stream, it always reads a long word from an even word address (A1/A0 = 00), regardless of port size or alignment.

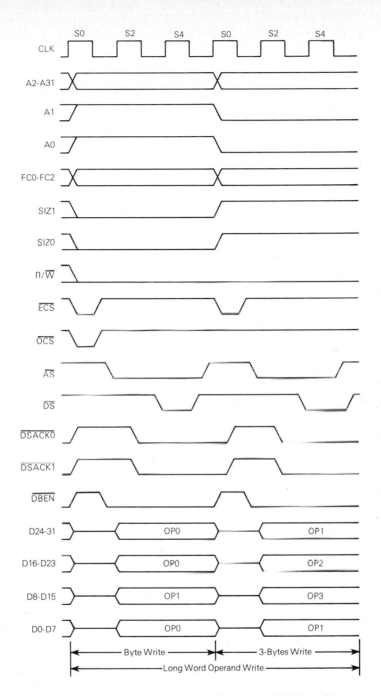

Figure 5-14. Misaligned Write Cycles to 32-Bit Data Port

5.1.4 Address, Size, and Data Bus Relationships

The dynamic bus capabilities of the MC68020, coupled with the allowance for misaligned operands, create an extremely powerful and flexible bus structure. Correct external interpretation of bus control signals is critical to ensure valid data transfer operation.

The MC68020 system designer should ensure that data ports are aligned as discussed in **5.1.1 Dynamic Bus Sizing** such that the MC68020 is able to route data to the correct locations. It is also required that the correct byte data strobes (four, for a long word memory) be generated which enable only those section of the data port(s) which are active during the current bus cycle. The MC68020 always drives all sections of the data bus during a write cycle, so this necessitates careful control of the enable signals for independent bytes of a data port.

For example, consider the bus transfer operation illustrated in Figure 5-9. The transfer described is a long word write to an odd address in word-organized memory, requiring three bus cycles to complete. Both the first and the last transfers require writing a single byte to a word address. In order not to overwrite those bytes which are not involved in these transfers, no byte data strobe should be asserted for those bytes.

The required active bytes of the data bus for any given bus transfer are a function of the size (SIZ1/SIZ0) and lower address (A1/A0) outputs of the MC68020 and are shown in Table 5-6. Individual data strobes for each byte of the bus can be generated by qualifying the above enables with data strobe ($\overline{\text{DS}}$). Devices residing on 8-bit ports can utilize $\overline{\text{DS}}$ alone since there is only one valid byte for any transfer.

Figure 5-15 shows a logic diagram of one method of generating byte data selects for 16 and 32-bit ports from the size and address encodings.

Table 5-6. Data Bus Activity for Byte, Word, and Long Word Ports

Transfer Size	SIZ1	SIZ0	A1	A0	Data Bus Active Sections Byte (B) — Word (W) — Long Word (L) Ports			
					D31-D24	D23-D16	D15-D8	D7-D0
Byte	0	1	0	0	B W L	—	—	—
	0	1	0	1	B	W L	—	—
	0	1	1	0	B W	—	L	—
	0	1	1	1	B	W	—	L
Word	1	0	0	0	B W L	W L	—	—
	1	0	0	1	B	W L	L	—
	1	0	1	0	B W	W	L	L
	1	0	1	1	B	W	—	L
Three-Byte	1	1	0	0	B W L	W L	L	—
	1	1	0	1	B	W L	L	L
	1	1	1	0	B W	W	L	L
	1	1	1	1	B	W	—	L
Long Word	0	0	0	0	B W L	W L	L	L
	0	0	0	1	B	W L	L	L
	0	0	1	0	B W	W	L	L
	0	0	1	1	B	W	—	L

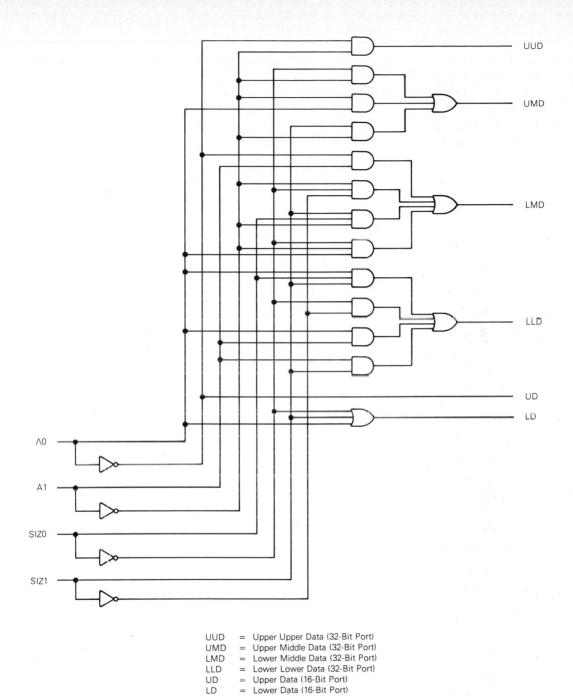

UUD	=	Upper Upper Data (32-Bit Port)
UMD	=	Upper Middle Data (32-Bit Port)
LMD	=	Lower Middle Data (32-Bit Port)
LLD	=	Lower Lower Data (32-Bit Port)
UD	=	Upper Data (16-Bit Port)
LD	=	Lower Data (16-Bit Port)

Figure 5-15. Byte Data Select Generation for 16- and 32-Bit Ports

5.2 BUS OPERATION

Transfer of data between the processor and other devices involves the following signals:

    1. Address Bus A0 through A31,

    2. Data Bus D0 through D31, and

    3. Control Signals.

The address and data buses are parallel, non-multiplexed buses used to transfer data with an asynchronous bus protocol. In all bus cycles, the bus master is responsible for deskewing all signals issued at both the start and the end of the cycle. In addition, the bus master is responsible for deskewing the acknowledge and data signals from the slave devices.

The following sections explain the data transfer operations, bus arbitration functions, and exception processing.

5.2.1 Read Cycles

During a read cycle, the processor receives data from a memory or peripheral device. The processor reads bytes in all cases. The MC68020 will read a byte, or bytes, as determined by the operand size and alignment. See **5.1 OPERAND TRANSFER MECHANISM.** If the $\overline{DSACKx}$ inputs or $\overline{BERR}$ are not asserted during the sample window of the falling edge of S2, wait cycles will be inserted in the bus cycle until either $\overline{DSACK1}/\overline{DSACK0}$ or $\overline{BERR}$ is recognized as being asserted.

A flowchart of a long word read cycle is shown in Figure 5-16 with positional signal information shown in Figure 5-17. A flowchart of a byte read cycle is shown in Figure 5-18 with byte and word read cycle timing shown in Figure 5-19. Actual read cycle timing diagrams specified in terms of clock periods are shown in **SECTION 10 ELECTRICAL SPECIFICATIONS.**

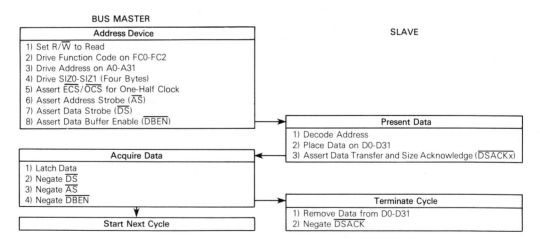

Figure 5-16. Long Word Read Cycle Flowchart

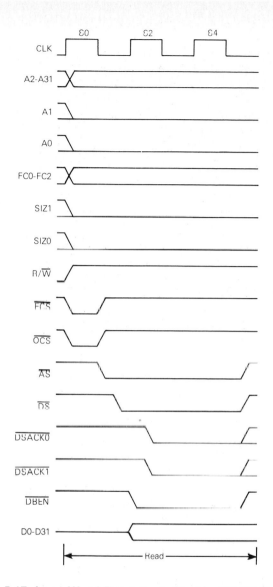

Figure 5-17. Long-Word Read Cycle Timing (32-Bit Data Port)

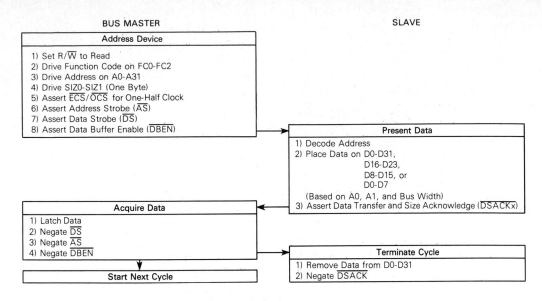

Figure 5-18. Byte Read Cycle Flowchart

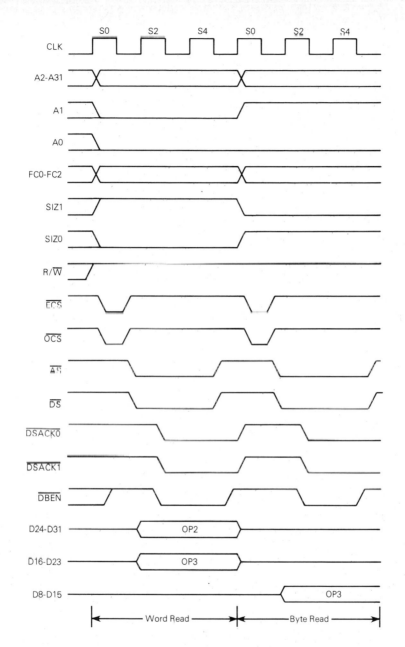

Figure 5-19. Byte and Word Read Cycle Timing (32-Bit Data Port)

5.2.2 Write Cycle

During a write cycle, the processor sends data to memory or a peripheral device. The function of the operand transfer mechanism during a write cycle is identical to that during a read cycle. See **5.1 OPERAND TRANSFER MECHANISM.**

A flowchart of write cycle operation for words is shown in Figure 5-20. Byte and word write cycle timing is shown in Figure 5-21. The actual write cycle timing diagrams specified in terms of clock periods and details of both word and byte write cycle operations are given in **SECTION 10 ELECTRICAL SPECIFICATIONS.**

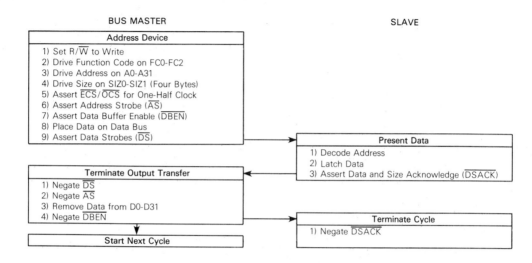

Figure 5-20. Write Cycle Flowchart

5.2.3 Read-Modify-Write Cycle

The read-modify-write cycle performs a read(s), modifies the data in the arithmetic-logic unit and writes the data back to the same address(es). In the M68000 architecture this process is indivisible. During the entire read-modify-write sequence the MC68020 asserts the $\overline{RMC}$ signal to indicate that an indivisible operation is occurring. The MC68020 will not issue a bus grant ($\overline{BG}$) in response to a bus request ($\overline{BR}$) during this operation.

The read-modify-write sequence is implemented to provide a means for secure inter-task and/or inter-processor communication.

The test and set (TAS) and compare and swap (CAS and CAS2) instructions are the only MC68020 instructions which utilize this feature.

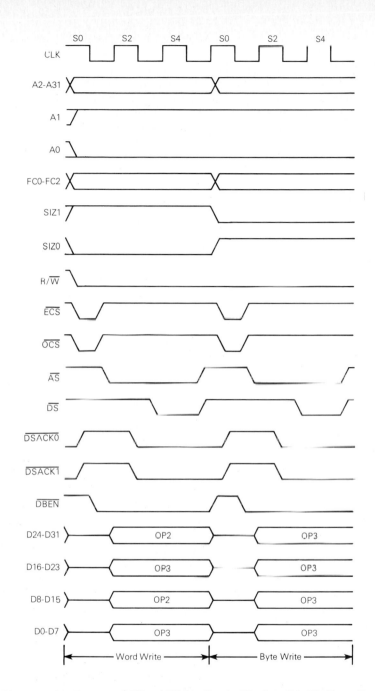

Figure 5-21. Byte and Word Write Cycle Timing (32-Bit Data Port)

A flowchart of the read-modify-write cycle operation is shown in Figure 5-22. For the CAS and CAS2 instructions, the operand read(s) and optional operand write(s) will use the dynamic bus sizing and operand misalignment capabilities of the processor to transfer up to two or four long word operands respectively. Thus, within both the read and write phases of the indivisible cycle, there may be up to eight bus cycles to different addresses. Note that this can impact bus arbitration latency if CAS or CAS2 operands are not long word aligned in a 32-bit port. Figure 5-23 depicts positional clock information for the read-modify-write operation. Actual timing diagrams specified in terms of clock periods are given in **SECTION 10 ELECTRICAL SPECIFICATIONS.**

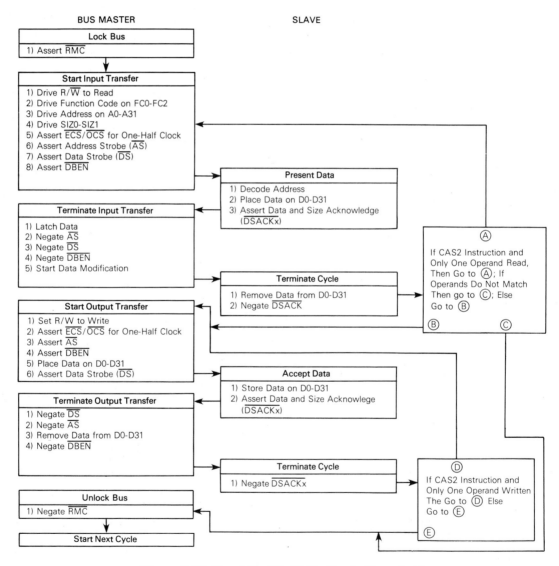

Figure 5-22. Read-Modify-Write Cycle Flowchart

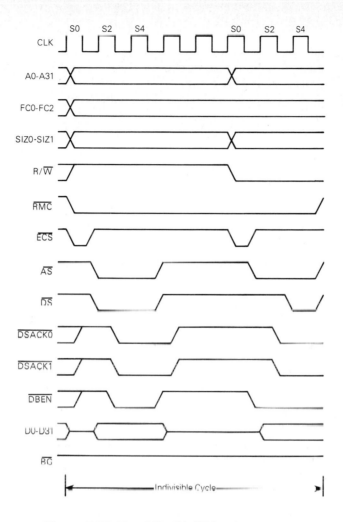

Figure 5-23. Read-Modify-Write Cycle Timing
(32-Bit Port, CAS Instruction)

5.2.4 CPU Space Cycles

Normal processor bus operations fall into two distinct classes: those which reference program areas and those which access data areas, as defined by the function code outputs. See **4.1 FUNCTION CODE SIGNALS (FC0-FC2).** A third class of operation incorporates those processor functions which do not properly fall into one of the above categories. These cycles are classified as CPU space cycles (FC0-FC2 = 111) and include interrupt acknowledge, breakpoint, module operations, and coprocessor communications. The CPU space type is encoded on A16-A19 during a CPU space operation and indicates the function that the processor is performing. On the MC68020, four of the encodings are implemented as shown in Figure 5-24.

All unused encodings are reserved by Motorola for future extension of CPU space functions.

5.2.4.1 INTERRUPT OPERATION. The following paragraphs describe the recognition and acknowledgement of interrupts for the MC68020. See **6.3.10 Interrupts** for interrupt processing details.

5.2.4.1.1 Interrupt Levels. The M68000 architecture supports seven levels of prioritized interrupts (level seven being the highest priority). Devices may be chained externally within interrupt priority levels, allowing an unlimited number of devices to interrupt the processor. Interrupt recognition and subsequent processing is based on the encoded state of the $\overline{IPL0}$-$\overline{IPL2}$ control inputs and the current processor priority set in the interrupt priority mask (I2, I1, I0) of MC68020 status register. Interrupt request level zero ($\overline{IPL0}/\overline{IPL1}/\overline{IPL2}$ = HHH) indicates that no interrupt service is requested. When an interrupt level one through six is requested via $\overline{IPL0}$-$\overline{IPL2}$, the processor compares the interrupt request level to the interrupt mask in order to determine whether the interrupt should be processed. Interrupt requests are ignored for all interrupt request levels that are less than or equal to the current processor priority determined by the interrupt mask. Level seven interrupts are non-maskable and are discussed further in **6.3.10 Interrupts.**

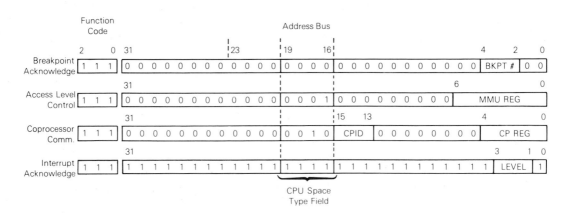

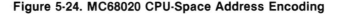

Figure 5-24. MC68020 CPU-Space Address Encoding

Table 5-7 shows the relationship between the actual requested interrupt level, the interrupt control lines ($\overline{\text{IPL0}}$-$\overline{\text{IPL2}}$), and the interrupt mask levels required for recognition of the requested interrupt.

Table 5-7. Interrupt Control Line Status for Each Requested Interrupt Level and Corresponding Interrupt Mask Levels

Requested Interrupt Level	Control Line Status			Interrupt Mask Level Required for Recognition
	$\overline{\text{IPL2}}$	$\overline{\text{IPL1}}$	$\overline{\text{IPL0}}$	
0*	High	High	High	N/A*
1	High	High	Low	0
2	High	Low	High	0-1
3	High	Low	Low	0-2
4	Low	High	High	0-3
5	Low	High	Low	0-4
6	Low	Low	High	0-5
7	Low	Low	Low	0-7

*Indicates that no interrupt is requested.

5.2.4.1.2 Recognition of Interrupts. To ensure that an interrupt will be recognized, the following rules should be followed:

1) The incoming interrupt request level must be at a higher priority level than the mask level set in the status register (except for level seven, the non-maskable interrupt).

2) The $\overline{\text{IPL0}}$-$\overline{\text{IPL2}}$ interrupt control lines must be held at the interrupt request level until the MC68020 acknowledges the interrupt. See **5.2.4.1.3 Interrupt Acknowledge Sequence (IACK).**

The above rules guarantee that the interrupt will be processed; however, the interrupt could also be processed if the request is taken away before the IACK bus cycle.

The MC68020 input synchronization circuitry for the $\overline{\text{IPL0}}$-$\overline{\text{IPL2}}$ control lines samples these inputs on consecutive falling edges of the processor clock in order to synchronize and debounce these signals. An interrupt request that is held constant for two consecutive clock periods is considered a valid input, and therefore it is possible that an interrupt request that is held for as short a period as two clock cycles could be recognized.

Interrupts recognized through the process described above do not force immediate exception processing but are made pending. Only those interrupt requests which exceed the current processor priority are made pending, after the synchronization and debounce delay, as described previously, and will cause the assertion of $\overline{\text{IPEND}}$, signalling to external devices that the MC68020 has an interrupt pending. Exception processing for a pending interrupt commences at the next instruction boundary, providing that a higher priority exception is not also valid. See **4.7.2 Interrupt Pending ($\overline{\text{IPEND}}$).**

5.2.4.1.3 Interrupt Acknowledge Sequence (IACK). When there is a pending interrupt at an instruction boundary, the MC68020 initiates interrupt processing, provided that no higher priority exceptions are pending. See **6.2 EXCEPTION PROCESSING.** In order to correctly service an interrupt request, the processor must first determine the starting location of the interrupt service routine corresponding to the requested service. The

M68000 Family supports acquisition of this information with the interrupt acknowledge cycle, during which the processor acquires externally, or generates internally, the interrupt vector number. See **6.2.1 Exception Vectors.**

The MC68020 supports acquisition of the interrupt vector number by two methods. For those devices that have a vector register, the device may pass the vector to the processor over the data bus during the IACK cycle. For those devices that cannot supply an interrupt vector, the MC68020 uses internally generated autovectors. The MC68020 IACK sequence is the same for both cases, but the response of the interrupting device differs.

At the beginning of the IACK cycle, the processor sets the function code and A16-A19 to indicate CPU space seven, echoes the interrupt level being acknowledged on A1-A3 and drives the remainder of the address bus high to indicate that the CPU space access is an interrupt acknowledge cycle. The interrupting device then either places an interrupt vector number on the least significant byte of its data port and asserts $\overline{DSACK0}/\overline{DSACK1}$ to indicate its port size, or it asserts $\overline{AVEC}$ to request that the processor internally generates the vector number corresponding to the requested interrupt level. Further detail of the IACK cycle is provided in Figures 5-25, 5-26, and 5-27.

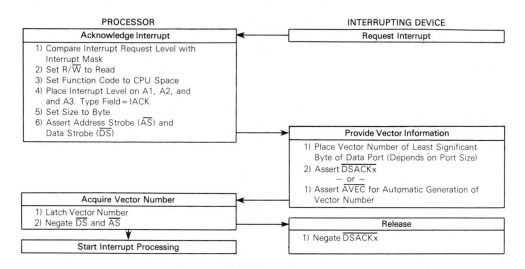

Figure 5-25. Interrupt Acknowledge Sequence Flowchart

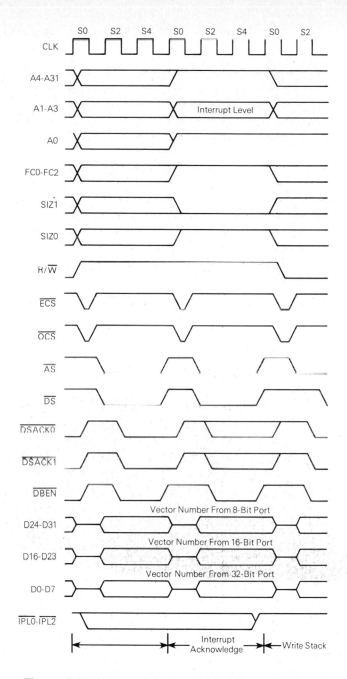

Figure 5-26. Interrupt Acknowledge Cycle Timing

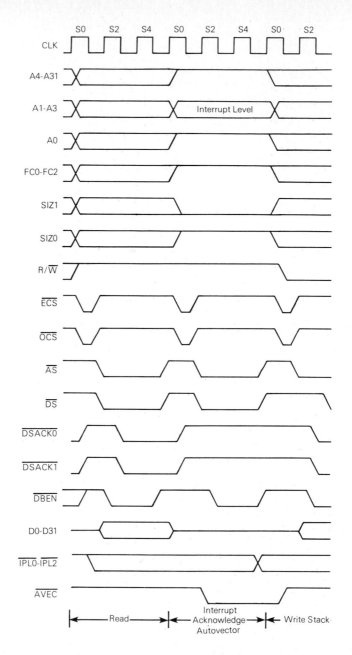

Figure 5-27. Autovector Operation Timing

5.2.4.1.4 Spurious Interrupt. If, during the interrupt acknowledge cycle, no device responds by asserting DSACK0/DSACK1 or AVEC, BERR should be asserted to terminate the vector acquisition. The processor separates the processing of this error from a bus error by fetching the spurious interrupt vector instead of the bus error vector. The processor then proceeds with the usual interrupt exception processing.

5.2.4.1.5 IACK Generation. In order to inform external devices that the processor is performing an interrupt acknowledge cycle, it is normal to generate IACK signals for each of the seven interrupt levels. The IACK signal for a particular level can be derived by decoding the interrupt level from A1-A3 and qualifying this with the function codes high (CPU space), the CPU space type (A16-A19) high (type $F), and address strobe (AS) asserted.

5.2.4.2 BREAKPOINT ACKNOWLEDGE CYCLE. When a breakpoint instruction is executed, the MC68020 performs a word read from the CPU space, type 0, at an address corresponding to the breakpoint number (bits [2:0] of the opcode). If this bus cycle is terminated by BERR, the processor then proceeds to perform illegal instruction exception processing. If the bus cycle is terminated by DSACKx, the processor uses the data returned on D16-D31 (for 16-bit or 32-bit ports) or two reads from D24-D31 (for 8-bit port) to replace the breakpoint instruction in the internal instruction pipeline, and begins execution of that instruction. The breakpoint operation flow is shown in Figure 5-28. Figures 5-29 and 5-30 show the timing diagrams for the breakpoint acknowledge cycle with the instruction opcodes supplied on the cycle and with an exception signaled, respectively.

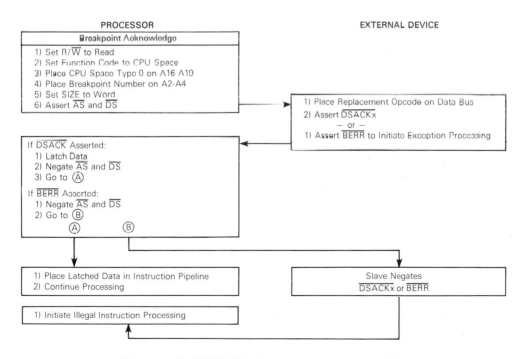

Figure 5-28. MC68020 Breakpoint Operation Flow

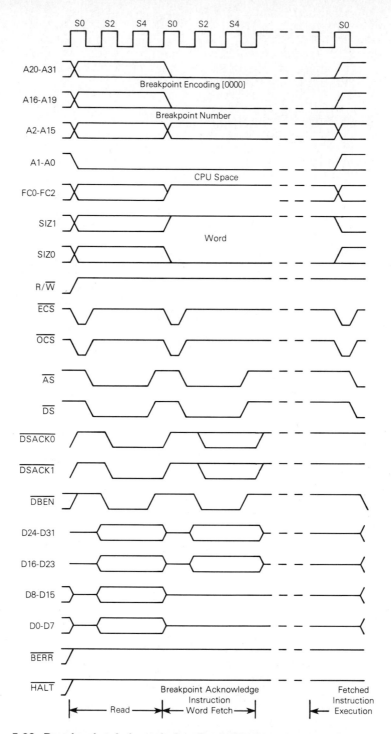

Figure 5-29. Breakpoint Acknowledge Cycle Timing (Opcode Returned)

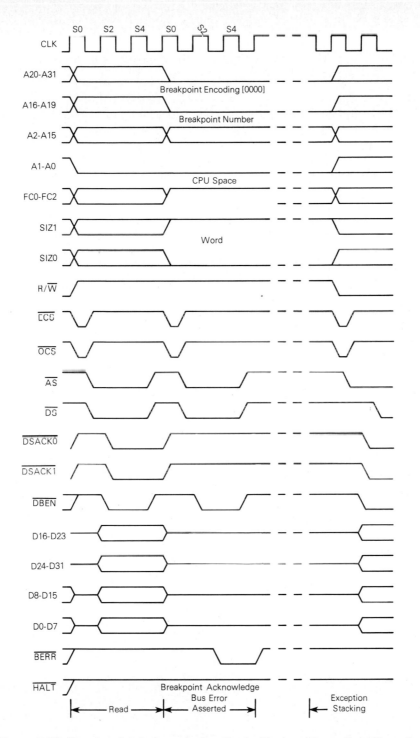

Figure 5-30. Breakpoint Acknowledge Cycle Timing (Exception Signalled)

5.2.4.3 COPROCESSOR OPERATIONS. The MC68020 coprocessor interface allows for instruction-oriented communication between the processor and up to eight coprocessors. The bus communication required to support coprocessor operations is carried out in the MC68020 CPU space.

Coprocessor accesses utilize standard bus protocol except that the address bus supplies access information rather than an address. The CPU space type field (A16-A19) for a coprocessor operation is 0010. The coprocessor identification number is encoded in A13-A15 and A0-A5 indicate the coprocessor interface register to be accessed. The memory management unit of an MC68020 system is always identified by coprocessor ID zero and has an extended register select field (A0-A7) in CPU space 0001 for use by the CALLM and RTM access level checking mechanism.

5.2.5 Bus Error and Halt Operation

In a bus architecture that requires a handshake from an external device to signal that a bus cycle is complete, the possibility exists that the handshake might not occur. Since different systems require different maximum response times, a bus error input is provided; see **4.9.3 Bus Error ($\overline{\text{BERR}}$)**. External circuitry must be used to determine the maximum duration between the assertion of address strobe ($\overline{\text{AS}}$) and data transfer and size acknowledge ($\overline{\text{DSACKx}}$) before issuing a bus error signal. When a $\overline{\text{BERR}}$ and/or $\overline{\text{HALT}}$ signal is received, the processor initiates a bus error exception sequence or retries the bus cycle.

In addition to a bus timeout indicator, the $\overline{\text{BERR}}$ input is used to indicate an access fault in a protected memory scheme or a page/segment fault in a virtual memory system. When an external memory management unit detects an invalid memory access, a bus error is generated to suspend execution of the current instruction.

5.2.5.1 BUS ERROR OPERATION. When the bus error signal is issued to terminate a bus cycle, the MC68020 may enter exception processing immediately following the bus cycle, or may defer processing the exception until it needs the data that it was attempting to access. Due to the highly pipelined architecture of the MC68020, the processor attempts to prefetch instructions ahead of the current program counter. If the MC68020 encounters a bus error during an instruction prefetch, the processor defers bus error exception processing until the faulted data is actually needed for execution. It is possible that bus error processing will not take place for a faulted access if changes in program flow (e.g., branches) make usage of the faulted data unnecessary.

The bus error signal will be recognized during a bus cycle in either of the following cases:
1) $\overline{\text{DSACKx}}$ and $\overline{\text{HALT}}$ are negated and $\overline{\text{BERR}}$ is asserted.
2) $\overline{\text{HALT}}$ and $\overline{\text{BERR}}$ are negated and $\overline{\text{DSACKx}}$ is asserted. $\overline{\text{BERR}}$ is then asserted within one clock cycle.
3) $\overline{\text{BERR}}$ and $\overline{\text{HALT}}$ asserted.

When the bus error condition is recognized, the current bus cycle is terminated in the normal fashion. Figures 5-31 and 5-32 show the timing diagrams for both the normal and the delayed bus error signals, assuming that the exception is taken. See **6.3.3 Bus Error** for exception processing details.

5.2.5.2 RETRY OPERATION When, during a bus cycle, the $\overline{BERR}$ and $\overline{HALT}$ inputs are both asserted by an external device, the processor enters the retry sequence. A delayed retry may be used, similar to the delayed bus error signal described above. Figures 5-33 and 5-34 show timing diagrams for both methods of retrying the bus cycle.

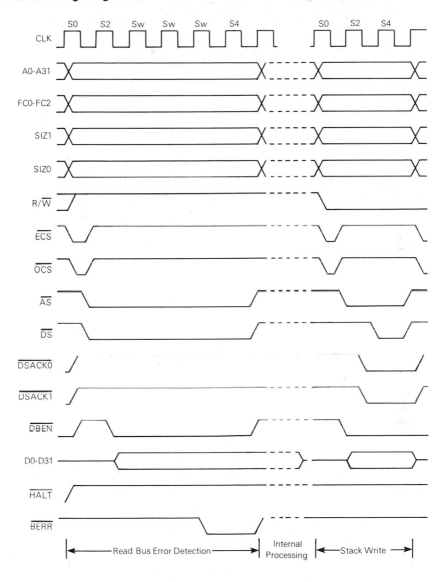

Figure 5-31. Bus Error Timing (Exception Taken)

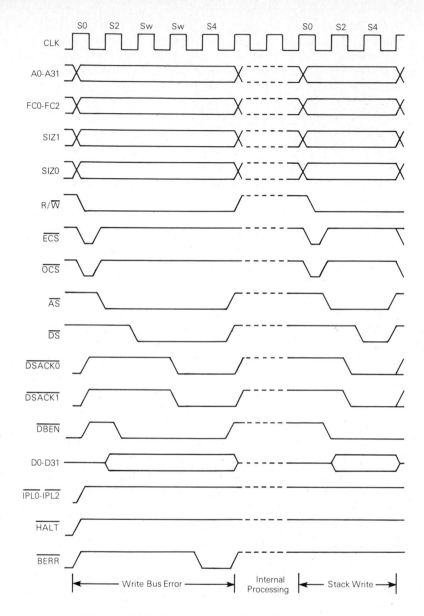

Figure 5-32. Delayed Bus Error (Exception Taken)

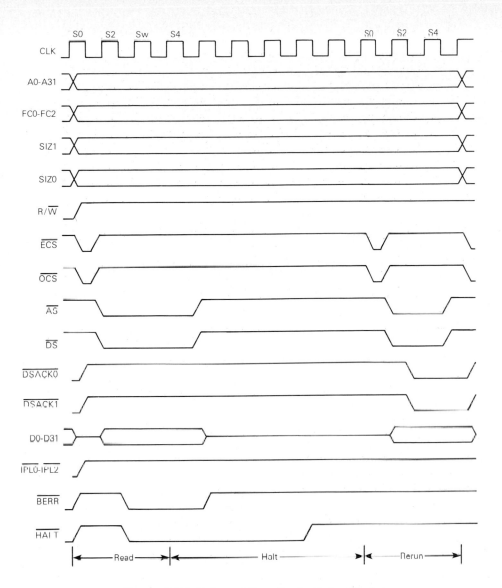

Figure 5-33. Delayed Bus Cycle Retry Timing

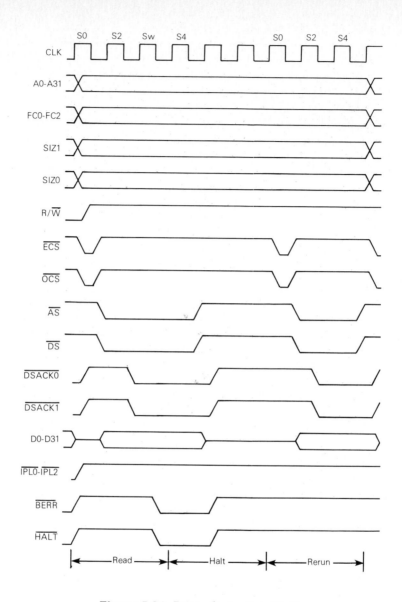

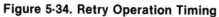

Figure 5-34. Retry Operation Timing

The processor terminates the bus cycle, places the control signals in their inactive state and does not run another bus cycle until the $\overline{\text{BERR}}$ and $\overline{\text{HALT}}$ signals are negated by external logic. The processor then retries the previous cycle using the same access information (address, function code, size, etc.). The $\overline{\text{BERR}}$ signal should be negated before or in conjunction with the $\overline{\text{HALT}}$ signal.

The MC68020 imposes no restrictions on retrying any type of bus cycle. Specifically, any read or write cycle of a read-modify-write operation may be separately retried, since the $\overline{\text{RMC}}$ signal will remain asserted during the entire retry sequence.

Systems designers who utilize the relinquish and retry operation ($\overline{\text{BERR}}$, $\overline{\text{HALT}}$, and $\overline{\text{BR}}$ asserted) must give special consideration to the read-modify-write operation since the MC68020 will not relinquish the bus during this operation. Any device requiring that the processor give up the bus and retry the bus operation during a read-modify-write cycle must assert $\overline{\text{BERR}}$ and $\overline{\text{BR}}$ ($\overline{\text{HALT}}$ must not be included). The bus error handler software should examine the RM bit in the special status word (see **6.4.1 Special Status Word**) and, if set, the handler can take the appropriate action to resolve the fault.

5.2.5.3 HALT OPERATION. The $\overline{\text{HALT}}$ input signal to the MC68020 performs a halt/run/single-step function. The halt and run modes are somewhat self explanatory in that when the halt signal is constantly asserted the processor "halts" (does nothing) and when the $\overline{\text{HALT}}$ signal is constantly negated the processor "runs" (does something). Note that the $\overline{\text{HALT}}$ signal only halts the operation of the external bus, not the internal bus and execution unit. Thus, a program that resides in the cache and does not require use of the external bus will not be affected by the $\overline{\text{HALT}}$ signal.

The single-step mode is derived from correctly timed transitions on the $\overline{\text{HALT}}$ input. If $\overline{\text{HALT}}$ is asserted when the processor begins a bus cycle and remains asserted, that bus cycle will complete, but another cycle will not be allowed to start. When it is desired to continue, $\overline{\text{HALT}}$ is then negated and re-asserted when the next bus cycle is started. Thus, the single-cycle mode allows the user to proceed through (and debug) processor operations, one bus cycle at a time.

The timing required for correct single-step operation is detailed in Figure 5-35. Some care must be exercised to avoid harmful interactions between the $\overline{\text{BERR}}$ and the $\overline{\text{HALT}}$ signals (see **5.2.5.2 RETRY OPERATION**) when using the single-cycle mode as a debugging tool.

When the processor completes a bus cycle after recognizing that the $\overline{\text{HALT}}$ signal is active, the bus control signals are placed in the inactive state; but the address, function code, size, and read/write lines remain driven.

While the processor is honoring the halt request, bus arbitration performs as usual. See **5.2.7 Bus Arbitration.** That is, halting has no effect on bus arbitration.

The single-step operation described above and the software trace capability allow the system debugger to trace single bus cycles, single instructions, or changes in program flow. These processor capabilities, along with a software debugging package, give complete debugging flexibility.

5.2.5.4 DOUBLE BUS FAULTS. When a bus error exception occurs, the processor attempts to stack several words containing information about the state of the machine. If a

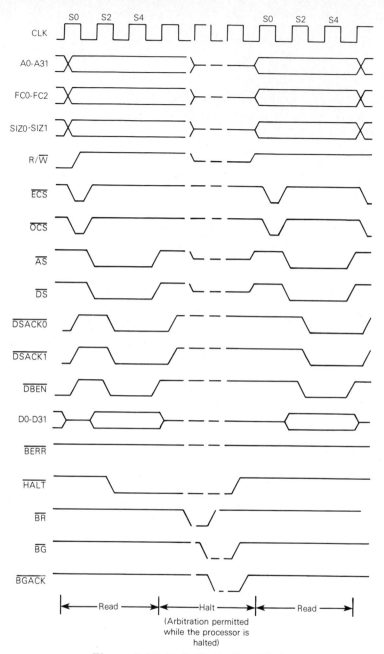

Figure 5-35. Halt Operation Timing

bus error exception occurs during the stacking operation, there have been two bus errors in a row. This is referred to as a double bus fault. When a double bus fault occurs, the processor halts and drives the HALT line low. Once a bus error exception has occurred, any additional bus error exception occurring before the execution of the first instruction of the bus error handler routine constitutes a double bus fault.

Note that a bus cycle that is re-tried does not constitute a bus error exception and does not contribute to a double bus fault. Note also that this means that as long as the external hardware requests it, the processor will continue to retry the same bus cycle.

The occurrance of an address error, similar to that of a bus error, is classified as an exception that may contribute to a double bus fault condition. See **6.3.2 Address Error.**

The bus error input also has an effect on processor operation after the processor receives an external reset input. After reset, the processor reads the vector table to determine the address to start program execution and the initial value of the interrupt stack pointer. If a bus error or address error occurs while reading the vector table (or at any time before the first instruction is executed), the processor reacts as if a double bus fault has occurred and halts. Only an external reset can re-start a halted processor.

From the above conditions a double bus fault is defined as the occurrance of an address error or bus error during the exception processing for an address error, bus error, or reset exception.

5.2.6 Reset Operation

The $\overline{\text{RESET}}$ signal is a bidirectional signal that allows either the processor or an external device to reset the system. Figure 5-36 is a timing diagram for the power-up reset operation.

When the $\overline{\text{RESET}}$ signal is driven by an external device (for a minimum of 520 clock periods), it is recognized as an entire system reset, including the processor. The processor responds by completing any active bus cycle in an orderly fashion, and then

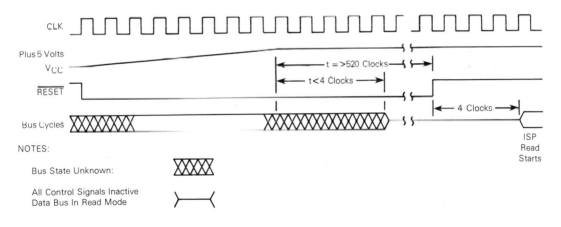

Figure 5-36. External Reset Operation Timing

reading the reset vector table entry (vector number zero, address $00000000) and loads it into the interrupt stack pointer (ISP). Vector table entry number one at address $00000004 is then read and loaded into the program counter. The processor initializes the status register to a mask level of seven with the T1/T0 and M bits cleared and the S bit set. The vector base register is initialized to $0000000 and the cache enable bit in the cache control register is cleared. No other registers are affected by the reset sequence.

When a reset instruction is executed, the processor drives the $\overline{RESET}$ pin for 512 clock cycles. In this case, the processor is resetting the rest of the system. Therefore, there is no effect on the internal state of the processor. All the internal registers of the processor and the status registers are unaffected by the execution of a reset instruction. All external devices connected to the $\overline{RESET}$ line are reset at the completion of the reset instruction. Figure 5-37 shows the timing information for the instruction.

Note that in order to cause an external reset in all cases, including when the processor is executing a reset instruction, the $\overline{RESET}$ signal must be driven as an input for 520 clock cycles. If the reset instruction will not be executed, or external logic can detect the assertion of $\overline{RESET}$ by the processor and compensate for that condition, the shorter assertion of $\overline{RESET}$ of ten clock cycles is all that is required to reset the processor.

5.2.7 Bus Arbitration

Bus arbitration is a technique used by bus master type devices to request, be granted, and acknowledge bus mastership. In its simplest form, the bus arbitration protocol consists of the following:

1. an external device asserts a bus request to the MC68020,
2. the processor asserts bus grant to indicate that the bus will be available at the end of the current bus cycle, and
3. the external device acknowledges that it has assumed bus mastership by asserting bus grant acknowledge.

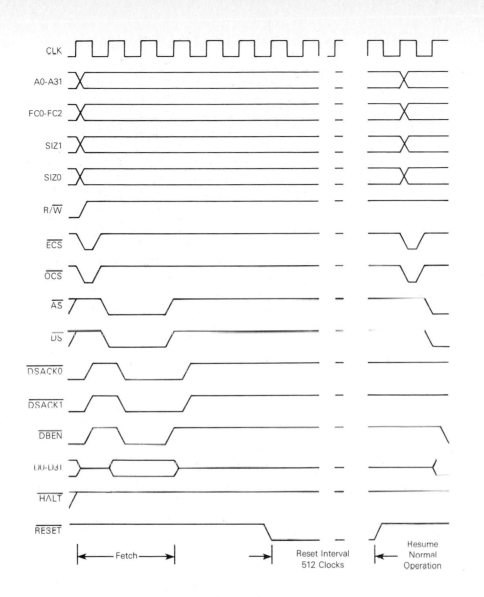

Figure 5-37. Processor Generated Reset Operation

Figure 5-38 is a flowchart showing the detail involved in bus arbitration for a single device. Figure 5-39 is a timing diagram for the same operation. This technique allows processing of bus requests during data transfer cycles.

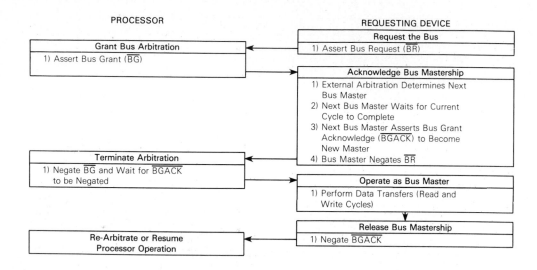

Figure 5-38. Bus Arbitration Flowchart for Single Request

The timing diagram shows that the bus request ($\overline{BR}$) is negated at the time that bus grant acknowledge ($\overline{BGACK}$) is asserted. This type of operation is true for a system consisting of the processor and one device capable of bus mastership. In systems having a number of devices capable of bus mastership, the bus request line from each device is wire ORed to the processor. In such a system, it is possible that there could be more than one bus request asserted simultaneously.

The timing diagram is Figure 5-39 shows that the bus grant ($\overline{BG}$) signal is negated a few clock cycles after the transition of the bus grant acknowledge signal. However, if bus requests are still pending after the negation of bus grant, the processor will assert another bus grant within a few clock cycles after it was negated. This additional assertion of bus grant allows external arbitration circuitry to select the next bus master before the current bus master has completed using the bus. The following paragraphs provide additional information about the three steps in the arbitration process.

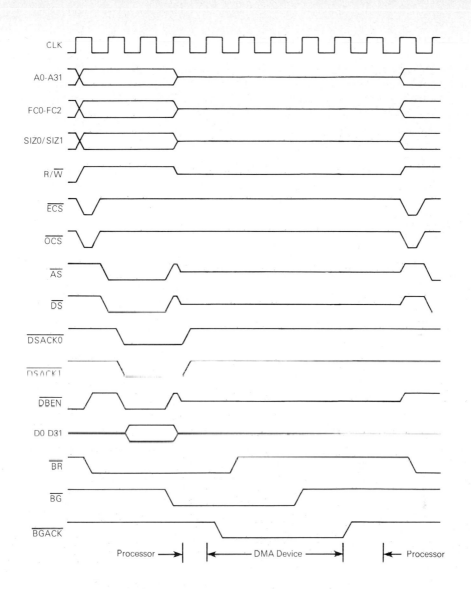

Figure 5-39. Bus Arbitration Operation Timing

5.2.7.1 REQUESTING THE BUS. External devices capable of becoming bus masters request the bus by asserting the bus request ($\overline{BR}$) signal. This is a wire-ORed signal (although it need not be constructed from open-collector devices) that indicates to the processor that some external device requires control of the bus. The processor is effectively at a lower bus priority level than the external device and relinquishes the bus after it has completed the current bus cycle if one has started.

If no acknowledge is received before the bus request signal is negated, the processor continues execution once it detects that the bus request is negated. This allows ordinary processing to continue if the arbitration circuitry inadvertently responded to noise or an external device determines that it no longer requires use of the bus before it has been granted mastership.

5.2.7.2 RECEIVING THE BUS GRANT. The processor asserts bus grant ($\overline{BG}$) as soon as possible after receipt of the bus request. Normally this is immediately following internal synchronization but there is one exception to this rule. The exception occurs when a read-modify-write (RMW) cycle is in progress. The processor will not assert bus grant until the entire RMW cycle is complete. During the RMW operation, the $\overline{RMC}$ signal will be asserted to indicate that the bus is locked.

The bus grant signal may be routed through a daisy-chained network or through a specific priority-encoded network. The processor is not affected by the external method of arbitration as long as the protocol is obeyed.

5.2.7.3 ACKNOWLEDGEMENT OF MASTERSHIP. Upon receiving a bus grant, the requesting device waits until address strobe, data transfer and size acknowledge, and bus grant acknowledge are negated before asserting its own $\overline{BGACK}$. The negation of the $\overline{AS}$ indicates that the previous master has completed its cycle; the negation of $\overline{BGACK}$ indicates that the previous master has released the bus. The negation of $\overline{DSACKx}$ indicates the previous slave has terminated its connection to the previous master. Note that in some applications $\overline{DSACKx}$ might not enter into this function. General purpose devices are then connected such that they are only dependent on address strobe. When bus grant acknowledge is asserted, the device is the bus master until it negates $\overline{BGACK}$. Bus grant acknowledge should not be negated until after all bus cycles required by the alternate bus master are completed. Bus mastership is terminated at the negation of bus grant acknowledge.

The bus request from the granted device should be negated after bus grant acknowledge is asserted. If a bus request is still pending after the assertion of $\overline{BGACK}$, another bus grant will be asserted within a few clocks of the negation of the bus grant. Refer to **5.2.7.4 BUS ARBITRATION CONTROL.** Note that the processor does not perform any external bus cycles before it reasserts bus grant.

5.2.7.4 BUS ARBITRATION CONTROL The bus arbitration control unit in the MC68020 is implemented with a finite state machine. As discussed previously, all asynchronous inputs to the MC68020 are internally synchronized in a maximum of two cycles of the system clock.

As shown in Figure 5-40, input signals labeled R and A are internally synchronized versions of the bus request and bus grant acknowledge pins respectively. The bus grant output is labeled G and the internal three-state control signal T. If T is true, the address, data, and control buses are placed in the high-impedance state when $\overline{AS}$ and $\overline{RMC}$ are negated. All signals are shown in positive logic (active high) regardless of their true active voltage level.

State changes occur on the next rising edge of the clock after the internal signal is valid. Outputs change on the falling edge of the clock after a state is reached.

A timing diagram of the bus arbitration sequence during a processor bus cycle is shown in Figure 5-39. The bus arbitration sequence while the bus is inactive (i.e., executing internal operations such as a multiply instruction) is shown in Figure 5-41.

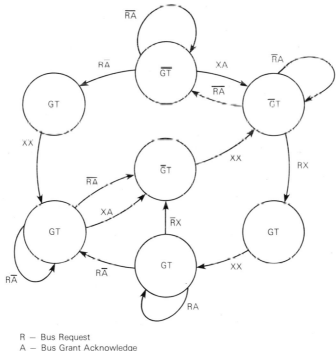

R — Bus Request
A — Bus Grant Acknowledge
G — Bus Grant
T — Three-State Control to Bus Control Logic
X — Don't Care
NOTE: The $\overline{BG}$ output will not be asserted while $\overline{RMC}$ is asserted.

5-40. Bus Arbitration State Diagram

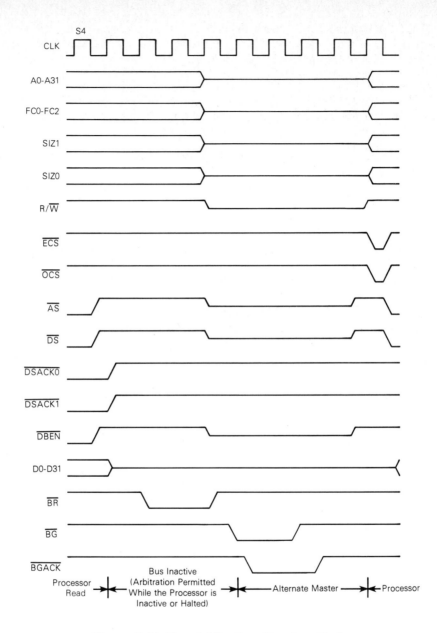

Figure 5-41. Bus Arbitration (Bus Inactive)

5.2.8 The Relationship of $\overline{DSACK}$, $\overline{BERR}$, and $\overline{HALT}$

In order to properly control termination of a bus cycle for a retry or a bus error condition, $\overline{DSACKx}$, $\overline{BERR}$, and $\overline{HALT}$ should be asserted and negated on the rising edge of the MC68020 clock. This will assure that when two signals are asserted simultaneously, the required setup time (#47) and hold time (#53) for both of them will be met during the same bus state. This, or some equivalent precaution, should be designed external to the MC68020.

The preferred bus cycle terminations may be summarized as follows (case numbers refer to Table 5-8).

Normal Termination: $\overline{DSACKx}$ is asserted, $\overline{BERR}$ and $\overline{HALT}$ remain negated (case 1).

Halt Termination: $\overline{HALT}$ is asserted at same time, or before $\overline{DSACKx}$ and $\overline{BERR}$ remains negated (case 2).

Bus Error Termination: $\overline{BERR}$ is asserted in lieu of, at the same time, or before $\overline{DSACKx}$ (case 3) or after $\overline{DSACKx}$ (case 4) and $\overline{HALT}$ remains negated; $\overline{BERR}$ is negated at the same time or after $\overline{DSACKx}$.

Retry Termination: $\overline{HALT}$ and $\overline{BERR}$ are asserted in lieu of, at the same time, or before $\overline{DSACKx}$ (case 5) or after $\overline{DSACKx}$ (case 6); $\overline{BERR}$ is negated at the same time or after $\overline{DSACKx}$, $\overline{HALT}$ may be negated at the same time, or after $\overline{BERR}$.

Table 5-8. $\overline{DSACK}$, $\overline{BERR}$, and $\overline{HALT}$ Assertion Results

Case No.	Control Signal	Asserted on Rising Edge of State		Result
		N	N+2	
1	$\overline{DSACKx}$	A	S	Normal cycle terminate and continue.
	$\overline{BERR}$	NA	NA	
	$\overline{HALT}$	NA	X	
2	$\overline{DSACKx}$	A	S	Normal cycle terminate and halt.
	$\overline{BERR}$	NA	NA	Continue when $\overline{HALT}$ removed.
	$\overline{HALT}$	A/S	S	
3	$\overline{DSACKx}$	NA/A	X	Terminate and take bus error trap, possibly
	$\overline{BERR}$	A	S	deferred.
	$\overline{HALT}$	NA	NA	
4	$\overline{DSACKx}$	A	X	Terminate and take bus error trap, possibly
	$\overline{BERR}$	NA	A	deferred.
	$\overline{HALT}$	NA	NA	
5	$\overline{DSACKx}$	NA/A	X	Terminate and retry when $\overline{HALT}$ removed.
	$\overline{BERR}$	A	S	
	$\overline{HALT}$	A/S	S	
6	$\overline{DSACKx}$	A	X	Terminate and retry when $\overline{HALT}$ removed.
	$\overline{BERR}$	NA	A	
	$\overline{HALT}$	NA	A	

LEGEND:

N — the number of current even bus state (e.g., S2, S4, etc.)
A — signal is asserted in this bus state
NA — signal is not asserted in this state
X — don't care
S — signal was asserted in previous state and remains asserted in this state

Table 5-8 details the resulting bus cycle termination under various combinations of control signal sequences. The correct timing for negation of $\overline{BERR}$ and $\overline{HALT}$ should also be utilized to ensure predictable operation. For the bus cycle retry operation $\overline{BERR}$ must be negated prior to, or at the same time as $\overline{HALT}$. $\overline{DSACKx}$, $\overline{BERR}$, and $\overline{HALT}$ may be negated when $\overline{AS}$ is negated. If $\overline{DSACKx}$ or $\overline{BERR}$ remain asserted into S2 of the next bus cycle, this may cause incorrect bus operation.

EXAMPLE A:
A system uses a watch-dog timer to terminate accesses to an unpopulated address space. The timer asserts $\overline{BERR}$ after time out (case 3).

EXAMPLE B:
A system uses error detection and correction on RAM contents. Designer may:
a) Delay $\overline{DSACKx}$ until data verified, and assert $\overline{BERR}$ and $\overline{HALT}$. simultaneously to retry error cycle (case 5), or if valid assert $\overline{DSACKx}$ (case 1).
b) Delay $\overline{DSACKx}$ until data verified, and assert $\overline{BERR}$ at same time as $\overline{DSACKx}$ if data in error (case 3).
c) Return $\overline{DSACKx}$ prior to data verification, as described in the next section. If data is invalid, $\overline{BERR}$ is asserted on next clock cycle (case 4).
d) Return $\overline{DSACKx}$ prior to data verification, if data is invalid assert $\overline{BERR}$ and $\overline{HALT}$ on next clock cycle (case 6). The memory controller may then correct the RAM prior to or during the retry.

5.2.9 Asynchronous Versus Synchronous Operation

5.2.9.1 ASYNCHRONOUS OPERATION. To achieve clock frequency independence at a system level, the MC68020 can be used in an asynchronous manner. This requires using only the bus handshake lines ($\overline{AS}$, $\overline{DS}$, $\overline{DSACK1}$, $\overline{DSACK0}$, $\overline{BERR}$, and $\overline{HALT}$) to control the data transfer. Using this method, $\overline{AS}$ signals the start of a bus cycle and $\overline{DS}$ is used as a condition for valid data on a write cycle. Decode of the size outputs and lower address lines A1 and A0 provide strobes which indicate which portion of the data bus is active. The slave device (memory or peripheral) then responds by placing the requested data on the correct portion of the data bus for a read cycle or latching the data on a write cycle and asserting data transfer and size acknowledge ($\overline{DSACK1}/\overline{DSACK0}$) corresponding to the port size to terminate the cycle. If no slave responds, or the access is invalid, external control logic asserts the $\overline{BERR}$, or $\overline{BERR}$ and $\overline{HALT}$ signal(s) to abort or retry the bus cycle.

The $\overline{DSACKx}$ signals are allowed to be asserted before the data from a slave device is valid on a read cycle. The length of time that $\overline{DSACKx}$ may precede data is given as parameter #31, and it must be met in any asynchronous system to insure that valid data is latched into the processor. Notice that there is no maximum time specified from the assertion of $\overline{AS}$ to the assertion of $\overline{DSACKx}$. This is because the MPU will insert wait cycles in one clock period increments until $\overline{DSACKx}$ is recognized as asserted.

The $\overline{BERR}$ and/or $\overline{HALT}$ signals are allowed to be asserted after the $\overline{DSACKx}$ signal is asserted. $\overline{BERR}$ and/or $\overline{HALT}$ must be asserted within the time given as parameter #48 after $\overline{DSACKx}$ is asserted in any asynchronous system to insure proper operation. If this maximum delay time is violated, the processor may exhibit erratic behavior.

5.2.9.2 SYNCHRONOUS OPERATION. To support those systems which use the system clock as a signal to generate $\overline{DSACKx}$ and other asynchronous inputs, the asynchronous input setup time is given (parameter #47), and the asynchronous input hold time is given (parameter #53). If this setup and hold time is met for the assertion or negation of an input, such as $\overline{DSACKx}$, the processor is guaranteed to recognize that signal level on that specific falling edge of the system clock. However, the converse is not true — if the input signal does not meet the setup and/or hold time, that level is not guaranteed not to be recognized. In addition, if the assertion of $\overline{DSACKx}$ is recognized on a falling edge of the clock, valid data will be latched into the processor (on a read cycle) on the next falling edge provided that the data meets the setup time (parameter #27). Given this situation, parameter #31 may be ignored. Note that if $\overline{DSACKx}$ is asserted for the required window around the falling edge of S2 (and obeys the proper bus protocol), no wait states will be incurred and the bus cycle will run at its maximum speed of three clock periods.

In order to assure proper operation in a synchronous system when $\overline{BERR}$ and/or $\overline{HALT}$ is asserted after $\overline{DSACKx}$, $\overline{BERR}$ and/or $\overline{HALT}$ must meet the setup time (parameter #27A) prior to the falling edge of the clock one clock cycle are $\overline{DSACKx}$ is recognized as asserted. This setup time is critical for proper operation, and the MC68020 may exhibit erratic behavior if it is violated.

The $\overline{ECS}$ (early cycle start) signal is provided on the MC68020 to provide the earliest possible indication that the processor is beginning a bus cycle. In a synchronous system, the $\overline{ECS}$ output can be utilized to initiate address decode in order to provide improved memory access time. However, the $\overline{ECS}$ output indicates only that the processor **may** be initiating a bus cycle. The MC68020 may initiate a bus cycle by driving the address, size, and function code outputs and asserting $\overline{ECS}$, but if the processor finds the data in the on-chip instruction cache, the cycle will be aborted before asserting $\overline{AS}$.

SECTION 6
PROCESSING STATES

This section describes the behavior of the processor during instruction execution as governed by the processing state of the machine. The functions of the bits in the supervisor portion of the status register are explained, as well as the actions taken by the processor in response to exception conditions.

The processor is always in one of three processing states: normal, exception, or halted. The normal processing state occurs during instruction execution, including the bus cycles to fetch instructions and operands, and to store the results and communicate with a coprocessor, if necessary. The stopped condition, which the processor enters when a STOP instruction is executed, is a special case of the normal state in which no further bus cycles are generated.

The exception processing state is associated with interrupts, trap instructions, tracing, and other exceptional conditions. The exception may be internally generated by an instruction or by an unusual condition arising during the execution of an instruction. Exception processing can also be initiated by conditions external to the processor such as an interrupt, a bus error, a reset, or a coprocessor primitive command. Exception processing is designed to provide an efficient context switch so that the processor may quickly and gracefully handle unusual conditions.

The halted processing state is caused by a catastrophic system failure. For example, if during the exception processing of a bus error another bus error occurs, the processor assumes that the system is unusable and halts. Only an external reset can restart a halted processor. Note, a processor in the stopped state is not in the halted state.

6.1 PRIVILEGE STATES

The processor operates at one of two levels of privilege: the user level or the supervisor level. These levels are ordered, with the supervisor level being of higher privilege than the user level. Not all processor instructions are permitted to execute in the lower-privileged user state, but all are available in the supervisor state. The privilege level can be used by external memory management devices to control and translate accesses, and internally by the processor in order to choose between the user stack pointer and the supervisor stack pointer during operand references.

The MC68020 provides a mechanism to allow external hardware to enforce up to 256 privilege levels within the user level of privilege. This mechanism is an optional part of the module call/return operations described in **APPENDIX D ADVANCED TOPICS.**

6.1.1 Use of Privilege States

The privilege level is a mechanism for providing security in a computer system. User programs may access only their own code and data areas, and can be restricted from accessing other information. User program behavior is more easily guaranteed when errors by other programs in the system cannot affect it.

The privilege mechanism provides security by allowing most programs to execute in user state. Here accesses are controlled, and their effects on other parts of the system are limited. The operating system typically executes in the supervisor state, has access to all resources, performs the overhead tasks for the user state programs, and coordinates their activities.

6.1.2 Supervisor States

The supervisor state is the higher privilege state. For instruction execution, the supervisor state is determined by the S bit of the status register; if the S bit is set, the processor is in the supervisor state, and all instructions are executable. The bus cycles generated by instructions that are executed in the supervisor state are normally classified as supervisor references, which is reflected in the values placed on the function code pins FC0-FC2.

The MC68020 allows a minor distinction of supervisor activities, based on the M bit of the status register. The purpose of the M bit is to allow separation of task related and asynchronous, I/O related supervisor tasks, since in a multi-tasking operating system it is more efficient to have a supervisor stack space associated with each user task and a separate stack space for interrupt associated tasks. Thus, the master stack may be used to contain task control information for the currently executing user task while the interrupt stack is used for interrupt task control information and temporary storage. When a user task switch is required, the master stack pointer is loaded with a new value that points to the new task context, while still maintaining a valid, independent stack space for interrupts.

When the M bit is clear, the MC68020 is in the interrupt state and operation is the same as the MC68000, MC68008, MC68010, and MC68012 supervisor state (this is the default condition after reset). The processor uses the interrupt stack pointer (ISP) when it references the system stack pointer (SSP). When the M bit is set, the processor is in the master state and the processor uses the master stack pointer (MSP) when it references the system stack pointer (SSP). Whether the M bit is set or clear does not affect execution of privileged instructions. The M bit may be set or cleared by an instruction that modifies the status register (MOVE to SR, ANDI to SR, EORI to SR, ORI to SR and RTE). Also, the processor saves the M bit configuration and clears it in the SR as part of the exception processing for interrupts.

All exception processing is done in the supervisor state. The bus cycles generated during exception processing are classified as supervisor references. All stacking operations during exception processing use the active supervisor stack pointer.

6.1.3 User State

The user state is the lower privilege state. For instruction execution, the user state is determined by the S bit of the status register; if the S bit is clear, the processor is executing instructions in the user state.

Most instructions execute both in the user state and in the supervisor state. However, some instructions which have important system effects are made privileged and are restricted to use in the supervisor state. For instance, user programs are not permitted to execute the STOP instruction or the RESET instruction. To insure that a user program cannot enter the privileged supervisor state, except in a controlled manner, the instructions which can modify the S bit in the status register are privileged. The TRAP #n instruction can be used to allow user program access to privileged services performed by the operating system in the supervisor state.

The bus cycles generated by an instruction executed in the user state are classified as user state references, as reflected by the address space values placed on the function code pins (FC0-FC2). This allows an external memory management device to distinguish between user and supervisor activity, and to control access to protected portions of the address map. While the processor is in the user state, those references made to either the system stack pointer implicitly, or address register seven (A7) explicitly, are always made relative to the user stack pointer (USP).

6.1.4 Change of Privilege State

The only way for the processor to change from the user to the supervisor privilege level is through exception processing, which causes a change from the user state to one of the supervisor states and can cause a change from the master state to the interrupt state. Exception processing saves the current state of the S and M bits of the status register on the active supervisor stack, and the S bit is set, forcing the processor into the supervisor state. Also, if the exception being processed is an interrupt and the M bit is set, it will be cleared to put the processor into the interrupt state. Instruction execution proceeds in the supervisor state to handle the exception condition.

A transition from supervisor to user state can be caused by the following instructions: RTE, MOVE to SR, ANDI to SR, and EORI to SR. The MOVE, ANDI, and EORI to SR instructions execute at the supervisor privilege level, and then fetch the next instruction at the next sequential program counter address at the new privilege level determined by the new value of the S bit.

The RTE instruction examines the supervisor stack contents to determine which state restorations are required. If the frame on top of the stack was created by an interrupt, trap, or instruction exception, the RTE instruction fetches the saved status register and program counter from the supervisor stack, and restores each into its respective register. The processor then continues execution at the restored program counter address and at the privilege level determined by the S bit of the restored status register.

If the frame on top of the stack was created by a faulted bus cycle, the RTE instruction restores the entire saved machine state from the stack.

6.1.5 Address Space Types

Address space classification is generated by the processor according to the type of access required during each bus cycle. This allows external translation of addresses, control of access, and differentiation of special processor states, such as interrupt acknowledge. Table 6-1 lists the types of accesses and their respective address space encodings.

Table 6-1. Address Space Encodings

FC2	FC1	FC0	Address Space
0	0	0	(Undefined, Reserved) *
0	0	1	User Data Space
0	1	0	User Program Space
0	1	1	(Undefined, Reserved) *
1	0	0	(Undefined, Reserved) *
1	0	1	Supervisor Data Space
1	1	0	Supervisor Program Space
1	1	1	CPU Space

*Address space 3 is reserved for user definition, while 0 and 4 are reserved for future use by Motorola.

User program and data accesses have no predefined memory locations. The supervisor data space also has no predefined locations. During reset, the first two long words at memory location zero in the supervisor program space are used for processor initialization. No other memory locations are explicitly defined by the processor.

6.1.6 CPU Space

The CPU space is not intended for general instruction execution, but is reserved for processor functions; that is, those bus cycles in which the processor must communicate with external devices for reasons beyond normal data movement associated with instructions. For example, all M68000 processors use the CPU space for interrupt acknowledge cycles. The MC68020 also makes CPU space accesses for breakpoints, coprocessor operations, and to support the module call/return mechanism.

Although the MOVES instruction can be used to generate CPU space bus cycles, this may interfere with proper system operation. Thus, the use of MOVES to access the CPU space should be done with caution.

6.2 EXCEPTION PROCESSING

A general description of exception processing is first presented to introduce the concepts of interrupts, traps, and tracing. Exception processing for coprocessor detected errors is not discussed in this section; refer to **SECTION 8 COPROCESSOR INTERFACE DESCRIPTION** for more details on coprocessor exception handling.

The processing of an exception occurs in four steps, with variations for different exception causes. During the first step, a temporary internal copy of the status register is made, and the status register is set for exception processing. In the second step, the exception vector is determined, and in the third step, the current processor context is saved. In the fourth step a new context is obtained, and the processor then proceeds with instruction processing.

6.2.1 Exception Vectors

The vector base register points to the base of the 1K byte exception vector table containing the 256 exception vectors. Exception vectors are memory pointers used by the processor to fetch the address of routines which will handle various exceptions. All exception vectors are one long word in length, except for the reset vector, which is two long words in length.

Exception vectors are selected by 8-bit vector numbers generated during exception processing. This vector number is multiplied by four to form the vector offset, which is added to the vector base register to obtain the address of the vector. All exception vectors are located in supervisor data space, except the reset vector which is located in supervisor program space. Vector numbers are generated internally or externally, depending on the cause of the exception. Table 6-2 provides the assignments of the exception vectors.

Table 6-2. Exception Vector Assignments (Sheet 1 of 2)

Vector Number(s)	Vector Offset		Assignment
	Hex	Space	
0	000	SP	Reset: Initial Interrupt Stack Pointer
1	004	SP	Reset: Initial Program Counter
2	008	SD	Bus Error
3	00C	SD	Address Error
4	010	SD	Illegal Instruction
5	014	SD	Zero Divide
6	018	SD	CHK, CHK2 Instruction
7	01C	SD	cpTRAPcc, TRAPcc, TRAPV Instructions
8	020	SD	Privilege Violation
9	024	SD	Trace
10	028	SD	Line 1010 Emulator
11	02C	SD	Line 1111 Emulator
12	030	SD	(Unassigned, Reserved)
13	034	SD	Coprocessor Protocol Violation
14	038	SD	Format Error
15	03C	SD	Uninitialized Interrupt
16 Through 23	040 ... 05C	SD SD	} (Unassigned, Reserved)
24	060	SD	Spurious Interrupt
25	064	SD	Level 1 Interrupt Auto Vector
26	068	SD	Level 2 Interrupt Auto Vector
27	06C	SD	Level 3 Interrupt Auto Vector
28	070	SD	Level 4 Interrupt Auto Vector
29	074	SD	Level 5 Interrupt Auto Vector
30	078	SD	Level 6 Interrupt Auto Vector
31	07C	SD	Level 7 Interrupt Auto Vector
32 Through 47	080 ... 0BC	SD SD	} TRAP #0-15 Instruction Vectors
48	0C0	SD	FPCP Branch or Set on Unordered Condition
49	0C4	SD	FPCP Inexact Result
50	0C8	SD	FPCP Divide by Zero
51	0CC	SD	FPCP Underflow
52	0D0	SD	FPCP Operand Error
53	0D4	SD	FPCP Overflow
54	0D8	SD	FPCP Signaling NAN
55	0DC	SD	Unassigned, Reserved
56	0E0	SD	PMMU Configuration
57	0E4	SD	PMMU Illegal Operation

Table 6-2. Exception Vector Assignments (Sheet 2 of 2)

Vector Number(s)	Vector Offset		Assignment
	Hex	Space	
58	0E8	SD	PMMU Access Level Violation
59 Through 63	0EC 0FC	SD SD	} Unassigned, Reserved
64 Through 255	100 3FC	SD SD	} User Defined Vectors (192)

SP = Supervisor Program Space
SD = Supervisor Data Space

As shown in Table 6-2, 192 vectors are reserved for user definition as interrupt vectors and 64 are defined by the processor. However, there is no protection on the first 64 vectors, so that external devices may use vectors reserved for internal purposes at the discretion of the system designer.

6.2.2. Exception Stack Frame

Exception processing saves the most volatile portion of the current processor context on the top of the supervisor stack. This context is organized in a format called the exception stack frame. This information always includes the status register, the program counter, and the vector offset used to fetch the vector. The processor also marks the frame with a frame format. The format field allows the RTE instruction to identify what information is on the stack so that it may be properly restored and the stack space deallocated. The general form of the exception stack frame is illustrated in Figure 6-1. Refer to **6.5 MC68020 EXCEPTION STACK FRAMES** for a complete list of exception stack frames.

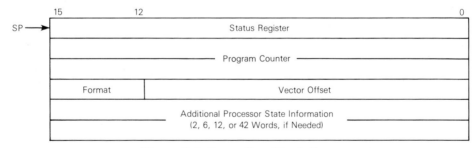

Figure 6-1. Exception Stack Frame

6.2.3 Exception Types

Exceptions can be generated by either internal or external causes. The externally generated exceptions are interrupts, bus errors, reset, and coprocessor detected errors. Interrupts are requests from peripheral devices for processor action, while the bus error and reset pins are used for access control and processor restart. The internally generated exceptions are caused by instructions, address errors, tracing, or breakpoints. The TRAP, TRAPcc, TRAPV, cpTRAPcc, CHK, CHK2, CALLM, RTM, RTE, and DIV instructions all can generate exceptions as part of their instruction execution. In addition, illegal instructions, address error, privilege violations, and coprocessor protocol violations cause exceptions.

6.2.4 Exception Processing Sequence

Exception processing occurs in four identifiable steps. During the first step, an internal copy is made of the status register. After the copy is made, the processor state bits in the status register are changed. The S bit is set, putting the processor into the supervisor privilege state. The T1 and T0 bits are cleared, which allows the exception handler to execute unhindered by tracing. For the reset and interrupt exceptions, the interrupt priority mask is also updated.

In the second step, the vector number of the exception is determined. For interrupts, the vector number is obtained by a processor read from CPU space $F, which is defined as an interrupt acknowledge cycle. For coprocessor detected exceptions, the vector number is included in the coprocessor exception primitive response. (Refer to **SECTION 8 COPROCESSOR INTERFACE DESCRIPTION** for a complete discussion of coprocessor exceptions.) For all other exceptions, internal logic provides the vector number. This vector number is then used to generate the address of the exception vector.

For all exceptions other than reset, the third step is to save the current processor context. An exception stack frame is created and filled on the active supervisor stack. Other information may also be stacked, depending on which exception is being processed and the context of the processor prior to the exception. If the exception is an interrupt and the M bit is set, the M bit is cleared, and a second stack frame is created on the interrupt stack.

The last step is the same for all exceptions. The exception vector offset is determined by multiplying the vector number by four. This offset is then added to the contents of the vector base register to determine the memory address of the exception vector. The program counter value (and ISP for the reset exception) is loaded with the value in the exception vector. The instruction at the address given in the exception vector is fetched, and normal instruction decoding and execution is resumed.

6.2.5 Multiple Exceptions

The following paragraphs describe the processing that occurs when multiple exceptions arise simultaneously. Exceptions can be grouped according to their characteristics and priority, as shown in Table 6-3.

The priority relationship between two exceptions determines which is processed first if both exceptions occur simultaneously. The term 'process' in this context means the execution of the four steps previously defined:
1) change processing states if needed,
2) determine exception vector,
3) save old context, and
4) load new context, including the first three instruction words at the new program counter location.

'Process' in this context **does not** include the execution of the routine pointed to by the fetched vector. As soon as the MC68020 has completed processing for an exception, it is then ready to begin execution of the exception handler routine, or begin exception processing for other pending exceptions. Also, a higher priority exception can be processed before the completion of exception processing for lower priority exceptions (for example,

Table 6-3. Exception Groups

Group/ Priority	Exception and Relative Priority	Characteristics
0	0.0 — Reset	Aborts all processing (instruction or exception) and does not save old context.
1	1.0 — Address Error 1.1 — Bus Error	Suspends processing (instruction or exception) and saves internal context.
2	2.0 — BKPT #n, CALLM, CHK, CHK2, cp Mid-Instruction, Cp Protocol Violation, cpTRAPcc, Divide-by-Zero, RTE, RTM, TRAP #n, TRAPV	Exception processing is part of instruction execution.
3	3.0 — Illegal Instruction, Line A, Unimplemented Line F, Privilege Violation, cp Pre-Instruction	Exception processing begins before instruction is executed.
4	4.0 — cp Post-Instruction 4.1 — Trace 4.2 — Interrupt	Exception processing begins when current instruction or previous exception processing is completed.

0.0 is the highest priority, 4.2 is the lowest.

if a bus error occurs during the processing for a trace exception, the bus error will be processed and handled before the trace exception processing is completed). However, most exceptions cannot occur during exception processing. Furthermore, very few combinations of the exceptions shown in Table 6-3 can be pending simultaneously.

This priority scheme is very important in determining the order in which exception handlers are executed in multiple exception situations. As a general rule, the lower the priority of an exception, the more quickly the handler routine for that exception will be executed. For example, if simultaneous trap, trace, and interrupt exceptions are pending, the trap exception is processed first, followed immediately by exception processing for the trace and then the interrupt. Thus, when the processor finally resumes normal instruction execution, it is in the interrupt handler, which returns to the trace handler, which returns to the trap exception handler. An exception to this rule is the reset exception, which is the highest priority and also the first exception handled, since all other exceptions are cleared by the reset condition.

6.3 EXCEPTION PROCESSING: DETAIL

Exceptions have a number of sources, and each exception has characteristics which are unique to it. The following paragraphs detail the sources of exceptions, how each arises, and how each is processed.

6.3.1 Reset

The $\overline{\text{RESET}}$ input provides the highest level of exception. The $\overline{\text{RESET}}$ signal provides for system initialization and recovery from catastrophic failure. Any processing in progress at the time of the reset is aborted, and cannot be recovered. The status register is initialized: tracing is disabled (both trace bits are cleared), supervisor interrupt state is entered (the supervisor bit is set and the master bit is cleared), and the processor interrupt priority mask is set to the highest priority level (level seven). The vector base register and cache control register are initialized to zero ($00000000). A vector number is internally generated to reference the reset exception vector at offset zero in the supervisor program address space (which is two long words instead of the normal one long word). Because no assumptions can be made about the validity of any register contents (in particular the supervisor stack pointer) neither the program counter nor the status register is saved. The address contained in the first long word of the reset exception vector is fetched for use as the initial interrupt stack pointer, and the address in the second long word of the reset exception vector is fetched for use as the initial program counter. Program execution then starts at the address loaded into the program counter.

The reset instruction does not affect any internal registers, but it does assert the $\overline{\text{RESET}}$ line, thus resetting all external devices. This allows software to reset the system to a known state and then continue processing at the next instruction.

6.3.2 Address Error

Address error exceptions occur when the processor attempts to prefetch an instruction from an odd address. The affect is much like an internally generated bus error, so that the bus cycle is not executed and the processor begins exception processing. After exception processing commences, the sequence is the same as that for bus error exceptions as described in **6.3.3 Bus Error**, except that the vector offset in the stack frame refers to the address error vector. Also, if an address error occurs during the exception processing for a bus error, address error, or reset, the processor is halted.

6.3.3 Bus Error

Bus error exceptions occur during a bus cycle when external logic aborts the cycle by asserting the $\overline{\text{BERR}}$ input. If the aborted bus cycle is a data space access, the processor immediately begins exception processing. If the aborted bus cycle is an instruction prefetch, the processor delays taking the exception (the processor will wait until the results of the aborted bus cycle are required for further instruction execution, and then takes the exception).

Exception processing for a bus error follows the usual sequence of steps. The status register is copied, the supervisor state is entered, and tracing is disabled. A vector number is generated to refer to the bus error vector. The vector offset, program counter, and the copy of the status register are then saved on the stack, in addition to information describing the non-user visible internal registers of the processor. This additional information is required to recover from the bus fault, since the processor may be in the middle of executing an instruction when the fault is detected. The saved program counter value is the address of the instruction that was executing at the time the fault was detected. This is not necessarily the instruction that generated the bus cycle, due to the overlapped execution allowed by the processor. The internal state information included in the stack frame contains sufficient information to determine the cause of the bus fault and recover from the error.

For improved efficiency, the MC68020 supports two different bus error stack frame formats as shown in Figures 6-7 and 6-8. If the bus error occurs in mid-instruction, the processor saves its entire state in order to properly continue execution of the instruction after the bus error is corrected. If the bus error is taken as the processor is beginning execution of an instruction, the processor can save a much smaller amount of information about the failed cycle in order to continue execution of that instruction when the exception handler returns. The two bus error stack frames are distinguished by the stack frame format code (refer to **6.5 MC68020 STACK FRAMES** for additional information).

If a bus error occurs during the exception processing for a bus error, address error, or reset, or while the processor is loading internal state information from the stack during the execution of an RTE instruction, the processor enters the halted state. This simplifies the detection of catastrophic system failures, since the processor removes itself from the system rather than modifying the current state of the stacks and memory. Only an external $\overline{\text{RESET}}$ can restart a processor halted due to a double bus fault.

6.3.4 Instruction Traps

Traps are exceptions caused by instruction execution. They arise either from processor recognition of abnormal conditions during instruction execution, or from use of the specific instructions whose normal behavior is to cause an exception.

Exception processing for traps follows the same steps outlined previously. The status register is copied internally, the supervisor state is entered, and the trace bits are cleared. Thus, if tracing was enabled when the trap causing instruction began execution, a trace exception will be generated by the instruction, but the trap handler routine will not be traced (the trap exception will be processed first, then the trace exception). A vector number is internally generated; for the TRAP #n instruction, part of the vector number comes from the instruction itself. The trap vector offset, the program counter, and the copy of the status register are saved on the supervisor stack. The saved value of the program counter is the address of the instruction after the instruction which generated the trap. For all instruction traps other than TRAP #n, a pointer to the instruction which caused the trap is also saved. Finally, instruction execution commences at the address contained in the exception vector.

Certain instructions are used specifically to generate traps. The TRAP #n instruction always forces an exception, and is useful for implementing system calls for user programs. The TRAPcc, TRAPV, cpTRAPcc, CHK, and CHK2 instructions force an exception if the user program detects a runtime error, which may be an arithmetic overflow or a subscript value out of bounds. The DIVS and DIVU instructions will force an exception if a division operation is attempted with a divisor of zero. The CALLM and RTM instructions will cause a format error if an illegal privilege change is requested or invalid parameters are present in the type or option fields.

6.3.5 Breakpoints

In order to use the MC68020 in a hardware emulator, it must provide a means of inserting breakpoints into the target code, and then give a clear announcement of when it has reached a breakpoint. For the MC68000 and MC68008, this can be done by inserting an illegal instruction at the breakpoint and detecting when the processor fetches from the illegal instruction exception vector location. Since the vector base register on the MC68010, MC68012, and MC68020 allows arbitrary relocation of the exception vectors, the exception vector address cannot serve as a reliable indicator that the processor is taking the breakpoint. On the MC68010, MC68012, and MC68020, this function is provided by extending the functionality of a set of the illegal instructions, $4848-$484F, to serve as breakpoint instructions. The breakpoint facility also allows external hardware to monitor the execution of a program residing in the on-chip cache, without severe performance degradation.

When a breakpoint instruction is executed, the MC68020 performs a read from CPU space $0 at an address corresponding to the breakpoint number. Refer to Figure 5-24 for the CPU space $0 encoding. If this bus cycle is terminated by $\overline{BERR}$, the processor then proceeds to perform illegal instruction exception processing. If the bus cycle is terminated by $\overline{DSACKx}$, the processor uses the data returned to replace the breakpoint instruction in the internal instruction pipe, and begins execution of that instruction.

6.3.6 Format Error

Just as the processor checks that prefetched instructions are valid, the processor (with the aid of a coprocessor, if needed) also performs some checks of data values for control operations, including the type and option fields of the descriptor for CALLM, the coprocessor save area format for cpRESTORE, and the stack format for RTE and RTM.

The RTE instruction checks the validity of the stack format code, and in the cases of the bus cycle fault formats, the validity of the data to be loaded into the various internal registers. The only data item checked for validity is the version number of the processor that generated the frame. This check ensures that the processor is not making erroneous assumptions about internal state information in the stack frame.

The CALLM and RTM both check the values in the option and type fields in the module descriptor and module stack frame, respectively. If these fields do not contain proper values, or if an illegal access rights change request is detected by an external memory management unit, then an illegal call or return is being requested and is not executed. Refer to **APPENDIX D.1 MODULE SUPPORT** for more information on the module call/return mechanism.

The cpRESTORE instruction passes the format field of the coprocessor save area to the coprocessor for validation. If the coprocessor does not recognize the format value, it indicates this to the main processor, and the MC68020 will take a format error exception. Refer to **8.15 EXCEPTION PROCESSING** for details of coprocessor related exceptions.

If any of these checks determine that the format of the control data is improper, the processor generates a format error exception. This exception saves a short format exception frame, and then continues execution at the address contained in the format exception vector. The stacked program counter is the address of the instruction that detected the format error.

6.3.7 Illegal or Unimplemented Instructions

An illegal instruction is any of the word bit patterns which do not correspond to the bit pattern of the first word of a legal MC68020 instruction, or a MOVEC instruction with an undefined register specification field in the first extension word. The word patterns with bits [15:12] equal to 1010 are distinguished as unimplemented instructions, referenced to as A-line opcodes. During instruction execution, when an attempt is made to execute an illegal instruction, an illegal instruction exception occurs. Unimplemented instructions utilize separate exception vectors, permitting more efficient emulation of unimplemented instructions.

The word patterns with bits [15:12] equal to 1111 (referred to as F-line opcodes) are used for coprocessor instructions, but may generate an unimplemented instruction exception. When the processor encounters an F-line instruction, it first runs a bus cycle referencing CPU space 2 and addressing one of eight coprocessors. If no coprocessor responds to the bus cycle and the access is terminated with a bus error, the processor will proceed with unimplemented instruction exception processing and fetch the F-line emulator vector. Thus, the function of the coprocessor may be emulated. Refer to **SECTION 8 COPROCESSOR INTERFACE DESCRIPTION** for more details.

Exception processing for illegal and unimplemented instructions is similar to that for traps. After the instruction is fetched and decoded, the processor determines that execution of an illegal or unimplemented instruction is being attempted and starts exception processing before executing the instruction. The status register is copied, the supervisor state is entered, and tracing is disabled. A vector number is generated to refer to the illegal instruction vector, or in the case of unimplemented instructions, to the corresponding emulation vector. The illegal or unimplemented instruction vector offset, current program counter, and copy of the status register are saved on the supervisor stack, with the saved value of the program counter being the address of the illegal or unimplemented instruction. Finally, instruction execution resumes at the address contained in the exception vector.

6.3.8 Privilege Violations

In order to provide system security, certain instructions are privileged (see Table 6-4). An attempt to execute one of the privileged instructions while in the user privilege state will cause an exception. Also, a privilege violation may occur if a coprocessor requests a privilege check and the processor is in the user state.

Table 6-4. Privileged Instructions

ANDI to SR	MOVEC
EORI to SR	MOVES
cpRESTORE	ORI to SR
cpSAVE	RESET
MOVE from SR	RTE
MOVE to SR	STOP
MOVE USP	

Exception processing for privilege violations is similar to that for illegal instructions. After the instruction is fetched and decoded, the processor determines that a privilege violation is being attempted, and the processor starts exception processing before executing the instruction. The status register is copied, the supervisor state is entered, and tracing is disabled. A vector number is generated to reference the privilege violation vector; the privilege violation vector offset, current program counter, and the status register are saved on the supervisor stack. The saved value of the program counter is the address of the first word of the instruction which caused the privilege violation. Finally, instruction execution resumes at the address contained in the privilege violation exception vector.

6.3.9 Tracing

To aid in program development, the M68000 processors include a facility to allow instruction-by-instruction tracing. The MC68020 also allows tracing of instructions that change program flow. In the trace mode, a trace exception is generated after an instruction is executed, allowing a debugger program to monitor the execution of a program under test.

The trace facility uses the T1 and T0 bits in the supervisor portion of the status register. If both T bits are clear, tracing is disabled, and instruction execution proceeds normally. If the T1 bit is clear and the T0 bit is set at the beginning of the execution of an instruction, and that instruction causes the program counter to be updated in a non-sequential manner, a trace exception will be generated after its execution is completed. Instructions that will be traced in this mode include all branches, jumps, instruction traps, returns, status register manipulations (since the processor must refetch any words that may have been prefetched from the supervisor program space rather than user program space), and coprocessor general instructions that modify the program counter flow. If the T1 bit is set and the T0 bit is clear at the beginning of the execution of any instruction, a trace exception will be generated after the execution of that instruction is completed. See Table 6-5.

Table 6-5. Tracing Control

TI	T0	Tracing Function
0	0	No Tracing
0	1	Trace on Change of Flow (BRA, JMP, etc.)
I	0	Trace on Instruction Execution (Any Instruction)
I	1	Undefined, Reserved

In general terms, a trace exception can be viewed as an extension to the function of any instruction. Thus, if a trace exception is generated by an instruction, the execution of that instruction is not complete until the trace exception processing associated with it is completed. If the instruction does not complete execution due to a bus error or address error exception, trace exception processing is deferred until after the execution of the suspended instruction is resumed (by the associated RTE), and the instruction execution is completed normally. If the instruction is executed and an interrupt is pending on completion, the trace exception processing is completed before the interrupt exception processing starts. If, during the execution of the instruction, an exception is forced by that instruction, the forced exception is processed before the trace exception is processed.

If the processor is in the trace mode when an attempt is made to execute an illegal or unimplemented instruction, that instruction will not cause a trace since it is not executed. This is of particular importance to an instruction emulation routine that performs the instruction function, adjusts the stacked program counter to beyond the unimplemented instruction and then returns. Before the return is executed, the status register on the stack should be checked to determine if tracing is on; and if so, then the trace exception processing should also be emulated in order for the trace exception handler to account for the emulated instruction.

The exception processing for a trace starts at the end of normal processing for the traced instruction, and before the start of the next instruction. An internal copy is made of the status register. The transition to supervisor state is made, and the T bits of the status register are cleared, disabling further tracing. A vector number is generated to reference the trace exception vector. The address of the instruction that caused the trace exception, the trace exception vector offset, program counter, and the copy of the status register are saved on the supervisor stack. The saved value of the program counter is the address of the next instruction to be executed. Instruction execution resumes at the address contained in the trace exception vector.

Note that there is one case where tracing affects the normal operation of one instruction. If the STOP instruction begins execution with T1 = 1, a trace exception will be taken after the STOP instruction loads the status register. Upon return from the trace handler routine, execution will continue with the instruction following the STOP, and the processor will never enter the stopped condition.

6.3.10 Interrupts

Exception processing can be caused by external devices requesting service through the interrupt mechanism described in **5.2.4.1 INTERRUPT OPERATION.** Interrupt requests arriving at the processor through the $\overline{IPL0}$-$\overline{IPL2}$ pins do not force immediate exception processing, but may be made pending. Pending interrupts are serviced between instruction execution, at the end of exception processing, or when permitted during coprocessor instructions. If the priority of the requested interrupt is less than or equal to the current interrupt mask level, execution continues with the next instruction and the interrupt request is ignored. (The recognition of level seven is slightly different, as explained below.) If the priority of the requested interrupt is greater than the current interrupt mask level it is made pending and exception processing will begin at the next instruction boundary.

Exception processing for interrupts follows the same steps as previously outlined. First, an internal copy of the status register is made, the privilege state is set to supervisor, tracing is suppressed, and the processor interrupt mask level is set to the level of the interrupt being serviced. The processor fetches a vector number from the interrupting device, classifying the bus cycle as an interrupt acknowledge and displaying the level number of the interrupt being acknowledged on pins A1-A3 of the address bus. If the vector number is not generated by the interrupting device, external logic requests automatic vectoring and the processor internally generates a vector number which is determined by the interrupt level number. However, if external logic indicates a bus error, the interrupt is taken to be spurious, and the generated vector number refers to the spurious interrupt vector.

Once the vector number is obtained, the processor proceeds with the usual exception processing, saving the exception vector offset, program counter, and status register on the supervisor stack. The saved value of the program counter is the address of the instruction which would have been executed had the interrupt not been present. If the interrupt was recognized during the execution of a coprocessor instruction, further internal information is saved on the stack so that the MC68020 can continue executing the coprocessor instruction when the interrupt handler completes execution. If the M bit of the status register is set, the M bit is cleared and a throwaway exception stack frame is created on top of the interrupt stack. This second frame contains the same program counter and vector offset as the frame created on top of the master stack, but has a format number of $1 instead of $0 or $9. The status register will be the same as that placed on the master stack except that the M and S bits will be set. The content of the exception vector corresponding to the vector number previously obtained is fetched and loaded into the program counter, and normal instruction execution resumes in the interrupt handler routine.

Priority level seven is a special case. Level seven interrupts cannot be inhibited by the interrupt priority mask, thus, providing a non-maskable interrupt capability. An interrupt request is generated each time the interrupt request level changes from some lower level to level seven. Note that a level seven interrupt may also be caused by level comparison if the request level and mask level are at seven and the priority mask is then set to a lower level (e.g., with the MOVE to SR or RTE instructions).

Most M68000 Family peripherals provide for programmable interrupt vector numbers to be used in the interrupt request/acknowledge mechanism of the system. If this vector number is not initialized after reset and the peripheral must acknowledge an interrupt request, the peripheral returns the vector number for the uninitialized interrupt vector, $0F.

6.3.11 Return From Exception

After exception stacking operations have been completed for all pending exceptions, the processor resumes normal instruction execution at the address contained in the vector rotoronocd by the last exception to be processed. Once the exception handler has completed execution, the processor must return to the system context prior to the exception (if possible). The mechanism used to accomplish this return for any exception is the RTE instruction.

When the RTE instruction is executed, the processor examines the stack frame on top of the active supervisor stack to determine if it is a valid frame and what type of context restoration should be performed. The actions taken by the processor for each of the stack frame types is described below. Refer to **6.5 MC68020 EXCEPTION STACK FRAMES** for the format of each framo typo.

For a normal four word frame, the processor updates the status register and program counter with the data pulled from the stack, increments the stack pointer by eight, and resumes normal instruction execution.

For the throwaway four word stack, the processor reads the status register from the frame, increments the active stack pointer by eight, loads the SR with the previously read value, and then begins RTE processing again. This means that the processor reads a new format word from the stack frame on top of the active stack (which may or may not be the same stack used for the previous operation) and performs the proper operations corresponding to that format. In most cases, the throwaway frame will be on the interrupt stack and when loaded, the S and M bits will be set. Then, there will be a normal four-word frame or a ten-word coprocessor mid-instruction frame on the master stack.

However, the second frame may be any format (including another throwaway frame) and may reside on any of the three system stacks.

For the six word stack frame, the status register and program counter are updated from the stack, the active supervisor stack pointer is incremented by twelve, and normal instruction execution resumes.

For the coprocessor mid-instruction stack frame the status register, program counter, instruction address, internal registers, and evaluated effective addresses are pulled from the stack and are restored to the corresponding internal registers, and the stack pointer is incremented by twenty. Then the processor reads from the response register of the coprocessor that generated the exception to determine the next operation to be performed. Refer to **8.15 EXCEPTION PROCESSING** for details of coprocessor related exceptions.

For both the short and long bus fault stack frames, the format value on the stack is first checked for validity. In addition, for the long stack frame, the version number contained in the stack must match the version number of the processor that is attempting to read the stack frame. The version number is located in the most significant nibble (bits 12 through 15) of the word at location SP + 54 in the long stack frame. This validity check is used to insure that in a dual processor system, the data will be properly interpreted by the RTE instruction. If the frame is found to be invalid or inaccessible, a format error or a bus error exception is taken, respectively. Otherwise, the processor reads the entire frame into the proper internal registers, deallocates the proper stack, and resumes normal processing. Once the processor begins to read the frame, a bus error must not occur or the processor will enter the halted state. Refer to **6.4 BUS FAULT RECOVERY** for more information on the behavior of the processor after the frame is read into the internal registers.

If a format error or bus error occurs during the execution of the RTE instruction, either due to any of the errors described above or due to an illegal format code, the processor will create a normal four word or a bus cycle fault stack frame above the frame that it was attempting to use. In this way, the faulty stack frame remains intact and may be examined by the format error or bus error exception handler and repaired, or used by another processor of a different type (e.g., an MC68010, MC68012, or a future M68000 processor) in a multiprocessor system.

6.4 BUS FAULT RECOVERY

There are two facets to recovery from a bus cycle fault: recognition of the fault and saving the processor state, and restoring the state at a later time.

A memory fault is indicated to the MC68020 by an address error (generated internally), or by a bus error (generated by external logic, generally by a memory management device or sub-system). The processor state is saved on the supervisor stack as described in **6.3.3 Bus Error,** and the state may be later restored by the RTE instruction as described in **6.3.11 Return From Exception.** The action taken by the processor after the return can be controlled, to some degree, by manipulating the data in the bus fault stack frame as described below.

The MC68020 can have faults occur on either instruction stream or data accesses. Faults on data accesses are taken when the bus cycle is terminated. Faults on instruction stream accesses are delayed until the processor attempts to use the information, if ever, which was not obtained due to the aborted bus cycle. Address error faults occur only on instruction stream accesses, and are taken before the bus cycle is attempted.

6.4.1 Special Status Word

There are several special registers saved as part of the bus fault exception stack frame information, including the internal special status word (see Figure 6-2). This word is placed in the stack frame, at offset $A, for both the short bus cycle fault format and the long bus cycle fault format. Refer to **6.5.5 Short Bus Cycle Fault Stack Frame** and **6.5.6 Long Bus Cycle Fault Stack Frame.**

15	14	13	12	11	10	9	8	7	6	5	4	3	2	1	0
FC	FB	RC	RB	0	0	0	DF	RM	RW	SIZ		0	FC2-FC0		

FC   — Fault on Stage C of the Instruction Pipe
FB   — Fault on Stage B of the Instruction Pipe
RC   — Rerun Flag for Stage C of the Instruction Pipe*
RB   — Rerun Flag for Stage B of the Instruction Pipe*
DF   — Fault/Rerun Flag for Data Cycle*
RM   — Read-Modify-Write on Data Cycle
RW   — Read/Write for Data Cycle — 1 = Read, 0 = Write
SIZ   — Size Code for Data Cycle
FC0 FC2 — Address Space for Data Cycle
*1 — Rerun Faulted Bus Cycle, or Run Pending Prefetch
  0 = Do Not Rerun Bus Cycle

Figure 6-2. Special Status Word (SSW)

The special status word (SSW) information defines whether the fault was on the instruction stream, data stream, or both. There are two status bits each for the B and C stages of the instruction pipe. The rerun flag bits (RB and RC) indicate that the processor will rerun the bus cycle for the corresponding stage during the RTE instruction. This can be due to either a prefetch that is pending or to a fault that occurred while executing a prefetch. The fault bits (FB and FC) indicate that the processor attempted to use a stage and found it to be marked as invalid due to a bus error on the prefetch for that stage. The fault bits are outputs only that can be used by a bus error handler to determine the cause(s) of a bus error exception; they are ignored when the processor reads the stack frame during an RTE. The rerun bits indicate if an element of the instruction pipe is valid, and can be used by a handler to repair the pipe due to a fault (either an address error or a bus error). RB and RC are used by the processor during an RTE to control the execution of bus cycles for each stage; if either, or both, of the rerun bits are set when the RTE instruction reads the frame, the processor will rerun the previously faulted prefetch cycle (or execute a pending prefetch for the first time). If a rerun bit is clear, it is assumed that there is no prefetch pending for the corresponding stage and that software has repaired or filled the image of the stage, if necessary. When the SSW is written to the stack frame during exception processing, the RB and/or RC bits will be set if the corresponding fault bit is set, or if a prefetch for the stage is pending, so that the default (if the handler does not modify RB and/or RC) is to have the processor execute the bus cycle(s). The address space for instruction stream faults is not presented explicitly, but is the program space for the privilege level indicated in the status register of the stack frame.

If an address error exception occurs, the fault bits written to the stack frame will not be set (since they are only set due to a bus error, as described above), and the rerun bits must be used to determine the cause of the exception. Depending on the state of the pipeline, either RB and RC will both be set, or RB alone will be set. If it is desired to repair the pipeline and continue execution of the suspended instruction, software must place the correct instruction stream data in the stage C and/or stage B images (and clear the corresponding rerun bits), depending on the state of the rerun bits.

If the DF bit of the SSW is set, a data fault has occurred. If the DF bit is set when the processor reads the stack frame, it will rerun the faulted data access; otherwise, it assumes that no data fault occurred, or software has corrected the fault. Other information about the data access, such as read/write, read-modify-write, the size of the operand access, and the address space for the access are present in the SSW. Data and instruction stream faults may be pending simultaneously; thus, the fault handler should be able to handle any combination of the FC, FB, RC, RB, and DF bits.

6.4.2 Completing the Bus Cycle(s)

There are two methods of completing faulted bus cycles. The first is to use a software handler to emulate the cycle and the second is to allow the processor to rerun the bus cycle(s) after the cause for the fault has been repaired.

6.4.2.1 COMPLETING THE BUS CYCLE(S) VIA SOFTWARE. Based on the information saved on the stack, the fault handler routine may emulate the faulted bus cycle in a manner that is transparent to the instruction that caused the fault. For instruction stream faults, there are separate images for the B and C stages of the instruction pipe that may need repair. If the fault indicator for a particular stage is set, the processor has faulted because the fetch of the instruction word was aborted by an address error or a bus error. For the short format frame, the address of the stage B word is the value in the program counter plus four, and the address of the stage C word is the value in the program counter plus two. For the long format, the address of the stage B word is given explicitly, and the address of the stage C word is the address of the stage B word minus 2. For each faulted stage, the software handler should fetch the instruction word from the proper address space as indicated by the S bit of the status register in the frame, and write it to the image of the stage in the stack frame. In addition, the handler must clear the rerun bit associated with the stage that it has completed. The fault bits for each stage should not be changed.

For data write operations, the handler must transfer the properly sized data in the image of the data output buffer (DOB) to the location indicated by the fault address in the address space defined by the SSW. For data read operations, the handler must transfer properly sized data from the location indicated by the fault address and address space to the image of the data input buffer (DIB). Byte, word, and 3-byte operands appear right-justified within the 4-byte image of the data buffers. In addition, the software handler must clear the DF bit of the SSW to inform the processor that the faulted data bus cycle has been completed.

In order to emulate a read-modify-write cycle, the exception handler must first determine what instruction, CAS, CAS2, or TAS, caused the fault. This may be accomplished by examining the operation word at the address contained in the stack frame program counter. Then the handler must modify not only the SSW of the stack frame, but also the status register image and the image of any data register(s) required for the CAS and CAS2 instructions (presumably, the user visible registers were saved upon entry to the handler with a MOVEM instruction and are restored later). In other words, the fault handler must emulate the entire instruction, rather than just the faulted bus cycle. This more detailed action is required due to the fact that the processor assumes that the entire read-modify-write operation (which may consist of up to four long word transfers), including condition code computations and register transfers, is completed by the handler if the DF bit is clear and the RM bit is set when the frame is read by an RTE instruction. This is true regardless of whether the fault occurred on the first read cycle, or subsequent read or write cycles of the operation.

After the handler has completed the software emulation, the stack frame and the memory state represent the state of the system after the bus cycle(s) has been successfully completed. Note that the software method must be used for address error faults.

To ensure proper operation of the processor, no modifications to a bus cycle fault stack frame other than those described above should be made.

6.4.2.2 COMPLETING THE BUS CYCLE(S) VIA RTE. If it is not necessary to complete the faulted bus cycle via software emulation, the RTE instruction, as the last instruction to be executed in the exception handler routine, is able to complete the faulted bus cycle(s). This is the default case and it is assumed that whatever caused the fault, such as a non-resident page in a virtual memory system, has been repaired or the fault will occur again. If a fault occurs when the RTE instruction attempts to rerun the bus cycle(s), a new stack frame will be created on the supervisor stack after the previous frame is deallocated; and address error or bus error exception processing will start in the normal manner.

The read-modify-write operations of the MC68020 provide for a special case of the bus fault recovery processing. While the bus recovery processing for all read and write operations are strictly on a cycle-by-cycle basis, that for a read-modify-write operation is on an instruction basis. This means that during an RTE from a bus error of a read-modify-write operation, if the DF bit in the SSW is set, indicating that the cycle should be rerun, then the processor will rerun the entire operation from beginning to completion regardless of which part of the operation caused the bus error. Similarly, if the DF bit is cleared, indicating that the operation has been completed in software, the processor assumes that the entire operation has been completed and will immediately proceed with the next instruction.

Systems programmers and designers both should be aware of this facet of the processor and its implications. Specifically, it is recommended that memory management mechanisms treat any bus cycle with $\overline{RMC}$ asserted as a write operation for protection checking operations regardless of the state of the R/$\overline{W}$ signal. Otherwise, the potential for partially destroying system pointers with the CAS and CAS2 instructions exists since one portion of the write operation could take place and the remainder aborted by a bus error.

6.5 MC68020 EXCEPTION STACK FRAMES

The MC68020 generates six different stack frames. These frames consist of the normal four and six word stack frames, the four word throwaway stack frame, the coprocessor mid-instruction exception stack frame, and the short and long bus fault stack frames.

Whenever the MC68020 writes or reads a stack frame, it will use long word operand transfers whenever possible. Thus, if the stack area resides in a 32-bit ported memory and the stack pointer is long word aligned, exception processing performance will be greatly enhanced. Also, the order of the bus cycles used by the processor to write or read a stack frame may not follow the order of the data in the frame.

6.5.1 Normal Four Word Stack Frame

This frame (see Figure 6-3) is created by interrupts, format errors, TRAP #n instructions, illegal instructions, A-line and F-line emulator traps, privilege violations, and coprocessor pre-instruction exceptions. The program counter value is the address of the next instruction to be executed, or the instruction that caused the exception, depending on the exception type.

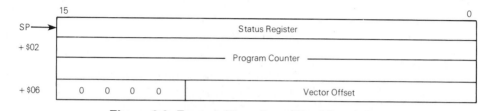

Figure 6-3. Format $0 — Four Word Stack Frame

6.5.2 Throwaway Four Word Stack Frame

This stack frame (see Figure 6-4) is the throwaway frame that is created on the interrupt stack during exception processing for an interrupt when a transition from the master state to the interrupt state occurs. The program counter value is equal to the value on the normal four word or coprocessor mid-instruction exception stack frame that was created on the master stack.

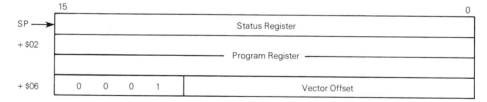

Figure 6-4. Format $1 — Throwaway Four Word Stack Frame

6.5.3 Normal Six Word Stack Frame

This stack frame (see Figure 6-5) is created by instruction related exceptions which include coprocessor post-instruction exceptions, CHK, CHK2, cpTRAPcc, TRAPcc, TRAPV trace, and zero divide. The instruction address value is the address of the instruction that caused the exception. The program counter value is the address of the next instruction to be executed, and the address to which the RTE instruction will return.

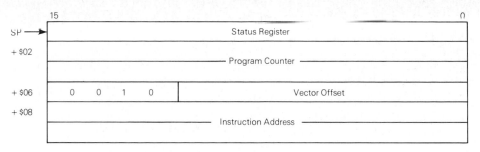

Figure 6-5. Format $2 — Six Word Stack Frame

6.5.4 Coprocessor Mid-Instruction Exception Stack Frame

This stack frame (see Figure 6-6) is created for three different exceptions, all related to coprocessor operations. The first occurs when the "take mid-instruction exception" primitive is read while processing a coprocessor instruction. The second occurs when the main processor detects a protocol violation during processing of a coprocessor instruction. The third occurs when a "null, come again with interrupts allowed" primitive is received, and the processor detects a pending interrupt. Refer to **SECTION 8 COPROCESSOR INTERFACE DESCRIPTION** for further details. The program counter value is the address of the next word to be fetched from the instruction stream. The instruction address value is the address of the first word of the instruction that was executing when the exception occurred.

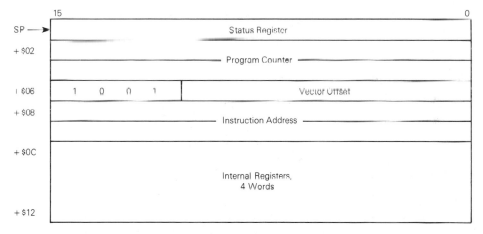

Figure 6-6. Format $9 — Coprocessor Mid-Instruction
Exception Stack Frame (10 Words)

6.5.5 Short Bus Cycle Fault Stack Frame

This stack frame (see Figure 6-7) is created whenever a bus cycle fault is detected, and the processor recognizes that it is at an instruction boundary and can use this reduced version of the bus fault stack frame. The program counter value is the address of the next instruction to be executed.

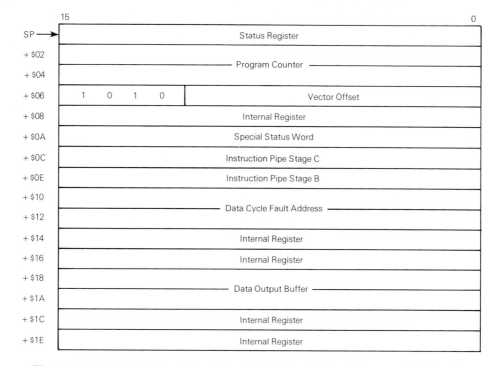

Figure 6-7. Format $A — Short Bus Cycle Fault Stack Frame (16 Words)

6.5.6 Long Bus Cycle Fault Stack Frame

This stack frame (see Figure 6-8) is created whenever the processor detects a bus cycle fault and recognizes that it is not on an instruction boundary. The program counter value is the address of the instruction that was executing when the fault occurred (which may not be the instruction that generated the faulted bus cycle).

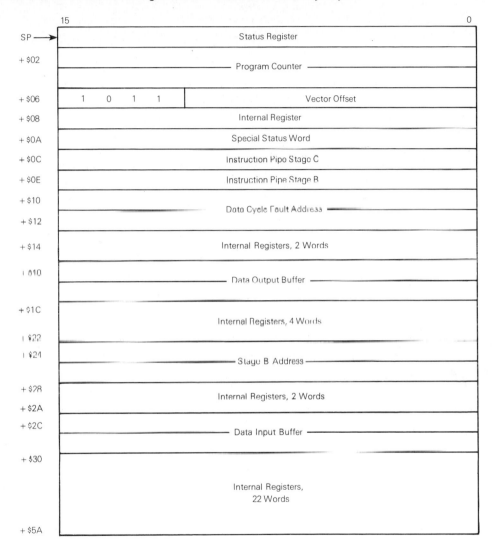

Figure 6-8. Format $B — Long Bus Cycle Fault Stack Frame (46 Words)

6.5.7 Stack Frame Summary

Figure 6-9 shows a summary of the M68000 Family defined stack frames.

Format	Frame Type
0000	Short Format (4 Words)
0001	Throwaway (4 Words)
0010	Instruction Exception (6 Words)
0011-0111	(Undefined, Reserved)
1000	MC68010 Bus Fault (29 Words)
1001	Coprocessor Mid-Instruction (10 Words)
1010	MC68020 Short Bus Fault (16 Words)
1011	MC68020 Long Bus Fault (46 Words)
1100-1111	(Undefined, Reserved)

Figure 6-9. Stack Frame Format Definitions

6

SECTION 7
ON-CHIP CACHE MEMORY

The MC68020 incorporates an on-chip cache memory as a means of improving the performance of the processor. The cache is implemented as a CPU instruction cache and is used to store the instruction stream prefetch accesses from the main memory.

Studies have shown that typical programs spend most of their execution time in a few main routines or tight loops. Therefore, once captured in the high-speed cache, these active code segments can execute directly from the cache. Thus, the processor does not suffer any external memory delays, and the total execution time of the program is significantly improved. The performance is also improved by allowing the MC68020 to make simultaneous accesses to instructions in the internal cache and to data in the external memory.

Another of the major benefits of using the cache is that the processor's external bus activity is greatly reduced. Thus, in a system with more than one bus master (such as a processor and DMA device) or a tightly-coupled multi-processor system, more of the bus bandwidth is available to the alternate bus masters without a major degradation in the performance of the MC68020.

7.1 CACHE DESIGN AND OPERATION

The following paragraphs describe the cache design and operation within the MC68020.

7.1.1 On-Chip Cache Organization

The MC68020 on-chip instruction cache is a direct-mapped cache of 64 long word entries. Each cache entry consists of a tag field made up of the upper 24 address bits and the FC2 value, one valid bit and 32 bits (two words) of instruction data.

Figure 7-1 shows a block diagram of the on-chip cache. Whenever an instruction fetch occurs, the cache (if enabled) is first checked to determine if the word required is in the cache. This is achieved by first using the index field (A2-A7) of the access address as an index into the on-chip cache. This selects one of the 64 entries in the cache. Next, the access address bits A8-A31, and FC2 are compared to the tag of the selected entry. If there is a match and the valid bit is set, a cache hit occurs. Address bit A1 is used to select the proper word from the cache entry and the cycle ends. If there is no match, or the valid bit is clear, a cache miss occurs and the instruction is fetched from external memory. This new instruction is automatically written into the cache entry, and the valid bit is set, unless the freeze cache bit has been set (see **7.1.2.3 F—FREEZE CACHE**) in the cache

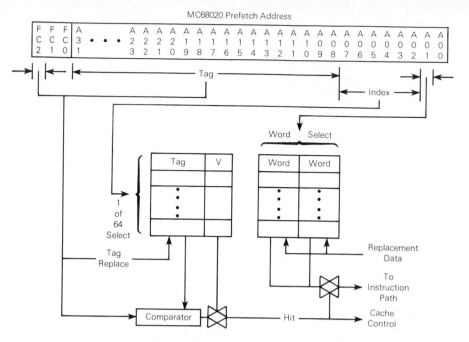

Figure 7-1. MC68020 On-Chip Cache Organization

control register. Since the processor always prefetches instructions externally with long word, aligned bus cycles, both words of the entry will be updated, regardless of which word caused the miss.

NOTE

Data accesses are not cached, regardless of their associated address space.

7.1.2 Cache Control

The cache itself is accessable only by the internal MC68020 control unit. The user has no direct method of accessing (read/write) individual entries (tag, data, etc.). To manipulate the cache entries, however, the user does have a set of control functions available in the form of a cache control register which is described below.

7.1.2.1 CACHE CONTROL REGISTER. Access to the cache control register (CACR) is provided by means of the Move Control Register (MOVEC) instruction. The MOVEC instruction is a privileged instruction. The CACR is a 32-bit register which is organized as shown in Figure 7-2. The unused bits (including bits [31:8] which are not shown) are always read as zeros.

```
31                                                    8  7                 0
┌──────────────────────────────────────────────────┬──┬──┬──┬──┬──┬──┬──┬──┬──┐
│ 0                                                  │ 0│ 0│ 0│ 0│ 0│ C│CE│ F│ E│
└──────────────────────────────────────────────────┴──┴──┴──┴──┴──┴──┴──┴──┴──┘
```

C = Clear Cache
CE = Clear Entry
F = Freeze Cache
E = Enable Cache

Figure 7-2. Cache Control Register

7.1.2.2 E—ENABLE CACHE. The cache enable function is necessary for system debug and emulation. This bit allows the designer to operate the processor with the cache disabled. Clearing this bit will disable the cache (force continuous misses, and suppress fills) and force the processor to always access external memory. The cache will remain disabled as long as this bit is cleared. The user must set this bit, which is automatically cleared whenever the processor is reset, to enable the cache.

7.1.2.3 F—FREEZE CACHE. The freeze bit keeps the cache enabled, but cache misses are not allowed to replace valid cache data. This bit can be used by emulators to freeze the cache during emulation function execution.

7.1.2.4 CE—CLEAR ENTRY. When the clear entry bit is set, the processor takes the address (index field, bits 2-7) in the cache address register (CAAR) and invalidates the associated entry (clears the valid bit) in the cache, regardless of whether or not it provides a hit; i.e., whether the tag field in the cache address register matches the cache tag or not. This function will occur only when a write to the cache control register is performed with the CE bit set. This bit always reads as a zero and the operation is independent of the state of the E or F bits, or the external Cache Disable ($\overline{\text{CDIS}}$) pin.

7.1.2.5 C—CLEAR CACHE. The cache clear bit is used to invalidate all entries in the cache. This function is necessary for operating systems and other software which must clear old data from the cache whenever a context switch is required. The setting of the clear cache bit in the cache control register causes all valid bits in the cache to be cleared, thus invalidating all entries. This function occurs only when a write to the cache control register is performed with the C bit set. This bit always reads as a zero.

7.2 CACHE ADDRESS REGISTER

The cache address register (CAAR) is a 32-bit register which provides an address for cache control functions (see Figure 7-3). The MC68020 only uses this register for the clear entry (CE) function. Access to the CAAR is provided by the Move Control Register (MOVEC) instruction.

```
31                                              8  7           2 1 0
┌──────────────────────────────────────────────┬──────────────┬────┐
│           Cache Function Address               │    Index     │    │
└──────────────────────────────────────────────┴──────────────┴────┘
```

Figure 7-3. Cache Address Register

7.3 CACHE DISABLE INPUT

The cache disable input is used to dynamically disable the cache. The input signal on this pin is synchronized before being used to control the internal cache. The cache is disabled on the first cache access after the synchronized $\overline{CDIS}$ signal is recognized as being asserted. The cache will be re-enabled on the first cache access after the synchronized $\overline{CDIS}$ signal is recognized as being negated. This pin disables the cache independent of the enable bit in the Cache Control Register and, therefore, can be used by external emulator hardware to force the MC68020 to make all accesses via the external bus.

7.4 CACHE INITIALIZATION

During processor reset, the cache is cleared by resetting all of the valid bits. The Cache Control Register (CACR) enable (E) and freeze (F) bits are also cleared.

7

SECTION 8
COPROCESSOR INTERFACE DESCRIPTION

This section describes the M68000 coprocessor interface. It is intended for designers who are implementing a coprocessor to interface to the MC68020. Motorola coprocessors will conform to the interface described in this section and their use does not require a detailed knowledge of the M68000 coprocessor interface. These coprocessors will execute Motorola defined instructions that are described in the respective coprocessor user manuals.

8.1 INTRODUCTION

The M68000 Family of general purpose microprocessors provide a level of performance which satisfies a wide range of computer applications. Special purpose hardware, however, can often provide higher levels of performance for a specific application. The coprocessor concept allows the capabilities and performance of a general purpose processor to be enhanced for a particular application without unduly encumbering the main processor architecture. A coprocessor can be designed to efficiently handle any number of specific capability requirements that must typically be implemented in software by a general purpose processor. Thus, the processing capabilities of a system can be tailored to a specific application by utilizing a general purpose main processor and the appropriate coprocessor(s).

It is important to make the distinction between standard peripheral hardware and a M68000 coprocessor. An M68000 coprocessor is a device or set of devices that have the capability of communicating with the main processor through the protocol defined as the M68000 coprocessor interface. A coprocessor differs from a peripheral particularly from the perspective of the main processor programming model. This programming model consists of the instruction set, register set, and memory map available to the programmer. A coprocessor adds additional instructions, and generally additional registers and data types which are not directly supported by the main processor architecture. Dedicated coprocessor instructions are provided to utilize the coprocessor capabilities. The interactions between the main processor and the coprocessor that are necessary for the coprocessor to provide a given service, are transparent to the programmer. That is, no knowledge of the communication protocol between the main processor and the coprocessor is required of the programmer since this protocol is implemented in hardware. Thus, the coprocessor can provide capabilities to the user without appearing as hardware external to the main processor.

In contrast, standard peripheral hardware is generally accessed through the use of interface registers mapped into the memory space of the main processor. The programmer uses standard processor instructions to access the peripheral interface registers and thus utilize the services provided by the peripheral. While a peripheral could conceivably provide capabilities equivalent to a coprocessor for many applications, the programmer must implement the communication protocol between the main processor and the peripheral necessary to use the peripheral hardware.

8.2 M68000 FAMILY COPROCESSOR INTERFACE OVERVIEW

The communication protocol defined for the M68000 coprocessor interface will be described under **8.3 COPROCESSOR INSTRUCTION TYPES.** The algorithms necessary to implement the M68000 coprocessor interface are provided in the microcode of the MC68020 and are completely transparent to the MC68020 programmer's model. For example, floating-point operations are not implemented in the MC68020 hardware. In a system utilizing both the MC68020 and the MC68881 Floating-Point Coprocessor, a programmer can use any of the instructions defined for the MC68881 without the knowledge that the actual computation is performed by the MC68881 hardware.

A M68000 coprocessor may be coupled with a main processor which does not have a coprocessor interface such as an MC68000, MC68008, MC68010, or MC68012. This is accomplished by providing instruction sequences that emulate the protocol of the coprocessor interface described in this section. The coprocessor will appear as a peripheral in the programming model of these processors.

8.2.1 Interface Features

The M68000 coprocessor interface design incorporates a number of flexible capabilities. The physical coprocessor interface is based on M68000 asynchronous bus cycles which simplifies the interface since there are no special purpose signals involved. Since standard M68000 asynchronous bus cycles are used to transfer information between the main processor and the coprocessor, the coprocessor can be implemented in the technology which is available to the coprocessor designer. A coprocessor can be implemented as a VLSI device, as a separate system board, or even as a separate computer system.

Since the main processor and a M68000 coprocessor communicate using an asynchronous bus, they are not required to operate at the same clock frequency. This feature allows the system designer to optimize the speed of the various sections of the processing hardware for a particular system application. The designer is free to choose the speeds of a main processor and coprocessor which provide the optimum performance for a given system.

The M68000 coprocessor interface also facilitates the design of coprocessors. The coprocessor design need only conform to the coprocessor interface and does not require extensive knowledge of the architecture of the main processor. The coprocessor must reflect the architecture of the main processor only to the extent that it must use the M68000 coprocessor interface protocol to communicate with the main processor. Also, the main processor can operate with a coprocessor without explicit provisions for the capabilities of that coprocessor being made in the main processor architecture. Since the capabilities of the coprocessor are not dictated by the architecture of the main processor, the coprocessor designer has a great deal of freedom in the implementation of a given coprocessor.

8.2.2 Concurrent Coprocessor Operation Support

The programmers model for the M68000 Family of microprocessors is based on sequential, non-concurrent instruction execution. This implies that the instructions in a given sequence are executed in the order which they occur and that all actions performed by an instruction will be completed by the time the next instruction in the sequence executes. In order to maintain a uniform programmers model, any coprocessor extensions should also maintain the model of sequential, non-concurrent instruction execution at the user level. That is, the programmer may assume that all services provided by a given instruction will have been completed when the next instruction in the sequence executes.

The M68000 coprocessor interface is designed to provide full support of all operations necessary for non-concurrent operation between the main processor and its associated coprocessors. While the M68000 coprocessor interface allows concurrency in coprocessor execution, it is the responsibility of the coprocessor designer to implement this concurrency while maintaining a programming model based on sequential, non-concurrent instruction execution.

8.2.3 Coprocessor Instruction Format

The instruction set for a given coprocessor is defined by the design of that coprocessor. When a coprocessor instruction is encountered in the main processor instruction stream, the MC68020 hardware initiates communication with the coprocessor and coordinates any interaction necessary for the instruction execution with the coprocessor. A programmer is required to know only the instruction set and register set defined by the coprocessor in order to utilize the functions provided by the coprocessor hardware.

The instruction set of an M68000 coprocessor is implemented by using the F-line operation words in the M68000 instruction set. The operation word is the first word of any M68000 Family instruction. The F-line operation word contains ones in bits 15 through 12 ([15:12] = [1111]; see Figure 8-1) and the remaining bits are used to specify the type of coprocessor instruction that will be executed. The F-line operation word may be followed by a number of extension words which provide additional information necessary for the execution of the coprocessor instruction.

Bits 11 through 9 of the F-line operation word are used to encode the coprocessor identification code (Cp-ID). The MC68020 uses the coprocessor identification field to indicate which coprocessor it is accessing for a given coprocessor instruction.

15	14	13	12	11	10	9	8	7	6	5	4	3	2	1	0
1	1	1	1		Cp-ID			Type				Type Dependent			

**Figure 8-1. F-line Coprocessor Instruction
Operation Word**

Cp-ID codes of 000-101 are reserved for current and future Motorola coprocessors and Cp-ID codes of 110-111 are reserved for user defined coprocessors. The Motorola Cp-ID codes which are currently defined are:

Cp-ID Code	Motorola Coprocessor
000	MC68851 Paged-Memory Management Unit
001	MC68881 Floating-Point Coprocessor

Thus, Motorola assemblers will by default use the Cp-ID codes specified above when generating the instruction operation codes for the MC68851 and MC68881 coprocessor instructions.

The encoding of bits 8 through 0 of the coprocessor instruction operation word is dependent on the particular instruction being implemented. These encodings are discussed in **8.3 COPROCESSOR INSTRUCTION TYPES.**

8.2.4 M68000 Coprocessor System Interface

The communication protocol between the main processor and coprocessor necessary to execute a coprocessor instruction is based on a group of interface registers which are defined for the M68000 coprocessor interface. The MC68020 hardware initiates a coprocessor instruction by accessing one of these registers. The coprocessor uses a set of response primitive codes and format codes defined for the M68000 coprocessor interface to communicate status and service requests to the main processor. The coprocessor interface registers are also used to pass operands between the main-processor and the coprocessor. The coprocessor interface register set, response primitives, and format codes will be discussed in **8.4 COPROCESSOR INTERFACE REGISTER (CIR) SET** and **8.6 COPROCESSOR RESPONSE PRIMITIVE SET DESCRIPTION.**

8.2.4.1 M68000 COPROCESSOR BUS INTERFACE. The MC68020 uses standard M68000 asynchronous bus cycles to access the registers in the coprocessor interface register set. Thus, the bus interface implemented by a coprocessor for its interface register set must only satisfy the MC68020 address, data, and control signal timing to guarantee proper communication with the main processor. The MC68020 timing information for read and write bus cycles is illustrated in Figures 10-5 and 10-6 found on foldout pages in the back of this manual. A detailed discussion of the MC68020 asynchronous bus operation is contained in **SECTION 5 BUS OPERATION.**

8.2.4.2 CPU ADDRESS SPACE. During coprocessor instruction execution, the MC68020 executes bus cycles in CPU space to access the interface register set of a coprocessor. The MC68020 indicates that it is accessing CPU space by driving the three function code outputs high during a CPU space bus cycle (FC2-FC0 = 111; see **5.2.4 CPU Space Cycles**). Thus, the coprocessor interface register set is mapped into CPU space in the same manner that a peripheral interface register set is generally mapped into data space. The information encoded on the function code lines and address bus of the

MC68020 during a coprocessor access is used to generate the chip select signal for the coprocessor being accessed. The address lines of the MC68020 are also used to specify which register in the interface set is being accessed during operand transfers between the main processor and the coprocessor.

The information that is encoded on the function code and address lines of the MC68020 during a coprocessor access is illustrated in Figure 8-2.

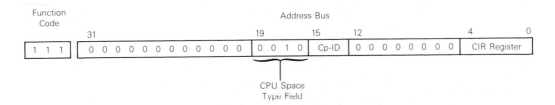

Figure 8-2. MC68020 CPU Space Address Encodings

Address signals A19-A16 specify the CPU space cycle type during a CPU space bus cycle. The types of CPU space cycles currently defined for the MC68020 are interrupt acknowledge, breakpoint acknowledge, module support operations, and coprocessor access cycles. CPU space type 2 (A19-A16 = 0010) specifies a coprocessor access cycle.

A15-A13 of the MC68020 address bus specify the coprocessor identification code (Cp-ID) for the coprocessor being accessed. This code is extracted from bits 11-9 of the coprocessor instruction operation word (see Figure 8-1) and placed on the address bus during each coprocessor access. Thus, a chip select signal for a given coprocessor can be generated by decoding the MC68020 function code signals and bits A19-A13 of the address bus. The function code signals and A19-A16 indicate a coprocessor access in CPU space, while A15-A13 indicate which of the possible eight coprocessors associated with the main processor is being accessed.

Bits A31-A20 and A12-A5 of the MC68020 address bus are always zero during a coprocessor access generated in conjunction with the execution of a coprocessor instruction. The MC68010 and MC68012 can emulate coprocessor access cycles in CPU space using the MOVES instruction.

8.2.4.3 COPROCESSOR INTERFACE REGISTER (CIR) SELECTION. The MC68020 must access the registers defined in the coprocessor interface register (CIR) set to communicate with the coprocessor during the exeuction of a coprocessor instruction. During coprocessor access bus cycles, A4-A0 of the MC68020 address bus are used to specify which register in the CIR set is being referenced. The register map for the M68000 coprocessor interface is depicted in Figure 8-3. A detailed description of the individual registers is provided in **8.4 COPROCESSOR INTERFACE REGISTER (CIR) SET.**

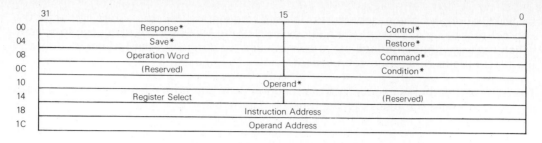

Figure 8-3. Coprocessor Interface Register Set Map

As a result of the values encoded on the MC68020 address bus during a coprocessor access, each coprocessor in a system is mapped into a unique region of the main processor's logical CPU address space. An address map for the coprocessor access portion of the MC68020 CPU space is presented in Figure 8-4. A4-A0 indicate the interface register offset from the coprocessor base address in CPU space.

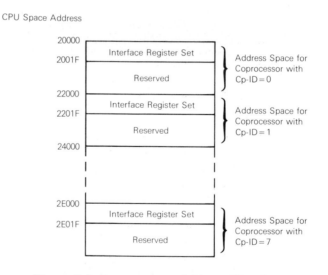

Figure 8-4. Coprocessor Address Map in MC68020 CPU Space

A block level diagram of the signals involved in the M68000 coprocessor interface is provided in Figure 8-5. Since the chip select for a given coprocessor is based in part on the Cp-ID encoded on A15-A13 of the MC68020 address bus, the system designer is free to use multiple coprocessors of the same type by simply assigning a unique Cp-ID to each one.

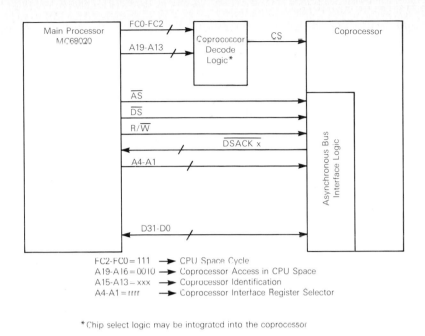

```
FC2-FC0 = 111      CPU Space Cycle
A19-A16 = 0010      Coprocessor Access in CPU Space
A15-A13 = xxx       Coprocessor Identification
A4-A1 = rrrr        Coprocessor Interface Register Selector
```

*Chip select logic may be integrated into the coprocessor

Address lines not specified above are "0" during coprocessor access.

Figure 8-5. M68000 Coprocessor Interface Signal Usage

The MC68851 Paged-Memory Management Unit, however, uses FC2-FC0 and A31-A0 as inputs to perform address translations. Thus, the MC68851 decodes the information on the MC68020 address bus and function code lines internally to determine when an access is made to one of its coprocessor interface registers. Since the MC68851 decodes the address and function code pins internally, it requires no external chip select logic and thus must be assigned the Cp-ID 000.

8.3 COPROCESSOR INSTRUCTION TYPES

Four categories of coprocessor instructions are defined for the M68000 coprocessor interface: general, conditional, context save, and context restore. These four categories are distinguished by the type of operations provided by the coprocessor instructions contained in each. The instruction category also determines the coprocessor interface register accessed by the MC68020 to initiate the coprocessor instruction and the communication protocol between the main processor and the coprocessor necessary for instruction completion.

During the execution of instructions in the general or conditional categories, the coprocessor can request services from and indicate status to the main processor using the set of coprocessor response primitive codes defined for the M68000 coprocessor interface. During the execution of the instruction in the context save and context restore categories, the coprocessor indicates its status to the main processor by utilizing the set of coprocessor format codes defined for the M68000 coprocessor interface.

8.3.1 Coprocessor General Instructions

The general coprocessor instruction category is used to implement data processing instructions and other general purpose instructions defined for a given coprocessor.

8.3.1.1 FORMAT. The format of a general type instruction is illustrated in Figure 8-6.

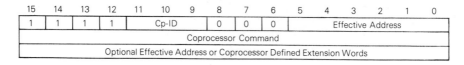

Figure 8-6. Coprocessor General Instruction Format (cpGEN)

For the purpose of this discussion, all coprocessor instructions in the general instruction category will be referred to using the cpGEN mnemonic. The actual mnemonic and syntax used to represent a coprocessor instruction is determined by the syntax of the assembler or compiler which generates the object code for the coprocessor instructions.

The coprocessor general type instructions always consists of at least two words. As in all coprocessor instructions, the first word of the instruction is an F-line operation code (bits [15-12] = 1111). The Cp-ID field of the F-line operation code is used by the MC68020 during the coprocessor access to indicate which of the coprocessors in the system will execute the coprocessor instruction. The Cp-ID is placed on A15-A13 during accesses to the coprocessor interface registers (see **8.2.4.2 CPU ADDRESS SPACE**).

Bits [8-6] = 000 indicate that the instruction is in the general instruction category. Bits 5-0 of the F-line operation code may be used to encode a standard M68000 effective address specifier (see **2.8 EFFECTIVE ADDRESS**). During the execution of a cpGEN instruction, the coprocessor can use a coprocessor response primitive to request that the MC68020 perform an effective address calculation necessary for that instruction. If the MC68020 receives one of these primitives, the processor will then utilize the effective address specifier field of the F-line operation code to determine the effective addressing mode being requested.

The second word of the general type instruction is the coprocessor command word. This command word is written to the command coprocessor interface register (command CIR) to initiate the coprocessor instruction.

An instruction in the coprocessor general instruction category may optionally include a number of extension words which follow the coprocessor command word in the instruction format. Additional information required for the coprocessor instruction execution can be included as coprocessor defined extension words. If the coprocessor requests that the MC68020 calculate an effective address during coprocessor instruction execution, information required for the calculation must be included in the instruction format as effective address extension words.

8.3.1.2 PROTOCOL. The execution of cpGEN instructions follows the protocol presented in Figure 8-7. The main processor initiates communication with the coprocessor by writing the instruction command word to the command CIR. The coprocessor then decodes the command word to begin processing associated with the execution of the cpGEN instruction. The interpretation of the coprocessor command word is specified by the coprocessor design and the MC68020 does not attempt to decode the information contained in this command word.

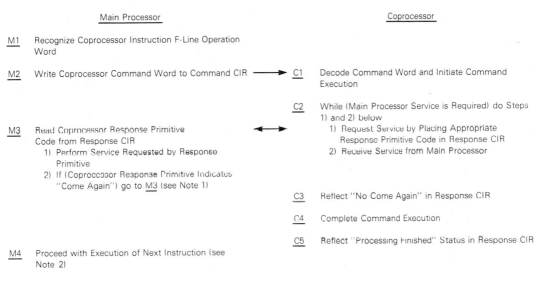

Main Processor   Coprocessor

M1   Recognize Coprocessor Instruction F-Line Operation
      Word

M2   Write Coprocessor Command Word to Command CIR ⟶ C1   Decode Command Word and Initiate Command
                                                              Execution

                                                        C2   While (Main Processor Service is Required) do Steps
                                                              1) and 2) below
M3   Read Coprocessor Response Primitive   ⟷   1) Request Service by Placing Appropriate
      Code from Response CIR   Response Primitive Code in Response CIR
      1) Perform Service Requested by Response   2) Receive Service from Main Processor
         Primitive
      2) If (Coprocessor Response Primitive Indicates
         "Come Again") go to M3 (see Note 1)
                                                        C3   Reflect "No Come Again" in Response CIR

                                                        C4   Complete Command Execution

                                                        C5   Reflect "Processing Finished" Status in Response CIR
M4   Proceed with Execution of Next Instruction (see
      Note 2)

NOTES:
   1. "Come Again" indicates that further service of the main processor is being requested by the coprocessor.
   2. The next instruction should be the operation word pointed to by the ScanPC at this point. The operation of the MC68020 ScanPC
       is discussed in **8.5.2 ScanPC**.

Figure 8-7. Coprocessor Interface Protocol for General Category Instructions

After writing to the command CIR, the main processor will read the response CIR to determine its next action. While the coprocessor is executing an instruction, it may request services from and communicate status to the main processor by placing the appropriate coprocessor response primitive codes in the response CIR. When the coprocessor has completed the execution of an instruction or no longer needs the services of the main processor to execute the instruction, it will reflect this status in the response CIR. The main processor will then proceed to the next instruction in the instruction stream. If a trace exception is pending, however, the MC68020 will not terminate communication with the coprocessor until the coprocessor indicates that it has completed all processing associated with the cpGEN instruction (see **8.8.2.5 TRACE EXCEPTIONS**).

The coprocessor interface protocol illustrated in Figure 8-7 allows the operation of a given general category instruction to be defined by the coprocessor. That is, the main processor simply initiates the instruction by writing the instruction command word to the command CIR and then reads the response CIR to determine its next action. The execution of the coprocessor instruction is then defined by the internal operation of the coprocessor and its use of response primitives to request services from the main processor. This instruction protocol allows a wide range of operations to be implemented in the general instruction category.

8.3.2 Conditional Coprocessor Instructions

The conditional instruction category allows program control, based on the operations of the coprocessor, to be implemented in a uniform manner. The execution of instructions in this category is inherently divided between the main processor and the coprocessor. The coprocessor is responsible for evaluating a condition and returning a true/false indicator to the main processor. The completion of the instruction execution is then handled by the main processor based on this true/false condition indicator.

The implementation of instructions in the conditional category promotes efficient utilization of the hardware provided by design in the main processor and the coprocessor. The condition on which the instruction execution is based is related to the coprocessor operation and is therefore evaluated by the coprocessor. The instruction completion following the condition evaluation is, however, directly related to the operation of the main processor. The portion of the instruction involving change of flow, setting a data alterable byte, or TRAP operations is executed by the main processor since its architecture inherently implements these operations to support its instruction set.

The protocol used to execute a conditional category coprocessor instruction is illustrated in Figure 8-8. The main processor initiates an instruction in this category by writing a condition selector to the condition CIR. The condition selector is decoded by the coprocessor to determine what condition it should evaluate. The coprocessor can use response primitives to request that the main processor provide services required for the condition evaluation. Upon completion of the condition evaluation, the coprocessor returns a true/false indicator to the main processor through the response CIR using the Null primitive (see **8.6.2 Null (No Operands)**). The main processor completes the coprocessor instruction execution when it receives the condition indicator from the coprocessor.

8.3.2.1 BRANCH ON COPROCESSOR CONDITION INSTRUCTIONS. There are two formats of the M68000 Family branch instruction provided in the conditional instruction category. These instructions allow the control of flow of instruction execution to be based on conditions related to the coprocessor operation. The execution of these instructions is based on the conditional branch instructions provided in the M68000 Family instruction set.

8.3.2.1.1 Format. The two formats of the branch on coprocessor condition instructions are illustrated in Figures 8-9 and 8-10.

Main Processor	Coprocessor

M1   Recognize Coprocessor Instruction F-Line Operation Word

M2   Write Coprocessor Condition Selector to Condition CIR   →   C1   Decode Condition Selector and Initiate Condition Evaluation

C2   While (Main Processor Service is Required) do Steps 1) and 2) Below

M3   Read Coprocessor Response Primitive Code from Response CIR   ↔   1) Request Service by Placing Appropriate Response Primitive Code in Response CIR

     1) Perform Service Requested by Response Primitive   2) Receive Service from Main Processor

     2) If (Coprocessor Response Primitive Indicates "Come Again") go to M3 (see Note 1)   C3   Complete Condition Evaluation

C4   Reflect "No Come Again" Status with True/False Condition Indicator in Response CIR

M4   Complete Execution of Instruction Based on the True/False Condition Indicator Returned in the Response CIR

NOTES:

1. All coprocessor response primitives, except the Null primitive, that allow the "Come Again" primitive attribute must indicate "Come Again" when used during the execution of a conditional category instruction. If a "Come Again" attribute is not indicated in one of these primitives, the main processor will initiate protocol violation exception processing (see **8.8.2.1 PROTOCOL VIOLATIONS**).

Figure 8-8. Coprocessor Interface Protocol for Conditional Category Instructions

15	14	13	12	11	10	9	8	7	6	5	4	3	2	1	0
1	1	1	1	Cp ID			0	1	0	Condition Selector					
Optional Coprocessor Defined Extension Words															
Displacement															

Figure 8-9. Branch On Coprocessor Condition Instruction (cpBcc.W)

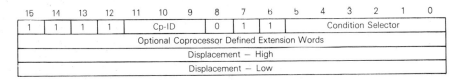

15	14	13	12	11	10	9	8	7	6	5	4	3	2	1	0
1	1	1	1	Cp-ID			0	1	1	Condition Selector					
Optional Coprocessor Defined Extension Words															
Displacement — High															
Displacement — Low															

Figure 8-10. Branch On Coprocessor Condition Instruction (cpBcc.L)

The first word of the branch on coprocessor condition instruction is the F-line operation word. As with all coprocessor instructions, bits [15-12] = 1111 and bits [11-9] contain the identification code of the coprocessor that will evaluate the condition. Bits [8-6] are used to distinguish between the word and long word displacement formats of the instruction, which are denoted by the cpBcc.W and cpBcc.L mnemonics respectively.

Bits [5-0] of the F-line operation word contain the coprocessor condition selector field. The MC68020 writes the entire operation word to the condition CIR to initiate the branch instruction. The coprocessor should then use bits [5-0] to determine the condition which it should evualate.

If the coprocessor requires additional information to evaluate the condition, this information can be included in the branch instruction format using coprocessor defined extension words. These extension words follow the F-line operation word and the number required for a given coprocessor instruction is determined by the coprocessor design. The final word(s) of the cpBcc instruction format contains the displacement used by the main processor to calculate the destination address when the branch is taken.

8.3.2.1.2 Protocol. The protocol used to implement the cpBcc.L and cpBcc.W instructions is depicted in Figure 8-8. The main processor transfers the condition selector to the coprocessor by writing the F-line operation word to the condition CIR to initiate the instruction. The main processor then reads the response CIR to determine its next action. The coprocessor can use the response primitive set to request services necessary to evaluate the condition. If the coprocessor returns the false condition indicator, the main processor proceeds with the execution of the next instruction in the instruction stream. If the coprocessor returns the true condition indicator, the displacement is added to the MC68020 scanPC (see **8.5.2 ScanPC**) to determine the destination address at which the main processor continues instruction execution. The scanPC must be pointing to the location of the first word of the displacement in the instruction stream when the destination address is calculated. The displacement is a two's complement integer that can be either a 16-bit word or a 32-bit long word. The 16-bit displacement is sign extended to a long word value before the destination address is calculated.

8.3.2.2 SET ON COPROCESSOR CONDITION. The set on coprocessor condition instructions are used to set or reset a flag (a data alterable byte) based on a condition evaluated by the coprocessor. The operation of this instruction is patterned after the operation of the Scc instruction in the M68000 Family instruction set. While the Scc instruction does not inherently cause a change of program flow, it is often used to set flags upon which program flow is based.

8.3.2.2.1 Format. The format for the set on coprocessor condition instruction, denoted by the cpScc mnemonic, is illustrated in Figure 8-11.

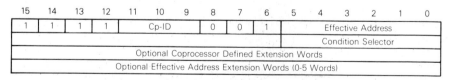

Figure 8-11. Set On Coprocessor Condition (cpScc)

The first word of the cpScc instruction is the F-line operation word. This word contains the Cp-ID field in bits [11-9] and bits [8-6] = 001 to identify the cpScc instruction. The lower six bits of the F-line operation word are used to encode an M68000 Family effective address mode (see **2.8 EFFECTIVE ADDRESS**).

The second word of the cpScc instruction format contains the coprocessor condition selector in bits [5-0]. Bits [15-6] of this word are reserved and should be zero to insure compatibility with future M68000 products. This word is written to the condition CIR to initiate the cpScc instruction.

If the coprocessor requires additional information to evaluate the condition, this information can be included in the cpScc instruction format using coprocessor defined extension words. These extension words follow the word containing the coprocessor condition selector field, and the number of extension words required for a given coprocessor instruction is determined by the coprocessor design.

The final portion of the cpScc instruction format contains zero to five effective address extension words. If the main processor requires additional information for the calculation of the effective address specified by bits [5-0] of the F-line operation word, this information is included in the effective address extension words.

8.3.2.2.2 Protocol. The protocol used to implement the cpScc instruction is depicted in Figure 8-8. The MC68020 transfers the condition selector to the coprocessor by writing the word following the operation word to the condition CIR. The main processor then reads the response CIR to determine its next action. The coprocessor can use the response primitive set to request services necessary to evaluate the condition. The operation of the cpScc instruction depends on the condition evaluation indicator returned to the main processor by the coprocessor. If the coprocessor returns the false condition indicator, the main processor evaluates the effective address specified by bits [5-0] of the F-line operation word and sets the byte at that effective address to FALSE (all bits to zero). If the coprocessor returns the true condition indicator, the main processor sets the byte specified by the effective address to TRUE (all bits set to one).

8.3.2.3 TEST COPROCESSOR CONDITION, DECREMENT AND BRANCH. The operation of the test coprocessor condition, decrement and branch instruction is patterned after the DBcc instructions provided in the M68000 Family instruction set. This operation is based on a coprocessor evaluated condition and a loop counter provided in the main processor and is useful in implementing the DO-UNTIL type constructs used in many high level languages.

8.3.2.3.1 Format. The format of the test coprocessor condition, decrement and branch instruction, denoted by the cpDBcc mnemonic, is illustrated in Figure 8-12.

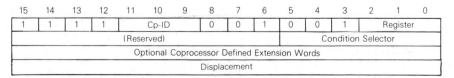

15	14	13	12	11	10	9	8	7	6	5	4	3	2	1	0
1	1	1	1		Cp-ID		0	0	1	0	0	1		Register	
				(Reserved)							Condition Selector				
			Optional Coprocessor Defined Extension Words												
			Displacement												

**Figure 8-12. Test Coprocessor Condition, Decrement and
Branch Instruction Format (cpDBcc)**

The first word of the cpDBcc instruction is the F-line operation word. Bits [2-0] of this operation word denote the main processor data register that will be used as the loop counter during instruction execution.

The second word of the cpDBcc instruction format contains the coprocessor condition selector in bits [5-0] and should contain zeroes in bits [15-6] to maintain compatibility with future M68000 products. This word is written to the condition CIR to initiate the cpDBcc instruction.

If the coprocessor requires additional information to evaluate the condition, this information can be included in the cpDBcc instruction format using coprocessor defined extension words. These extension words follow the word containing the coprocessor condition selector field in the cpDBcc instruction format.

The displacement for the cpDBcc instruction is contained in the last word of the instruction format. This displacement is a two's complement 16-bit value that is sign extended to long word size when it is used for a destination address calculation.

8.3.2.3.2 Protocol. The protocol used to implement the cpDBcc instructions is depicted in Figure 8-8. The MC68020 transfers the condition selector to the coprocessor by writing the word following the operation word to the condition CIR. The main processor then reads the response CIR to determine its next action. The coprocessor can use the response primitive set to request any services necessary to evaluate the condition. If the coprocessor returns the true condition indicator, the main processor proceeds with the execution of the next instruction in the instruction stream. If the coprocessor returns the false condition indicator, the main processor decrements the low-order word of the register specified by bits [2-0] of the F-line operation word. If this register is equal to minus one (− 1) after being decremented, the main processor proceeds with the execution of the next instruction in the instruction stream. If the register is not equal to minus one (− 1) after being decremented, the main processor branches to the destination address to continue instruction execution.

The destination address calculation is identical to that used for the cpBcc.W instruction. That is, the displacement is added to the MC68020 scanPC (see **8.5.2 ScanPC**) to determine the destination address at which the main processor continues instruction execution. The scanPC must be pointing to the location of the 16-bit displacement in the instruction stream when the destination address is calculated.

8.3.2.4 TRAP ON COPROCESSOR CONDITION. The operation of the trap on coprocessor condition instruction allows the programmer to initiate exception processing based on conditions related to the coprocessor operation.

8.3.2.4.1 Format. The format for the trap on coprocessor condition instruction, denoted by the cpTRAPcc mnemonic, is illustrated in Figure 8-13.

15	14	13	12	11	10	9	8	7	6	5	4	3	2	1	0
1	1	1	1		Cp-ID		0	0	1	1	1	1		Opmode	
(Reserved)										Condition Selector					
Optional Coprocessor Defined Extension Words															
Optional Word															
or Long Word Operand															

Figure 8-13. Trap On Coprocessor Condition (cpTRAPcc)

Bits [2-0] of the cpTRAPcc F-line operation word specify the number of optional operand words included in the instruction format. The instruction format can include zero, one, or two operand words.

The second word of the cpTRAPcc instruction format contains the coprocessor condition selector in bits [5-0] and should contain zeroes in bits [15-6] to maintain compatibility with future M68000 products. This word is written to the condition CIR to initiate the cpTRAPcc instruction.

If the coprocessor requires additional information to evaluate a condition, this information can be Included in coprocessor defined extension words. These extension words follow the word containing the coprocessor condition selector field in the cpTRAPcc Instruction format.

The number of operand words indicated by bits [2-0] of the cpTRAPcc F-line operation word follow the coprocessor defined extension words. These operand words are not explicitly used by the MC68020, but can be used to encode information referenced by the cpTRAPcc exception handling routines. The legal encodings for bits [2-0] are provided in Table 8-1. Other encodings of these bits map to the encodings of the cpScc instruction or if undefined, cause an F-line emulator exception (see **APPENDIX B INSTRUCTION SET**).

Table 8-1. cpTRAPcc Opmode Encodings

Opmode	Optional Words in Instruction Format
010	One
011	Two
100	Zero

8.3.2.4.2 Protocol. The protocol used to implement the cpTRAPcc instructions is depicted in Figure 8-8. The MC68020 transfers the condition selector to the coprocessor by writing the word following the operation word to the condition CIR. The main processor then reads the response CIR to determine its next action. The coprocessor can use the response primitive set to request any services necessary to evaluate the condition. If the coprocessor returns the true condition indicator, the main processor initiates exception processing for the cpTRAPcc exception (see **8.8.2.4 cpTRAPcc INSTRUCTION TRAPS**). If the coprocessor returns the false condition indicator, the main processor proceeds with the exception of the next instruction in the instruction stream.

8

8.3.3 Coprocessor Context Save and Context Restore

The coprocessor context save and context restore instruction categories are included in the M68000 coprocessor interface in order to support multitasking programming environments. In a multitasking environment, the context of a coprocessor may need to be changed in an asynchronous manner with respect to the operation of that coprocessor. That is, the coprocessor may be interrupted at any point in the execution of an instruction in the general or conditional category in order to commence context change operations.

In contrast to the general and condition instruction categories, the context save and context restore instruction categories do not use the coprocessor response primitives during the instruction execution. A set of format codes is defined for the M68000 coprocessor interface to allow the coprocessor to communicate status information to the main processor during the execution of instructions in the context save and context restore categories. These coprocessor format codes are discussed in detail in **8.3.3.4 COPROCESSOR FORMAT WORDS.**

8.3.3.1 COPROCESSOR CONTEXT SAVE. There is one instruction defined for the M68000 coprocessor context save instruction category. The coprocessor context save instruction, denoted by the cpSAVE mnemonic, allows the context of a coprocessor to be saved in an asynchronous manner with respect to the execution of coprocessor instructions in the general or conditional instruction categories. During the execution of a cpSAVE instruction, the coprocessor can communicate status information to the main processor by using the coprocessor format codes.

8.3.3.1.1 Format. The format of the cpSAVE instruction is illustrated in Figure 8-14.

15	14	13	12	11	10	9	8	7	6	5	4	3	2	1	0
1	1	1	1		Cp-ID		1	0	0			Effective Address			
					Effective Address Extension Words (0-5 Words)										

Figure 8-14. Coprocessor Context Save Instruction Format (cpSAVE)

The first word of the instruction is the F-line operation code which contains the coprocessor identification specifier in bits [11-9] and an M68000 effective address specifier in bits [5-0]. The effective address encoded in the cpSAVE instruction is used to determine where the state frame associated with the current context of the coprocessor will be saved in memory.

The control alterable and pre-decrement addressing modes are legal with the cpSAVE instruction. Other addressing modes encoded within this instruction will cause the MC68020 to initiate F-line emulator exception processing as described in **8.8.2.2 F-LINE EMULATOR EXCEPTIONS.**

There can be up to five effective address extension words following the cpSAVE instruction operation word. If the main processor requires additional information for the calculation of the effective address specified by bits [5-0] of the operation word, this information is included in the effective address extension words.

8.3.3.1.2 Protocol. The protocol for the coprocessor context save instruction is illustrated in Figure 8-15. The main processor initiates the cpSAVE instruction by reading the save CIR. Thus, the cpSAVE instruction is the only coprocessor instruction that is initiated by reading from (as opposed to writing to) a register in the coprocessor interface register set. The coprocessor communicates status information associated with the context save operation to the main processor by placing coprocessor format codes in the save CIR.

	Main Processor		Coprocessor
M1	Recognize Coprocessor Instruction F-Line Operation Word		
M2	Read Save CIR to Initiate the cpSAVE Instruction	C1	If (Not Ready to Begin Context Save Operation) do Steps 1) and 2) Below
M3	If (Format = Not Ready) do Steps 1) and 2) Below ←		1) Place Not Ready Format Code in Save CIR
	1) Service Pending Interrupts		2) Suspend or Complete Current Operations
	2) Go to M2		
		C2	Place Appropriate Format Word in Save CIR
M3	Evaluate Effective Address Specified in F-Line Opword and Store Format Word at Effective Address	C3	Transfer Number of Bytes Indicated in Format Word Through Operand CIR
M4	If (Format = Empty) go to M5 Else, Transfer Number of Bytes Indicated in Format Word From Operand CIR to Effective Address		
M5	Proceed with Execution of Next Instruction		

Figure 8-15. Coprocessor Context Save Instruction Protocol

If the coprocessor is not ready to immediately suspend its current operation when the main processor reads the save CIR, the coprocessor may return a format code indicating "Not Ready" to the main processor. The main processor will then service any pending interrupts and return to read the save CIR and thus re-initiate the cpSAVE instruction. After placing the not ready format code in the save CIR, the coprocessor should proceed to either suspend or complete the operations associated with the instruction it is currently executing.

Once the coprocessor has suspended or completed all operations associated with the instruction it is executing, it will place a format code in the save CIR representing the internal coprocessor state. When the main processor reads the save CIR, it transfers the format word to the effective address encoded in the cpSAVE instruction. The lower byte of the coprocessor format word specifies the number of bytes of state information, not including the format word, which will be transferred from the coprocessor to the effective address specified. If the state information is not a multiple of four bytes in size, the MC68020 will initiate format error exception processing (see **8.8.1.5 FORMAT ERRORS**). The coprocessor and main processor coordinate the transfer of the internal state of the coprocessor through the use of the operand CIR. The MC68020 completes the coprocessor context save by repeatedly reading the operand CIR and writing the information obtained into memory until the number of bytes specified in the coprocessor format word have been transferred. Following a cpSAVE instruction, the coprocessor should be in an idle state, that is, not executing any coprocessor instructions.

The cpSAVE instruction is a privileged instruction. Thus, when the main processor encounters the cpSAVE instruction, it checks the supervisor bit in the status register to determine if it is operating in the supervisor state. If the MC68020 attempts to execute a cpSAVE instruction while in the user state (bit [13] = 0 in status register), it will initiate privilege violation exception processing without accessing any of the coprocessor interface registers (see **8.8.2.3 PRIVILEGE VIOLATIONS**).

The MC68020 will initiate format error exception processing if it reads an invalid format word of a valid format word whose length field is not a multiple of four bytes from the save CIR during the execution of a cpSAVE instruction (see **8.3.3.4.3. Invalid Format Words**). The MC68020 will write a $0001 to the control CIR to abort the coprocessor instruction in this situation prior to exception processing. This case is not included in Figure 8-15 since a coprocessor should generally only return a not ready or a valid format code in the context of the cpSAVE instruction. The coprocessor may return the invalid format word, however, if a cpSAVE is initiated while the coprocessor is executing a cpSAVE or cpRESTORE instruction and the coprocessor is not able to support the suspension of these two instructions.

8.3.3.2 COPROCESSOR CONTEXT RESTORE. There is one instruction defined for the M68000 coprocessor context restore instruction category. The coprocessor context restore instruction, denoted by the cpRESTORE mnemonic, provides a mechanism by which a coprocessor can be forced to terminate any current operations and restore a state associated with a different context of execution. During the execution of a cpRESTORE instruction, the coprocessor can communicate status information to the main processor by placing format codes in the restore CIR.

8.3.3.2.1 Format. The format of the cpRESTORE instruction is illustrated in Figure 8-16.

15	14	13	12	11	10	9	8	7	6	5	4	3	2	1	0
1	1	1	1		Cp-ID		1	0	1			Effective Address			
			Effective Address Extension Words (0-5 Words)												

Figure 8-16. Coprocessor Context Restore Instruction Format (cpRESTORE)

The first word of the instruction is the F-line operation code which contains the coprocessor identification specifier in bits [11-9] and an M68000 effective address specifier in bits [5-0]. The effective address encoded in the cpRESTORE instruction is used to determine where in memory the coprocessor context is stored. The effective address points to the coprocessor format word containing information related to the context that will be restored to the coprocessor.

There can be up to five effective address extension words following the first word in the cpRESTORE instruction format. If the main processor requires additional information for the calculation of the effective address specified by bits [5-0] of the operation word, this information is included in the effective address extension words.

All memory addressing modes except the pre-decrement addressing mode are legal. Illegal effective address encodings cause the MC68020 to initiate F-line emulator exception processing (see **8.8.2.2 F-LINE EMULATOR EXCEPTIONS**).

8.3.3.2.2 Protocol. The protocol for the coprocessor context restore instruction is illustrated in Figure 8-17. When the main processor encounters a cpRESTORE instruction it first reads a coprocessor format word from the effective address specified in the instruction. This format word contains a format code and length field. The main processor retains a copy of the length field to determine the number of bytes which will be transferred to the coprocessor during the cpRESTORE operation and writes the format word to the restore CIR to initiate the coprocessor context restore.

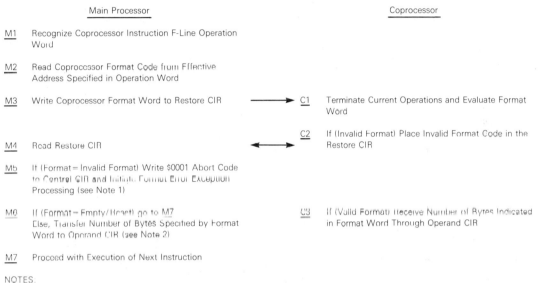

Main Processor		Coprocessor
M1	Recognize Coprocessor Instruction F-Line Operation Word	
M2	Read Coprocessor Format Code from Effective Address Specified in Operation Word	
M3	Write Coprocessor Format Word to Restore CIR	C1 Terminate Current Operations and Evaluate Format Word
		C2 If (Invalid Format) Place Invalid Format Code in the Restore CIR
M4	Read Restore CIR	
M5	If (Format = Invalid Format) Write $0001 Abort Code to Control CIR and Initiate Format Error Exception Processing (see Note 1)	
M6	If (Format = Empty/Reset) go to M7 Else, Transfer Number of Bytes Specified by Format Word to Operand CIR (see Note 2)	C3 If (Valid Format) Receive Number of Bytes Indicated in Format Word Through Operand CIR
M7	Proceed with Execution of Next Instruction	

NOTES:
1. See **8.8.1.5 FORMAT ERROR**.
2. The MC68020 uses the length field in the format word read during M2 to determine the number of bytes to read from memory and write to the operand CIR.

Figure 8-17. Coprocessor Context Restore Instruction Protocol

When the coprocessor receives the format word in the restore CIR it must terminate any current operations and evaluate the format word. If the format word represents a valid coprocessor context as determined by the coprocessor design, the coprocessor will return the format word to the main processor through the restore CIR and prepare to receive the number of bytes specified in the format word through its operand CIR.

The main processor follows its write of the format word to the restore CIR by reading that same register. If the coprocessor returns a valid format word, the main processor will proceed to transfer the number of bytes specified (by the format word read from the cpRESTORE effective address previously) through the operand CIR.

If the format word written to the restore CIR does not represent a valid coprocessor state frame, the coprocessor will place an invalid format word in the restore CIR and terminate any current operations. Upon receipt of the invalid format code, the main processor acknowledges the format error by writing a $0001 to the control CIR and initiating format error exception processing (see **8.8.1.5 FORMAT ERROR**).

The cpRESTORE instruction is a privileged instruction. Thus, when the main processor encounters a cpRESTORE instruction, it checks the supervisor bit in the status register to determine if it is operating in the supervisor state. If the MC68020 attempts to execute a cpRESTORE instruction while in the user state (bit[13] = 0 in status register), it will initiate privilege violation exception processing without accessing any of the coprocessor interface registers (see **8.8.2.3 PRIVILEGE VIOLATIONS**).

8.3.3.3 COPROCESSOR INTERNAL STATE FRAMES. The cpSAVE and cpRESTORE instructions transfer an internal coprocessor state frame between memory and a coprocessor. This internal coprocessor state frame represents the state of coprocessor operations. Using the cpSAVE and cpRESTORE instructions it is possible to interrupt coprocessor operation, save the context associated with the current operation, and initiate coprocessor operations in a new context.

A coprocessor's internal state frame is stored as a sequence of long word entries in memory as a result of a cpSAVE instruction execution. The format of a coprocessor state frame stored in memory is illustrated in Figure 8-18.

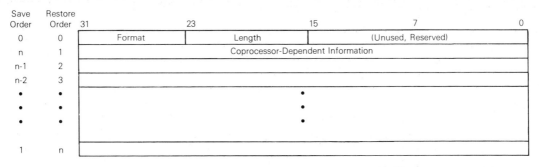

Figure 8-18. Coprocessor State Frame Format in Memory

During the cpSAVE instruction, the effective address contained in the operation word is calculated and the format word is stored at this effective address. The long words that form the coprocessor state frame are then written to descending memory addresses beginning with the address specified by the sum of the effective address and the format word length field x4. During the cpRESTORE instruction, the format word and long words that are contained in the state frame are read from ascending addresses beginning with the effective address specified in the instruction operation word.

The coprocessor format word is stored at the lowest address of the state frame in memory and is the first word transferred for both the cpSAVE and the cpRESTORE instructions. The word following the format word does not contain information relevant to the coprocessor state frame, but serves to keep the information in the state frame a multiple of four bytes in size. The number of entries following the format word (at higher addresses) is determined by the format word length for a given coprocessor state.

The information contained in a coprocessor state frame describes a context of operation for that coprocessor. This description of a coprocessor context includes the program invisible state information and, optionally, the program visible state information. The program invisible state information is any internal registers or status information which cannot be accessed by the programmer, but is still necessary for the coprocessor to continue its operation at the point of suspension. Program visible state information includes the contents of all registers which appear in the coprocessor programming model and which can be directly accessed using the coprocessor instruction set. The information saved by the cpSAVE instruction must include the program invisible state information. If cpGEN instructions are provided to save the program visible state of the coprocessor, the cpSAVE and cpRESTORE instructions should only transfer the program invisible state information to minimize interrupt latency during a save or restore operation.

8.3.3.4 COPROCESSOR FORMAT WORDS. The coprocessor communicates status information to the main processor during the cpSAVE and cpRESTORE instructions by utilizing coprocessor format words. The format words defined for the M68000 coprocessor interface are listed in Table 8-2.

Table 8-2. Coprocessor Format Word Encodings

Format Code	Length	Meaning
00	xx	Empty/Reset
01	xx	Not Ready, Come Again
02	xx	Invalid Format
03-0F	xx	Undefined, Reserved
10-FF	Length	Valid Format, Coprocessor Defined

The upper byte of the coprocessor format word contains the code used to communicate coprocessor status information to the main processor. The MC68020 recognizes four types of format words: empty/reset, not ready, invalid format, and valid format. The MC68020 interprets the reserved format codes ($03-$0F) as invalid format words. The lower byte of the coprocessor format word is used to specify the size in bytes (which must be a multiple of four) of the coprocessor state frame in conjunction with the valid format code (see **8.3.3.4.4 Valid Format Words**).

8.3.3.4.1 Empty/Reset Format Word. The empty/reset format code Is returned by the coprocessor during a cpSAVE instruction to indicate that the coprocessor contains no user loaded information. That is, no coprocessor instructions have been executed since either the previous cpRESTORE with the empty/reset format code or the previous hardware reset. If the main processor reads the empty/reset format word from the save CIR during the initiation of a cpSAVE instruction, it will simply store the format word at the effective address specified in the cpSAVE instruction, and proceed with the execution of the next instruction.

If the main processor reads the empty/reset format word from memory during the execution of the cpRESTORE instruction, it will write the format word to the restore CIR. The main processor will then read the restore CIR and if the empty/reset format word is returned by the coprocessor, the main processor will then continue with the execution of the next instruction. The main processor can initialize the coprocessor by writing the empty/reset format code to the restore CIR. When the coprocessor receives the empty/reset format code, it will terminate any current operations and wait for the main processor to initiate the next coprocessor instruction. In particular, the cpRESTORE of the empty/reset format word should cause the coprocessor to return this same format word if a cpSAVE instruction is executed before any other coprocessor instructions. Thus, an empty/reset state frame consists only of the format word and the following reserved word in memory (see Figure 8-18).

8.3.3.4.2 Not Ready Format Word. When the main processor initiates a cpSAVE instruction by reading the save CIR, the coprocessor may return a not ready format word. The main processor will then service any pending interrupts and return to re-read the save CIR. The not ready format word allows the coprocessor to delay the save operation until it is ready to save its internal state. The cpSAVE instruction may cause the suspension of a coprocessor instruction in the general or conditional category with the capability of resuming the suspended instruction at a later time. If no further main processor services are required to complete coprocessor instruction execution, it may be more efficient to complete the instruction and thus reduce the size of the saved state. The coprocessor designer should consider the efficiency of instruction completion versus instruction suspension and resumption when a cpSAVE instruction is initiated by the main processor.

When the main processor initiates a cpRESTORE instruction by writing a format word to the restore CIR, the coprocessor should generally terminate any current operations and restore the state frame supplied by the main processor. Thus, the not ready format word should generally not be returned by the coprocessor during the execution of a cpRESTORE instruction. If the coprocessor must delay the cpRESTORE operation for any reason, it can return the not ready format word when the main processor reads the restore CIR. If the main processor does read the not ready format word from the restore CIR during the cpRESTORE instruction, it will re-read the restore CIR **without** servicing any pending interrupts.

8.3.3.4.3 Invalid Format Words. A coprocessor may place the invalid format word in the restore CIR in response to the main processor's initiation of the cpRESTORE instruction. This invalid format indicates that the format word written to the restore CIR does not describe a valid coprocessor state frame. If the main processor reads this format word during the cpRESTORE instruction, it will write the abort mask ($0001) to the control CIR and initiate format error exception processing.

A coprocessor should generally not place an invalid format word in the save CIR when the main processor initiates a cpSAVE instruction. A coprocessor, however, may not be able to support the initiation of a cpSAVE instruction while it is executing a previously initiated cpSAVE or cpRESTORE instruction. In this situation, the coprocessor can return the invalid format word when the main processor reads the save CIR to initiate the cpSAVE instruction while either another cpSAVE or cpRESTORE instruction is executing. If the main processor reads an invalid format word from the save CIR it will write the abort mask to the control CIR and initiate format error exception processing (see **8.8.1.5 Format Error**).

8.3.3.4.4 Valid Format Words. Valid format words are the only type of format words in which the length field, contained in the lower eight bits, is relevant. When the main processor reads a valid format word from the save CIR during the cpSAVE instruction, it will use the length field to determine the size of the coprocessor state frame to save. During the cpRESTORE instruction, the main processor uses the length field in the valid format word read from the effective address specified in the instruction to determine the size of the coprocessor state frame that will be restored.

The length field of a valid format word must be a multiple of four bytes in size. If the main processor detects a valid format length field that is not a multiple of four bytes in size during the execution of a cpSAVE or cpRESTORE instruction, the main processor will write the abort mask ($0001) to the control CIR and initiate format error exception processing.

8.4 COPROCESSOR INTERFACE REGISTER (CIR) SET

The M68000 coprocessor interface is implemented using a protocol based on the coprocessor interface register set. During the execution of a coprocessor instruction, the MC68020 accesses the registers defined in the CIR set to communicate with the coprocessor. It should be noted that the interface register set is not directly related to the register set that appears in the coprocessor's programming model.

A memory map of the coprocessor interface register set is illustrated in Figure 8-3. The registers denoted by an asterisk (*) must be included in a coprocessor interface in order to allow coprocessor instructions in all four categories to be implemented. The complete register model must be implemented if the system is to utilize all of the coprocessor response primitives defined for the M68000 coprocessor interface. A detailed description of each register in the CIR set is given in the following paragraphs. The hexidecimal value in parenthesis following each register name in the following paragraph titles is the register offset from the base address of the CIR set.

8.4.1 Response CIR ($00)

The response CIR is a 16-bit register through which the coprocessor communicates all service requests to the main processor using the coprocessor response primitives. The main processor reads the response CIR to receive the coprocessor response primitives during the execution of instructions in the general and conditional instruction categories.

8.4.2 Control CIR ($02)

The control CIR is a 16-bit register which is accessed by the main processor to acknowledge coprocessor requested exception processing or to abort the execution of a coprocessor instruction. The format of this register is illustrated in Figure 8-19.

15	14	13	12	11	10	9	8	7	6	5	4	3	2	1	0
(Undefined, Reserved)														XA	AB

Figure 8-19. Control CIR Format

The MC68020 writes the hexidecimal value $0002 to the control CIR to acknowledge the receipt of one of the three "Take Exception" coprocessor response primitives. The MC68020 writes the hexidecimal value $0001 to the control CIR to abort any coprocessor instruction that is in progress. The MC68020 will abort a coprocessor instruction when it detects one of three exception conditions: F-line emulator detected after a response primitive is read, privilege violation caused by the supervisor check primitive, or a format error (see **8.8 EXCEPTIONS**).

8.4.3 Save CIR ($04)

The save CIR is a 16-bit register through which the coprocessor communicates status and state frame format information to the main processor during the execution of a cpSAVE instruction. The main processor reads the save CIR to initiate the cpSAVE instruction.

8.4.4 Restore CIR ($06)

The restore CIR is a 16-bit register. The main processor initiates the cpRESTORE instruction by writing a coprocessor format word read from memory into this register. During the execution of the cpRESTORE instruction, the coprocessor communicates status and state frame format information to the main processor through the use of the restore CIR.

8.4.5 Operation Word CIR ($08)

The operation word CIR is a 16-bit register to which the main processor writes the F-line operation word of the coprocessor instruction in progress when it is requested by the transfer operation word coprocessor response primitive (**8.6.4 Transfer Operation Word**).

8.4.6 Command CIR ($0A)

The command CIR is a 16-bit register. The main processor initiates an instruction in the coprocessor general instruction category by writing the instruction command word, which follows the instruction F-line operation word, to this register.

8.4.7 Condition CIR ($0E)

The condition CIR is a 6-bit register through which the main processor initiates an instruction in the coprocessor conditional category by writing the condition selector associated with the instruction. The format of the condition CIR is illustrated in Figure 8-20.

15	14	13	12	11	10	9	8	7	6	5	4	3	2	1	0
Undefined Reserved										Condition Selector					

Figure 8-20. Condition CIR Format

8.4.8 Operand CIR ($10)

The operand CIR is a 32-bit register. If the coprocessor requests the transfer of an operand necessary to execute an instruction, the operand transfer is performed by the main processor reading from or writing to this register.

The MC68020 transfers all operands to and from the operand CIR aligned with the most significant byte of this register. Any operand larger than four bytes is read from or written to this register using a sequence of long word transfers. If the operand is not a multiple of four bytes in size, the portion remaining after the initial long word transfers will be aligned with the most significant byte of the operand CIR. Figure 8-21 illustrates the operand alignment used by the MC68020 when accessing the operand CIR.

31	24	23	16	15	8	7	0
Byte Operand		No Transfer					
Word Operand			No Transfer				
Three Byte Operand				No Transfer			
Long Word Operand							
Ten -							
Byte -							
Operand			No Transfer				

Figure 8-21. Operand Alignment for Operand CIR Accesses

8.4.9 Register Select CIR ($14)

The register select CIR is a 16-bit register. When the coprocessor uses a response primitive to request the transfer of a main processor control register, multiple main processor registers, or multiple coprocessor registers, the main processor reads this register to identify the number or type of registers to be transferred.

8.4.10 Instruction Address CIR ($18)

The instruction address CIR is a 32-bit register. If the coprocessor uses a response primitive to request the address of the instruction it is currently executing, the main processor will transfer this address to the instruction address CIR. Any transfer of the scanPC is also performed through the instruction address CIR (see **8.6.15 Transfer Status Register and ScanPC**).

8.4.11 Operand Address CIR ($1C)

The operand address CIR is a 32-bit register. If a coprocessor uses a response primitive to request an operand address transfer between the main processor and the coprocessor, the address is transferred through this register.

8.5 COPROCESSOR RESPONSE PRIMITIVES INTRODUCTION

The response primitives are essentially primitive instructions that the coprocessor issues to the main processor during the execution of a coprocessor instruction. The coprocessor can communicate status information and service requests to the main processor through the use of the coprocessor response primitives. Within the general and conditional instruction categories, individual instructions are distinguished by the operation of the coprocessor hardware and the services specified by coprocessor response primitives and provided by the main processor.

8.5.1 Coprocessor Response Primitive Format

The M68000 coprocessor response primitives are encoded in a 16-bit word which is transferred to the main processor through the use of the response CIR. The format of the coprocessor response primitives is illustrated in Figure 8-22.

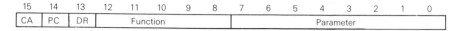

Figure 8-22. Coprocessor Response Primitive Format

The encoding of bits [12-0] of a coprocessor response primitive is dependent on the individual primitive being implemented. Bits [15-13], however, are used to specify particular attributes of the response primitive which can be utilized in most of the primitives defined for the M68000 coprocessor interface.

Bit [15] in the coprocessor response primitive format, denoted by CA, is used to specify the come again operation of the main processor. Whenever the main processor receives a response primitive from the response CIR with the come again bit set to one, it will perform the service indicated by the primitive and then return to read the response CIR. This protocol allows a coprocessor to communicate multiple response primitives to the main processor during the execution of a single coprocessor instruction.

Bit [14] in the coprocessor response primitive format, denoted by PC, is used to specify the pass program counter operation. If the main processor reads a primitive from the response CIR that has the PC bit set, the main processor will immediately pass the current value of its program counter to the instruction address CIR as the first operation in servicing the primitive request. The value of the program counter passed from the main processor to the coprocessor is the address of the operation word of the coprocessor instruction executing when the primitive is received.

The PC bit is implemented in all of the coprocessor response primitives currently defined for the M68000 coprocessor interface. If an undefined primitive or a primitive that requests an illegal operation is passed to the main processor, the main processor will initiate exception processing for either an F-line emulator or a protocol violation (see **8.8.2 Main Processor Detected Exceptions**). If the PC bit is set in one of these response primitives, however, the main processor will pass the program counter to the instruction address CIR before it initiates exception processing.

The PC bit will generally be set in the first primitive returned by the coprocessor after the main processor initiates a cpGEN instruction that can be executed concurrently by the coprocessor. Since the main processor may proceed with instruction stream execution once the coprocessor releases it, the coprocessor must record the instruction address to support any possible exception processing related to the instruction operation. Exception processing related to concurrent coprocessor instruction execution is discussed in **8.6.16.1 TAKE PRE-INSTRUCTION EXCEPTION**.

Bit [13] of the coprocessor response primitive format, denoted by DR, is the direction bit and is used in conjunction with operand transfers between the main processor and the coprocessor. If DR = 0, the direction of transfer is from the main processor to the coprocessor (main processor write). If DR = 1, the direction of transfer is from the coprocessor to the main processor (main processor read). If the operation indicated by a given response primitive does not involve an explicit operand transfer, the value of this bit is dependent on the particular primitive encoding.

8.5.2 ScanPC

During the execution of a coprocessor instruction, the program counter in the MC68020 will contain the address of the operation word of that instruction. A second register is used to sequentially address the words that compose the remaining portion of a given instruction. This second register is referred to as the scanPC, since it is used to scan the instruction stream during the instruction execution.

If the main processor requires extension words in order to calculate an effective address or destination address of a branch operation, it uses the scanPC to address these extension words in the instruction stream. Also, if a coprocessor requests the transfer of information contained in the instruction stream, the scanPC is used to address coprocessor defined extension words (which are provided in the instruction format) during the transfer. As each word is referenced, the scanPC is incremented to point to the next word in the instruction stream. When an instruction is completed, the value contained in the scanPC is transferred to the program counter to address the operation word of the next instruction to be executed.

The value of the scanPC at the time that the main processor reads the first response primitive after an instruction initiation is dependent on the instruction being executed. For a cpGEN instruction, the scanPC points to the word following the coprocessor command word. For the cpBcc instructions, the scanPC points to the word following the instruction operation word. For the cpScc, cpTRAPcc, or cpDBcc instructions, the scanPC points to the word following the coprocessor condition specifier word.

If a coprocessor implementation uses optional instruction extension words to define a general or conditional instruction, these words must be used consistently during the instruction execution. Specifically, during the execution of general category instructions, when the coprocessor terminates the instruction protocol the MC68020 assumes that the scanPC is pointing to the operation word of the next instruction to be executed. During the execution of conditional category instructions, when the coprocessor terminates the instruction protocol the MC68020 assumes that the scanPC is pointing to the word following the last of any coprocessor defined extension words in the instruction format.

8.6 COPROCESSOR RESPONSE PRIMITIVE SET DESCRIPTION

The following sections present a detailed description of the M68000 coprocessor response primitives which are supported by the MC68020. Any response primitive that the MC68020 does not recognize will cause the MC68020 to initiate protocol violation exception processing (see **8.8.2.1 PROTOCOL VIOLATIONS**). This method of handling undefined primitives allows the support of extensions to the M68000 coprocessor response primitive set to be emulated by the protocol violation exception handler. Exception processing related to the coprocessor interface is discussed in **8.8 EXCEPTIONS**.

8

8.6.1 Busy

The busy response primitive causes the main processor to re-initiate a coprocessor instruction. This primitive can be used with instructions in the general or conditional category.

8.6.1.1 FORMAT. The format of this primitive is illustrated in Figure 8-23.

15	14	13	12	11	10	9	8	7	6	5	4	3	2	1	0
0	PC	1	0	0	1	0	0	0	0	0	0	0	0	0	0

Figure 8-23. Busy Primitive Format

The PC bit is allowed and is interpreted as described in **8.5.1 Coprocessor Response Primitive Format**.

8.6.1.2 OPERATION. The busy primitive is utilized by coprocessors which can operate concurrently with the main processor but cannot buffer writes to their command or condition CIR. A coprocessor may execute a cpGEN instruction concurrently with instruction execution in the main processor. If the main processor attempts to initiate an instruction in the general or conditional instruction category while the coprocessor is concurrently executing a cpGEN instruction, the coprocessor can place the busy primitive in the response CIR. When the main processor reads this primitive, it services pending interrupts (using a pre-instruction exception stack frame, see Figure 8-41) and then restarts the general or conditional coprocessor instruction which it had attempted to initiate earlier by writing to the command or condition CIR respectively.

The busy primitive should only be used as the first primitive returned after the main processor attempts to initiate an instruction in the general or conditional category. Thus, this primitive will be used only in response to a write to the command or condition CIR. In particular, the busy primitive should not be issued at a point in instruction execution after program visible resources (coprocessor or main processor program visible registers or operands in memory) have been altered by that instruction operation. The restart of an instruction after it has altered program visible resources will cause those resources to have inconsistent values when the instruction execution is reinitiated. The scanPC is not considered a program visible register.

A special case of the operations of the MC68020 in response to the busy primitive occurs in relation to breakpoint cycles (see **6.3.5 Breakpoints**). This special case occurs when a coprocessor F-line instruction is initiated through a breakpoint cycle, the busy primitive is returned in response to the instruction initiation, and an interrupt is pending. If these three conditions are met, the breakpoint cycle is re-executed after the interrupt exception processing has been completed. This is of particular interest to designers that intend to use breakpoints to increment or decrement a counter in order to monitor the number of passes through a loop, since this special case may cause multiple breakpoint acknowledge cycles to be executed during a single pass through a loop.

8.6.2 Null (No Operands)

The null coprocessor response primitive is used to communicate coprocessor status information to the main processor. This primitive can be used in conjunction with instructions in the general and conditional categories.

8.6.2.1 FORMAT. The format of the null primitive is illustrated in Figure 8-24.

15	14	13	12	11	10	9	8	7	6	5	4	3	2	1	0
CA	PC	0	0	1	0	0	IA	0	0	0	0	0	0	PF	TF

Figure 8-24. Null Primitive Format

The CA and PC bits are implemented and are interpreted as described in **8.5.1 Coprocessor Response Primitive Format**.

Bit [8] of the primitive format, denoted by IA, is used to indicate the interrupts allowed primitive attribute. This bit determines whether the MC68020 will service pending interrupts prior to re-reading the response CIR after receiving a null primitive.

Bit [1] in the null primitive format, denoted by PF, is used to indicate the processing finished status of the coprocessor. That is, PF = 1 indicates that the coprocessor has completed all processing associated with an instruction.

Bit [0] of the primitive format, denoted by TF, is used to provide the true/false condition indicator to the main processor during the execution of a conditional category instruction. TF = 1 is the true condition specifier and TF = 0 is the false condition specifier. The TF bit is only relevant for null primitives in which CA = 0 that are used by the coprocessor during the execution of a conditional type instruction.

8.6.2.2 OPERATION. A null primitive with CA = 1 is handled in the same manner by the MC68020 whether executing a general or conditional type coprocessor instruction. If the null primitive is issued by the coprocessor with CA = 1 and IA = 1, the main processor will service pending interrupts (generating a mid-instruction stack frame, see Figure 8-43) and return to read the response CIR. If the null primitive is issued with CA = 1 and IA = 0, the main processor will simply re-read the response CIR without servicing any pending interrupts.

The main processor completes the execution of a conditional category coprocessor instruction when it receives a null, CA = 0 primitive. A null, CA = 0 primitive is used to communicate a condition evaluation indicator to the main processor during the execution of a conditional instruction and thus end the dialogue between the main processor and coprocessor for that instruction. The PF bit is not relevant during conditional instruction execution since there is an implied "coprocessor processing finish" by the null, CA = 0 primitive.

The dialogue between the main processor and coprocessor for instructions in the general category is normally terminated after any primitive which does not have CA = 1. If a trace exception is pending, however, the instruction dialogue is not terminated until the main processor reads a null, CA = 0, PF = 1 primitive from the response CIR (see **8.8.2.5 TRACE EXCEPTIONS**). Thus, the main processor will continue to re-read the response

CIR until it receives a null, CA = 0, PF = 1 primitive, and will then proceed with trace exception processing. Under these circumstances, the main processor will service pending interrupts before re-reading the response CIR if IA = 1.

A coprocessor may be able to execute a cpGEN instruction concurrently with the execution of main processor instructions and buffer one write to either its command or condition CIR. In this situation, a null primitive with CA = 1 can be issued when the coprocessor is concurrently executing a cpGEN instruction and the main processor initiates another general or conditional coprocessor instruction. This primitive indicates that the coprocessor is currently busy and the main processor should re-read the response CIR without reinitiating the instruction. The IA bit of this null primitive should generally be set to minimize interrupt latency while the main processor is waiting for the coprocessor to complete the general category instruction.

A summary of the encodings of the null primitive is provided in Table 8-3.

Table 8-3. Null Coprocessor Response Primitive Encodings

CA	PC	IA	PF	TF	General Instructions	Conditional Instructions
x	1	x	x	x	Pass Program Counter to Instruction Address CIR, Clear PC Bit and Proceed with Operation Specified by CA, IA, PF, and TF Bits	Same as General Category
1	0	0	x	x	Re-Read Response CIR, Do Not Service Pending Interrupts	Same as General Category
1	0	1	x	x	Service Pending Interrupts and Re-Read the Response CIR	Same as General Category
0	0	0	0	c	If (Trace Pending) Re-Read Response CIR Else, Execute Next Instruction	Main Processor Completes Instruction Execution Based on TF = c
0	0	1	0	c	If (Trace Pending) Service Pending Interrupts and Re-Read Response CIR Else, Execute Next Instruction	Main Processor Completes Instruction Execution Based on TF = c
0	0	x	1	c	Coprocessor Instruction Completed; Service Pending Exceptions or Execute Next Instruction	Main Processor Completes Instruction Execution Based on TF = c

x = Don't Care
c = 1 or 0 Depending on Coprocessor Condition Evaluation

8.6.3 Supervisor Check

The supervisor check primitive allows the coprocessor to verify that the main processor is operating in the supervisor state during the coprocessor instruction execution. This primitive can be used in conjunction with instructions in the general and conditional coprocessor instruction categories.

8.6.3.1 FORMAT. The format of the supervisor check primitive is illustrated in Figure 8-25.

15	14	13	12	11	10	9	8	7	6	5	4	3	2	1	0
1	PC	0	0	0	1	0	0	0	0	0	0	0	0	0	0

Figure 8-25. Supervisor Check Primitive Format

The PC bit is allowed and is interpreted as described in **8.5.1 Coprocessor Response Primitive Format**. While bit [15] is shown as 1, this bit is actually a "don't care" value for this primitive. That is, the primitive will result in the actions specified below regardless of the value of this bit. If this primitive is issued with bit [15] = 0 during a conditional category instruction, however, the main processor will initiate protocol violation exception processing.

8.6.3.2 OPERATION. When the main processor reads the supervisor check primitive from the response CIR, it checks the value of the S bit in the status register. If S = 0 (main processor operating in user mode), the main processor aborts the coprocessor instruction execution by writing a $0001 mask to the control CIR. The main processor then initiates privilege violation exception processing (see **8.8.2.3 PRIVILEGE VIOLATIONS**). If the main processor is in the supervisor mode when it receives this primitive, it will simply re-read the response CIR.

The purpose of the supervisor check primitive is to allow the implementation of privileged instructions in the coprocessor general and conditional instruction categories. Thus, this primitive should be the first one issued by the coprocessor during the dialog for an instruction which is implemented as privileged.

8.6.4 Transfer Operation Word

The transfer operation word primitive allows the coprocessor to obtain a copy of the coprocessor instruction operation word. This primitive can be used with general or conditional category instructions.

8.6.4.1 FORMAT. The format of the transfer operation word primitive is illustrated in Figure 8-26.

15	14	13	12	11	10	9	8	7	6	5	4	3	2	1	0
CA	PC	0	0	0	1	1	1	0	0	0	0	0	0	0	0

Figure 8-26. Transfer Operation Word Primitive Format

Both the CA and PC bits are allowed and are interpreted as described in **8.5.1 Coprocessor Response Primitive Format**. If this primitive is issued with CA = 0 during a conditional category instruction, the main processor will initiate protocol violation exception processing.

8.6.4.2 OPERATION. After reading this primitive from the response CIR, the main processor transfers the operation word of the currently executing coprocessor instruction to the operation word CIR. The value of the scanPC is not affected by this primitive.

8.6.5 Transfer From Instruction Stream

The main processor transfers operands from the instruction stream to the coprocessor. This primitive is allowed with general and conditional category instructions.

8.6.5.1 FORMAT. The format of the transfer from instruction stream primitive is illustrated in Figure 8-27.

15	14	13	12	11	10	9	8	7	6	5	4	3	2	1	0
CA	PC	0	0	1	1	1	1					Length			

Figure 8-27. Transfer From Instruction Stream Primitive Format

Both the CA and PC bits are allowed and are interpreted as described in **8.5.1 Coprocessor Response Primitive Format**. If this primitive is issued with CA = 0 during a conditional category instruction, the main processor will initiate protocol violation exception processing.

Bits [7-0] of the primitive format specify the length, in bytes, of the operand to be transferred from the instruction stream to the coprocessor. The length must be an even number of bytes. If an odd length is specified, the main processor will initiate protocol violation exception processing (see **8.8.2.1 PROTOCOL VIOLATIONS**).

8.6.5.2 OPERATION. When the main processor reads this primitive from the response CIR it copies the number of bytes indicated by the length field from the instruction stream to the operand CIR. Thus, coprocessor defined extension words provided in the instruction format can be transferred to the coprocessor in response to this primitive. The first word or long word transferred is at the location pointed to by the scanPC when the primitive is read by the main processor and the scanPC is incremented by two after each word is transferred. Thus, the scanPC is incremented by the total number of bytes transferred and points to the word following the last word transferred when the primitive execution has completed. The main processor will transfer the operands from the instruction stream using a sequence of long word writes to the operand CIR. If the length field is not an even multiple of four bytes, the last two bytes form the instruction stream are transferred using a word write to the operand CIR.

8.6.6 Evaluate and Transfer Effective Address

The effective address specified in the coprocessor instruction operation word is evaluated by the main processor and transferred to the coprocessor. This primitive is allowed with general category instructions. If this primitive is issued by the coprocessor during the execution of a conditional category instruction, the main processor will initiate protocol violation exception processing.

8.6.6.1 FORMAT. The format of the evaluate and transfer effective address primitive is illustrated in Figure 8-28.

15	14	13	12	11	10	9	8	7	6	5	4	3	2	1	0
CA	PC	0	0	1	0	1	0	0	0	0	0	0	0	0	0

Figure 8-28. Evaluate and Transfer Effective Address Primitive Format

Both the CA and PC bits are allowed and are interpreted as described in **8.5.1 Coprocessor Response Primitive Format**.

8.6.6.2 OPERATION. When the main processor receives this primitive during the execution of a general category instruction, the main processor evaluates the effective address specified in the instruction operation word. If the effective address requires any extension words, the scanPC is assumed to be pointing to the first of these words when the main processor receives this primitive. The scanPC is incremented by two after each of these extension words is referenced by the main processor. After the effective address is calculated, the resulting 32-bit value is written to the operand address CIR.

Only alterable control addressing modes are calculated by the MC68020 in response to this primitive. If the addressing mode in the operation word is not an alterable control mode, the main processor aborts the instruction by writing a $0001 to the control CIR and initiates F-line emulation exception processing (see **8.8.2.2 F-LINE EMULATOR EXCEPTIONS**).

8.6.7 Evaluate Effective Address and Transfer Data

The main processor transfers an operand between the coprocessor and the effective address specified in the coprocessor instruction operation word. This primitive is allowed with general category instructions. If this primitive is used by the coprocessor during the execution of a conditional category instruction, the main processor will initiate protocol violation exception processing.

8.6.7.1 FORMAT. The format of the evaluate effective address and transfer data primitive is illustrated in Figure 8-29.

15	14	13	12	11	10	9	8	7	6	5	4	3	2	1	0
CA	PC	DR	1	0		Valid EA					Length				

Figure 8-29. Evaluate Effective Address and Transfer Data Primitive Format

The CA, PC, and DR bits are allowed and are interpreted as described in **8.5.1 Coprocessor Response Primitive Format**.

The valid effective address field (bits [10-8]) of the primitive format allows the coprocessor to specify the legal effective address categories for this primitive. If the effective address specified in the instruction operation word is not a member of the class specified by bits [10-8], the main processor aborts the coprocessor instruction by writing $0001 to the control CIR, and initiates F-line emulation exception processing. The valid effective address field encodings are listed in Table 8-4.

Table 8-4. Valid Effective Address Codes

000	Control Alterable
001	Data Alterable
010	Memory Alterable
011	Alterable
100	Control
101	Data
110	Memory
111	Any Effective Address (No Restriction)

Note that the control alterable, data alterable, and memory alterable categories are determined by the intersection of the alterable effective addressing category with the control, data, and memory effective addressing categories respectively (see Table C-2. Effective Addressing Mode Categories). If the valid effective address fields specified in the primitive and in the instruction operation word match, the MC68020 will initiate protocol violation exception processing if the primitive requests a write to a non-alterable effective address.

The length in bytes of the operand to be transferred is specified by bits [7-0] of the primitive format. There are several restrictions on the operand length field used with certain effective addressing modes. If the effective address is a main processor register (register direct mode), only operand lengths of one, two, or four bytes are legal; other lengths cause the main processor to initiate protocol violation exception processing. Thus, a length of zero for a register direct effective address will result in a protocol violation. Operand lengths of zero through 255 bytes are legal in conjunction with the memory addressing mode.

There is one exception to the length field for the memory effective address category. If the effective address is immediate, the operand length must be one or even and the direction of transfer must be to the coprocessor; otherwise, the main processor will initiate protocol violation exception processing.

8.6.7.2 OPERATION. When the main processor receives this primitive during the execution of a general category instruction, it first verifies that the effective address encoded in the instruction operation word is in the effective address category specified by the primitive. If this condition is satisfied, the effective address is calculated using any necessary effective address extension words located at the current scanPC address and the scanPC is incremented by two for each word referenced. The main processor then transfers the number of bytes specified in the primitive between the operand CIR and the effective address using long word transfers whenever possible. Refer to **8.4.8 Operand CIR** for information concerning operand alignment for tranfers involving the operand CIR.

The direction of the operand transfer is specified by the DR bit. DR = 0 indicates a transfer from the effective address to the operand CIR and DR = 1 indicates a transfer from the operand CIR to the effective address.

If the effective address is the predecrement mode, the address register used is decremented by the size of the operand before the transfer. The bytes within the operand are then transferred to/from ascending addresses beginning with the location specified by the decremented address register. If the effective addressing mode is predecrement, A7 is used as the address register, and the operand is one byte in length, A7 will be decremented by two to maintain a word aligned stack.

For the postincrement effective addressing mode, the address register used is incremented by the size of the operand after the transfer. The bytes within the operand are transferred to/from ascending addresses beginning with the location specified by the address register. If the effective addressing mode is postincrement, A7 is used as the address register, and the operand is one byte in length, A7 will be incremented by two after the transfer to maintain a word aligned stack. It should be noted that the transfer of odd length operands of lengths greater than one using the − (A7) or (A7) + addressing modes can result in a stack pointer which is not word aligned.

The effective address calculation is repeated each time that this primitive is issued during the execution of a given instruction. The effective address is calculated using the current contents of any address and data registers used in the addressing mode. The main processor locates any necessary effective address extension words at the current scanPC location and increments the scanPC by two for each extension word referenced in the instruction stream.

The MC68020 sign extends byte and word size operands to a long word value when they are transferred to an address register (A0-A7) using this primitive and the register direct effective addressing mode. Byte and word size operands transferred to a data register (D0-D7) will only overwrite the lower byte or word respectively of the data register referenced.

8.6.8 Write to Previously Evaluated Effective Address

The main processor transfers an operand from the coprocessor to a previously evaluated effective address. This primitive is allowed with general category instructions. If this primitive is used by the coprocessor during the execution of a conditional category instruction, the main processor will initiate protocol violation exception processing.

8.6.8.1 FORMAT The format of the write to previously evaluated effective address primitive is illustrated in Figure 8-30.

15	14	13	12	11	10	9	8	7	6	5	4	3	2	1	0
CA	PC	1	0	0	0	0	0				Length			

Figure 8-30. Write to Previously Evaluated Effective Address Primitive Format

The CA, and PC bits are allowed and are interpreted as described in **8.5.1 Coprocessor Response Primitive Format**.

The length in bytes of the operand transferred is specified in bits [7-0] of the primitive format. The MC68020 will transfer operands between zero and 255 bytes in length.

8.6.8.2 OPERATION. When the main processor receives this primitive during the execution of a general category instruction, it transfers an operand from the operand CIR to an effective address specified by a temporary register within the MC68020. This temporary register will contain the evaluated effective address specified in the coprocessor instruction operation word if this primitive is used after either the evaluate and transfer effective address, evaluate effective address and transfer data, or transfer multiple coprocessor registers coprocessor response primitive has been executed during the coprocessor instruction. If this primitive is used during an instruction in which the effective address specified in the instruction operation word has not been calculated, the effective address used for the write is undefined. Also, if the previously evaluated effective address was register direct, the value written to in response to this primitive is undefined.

The value on the MC68020 function code signals during the write operation will indicate either supervisor or user data space depending on whether the S bit in the MC68020 status register is one or zero respectively when this primitive is received. While a coprocessor should request writes to only alterable effective addressing modes, the MC68020 does not check the type of effective address used in conjunction with the execution of this primitive. For example, if the previously evaluated effective address was program counter relative and the MC68020 is in the user state (S = 0 in status register) when this primitive is received, the MC68020 will write to **user data space** at the previously calculated program relative address (the 32-bit value contained in the temporary internal register of the processor).

Operands of length greater than four bytes are transferred in increments of four bytes (operand parts) when possible. The main processor will first read a long word operand part from the operand CIR and then transfer this part to the current effective address location. The transfers continue in this manner using ascending memory locations until all of the long word operand parts are transferred and any remaining operand part is then transferred using a one, two, or three byte transfer. For all effective addresses in the memory category, the operand parts are stored in memory using ascending addresses beginning with the address contained in the MC68020 temporary register.

The execution of this primitive will not modify any of the registers that appear in the MC68020 programmers model. If the previously evaluated effective addressing mode utilized any of the MC68020 internal address or data registers, the effective address value used will be the last value generated by the evaluate and transfer effective address, evaluate effective address and transfer data, or transfer multiple coprocessor registers primitives. Thus, the write to previously evaluated effective address primitive will not modify any data or address registers even if the previously evaluated effective address is predecrement or postincrement mode.

Note that the take address and transfer data primitive described in **8.6.9 Take Address and Transfer Data** does not replace the effective address value which has been calculated by the MC68020. Thus, the address that the main processor obtains in response to the take address and transfer data primitive cannot be referenced by the write to previously evaluated effective address primitive.

It is possible to implement read-modify-write instructions (but not indivisible bus cycles) using this primitive and the evaluate effective address and transfer data primitive.

8.6.9 Take Address and Transfer Data

The main processor transfers an operand between the coprocessor and an address supplied by the coprocessor. This primitive can be used with general or conditional category instructions.

8.6.9.1 FORMAT. The format of the take address and transfer data primitive is illustrated in Figure 8-31.

15	14	13	12	11	10	9	8	7	6	5	4	3	2	1	0
CA	PC	DR	0	0	1	0	1				Length				

Figure 8-31. Take Address and Transfer Data Primitive Format

The CA, PC, and DR bits are allowed and are interpreted as described in **8.5.1 Coprocessor Response Primitive Format**. If this primitive is issued with CA = 0 during a conditional category instruction, the main processor will initiate protocol violation exception processing.

The operand length, which can be from zero to 255 bytes, is specified by bits [7-0] of the primitive format.

8.6.9.2 OPERATION. The main processor first reads a 32-bit address from the operand address CIR. The operand is then transferred, using a series of long word transfers, between this address and the operand CIR. The operand parts are read or written to ascending addresses starting with the address read from the operand address CIR. If the operand length is not a multiple of four bytes, the final operand part is transferred using a one, two, or three byte transfer.

The function code signals used with the address read from the operand address CIR indicate either supervisor or user data space depending on whether the S bit in the MC68020 status register is one or zero respectively when this primitive is received.

8.6.10 Transfer To/From Top of Stack

The main processor transfers an operand between the coprocessor and the top of the currently active main processor stack (see **2.10 SYSTEM STACK**). This primitive can be used with general or conditional category instructions.

8.6.10.1 FORMAT. The format of the transfer to/from top of stack primitive is illustrated in Figure 8-32.

15	14	13	12	11	10	9	8	7	6	5	4	3	2	1	0
CA	PC	DR	1	1	1	0				Length					

Figure 8-32. Transfer To/From Top of Stack Primitive Format

The CA, PC, and DR bits are allowed and are interpreted as described in **8.5.1 Coprocessor Response Primitive Format**. If this primitive is issued with CA = 0 during a conditional category instruction, the main processor will initiate protocol violation exception processing.

Bits [7-0] of the primitive format specify the length in bytes of the operand to be transferred. The operand may be one, two, or four bytes in length; other length field values cause the main processor to initiate protocol violation exception processing.

8.6.10.2 OPERATION. If DR = 0, the main processor transfers the operand from the currently active system stack to the operand CIR. The implied effective address used for the transfer is therefore the (A7) + addressing mode. Operands of length one cause the stack pointer to be incremented by two after the transfer to maintain word alignment of the stack.

If DR = 1, the main processor transfers the operand from the operand CIR to the currently active stack. The implied effective address used for the transfer is therefore the − (A7) addressing mode. Operands of length one cause the stack pointer to be decremented by two before the transfer to maintain word alignment of the stack.

8.6.11 Transfer Single Main Processor Register

The main processor transfers an operand between one of its data or address registers and the coprocessor. This primitive can be used with general or conditional category instructions.

8.6.11.1 FORMAT. The format of the transfer single main processor register primitive is illustrated in Figure 8-33.

15	14	13	12	11	10	9	8	7	6	5	4	3	2	1	0
CA	PC	DR	0	1	1	0	0	0	0	0	0	D/A		Register	

Figure 8-33. Transfer Single Main Processor Register Primitive Format

The CA, PC, and DR bits are allowed and are interpreted as described in **8.5.1 Coprocessor Response Primitive Format.** If this primitive is issued with CA = 0 during a conditional category instruction, the main processor will initiate protocol violation exception processing.

Bit [3], denoted by D/A, indicates whether an address or data register is referenced. D/A = 0 indicates a data register and D/A = 1 indicates an address register. Bits [2-0] identify the register number referenced.

8.6.11.2 OPERATION. If DR = 0, the main processor writes the long word operand contained in the specified register to the operand CIR. If DR = 1, the main processor reads a long word operand from the operand CIR and transfers it to the indicated data or address register.

8.6.12 Transfer Main Processor Control Register

The main processor transfers a long word operand between one of its control registers and the coprocessor. This primitive can be used with general or conditional category instructions.

8.6.12.1 FORMAT. The format of the transfer main processor control register primitive is illustrated in Figure 8-34.

15	14	13	12	11	10	9	8	7	6	5	4	3	2	1	0
CA	PC	DR	0	1	1	0	1	0	0	0	0	0	0	0	0

Figure 8-34. Transfer Main Processor Control Register Primtive Format

The CA, PC, and DR bits are allowed and are interpreted as described in **8.5.1 Coprocessor Response Primitive Format**. If this primitive is issued with CA = 0 during a conditional category instruction, the main processor will initiate protocol violation exception processing.

8.6.12.2 OPERATION. When the main processor receives this primitive it first reads a control register select code from the register select CIR. This code determines which main processor control register is referenced during the transfer. The control register select codes recognized by the MC68020 are shown in Table 8-5. If the control register selector code is not recognized by the MC68020, the MC68020 will initate protocol violation exception processing (see **8.8.2.1 PROTOCOL VIOLATIONS**).

Table 8-5. Main Processor Control Register Selector Codes

Hex	Control Register
x000	Source Function Code (SFC) Register
x001	Destination Function Code (DFC) Register
x002	Cache Control Register (CACR)
x800	User Stack Pointer (USP)
x801	Vector Base Register (VBR)
x802	Cache Address Register (CAAR)
x803	Master Stack Pointer (MSP)
x804	Interrupt Stack Pointer (ISP)
All other codes cause a protocol violation exception	

After reading a valid code from the register select CIR, if DR = 0, the main processor writes the long word operand from the specified control register to the operand CIR. If DR = 1, the main processor reads a long word operand from the operand CIR and places it in the specified control register.

8.6.13 Transfer Multiple Main Processor Registers

The main processor transfers long word operands between one or more of its data or address registers and the coprocessor. This primitive can be used with general or conditional category instructions.

8.6.13.1 FORMAT. The format of the transfer multiple main processor registers primitive is illustrated in Figure 8-35.

15	14	13	12	11	10	9	8	7	6	5	4	3	2	1	0
CA	PC	DR	0	0	1	1	0	0	0	0	0	0	0	0	0

Figure 8-35. Transfer Multiple Main Processor Registers Primitive Format

The CA, PC, and DR bits are allowed and are interpreted as described in **8.5.1 Coprocessor Response Primitive Format**. If this primitive is issued with CA = 0 during a conditional category instruction, the main processor will initiate protocol violation exception processing.

8.6.13.2 OPERATION. When the main processor receives this primitive it first reads a 16-bit register select mask from the register select CIR. The format of the register select mask is illustrated in Figure 8-36. A register will be transferred if the bit corresponding to that register in the register select mask is set to one. The selected registers are transferred in the order D0-D7 and then A0-A7.

15	14	13	12	11	10	9	8	7	6	5	4	3	2	1	0
A7	A6	A5	A4	A3	A2	A1	A0	D7	D6	D5	D4	D3	D2	D1	D0

Figure 8-36. Register Select Mask Format

If DR = 0, the main processor writes the contents of each register indicated in the register select mask to the operand CIR using a sequence of long word transfers. If DR = 1, the main processor reads a long word operand from the operand CIR into each register indicated in the register selector mask. The registers are transferred in the same order regardless of the direction of transfer indicated by the DR bit in the primitive.

8.6.14 Transfer Multiple Coprocessor Registers

From zero to sixteen operands are transferred between the effective address specified in the coprocessor instruction and the coprocessor. This primitive is allowed with general category instructions. If this primitive is issued by the coprocessor during the execution of a conditional category instruction, the main processor will initiate protocol violation exception processing.

8.6.14.1 FORMAT. The format of the transfer multiple coprocessor registers primitive is illustrated in Figure 8-37.

15	14	13	12	11	10	9	8	7	6	5	4	3	2	1	0
CA	PC	DR	0	0	0	0	1				Length				

Figure 8-37. Transfer Multiple Coprocessor Registers Primitive Format

The CA, PC, and DR bits are allowed and are interpreted as described in **8.5.1 Coprocessor Response Primitive Format.**

Bits [7-0] of the primitive format indicate the length in bytes of each operand transferred. The operand length must be an even number of bytes, odd length operands will cause the MC68020 to initiate protocol violation exception processing (see **8.8.2.1 PROTOCOL VIOLATIONS**).

8.6.14.2 OPERATION. When the main processor receives this primitive it will calculate the effective address specified in the coprocessor instruction operation word. The scanPC should be pointing to the first of any necessary effective address extension words when this primitive is read from the response CIR and the scanPC will be incremented by two for each extension word reference during the effective address calculation. For transfers from the effective address to the coprocessor (DR = 0), the control addressing modes and the postincrement addressing mode are legal. For transfers from the coprocessor to the effective address (DR = 1), the alterable control and predecrement addressing modes are legal. Illegal addressing modes causes the MC68020 to abort the instruction by writing a $0001 to the control CIR and initiate F-line emulator exception processing (see **8.8.2.2 F-LINE EMULATOR EXCEPTIONS**).

After performing the effective address calculation, the MC68020 reads a 16-bit register select mask from the register select CIR. While the coprocessor can use the register select mask to indicate which register it will transfer, the MC68020 simply counts the number of ones in the register select mask to determine the number of operands that will be transferred. Thus, the order of the ones in the register select mask is not relevant to the operation of the main processor and up to 16 operands can be transferred by the main processor in response to this primitive. Thus, the total number of bytes transferred is the product of the number of operands transferred and the length of each operand specified by bits [7-0] of the primitive format.

If DR = 1, the main processor will read the number of operands specified in the register select mask from the operand CIR and write these operands to the effective address specified in the instruction operation word using long word transfers whenever possible. If DR = 0, the main processor will read the number of operands specified in the register select mask from the effective address and write them to the operand CIR.

For the control addressing modes, the operands are transferred to/from memory using ascending addresses. For the postincrement addressing mode, the operands are read from memory with ascending addresses and the address register used is incremented by the size of each operand after that operand is transferred. Thus, the final value of the address register used with the (An) + addressing mode will be incremented by the total number of bytes transferred during the primitive execution.

For the predecrement addressing mode, the operands are written to memory with descending addresses, while the bytes within each operand are written to memory with ascending addresses. As an example, the format in a long word wide memory for two 12 byte operands transferred from the coprocessor to the effective address using the − (An) addressing mode is illustrated in Figure 8-38. The address register used is decremented by the size of each operand before that operand is transferred. The bytes within each operand are then written to memory with ascending addresses. Thus, the address register used is decremented by the total number of bytes transferred by the end of the primitive execution. The MC68020 will transfer the data using long word transfers whenever possible.

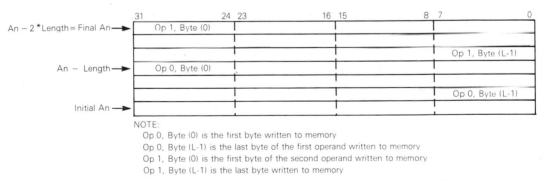

NOTE:
Op 0, Byte (0) is the first byte written to memory
Op 0, Byte (L-1) is the last byte of the first operand written to memory
Op 1, Byte (0) is the first byte of the second operand written to memory
Op 1, Byte (L-1) is the last byte written to memory

Figure 8-38. Operand Format in Memory for Transfer to − (An)

8.6.15 Transfer Status Register and ScanPC

The main processor transfers operands between the coprocessor and either the main processor status register or both the status register and scanPC. This primitive is allowed with general category instructions. If this primitive is used by the coprocessor during the execution of a conditional category instruction, the main processor will initiate protocol violation exception processing.

8.6.15.1 FORMAT. The format of the transfer status register and scanPC primitive is illustrated in Figure 8-39.

15	14	13	12	11	10	9	8	7	6	5	4	3	2	1	0
CA	PC	DR	0	0	0	1	SP	0	0	0	0	0	0	0	0

Figure 8-39. Transfer Status Register and ScanPC Primitive Format

The CA, PC, and DR bits are allowed and are interpreted as described in **8.5.1 Coprocessor Response Primitive Format**.

Bit [8] of the primitive format, denoted by SP, indicates whether the scanPC, in addition to the status register, will be transferred during the primitive execution. If SP = 1, both the scanPC and status register will be transferred. If SP = 0, only the status register will be transferred.

8.6.15.2 OPERATION. If SP = 0 and DR = 0, the main processor will write a 16-bit operand from its status register to the operand CIR. If SP = 0 and DR = 1, the main processor will read a 16-bit operand from the operand CIR into the status register.

If SP = 1, operands will be transferred between the status register and the operand CIR and between the scanPC and instruction address CIR. The order and direction of the transfer depends on the DR bit in the primitive format. If SP = 1 and DR = 0, the main processor first writes the long-word value in the scanPC to the instruction address CIR and then writes the status register to the operand CIR. If SP = 1 and DR = 1, the main processor first reads a 16-bit value from the operand DIR into the status register and then reads a long word value from the instruction address CIR into the scanPC.

This primitive allows the implementation of instructions in the general instruction category which change the main processor program flow. The main processor change of flow can occur due to transfers to the status register, the scanPC, or both. Access to the status register enables the coprocessor to determine and manipulate the main processor condition codes, supervisor status, trace modes, master or interrupt stack usage, and interrupt mask level.

Any instruction words that have been prefetched by the main processor beyond the current scanPC location are discarded by the MC68020 when this primitive is issued with DR = 1 (transfer to main processor). The MC68020 will then refill the instruction pipe from the scanPC address in the address space indicated by the status register S bit. If the scanPC was not altered by the primitive, the instruction pipe will be refilled using the value of the scanPC before the primitive execution.

If T1/T0 = 01 in the MC68020 status resgister (trace on change of flow, see **6.3.9 Tracing**) when the coprocessor instruction begins execution and this primitive is issued with

DR = 1, a trace exception will be made pending within the MC68020. This trace exception will be taken when the coprocessor signals that it has completed all processing associated with the instruction by returning the null primitive with CA = 0 and PF = 1 (see **8.8.2.5 TRACE EXCEPTIONS**).

8.6.16 Exception Processing Request Primitives

There are three primitives defined for the M68000 coprocessor interface that allow the coprocessor to cause exception processing based on its operations. When the main processor receives one of these three primitives from the coprocessor, the main processor will initiate exception processing. These primitives enable a coprocessor to suspend or abort an instruction due to an exception that occurred during the coprocessor operation.

The three "Take Exception" coprocessor response primitives differ mainly in the stack frame saved by the MC68020 in response to the primitive. Since different stack frames are saved for each of the primitives, the RTE instruction executed to exit the exception handler routine will cause the M68020 to operate differently for each of the stack frames. When the RTE instruction is executed in the exception handler, the MC68020 will either restart the instruction during which the primitive was received, continue the instruction, or proceed with the execution of the next instruction in the instruction stream.

8.6.16.1 TAKE PRE-INSTRUCTION EXCEPTION. The main processor initiates exception processing using a coprocessor supplied exception vector and the pre-instruction exception stack frame format. This primitive can be used with general or conditional category instructions.

8.6.16.1.1 Format. The format of the take pre-instruction exception primitive is illustrated in Figure 8-40.

15	14	13	12	11	10	9	8	7	6	5	4	3	2	1	0
0	PC	0	1	1	1	0	0				Vector Number				

Figure 8-40. Take Pre-Instruction Exception Primitive Format

The PC bit is allowed and is interpreted as described in **8.5.1 Coprocessor Response Primitive Format**.

Bits [7-0] of the primitive format are used to specify the exception vector number used by the main processor to initiate exception processing.

8.6.16.1.2 Operation. When the main processor receives this primitive, it first acknowledges the coprocessor exception request by writing a $0002 to the control CIR. The MC68020 then proceeds with exception processing as detailed in **6.2.4 Exception Processing Sequence**. The vector number for the exception is taken from bits [7-0] of the primitive and the MC68020 uses the four word stack frame format illustrated in Figure 8-41.

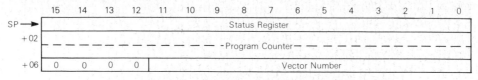

Figure 8-41. MC68020 Pre-Instruction Stack Frame

The value of the program counter saved in this stack frame is the operation word address of the coprocessor instruction during which the primitive was received. Thus, if no modificiations are made to the stack frame within the exception handler routine, an RTE instruction will cause the MC68020 to return to re-initiate the instruction during which the take pre-instruction exception primitive was received.

This primitive can be used in a number of circumstances in which the coprocessor must request exception processing related to its operation. The take pre-instruction exception primitive can be used when the coprocessor does not recognize a value written to either its command CIR or condition CIR to initiate a general or conditional instruction respectively. This primitive can also be used if an exception occurred in the coprocessor instruction before any program visible resources where modified by the instruction operation. This primitive should not be used during a coprocessor instruction if program visible resources have been modified by that instruction. Since the MC68020 will re-initiate the instruction when it returns from exception processing, the restarted instruction would receive the previously modified resources in an inconsistent state.

One of the most important uses of the take pre-instruction exception primitive is to signal an exception condition in a cpGEN instruction that was executing concurrently with the main processor's instruction execution. If the coprocessor no longer requires the services of the main processor to complete a cpGEN instruction and the concurrent instruction completion is transparent to the programmer's model, the coprocessor can release the main processor by issuing a primitive with CA = 0. Thus, the main processor will generally proceed to execute the next instruction in the instruction stream and the coprocessor will complete its operations concurrently with the main processor operation. If an exception occurs while the coprocessor is executing an instruction concurrently, the coprocessor must wait until the main processor attempts to initiate the next general or conditional instruction before the exception can be processed. After the main processor writes to the command or condition CIR to initiate a general or conditional instruction respectively, it will then read the response CIR. At this time, the coprocessor can return the take pre-instruction exception primitive. This protocol allows the main processor to proceed with exception processing related to the previous concurrently executing coprocessor instruction and then return to re-initiate the coprocessor instruction during which the exception was signalled.

The coprocessor should record the address of all general category instructions which can be executed concurrently with the main processor if exception processing and exception recovery is to be supported for that instruction. Since the exception will not be reported until the next coprocessor instruction is initiated, the instruction address is generally necessary to determine which instruction the coprocessor was executing when the exception occurred. A coprocessor can record the instruction address by setting

PC = 1 in one of the primitives used before the main processor is released after servicing a primitive with CA = 0.

8.6.16.2 TAKE MID-INSTRUCTION EXCEPTION. The main processor initiates exception processing using a coprocessor supplied exception vector and the mid-instruction exception stack frame format. This primitive can be used with general or conditional category instructions.

8.6.16.2.1 Format. The format of the take mid-instruction exception primitive is illustrated in Figure 8-42.

15	14	13	12	11	10	9	8	7	6	5	4	3	2	1	0
0	PC	0	1	1	1	0	1				Vector Number				

Figure 8-42. Take Mid-Instruction Exception Primitive Format

The PC bit is allowed and is interpreted as described in **8.5.1 Coprocessor Response Primitive Format.**

Bits [7-0] of the primitive format are used to specify the exception vector number used by the main processor to initiate exception processing.

8.6.16.2.2 Operation. When the main processor receives this primitive, it first acknowledges the coprocessor exception request by writing a $0002 to the control CIR. The MC68020 then proceeds with exception processing as detailed in **6.2.4 Exception Processing Sequence.** The vector number for the exception is taken from bits [7-0] of the primitive and the MC68020 uses the ten word stack frame format illustrated in Figure 8-43.

The value of the program counter saved in this stack frame is the operation word address of the coprocessor instruction during which the primitive was received. The scanPC field contains the value of the MC68020 scanPC when the primitive was received. If no primitive caused the evaluation of the effective address in the coprocessor instruction operation word prior to the exception request primitive, the value of the effective address field in the stack frame is undefined.

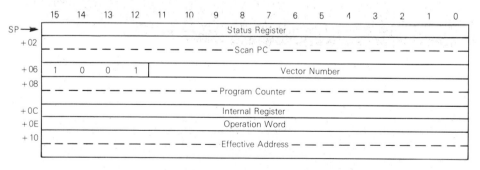

Figure 8-43. MC68020 Mid-Instruction Stack Frame

This primitive allows the coprocessor to request exception processing to handle an exception that occurred while the coprocessor is engaged in the instruction dialog with the main processor. If no modifications are made to the stack frame within the exception handler, the MC68020 will return from the exception handler after an RTE instruction and read the response CIR. Thus, the main processor will attempt to continue the execution of an instruction suspended by the take mid-instruction exception primitive by reading the response CIR and processing the primitive it receives.

8.6.16.3 TAKE POST-INSTRUCTION EXCEPTION. The main processor initiates exception processing using a coprocessor supplied exception vector and the post-instruction exception stack frame format. This primitive can be used with general or conditional category instructions.

8.6.16.3.1 Format. The format of the take post-instruction exception primitive is illustrated in Figure 8-44.

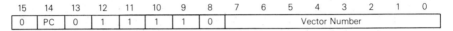

15	14	13	12	11	10	9	8	7	6	5	4	3	2	1	0
0	PC	0	1	1	1	1	0	Vector Number							

Figure 8-44. Take Post-Instruction Exception Primitive Format

The PC bit is allowed and is interpreted as described in **8.5.1 Coprocessor Response Primitive Format**.

Bits [7-0] of the primitive format are used to specify the exception vector number used by the main processor to initiate exception processing.

8.6.16.3.2 Operation. When the main processor receives this primitive, it first acknowledges the coprocessor exception request by writing a $0002 to the control CIR. The MC68020 then proceeds with exception processing as detailed in **6.2.4 Exception Processing Sequence**. The vector number for the exception is taken from bits [7-0] of the primitive and the MC68020 uses the six word stack frame format illustrated in Figure 8-45.

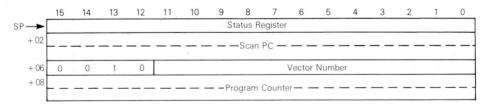

Figure 8-45. MC68020 Post-Instruction Stack Frame

The value of the main processor scanPC at the time this primitive is received is saved in the scanPC field of the post-instruction exception stack frame. The value of the program counter saved is the operation word address of the coprocessor instruction during which the primitive was received.

When the MC68020 receives the take post-instruction exception primitive it assumes that the coprocessor either completed or aborted the instruction in progress with an exception. If no modifications are made to the stack frame within the exception handler, the MC68020 will return from the exception handler after an RTE instruction to begin execution at the location specified by the scanPC field of the stack frame, which should be the address of the next instruction to be executed.

This primitive allows the coprocessor to request exception processing when the coprocessor completes or aborts an instruction with an exception while the main processor was waiting for either a release (for general category instructions) or an evaluated true/false condition indicator (for conditional category instructions). Thus, the operation of the MC68020 in response to this primitive is analogous to standard M68000 Family instruction related exception processing, for example the divide-by-zero exception.

8.7 COPROCESSOR CLASSIFICATIONS

M68000 coprocessors can be classified into two categories depending on their bus interface capabilities. The first category, non-DMA coprocessors, always operate as bus slaves. The second category, DMA coprocessors, operate as bus slaves while communicating with the main processor across the coprocessor interface, but also have the ability to operate as bus masters and directly control the system bus.

Since non-DMA coprocessors always operate as bus slaves, all external bus related functions that the coprocessor requires are handled by the main processor. The main processor will transfer operands from the coprocessor by first reading the operand from the appropriate CIR and then writing the operand to a specified effective address. Likewise, the main processor transfers operands to the coprocessor by first reading the operand from a specified effective address and then writing that operand to the appropriate CIR. If the operation of a coprocessor does not require a large portion of the available bus bandwidth, that coprocessor can be efficiently implemented as a non-DMA coprocessor. Since non-DMA coprocessors only operate as bus slaves, the bus interface circuitry of the coprocessor does not need to be as complex as that of a device which can operate as a bus master.

DMA coprocessors have the capability to operate as bus masters. This implies that the coprocessor implements all control, address, and data signals necessary to request and obtain the bus, and then perform DMA transfers using the bus. If the operation of a coprocessor requires a relatively high amount of bus bandwidth, that coprocessor can be implemented as a DMA coprocessor to improve the efficiency of operand transfers between memory and the coprocessor. DMA coprocessors, however, must still act as bus slaves when they require information or services of the main processor using the M68000 coprocessor interface protocol. In particular, if the coprocessor must access data contained in the main processor registers, the coprocessor must communicate this request to the main processor using the response primitives and operate as a bus slave during the execution of those primitives.

8.8 EXCEPTIONS

A number of exception conditions may occur related to the execution of coprocessor instructions. While these exceptions may be detected by either the main processor or the coprocessor, exception processing is coordinated and handled by the main processor. This protocol allows the service of coprocessor related exceptions to be a simple extension of the protocol used to service standard M68000 Family exceptions. That is, when either the main processor detects an exception or is signalled by the coprocessor that an exception condition has occurred, the main processor proceeds with exception processing as described in **6.2.4 Exception Processing Sequence**.

8.8.1 Coprocessor Detected Exceptions

Exceptions which are perceptible to the coprocessor, whether or not they are also perceptible to the main processor, are generally classified as coprocessor detected exceptions. These exceptions can arise from the M68000 coprocessor interface operations, internal operations, or other system related operations of the coprocessor.

Most coprocessor detected exceptions are signalled to the main processor through the use of one of the three "Take Exception" primitives defined for the M6800 coprocessor interface. When the main processor receives one of these exception signalling primitives, it proceeds as described in **8.6.16 Exception Processing Request Primitives**. There is one type of coprocessor detected exception which is not signalled to the coprocessor by a response primitive. Coprocessor detected format errors during the cpSAVE or cpRESTORE instruction are signalled to the main processor using the invalid format word as described in **8.3.3.4.3 Invalid Format Words**.

8.8.1.1 COPROCESSOR DETECTED PROTOCOL VIOLATIONS.
Protocol violation exceptions are communication failures between the main processor and coprocessor across the M68000 coprocessor interface. Coprocessor detected protocol violations occur when the main processor accesses entries in the coprocessor interface register set in a sequence that is determined to be illegal by the coprocessor. The sequence of operations that the main processor will perform for a given coprocessor instruction or coprocessor response primitive have been described previously in this section. Thus, a given CIR access by the main processor can be considered illegal by the coprocessor if the coprocessor was not expecting that access to occur.

Coprocessors can be implemented with a range of interface protocol violation detection capabilities. According to the M68000 coprocessor interface protocol, the main processor always accesses the operation word, operand, register select, instruction address, or operand address CIRs in a synchronous manner with respect to the operation of the coprocessor. That is, both the main processor and the coprocessor are aware of the sequence in which these five registers will be accessed during the execution of a given coprocessor response primitive. As a minimum, all M68000 coprocessors should detect a protocol violation if the main processor accesses any of these five registers when the coprocessor is expecting an access to either the command or condition CIR. Likewise, if the coprocessor is expecting an access of the command or condition CIR and the main processor accesses one of these five registers, the coprocessor should detect and signal a protocol violation.

According to the M68000 coprocessor interface protocol, the main processor can perform a read of either the save or response CIRs or a write of either the restore or control CIRs asynchronously to the operation of the coprocessor. That is, valid accesses can be made to these registers without the coprocessor explicitly expecting these accesses at a given point in its operation. While the coprocessor can anticipate certain accesses to either the restore, response, and control coprocessor interface registers, these registers can also be accessed when not anticipated by the coprocessor operation.

Protocol violations can not be signalled to the main processor during the execution of cpSAVE or cpRESTORE instructions. If a coprocessor detects a protocol violation during the cpSAVE or cpRESTORE instruction, it should signal the exception to the main processor when the next coprocessor instruction is initiated.

The main philosophy of the coprocessor detected protocol violation is that the coprocessor should always respond when one of its interface registers is accessed. If the access is determined to be not valid by the coprocessor, it should still assert $\overline{\text{DSACKx}}$ to the main processor and signal a protocol violation when the main processor next reads the response CIR. This protocol ensures that an access to one of the coprocessor interface registers will never halt the main processor by not having $\overline{\text{DSACKx}}$ asserted by the coprocessor.

Coprocessor detected protocol violations can be signalled to the main processor with the take mid-instruction exception primitive encoded with the coprocessor protocol violation exception vector number 13 to maintain consistency with main processor detected protocol violations. When the main processor reads this primitive, it will proceed as described in **8.6.16.2 TAKE MID-INSTRUCTION EXCEPTION**. If no modifications are made to the stack frame within the exception handler, the MC68020 will return from the exception handler after an RTE instruction and read the response CIR.

All Motorola M68000 coprocessors signal protocol violations using the take mid-instruction exception primitive with the coprocessor protocol violation exception vector number.

8.8.1.2 COPROCESSOR DETECTED ILLEGAL COMMAND OR CONDITION WORDS. Illegal coprocessor command or condition words are values written to the command CIR or condition CIR respectively that are not recognized by the coprocessor. If a value written to either of these registers is not valid, the coprocessor should place the take pre-instruction exception prmimitive in the response CIR. When it receives this primitive, the main processor will proceed as described in **8.6.16.1 TAKE PRE-INSTRUCTION EXCEPTION**. If no modifications are made to the main processor stack frame within the exception handler, an RTE instruction will cause the MC68020 to return to re-initiate the instruction during which the take pre-instruction exception primitive was received. The coprocessor designer should ensure that the state of the coprocessor is not unrecoverably altered by an illegal command or condition exception if emulation of the unrecognized command or condition word is to be supported.

All Motorola M68000 coprocessors signal illegal command and condition words by returning the take pre-instruction exception primitive with the F-line emulator exception vector number 11.

8.8.1.3 COPROCESSOR DATA PROCESSING EXCEPTIONS. Exceptions related to the internal operation of a coprocessor are classified as data processing related exceptions. These exceptions are analogous to the divide-by-zero exception defined by M68000 microprocessors and should be signalled to the main processor using one of the three "Take Exception" primitives containing an appropriate exception vector number. Which of these three primitives is used to signal the exception is generally determined by the point in the instruction operation where the main processor should continue the program flow after exception processing. These considerations are discussed in **8.6.16 Exception Processing Request Primitives**.

8.8.1.4 COPROCESSOR SYSTEM RELATED EXCEPTIONS. System related exceptions detected by a DMA coprocessor include those associated with bus activity, and any other exceptions generated external to the coprocessor. These externally generated exceptions could include non-bus cycle associated events (like interrupts) detected by the coprocessor. The actions taken by the coprocessor and the main processor depend on the type of exception encountered and are thus not general.

When an address or bus error is detected by a DMA coprocessor, any information necessary for the main processor exception handling routines should be recorded in system accessible registers by the coprocessor. The coprocessor should place one of the three "Take Exception" primitives encoded with an appropriate exception vector number in the response CIR. Which of the three primitives is used depends upon the point in the coprocessor instruction at which the exception was detected, and the point in the instruction execution where the main processor should continue the program flow after exception processing.

8.8.1.5 FORMAT ERROR. Format errors are the only coprocessor detected exceptions that are not signalled to the main processor with one of the three "Take Exception" coprocessor response primitives. When the main processor writes a format word to the restore CIR during the execution of a cpRESTORE instruction, the coprocessor decodes this word to determine if it is valid (see **8.3.3.2 COPROCESSOR CONTEXT RESTORE**). If the format word is not valid, the coprocessor will place the invalid format code in the restore CIR. When the main processor reads the invalid format code, it will first abort the coprocessor instruction by writing a $0001 to the control CIR. The main processor then proceeds with exception processing using a four word pre-instruction stack frame and the format error exception vector number 14. Thus, if the stack frame is not modified by the exception handler, the MC68020 will restart the cpRESTORE instruction after an RTE is executed to exit the handler. If the coprocessor returns the invalid format code when the main processor reads the save CIR to initiate a cpSAVE instruction the main processor will proceed with format error exception processing as outlined above for the cpRESTORE instruction.

8.8.2 Main Processor Detected Exceptions

A number of exceptions related to coprocessor instruction execution are not directly perceptible to the coprocessor, but can be detected and serviced by the main processor. These exceptions can be related to the execution of coprocessor response primitives, communication across the M68000 coprocessor interface, or the completion of conditional coprocessor instructions by the main processor.

8.8.2.1 PROTOCOL VIOLATIONS. The main processor detects a protocol violation when it reads a primitive from the response CIR that is not a valid primitive encoding. The protocol violations that can be generated by the MC68020 in response to the primitives defined for the M68000 coprocessor interface are summarized in Table 8-6.

When the MC68020 detects a protocol violation it does **not** automatically notify the coprocessor of the resulting exception processing by writing to the control CIR. The exception handling routine may, however, use the MOVES instruction to re-read the response CIR and thus determine the primitive that caused the MC68020 to initiate protocol violation exception processing. The main processor initiates exception processing using the mid-instruction stack frame (see Figure 8-43) and the coprocessor protocol violation exception vector number 13. If the stack frame is not modified within the exception handler, the main processor will return and read the response CIR following the execution of an RTE instruction in the exception handler. This protocol allows extensions to the M68000 coprocessor interface to be emulated in software by a main processor that does not provide hardware support for these extensions. Thus, the protocol violation is transparent to the coprocessor if the primitive execution can be emulated in software by the main processor.

8.8.2.2 F-LINE EMULATOR EXCEPTIONS. The F-line emulator exceptions detected by the MC68020 are either explicitly or implicitly related to the encodings of F-line operation words encountered in the instruction stream. If the main processor determines the F-line operation word is not a legal encoding, it will initiate F-line emulator exception processing. Any F-line operation word with bits [8-6] = 110 or 111 causes the MC68020 to initiate exception processing without any communication being initiated with the coprocessor for that instruction. Also, an operation word with bits [8-6] = 000-101 that does not map to one of the legal coprocessor instruction encodings in **APPENDIX B INSTRUCTION SET**, causes the MC68020 to initiate F-line emulator exception processing. If the F-line emulator exception is generated as a result of one of these two situations, the main processor will not write to the control CIR prior to initiating exception processing.

F-line exceptions can also occur if the operations requested by a coprocessor response primitive are not compatible with the effective address type encoded in bits [5-0] of the coprocessor instruction operation word. The F-line emulator exceptions that can result from the use of the M68000 coprocessor response primitives are summarized in Table 8-6. If the exception is caused by the receipt of a primitive, the coprocessor instruction in progress is aborted by the main processor writing a $0001 to the control CIR prior to F-line emulator exception processing.

When the main processor initiates F-line emulator exception processing, it uses a four word pre-instruction exception stack frame (see Figure 8-41) and the F-line emulator exception vector number 11. Thus, if the stack frame is not modified within the exception handler, the main processor will attempt to restart the instruction that caused the exception after an RTE is executed.

Generally, if the cause of the F-line exception can be emulated in software, the handler will reflect the results of the emulation in the programmer's model and in the status register field of the saved stack frame. The exception handler will adjust the program

Table 8-6. Exceptions Related to Primitive Processing

Primitive	Protocol	F-Line	Other
Busy			
NULL			
Supervisory Check* Other: Privilege Violation if "S" Bit = 0			X
Transfer Operation Word*			
Transfer from Instruction Stream* Protocol: If Length Field is Odd (Zero Length Legal)	X		

Evaluate and Transfer Effective Address
   Protocol: If Used with Conditional Instruction
   F-Line: If EA in Op-Word is NOT Control Alterable
	X	X	

Evaluate Effective Address and Transfer Data
   Protocol:
     1. If Used with Conditional Instructions
     2. Length is Not 1, 2, or 4 and EA = Register Direct
     3. If EA = Immediate and Length Odd and Greater Than 1
     4. Attempt to Write to Non-Alterable Address Even if Address Declared Legal in Primitive
   F-Line: Valid EA Field Does Not Match EA in Op-Word
	X	X	

Write to Previously Evaluated Effective Address Protocol: If Used with Conditional Instruction	X		
Take Address and Transfer Data*			
Transfer To/From Top-of-Stack* Protocol: Length Field Other Than 1, 2, or 4	X		
Transfer To/From Main Processor Register*			
Transfer To/From Main Processor Control Register Protocol: Invalid Control Register Select Code	X		
Transfer Multiple Main Processor Registers*			

Transfer Multiple Coprocessor Registers
   Protocol:
     1. If Used with Conditional Instructions
     2. Odd Length Value
   F-Line:
     1. EA Not Control Alterable or (An) + for CP to Memory Transfer
     2. EA Not Control Alterable or − (An) for Memory to CP Transfer
	X	X	

Transfer Status and/or ScanPC
   Protocol: If Used with Conditional Instruction
   Other:
     1. Trace — Trace Made Pending if MC68020 in "Trace on Change of Flow" Mode and DR = 1
     2. Address Error — If Odd Value Written to ScanPC
	X		X

Take Pre-Instruction, Mid-Instruction, or Post-Instruction Exception Exception Depends on Vector Supplied in Primitive	X	X	X

*Use of this primitive with CA = 0 will cause protocol violation on conditional instructions.

Abbreviations: EA = Effective Address
                CP = Coprocessor

counter field of the saved stack frame to point to the next instruction operation word and execute the RTE instruction. The MC68020 will then proceed with the execution of the instruction following the instruction that was emulated.

8.8.2.3 PRIVILEGE VIOLATIONS. Privilege violations can result from the use of the cpSAVE and cpRESTORE instructions as well as from the use of the supervisor check coprocessor response primitive. The main processor will initiate privilege violation exception processing if it encounters either the cpSAVE or cpRESTORE instruction when it is in the user state (S = 0 in status register). The main processor will initiate this exception processing prior to any communication with the coprocessor associated with the cpSAVE or cpRESTORE instructions.

If the main processor is in the user state while executing a coprocessor instruction when it reads the supervisor check primitive, it will first abort the coprocessor instruction in progress by writing a $0001 to the control CIR. The main processor will then proceed with privilege violation exception processing.

If a privilege violation occurs, the main processor initiates exception processing using a four word pre-instruction stack frame (see Figure 8-41) and the privilege violation exception vector number 8. Thus, if the stack frame is not modified within the exception handler, the main processor will attempt to restart the instruction during which the exception occurred after an RTE is executed to exit the handler.

8.8.2.4 cpTRAPcc INSTRUCTION TRAPS. The main processor may initiate trap exception processing during the execution of the cpTRAPcc instruction. If the coprocessor returns the TRUE condition indicator to the main processor with a null primitive, the main processor will initiate trap exception processing. The main processor will use a six word post-instruction exception stack frame (see Figure 8-45) and the trap exception vector number 7. The scanPC field of this stack frame will contain the address of the instruction following the cpTRAPcc instruction. The processing associated with the cpTRAPcc instruction can then proceed and the exception handler can locate any immediate operand words encoded in the cpTRAPcc instruction using the information contained in the six word stack frame. If the stack frame is not modified within the exception handler, the main processor will proceed with the instruction following the cpTRAPcc instruction after an RTE is executed to exit the handler.

8.8.2.5 TRACE EXCEPTIONS. The MC68020 supports two modes of instruction tracing which are discussed in **6.3.9 Tracing**. In the trace on instruction execution mode, the MC68020 takes a trace exception after the completion of each instruction. In the trace on change of flow mode, the MC68020 takes a trace exception after each instruction that alters the status register or causes the program counter to be updated in a non-sequential manner.

The protocol used to execute coprocessor cpSAVE, cpRESTORE, or conditional category instructions does not change when a trace exception is pending in the main processor. The main processor will proceed with a pending trace on instruction execution exception after completing the execution of that instruction. If the main processor is in trace on change of flow mode, it will take a trace exception after the instruction execution if the instruction caused the program counter to be updated in a non-sequential fashion, for example a branch was taken.

The conditions on which the main processor will terminate communication with the coprocessor during the execution of a cpGEN instruction and proceed with the next instruction are altered when the main processor is in a trace mode. When a trace exception is pending, the main processor will not take the trace exception until the coprocessor indicates that all processing associated with a cpGEN instruction has completed.

8

If a trace exception is not pending during a general category instruction, the main processor will terminate communication with the coprocessor after reading any primitive with CA = 0. This protocol allows the coprocessor to complete a cpGEN instruction concurrently with the instruction execution of the main processor. When a trace exception is pending, however, the main processor must insure that all processing associated with cpGEN instruction has been completed before the trace exception is taken. Under these circumstances, the main processor will continue to read the response CIR and service the primitives received until it receives either a null, CA = 0, PF = 1 primitive or after exception processing caused by a take post-instruction exception primitive. The coprocessor should return the null, CA = 0 primitive with PF = 0 while it is completing the execution of the cpGEN instruction. The main processor may service pending interrupts between reads of the response CIR if IA = 1 in these null, CA = 0 primitives (see Table 8-3). This protocol insures that a trace exception will not be taken until all processing associated with a cpGEN instruction has been completed.

If T1/T0 = 01 in the MC68020 status register (trace on change of flow) when a general category instruction is initiated, a trace exception will be taken after the instruction only when the transfer status register and scan PC primitive is issued with DR = 1 during the execution of that instruction. If an instruction following the cpGEN instruction does cause a change of flow, the coprocessor may be executing the previous cpGEN instruction concurrently when the main processor begins execution of the trace exception handler. A cpSAVE instruction used within the trace on change of flow exception handler could thus suspend the execution of a concurrently operating cpGEN instruction.

8.8.2.6 INTERRUPTS. Interrupt processing by the main processor can occur at any instruction boundary and is discussed in **6.3.10 Interrupts.** Interrupts may also be serviced during the execution of a general or conditional category instruction under either of two conditions. If the main processor reads a null primitive with CA = 1 and IA = 1 the main processor will service any pending interrupts prior to reading the response CIR. Likewise, if a trace exception is pending during cpGEN instruction execution and the main processor reads a null primitive with CA = 0, IA = 1, and PF = 0 (see **8.8.2.5 TRACE EXCEPTIONS**) the main processor will service pending interrupts prior to re-reading the response CIR.

The MC68020 uses the ten word mid-instruction stack frame when it services interrupts during the execution of a general or conditional category coprocessor instruction. The use of this stack frame allows the mainprocessor to perform all necessary processing and then return to read the response CIR and thus continue the coprocessor instruction during which the interrupt exception was taken.

The MC68020 will also service interrupts if it reads the not ready format word from the save CIR during a cpSAVE instruction. The MC68020 uses the normal four word preinstruction stack frame when it services interrupts after reading the not ready format word. Thus, the processor can service any pending interrupts and execute an RTE to return and re-initiate the cpSAVE instruction by reading the save CIR.

8.8.2.7 ADDRESS AND BUS ERRORS. Coprocessor instruction related bus faults can occur during main processor bus cycles to CPU space to communicate with a coprocessor or during memory cycles run as part of the coprocessor instruction execution. If a bus error occurs during the coprocessor interface register access that is used to **initiate** a coprocessor instruction, the main processor assumes that the coprocessor is not present in the system and takes an F-line emulator exception as described in **8.8.2.2 F-LINE EMULATOR EXCEPTIONS.** Thus an F-line emulator exception will be taken if a bus error occurs during the initial access to the command, condition, restore, or save CIR that was made to initiate a general, conditional, context restore, or context save instruction respectively. If a bus error occurs on any other coprocessor access or on a memory access made during the execution of a coprocessor instruction, the main processor proceeds with bus error exception processing as described in **6.3.3. Bus Error.** After the exception handler has corrected the cause of the bus error, the main processor can return to the point in the coprocessor instruction at which the fault occurred.

An address error will occur if the MC68020 attempts to prefetch an instruction from an odd address. This can occur if the calculated destination address of a cpBcc or cpDBcc instruction is odd, or if an odd value is transferred to the scanPC with the transfer status register and scanPC response primitive. If an address error occurs, the MC68020 proceeds with exception processing as described in **6.3.2 Address Error.**

8.8.2.8 MAIN PROCESSOR DETECTED FORMAT ERRORS. The MC68020 can detect a format error during the execution of a cpSAVE or cpRESTORE instruction if the length field of a valid format word is not a multiple of four bytes in length. If the MC68020 reads a format word with an invalid length field from the save CIR during the cpSAVE instruction, it will abort the coprocessor instruction by writing a $0001 to the control CIR and initiate format error exception processing. If the MC68020 reads a format word with an invalid length field from the effective address specified in the cpRESTORE instruction, the MC68020 will write that format word to the coprocessor restore CIR and then read the coprocessor response from the restore CIR. The MC68020 will then abort the cpRESTORE instruction by writing a $0001 to the control CIR and initiate format error exception processing.

The MC68020 uses the four word pre-instruction stack frame and the format error vector number 14 when it initiates format error exception processing. Thus, if the stack frame is not modified within the exception handler, the main processor will attempt to restart the instruction during which the exception occurred after an RTE is executed to exit the handler.

8.8.3 Coprocessor Reset

When a system (hardware) reset occurs, the coprocessor should be reset and initialized appropriately. At the discretion of the system designer, there may be a distinction made between an entire system reset and the execution of the RESET instruction by the main processor. In keeping with the function of the RESET instruction, it is generally desirable that the internal state of a coprocessor is only affected by an external system reset and not by the RESET instruction. This convention is desirable since the coprocessor is viewed as an extension to the main processor programming model, and thus an extension to the internal state of the MC68020.

8.9 COPROCESSOR INSTRUCTION FORMAT SUMMARY

A summary of the coprocessor instruction formats is presented in Figure 8-46.

8.10 COPROCESSOR RESPONSE PRIMITIVE FORMAT SUMMARY

The M68000 coprocessor response primitive formats are illustrated in **APPENDIX C IN-STRUCTION FORMAT SUMMARY.** Any response primitive with bits [13-8] = $00 or $3F will always cause a protocol violation. Response primitives with bits [13-8] = $0B, $18-$1B, $1F, $28-$2B, and $38-$3E currently cause a protocol, but are undefined and reserved for future use by Motorola.

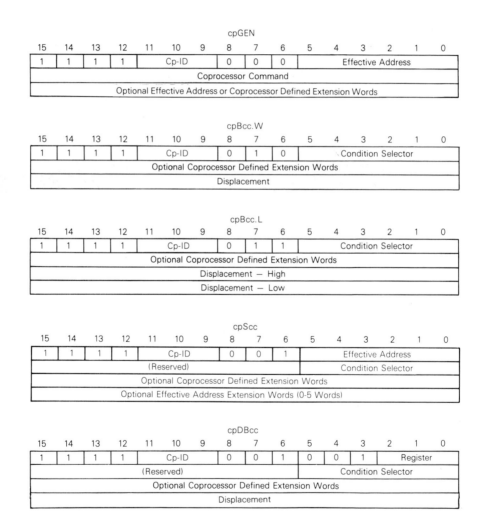

Figure 8-46. Coprocessor Instruction Formats (Sheet 1 of 2)

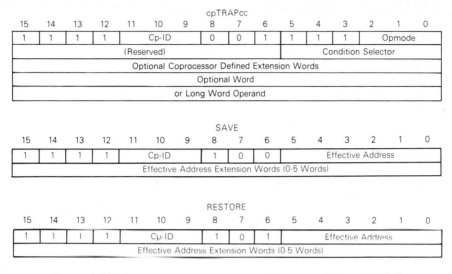

cpTRAPcc

15	14	13	12	11	10	9	8	7	6	5	4	3	2	1	0
1	1	1	1	Cp-ID			0	0	1	1	1	1	Opmode		
(Reserved)										Condition Selector					
Optional Coprocessor Defined Extension Words															
Optional Word															
or Long Word Operand															

SAVE

15	14	13	12	11	10	9	8	7	6	5	4	3	2	1	0
1	1	1	1	Cp-ID			1	0	0	Effective Address					
Effective Address Extension Words (0-5 Words)															

RESTORE

15	14	13	12	11	10	9	8	7	6	5	4	3	2	1	0
1	1	1	1	Cp-ID			1	0	1	Effective Address					
Effective Address Extension Words (0-5 Words)															

Figure 8-46. Coprocessor Instruction Formats (Sheet 2 of 2)

8

SECTION 9
INSTRUCTION EXECUTION TIMING

This section describes the instruction execution times of the MC68020 in terms of external clock cycles.

9.1 TIMING ESTIMATION FACTORS

The advanced architecture of the MC68020 makes exact instruction timing calculations difficult due to the effects of:

1) An On-Chip Instruction Cache and Instruction Prefetch,
2) Operand Misalignment, and
3) Instruction Execution Overlap.

These factors make MC68020 instruction set timing difficult to calculate on a single instruction basis since instructions vary in execution time from one context to another. A detailed explanation of each of these factors follows.

9.1.1 Instruction Cache and Prefetch

The on-chip cache of the MC68020 is an instruction-only cache. Its purpose is to increase execution efficiency by providing a quick-store for instructions.

Instruction prefetches that hit in the cache will occur with no delay in instruction execution. Instruction prefetches that miss in the cache will cause an external memory cycle to be performed, which may overlap with internal instruction execution. Thus, while the execution unit of the microprocessor is busy, the bus controller prefetches the next instruction from external memory. Both cases are illustrated in later examples.

When prefetching instructions from external memory, the microprocessor will utilize long word read cycles. When the read is aligned on a long word address boundary, the processor reads two words, which may load two instructions at once, or two words of a multi-word instruction. The subsequent instruction prefetch will find the second word is already available and there is no need to run an external bus cycle (read).

The MC68020 always prefetches long words. When an instruction prefetch falls on an odd word boundary (e.g., due to a branch to an odd word location), the MC68020 will read the even word associated with the long word base address at the same time as (32-bit memory) or before (8- or 16-bit memory) the odd word is read. When an instruction prefetch falls on an even word boundary (as would be the normal case), the MC68020 reads both words at the long word address, thus effectively prefetching the next two words.

9.1.2 Operand Misalignment

Another significant factor affecting instruction timing is operand misalignment. Operand misalignment has impact on performance when the microprocessor is reading or writing external memory. In this case the address of a word operand falls across a long word boundary or a long word operand falls on a byte or word address which is not a long word boundary. While the MC68020 will automatically handle all occurrences of operand misalignment, it must use multiple bus cycles to complete such transfers.

9.1.3 Concurrency

The MC68020 allows concurrency to take place when executing instructions. The main elements participating in this concurrency are the bus controller and the sequencer. The bus controller is responsible for all bus activity. The sequencer controls the bus controller, instruction execution, and internal processor operation, such as calculation of effective addresses and setting of condition codes. The sequencer is responsible for initiating instruction prefetches, decoding and validating incoming instructions in the pipe.

The bus controller and sequencer can operate on an instruction concurrently. The bus controller can perform a read or write while the sequencer controls an effective address calculation or sets the condition codes. The sequencer may also request a bus cycle that the bus controller cannot immediately perform. In this case the bus cycle is queued and the bus controller runs the cycle when the current cycle is complete.

Concurrency of operation between the sequencer and bus controller introduces ambiguity into the calculation of instruction timing due to potential overlap of instruction execution.

9.1.4 Overlap

Overlap is the time, measured in clocks, when two instructions execute simultaneously. Overlap is measured as the time that an instruction is executing concurrent to the previous instruction. In Figure 9-1, instructions A and B execute simultaneously and the overlapped portion of instruction B is absorbed in the instruction execution time of A (the previous instruction). The overlap time is deducted from the execution time of instruction B. Similarly, there is an overlap period between instruction B and instruction C, which reduces the attributed execution time for C.

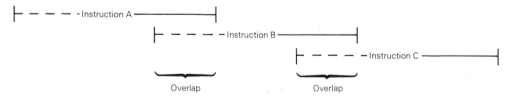

Figure 9-1. Simultaneous Instruction Execution

The execution time attributed to instructions A, B, and C (after considering the overlap) is depicted in Figure 9-2.

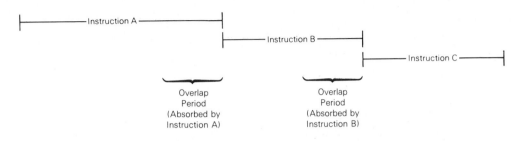

Figure 9-2. Instruction Execution for Instruction Timing Purposes

It is possible that the execution time of an instruction will be absorbed by the overlap with a previous instruction for a net execution time of zero clocks.

9.1.5 Instruction Stream Timing Examples

A programming example allows a more detailed examination of these effects. The effect of instruction execution overlap on instruction timing is illustrated by the following example instruction stream:

> **Instruction**
> #1) MOVE.L   D4,(A1) +
> #2) ADD.L   D4,D5
> #3) MOVE.L   (A1), – (A2)
> #4) ADD.L   D5,D6

For the first example, the assumptions are:
1) The data bus is 32 bits,
2) The first instruction is prefetched from an ODD word address,
3) Memory access with no wait states, and
4) The instruction cache is disabled.

For this example, the instruction stream is positioned in 32-bit memory as:

Address	n	· · ·	MOVE #1
	n + 4	ADD #2	MOVE #3
	n + 8	ADD #4	· · ·

Figure 9-3 shows processor activity on the first example instruction stream. It shows the activity of the external bus, and bus controller, the sequencer, and the attributed instruction execution time.

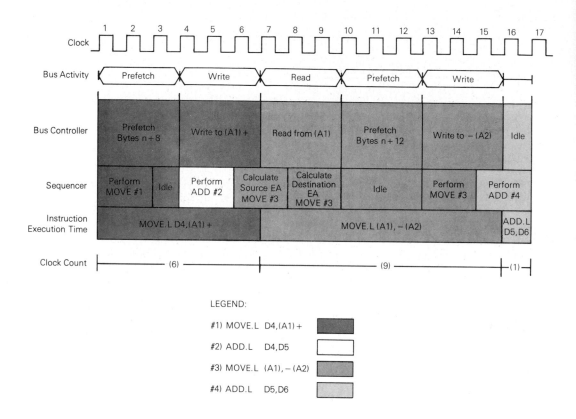

Figure 9-3. Processor Activity Example 1

For the first three clocks of this example, the bus controller and sequencer are both performing tasks associated with the MOVE #1 instruction. The next three clocks (clocks four, five, and six) demonstrate instruction overlap. The bus controller is performing a write to memory as part of the MOVE #1 instruction. The sequencer, on the other hand, is performing the ADD #2 instruction for two clocks (clocks four and five) and beginning source effective address (EA) calculations for the MOVE #3 instruction. The bus controller activity completely overlaps the execution of the ADD #2 instruction, causing the ADD #2 attributed execution time to be zero clocks. This overlap also shortens the effective execution time of the MOVE #3 instruction by the one clock because the bus controller completes the MOVE #1 write operation while the sequencer begins the MOVE #3 effective address calculation.

The sequencer continues the source EA calculation for one more clock period (clock seven) while the bus controller begins a read for MOVE #3. When counting instruction execution time in bus clocks, the MOVE #1 completes at the end of clock 6 and the execution of MOVE #3 begins on clock 7.

Both the sequencer and bus controller continue with MOVE #3 until the end of clock 14, when the sequencer begins to perform ADD #4. Timing for MOVE #3 continues, because the bus controller is still performing the write to the destination of MOVE #3. The bus activity for MOVE #3 completes at the end of clock 15. The effective execution time for MOVE #3 is 9 clocks.

The one clock cycle (clock 15) when the sequencer is performing ADD #4 and the bus controller is writing to the destination of MOVE #3 is absorbed by the execution time of MOVE #3. This shortens the effective execution time of ADD #4 by one clock, giving it an attributed execution time of one clock.

Using the same instruction stream, the second example demonstrates the different effects of instruction execution overlap on instruction timing when the same instructions are positioned slightly differently, in 32-bit memory:

Address	n	MOVE #1	ADD #2
	n + 4	MOVE #3	ADD #4
	n + 8	· · ·	· · ·

The assumptions for the second example in Figure 9-4 are:
  1) The data bus is 32 bits,
  2) The first instruction is prefetched from an EVEN word address,
  3) Memory access occur with no wait states, and
  4) The cache is disabled.

While the total execution time of the instruction segment does not change in this example, the individual instruction times are significantly different. This demonstrates that the effects of overlap are not only instruction sequence dependent, but are also dependent upon the alignment of the instruction stream in memory.

Both Figures 9-3 and 9-4 show instruction execution without benefit of the MC68020 instruction cache. Figure 9-5 shows a third example for the same instruction stream executing in the cache. The assumptions for Example 3 are:
  1) The data bus is 32 bits,
  2) The cache is enabled and instructions are in the cache, and
  3) Memory access occur with no wait states.

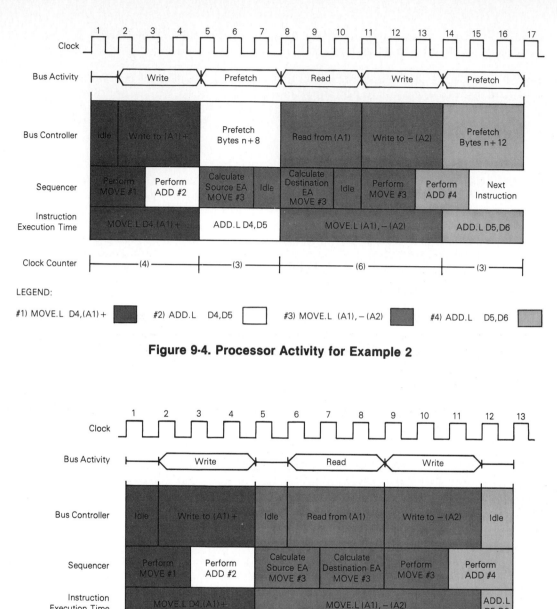

Figure 9-4. Processor Activity for Example 2

Figure 9-5. Processor Activity for Example 3

Note that once the instructions are in the cache, the original location in external memory is no longer a factor in timing.

Figure 9-5 illustrates the benefits of the instruction cache. The total number of clock cycles is reduced from 16 to 12 clocks. Since the instructions are resident in the cache, the instruction prefetch activity does not require the bus controller to perform external bus cycles. Prefetch occurs with no delay, and subsequently, the bus controller is idle more often.

Such idle clock cycles are useful in MC68020 systems that require wait states when accessing external memory. This is illustrated by the fourth example in Figure 9-6 with the following assumptions:
1) The data bus is 32 bits,
2) The cache is enabled and instructions are in the cache, and
3) Memory access occur with one wait state.

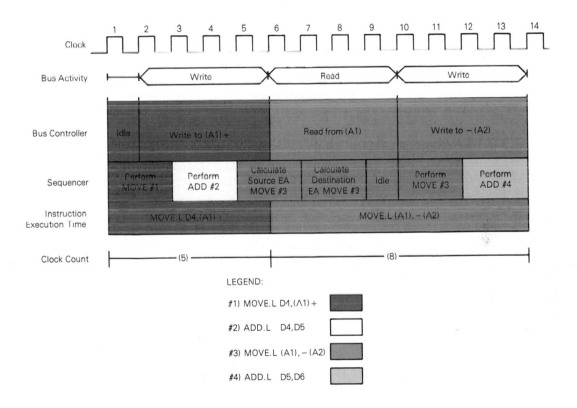

Figure 9-6. Processor Activity for Example 4

Figure 9-6 shows the same instruction stream executing with four clocks for every read and write. The idle bus cycles coincide with the wait states of the memory access, so the total execution time is only 13 clocks.

These examples demonstrate the complexity of instruction timing calculation for the MC68020. It is impossible to anticipate individual instruction timing as an absolute number of clock cycles due to the dependency of overlap on the instruction sequence and alignment, as well as the number of wait states in memory. This can be seen by comparing individual and composite time for Figure 9-3 through 9-6. These instruction timings are compared in Table 9-1, where timing varies for each instruction as the context varies.

Table 9-1. Example Instruction Stream Execution Comparison

Instruction	Example 1 (Odd Alignment)	Example 2 (Even Alignment)	Example 3 (Cache)	Example 4 (Cache With Wait States)
#1) MOVE.L D4,(A1)+	6	4	4	5
#2) ADD.L D4,D5	0	3	0	0
#3) MOVE.L (A1),−(A2)	9	6	7	8
#4) ADD.L D5,D6	1	3	1	0
Total Clock Cycles	16	16	12	13

9.2 INSTRUCTION TIMING TABLES

The instruction times below include the following assumptions about the MC68020 system:

1) All operands are long word aligned as is the stack,
2) 32-bit data bus, and
3) No wait state memory (3 cycle read/write).

There are three values given for each instruction and addressing mode:

1) The best case (BC) which reflects the time (in clocks) when the instruction is in the cache and benefits from maximum overlap due to other instructions.
2) Cache-only-case (CC) when the instruction is in the cache but has no overlap, and
3) Worst case (WC) when the instruction is not in cache or the cache is disabled and there is no instruction overlap.

The only instances for which the size of the operand has any effect are the instructions with immediate operands. Unless specified otherwise, immediate byte and word operands have identical execution times.

Within each set or column of instruction timings are four sets of numbers, three of which are enclosed in parentheses. The outer number is the total number of clocks for the instruction. The first number inside the parentheses is the number of operand read cycles performed by the instruction. The second value inside parentheses is the number of instruction accesses performed by the instruction, including all prefetches to keep the instruction pipe filled. The third value within parentheses is the number of write cycles performed by the instruction. One example from the instruction timing table is:

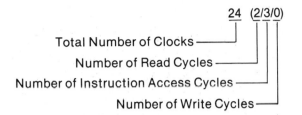

The total number of bus activity clocks for the above example is derived in the following way:

(2 Reads * 3 Clocks/Read) + (3 Instruction Accesses * 3 Clocks/Access)
+ (0 Writes * 3 Clocks/Write) = 15 Clocks of Bus Activity
24 Total Clocks − 15 Clocks (Bus Activity) = 9 Internal Clocks

The example used here was taken from a worst-case "fetch effective address" time. The addressing mode was ([d32,B],I,d32). The same addressing mode under the best case entry is 17 (2/0/0). For the best case, there are no instruction accesses because the cache is enabled, and the sequencer does not have to go to external memory for the instruction words.

The first tables deal exclusively with fetching and calculating effective addresses and immediate operands. The tables are arranged in this manner because some instructions do not require effective address calculation or fetching. For example, the instruction CLR<ea> (found in the table under **9.2.11 Single Operand Instruction**) only needs to have a calculated EA time added to its table entry because no fetch of an operand is required. This instruction only writes to memory or a register. Some instructions use specific addressing modes which exclude timing for calculation or fetching of an operand. When these instances arise, they are footnoted to indicate which other tables are needed in the timing calculation.

The MOVE instruction timing tables include all necessary timing for extension word fetch, address calculation, and operand fetch.

The instruction timing tables are used to calculate a best case and worst case bounds for some target instruction stream. Calculating exact timing from the timing tables is impossible because the tables cannot anticipate how the combination of factors will influence every particular sequence of instructions. This is illustrated by comparing the observed instruction timing from the prior four examples with instruction timing derived from the instruction timing tables.

Table 9-2 shows the original instruction stream and the corresponding clock timing from the appropriate timing tables for the best case (BC), cache only case (CC), and worst case (WC).

Table 9-2. Instruction Timings from Timing Tables

Instruction		Best Case	Cache Case	Worst Case
#1) MOVE.L	D4,(A1) +	4	4	6
#2) ADD.L	D4,D5	0	2	3
#3) MOVE.L	(A1), − (A2)	6	7	9
#4) ADD.L	D5,D6	0	2	3
Total		10	15	21

Table 9-3 summarizes the observed instruction timings for the same instruction stream as executed according to the assumptions of the four examples. For each example, Table 9-3 shows which entry (BC/CC/WC) from the timing tables corresponds to the observed timing for each of the four instructions. Some of the observed instruction timings cannot be found in the timing tables and appear in Table 9-3 within parenthesis in the most appropriate column. These occur when instruction execution overlap dynamically alters what would otherwise be a BC, CC, or WC timing.

Table 9-3. Observed Instruction Timings

Instruction		Example 1 BC	CC	WC	Example 2 BC	CC	WC	Example 3 BC	CC	WC	Example 4 BC	CC	WC
#1) MOVE.L	D4,(A1) +			6	4				4			(5)	
#2) ADD.L	D4,D5	0					3	0			0		
#3) MOVE.L	(A1), − (A2)			9	6				7			(8)	
#4) ADD.L	D5,D6		(1)				3	(1)			0		
Total			(16)			(16)			(12)			(13)	

Comparing Tables 9-2 and 9-3 demonstrates that calculation of instruction timing cannot be a simple lookup of only BC or only WC timings. Even when the assumptions are known and fixed, as in the four examples summarized in Table 9-3, the microprocessor can sometimes achieve best case timings under worst case assumptions.

Looking across the four examples in Table 9-3 for an individual instruction, it is difficult to predict which timing table entry is used, since the influence of instruction overlap may or may not improve the BC, WC, or CC timings. When looking at the observed instruction timings for one example, it is also difficult to determine which combination cf BC/CC/WC timing is required. Just how the instruction stream will fit and run with cache enabled, how instructions are positioned in memory, and the degree of instruction overlap are factors that are impossible to be accounted for in all combinations of the timing tables.

Although the timing tables cannot accurately predict the instruction timing that would be observed when executing an instruction stream on the MC68020, the tables can be used to calculate best case and worst case bounds for instruction timing. Absolute instruction timing must be measured by using the microprocessor itself, to execute the target instruction stream.

9.2.1 Fetch Effective Address

The fetch effective address table indicates the number of clock periods needed for the processor to calculate and fetch the specified effective address. The total number of clock cycles is outside the parentheses, the number of read, prefetch, and write cycles are given inside the parentheses as (r/p/w). They are included in the total clock cycle number.

Address Mode	Best Case	Cache Case	Worst Case
Dn	0 (0/0/0)	0 (0/0/0)	0 (0/0/0)
An	0 (0/0/0)	0 (0/0/0)	0 (0/0/0)
(An)	3 (1/0/0)	4 (1/0/0)	4 (1/0/0)
(An) +	4 (1/0/0)	4 (1/0/0)	4 (1/0/0)
−(An)	3 (1/0/0)	5 (1/0/0)	5 (1/0/0)
(d_{16},An) of (d_{16},PC)	3 (1/0/0)	5 (1/0/0)	6 (1/1/0)
(xxx).W	3 (1/0/0)	4 (1/0/0)	6 (1/1/0)
(xxx).L	3 (1/0/0)	4 (1/0/0)	7 (1/1/0)
#<data>.B	0 (0/0/0)	2 (0/0/0)	3 (0/1/0)
#<data>.W	0 (0/0/0)	2 (0/0/0)	3 (0/1/0)
#<data>.l	0 (0/0/0)	4 (0/0/0)	5 (0/1/0)
(d_8,An,Xn) or (d_8, PC, Xn)	4 (1/0/0)	7 (1/0/0)	8 (1/1/0)
(d_{16},An,Xn) or (d_{16},PC,Xn)	4 (1/0/0)	7 (1/0/0)	9 (1/1/0)
(B)	4 (1/0/0)	7 (1/0/0)	9 (1/1/0)
(d_{16},B)	6 (1/0/0)	9 (1/0/0)	12 (1/1/0)
(d_{32},B)	10 (1/0/0)	13 (1/0/0)	16 (1/2/0)
([B],I)	9 (2/0/0)	12 (2/0/0)	13 (2/1/0)
$([B],I,d_{16})$	11 (2/0/0)	14 (2/0/0)	16 (2/1/0)
$([B],I,d_{32})$	11 (2/0/0)	14 (2/0/0)	17 (2/2/0)
$([d_{16},B],I)$	11 (2/0/0)	14 (2/0/0)	16 (2/1/0)
$([d_{16},B],I,d_{16})$	13 (2/0/0)	16 (2/0/0)	19 (2/2/0)
$([d_{16},B],I,d_{32})$	13 (2/0/0)	16 (2/0/0)	20 (2/2/0)
$([d_{32},B],I)$	15 (2/0/0)	18 (2/0/0)	20 (2/2/0)
$([d_{32},B],I,d_{16})$	17 (2/0/0)	20 (2/0/0)	22 (2/2/0)
$([d_{32},B],I,d_{32})$	17 (2/0/0)	20 (2/0/0)	24 (2/3/0)

B = Base address; 0, An, PC, Xn, An + Xn, PC + Xn. Form does not affect timing.

I = Index; 0, Xn

NOTE: Xn cannot be in B and I at the same time. Scaling and size of Xn does not affect timing.

9.2.2 Fetch Immediate Effective Address

The fetch immediate effective address table indicates the number of clock periods needed for the processor to fetch the immediate source operand, and calculate and fetch the specified destination operand. The total number of clock cycles is outside the parentheses, the number of read, prefetch, and write cycles are given inside the parentheses as (r/p/w). They are included in the total clock cycle number.

Address Mode	Best Case	Cache Case	Worst Case
#<data>.W,Dn	0 (0/0/0)	2 (0/0/0)	3 (0/1/0)
#<data>.L,Dn	1 (0/0/0)	4 (0/0/0)	5 (0/1/0)
#<data>.W,(An)	3 (1/0/0)	4 (1/0/0)	4 (1/1/0)
#<data>.L,(An)	3 (1/0/0)	4 (1/0/0)	7 (1/1/0)
#<data>.W,(An)+	4 (1/0/0)	6 (1/0/0)	7 (1/1/0)
#<data>.L,(An)+	5 (1/0/0)	8 (1/0/0)	9 (1/1/0)
#<data>.W,-(An)	3 (1/0/0)	5 (1/0/0)	6 (1/1/0)
#<data>.L,-(An)	4 (1/0/0)	7 (1/0/0)	8 (1/1/0)
#<data>.W,(bd,An)	3 (1/0/0)	5 (1/0/0)	7 (1/1/0)
#<data>.L,(bd,An)	4 (1/0/0)	7 (1/0/0)	10 (1/2/0)
#<data>.W,xxx.W	3 (1/0/0)	5 (1/0/0)	7 (1/1/0)
#<data>.L,xxx.W	4 (1/0/0)	7 (1/0/0)	10 (1/2/0)
#<data>.W,xxx.L	3 (1/0/0)	6 (1/0/0)	10 (1/2/0)
#<data>.L,xxx.L	4 (1/0/0)	8 (1/0/0)	12 (1/2/0)
#<data>.W,#<data>.B,W	0 (0/0/0)	4 (0/0/0)	6 (0/2/0)
#<data>.W,#<data>.B,W	1 (0/0/0)	6 (0/0/0)	8 (0/2/0)
#<data>.W,#<data>.L	0 (0/0/0)	6 (0/0/0)	8 (0/2/0)
#<data>.L,#<data>.L	1 (0/0/0)	8 (0/0/0)	10 (0/2/0)
#<data>.W,(d8,An,Xn) or (d8,PC,Xn)	4 (1/0/0)	9 (1/0/0)	11 (1/2/0)
#<data>.L,(d8,An,Xn) or (d8,PC,Xn)	5 (1/0/0)	11 (1/0/0)	13 (1/2/0)
#<data>.W,(d16,An,Xn) or (d16,PC,Xn)	4 (1/0/0)	9 (1/0/0)	12 (1/2/0)
#<data>.L,(d16,An,Xn) or (d16,PC,Xn)	5 (1/0/0)	11 (1/0/0)	15 (1/2/0)
#<data>.W,(B)	4 (1/0/0)	9 (1/0/0)	12 (1/2/0)
#<data>.L,(B)	5 (1/0/0)	11 (1/0/0)	14 (1/2/0)
#<data>.W,(bd,PC)	10 (1/0/0)	15 (1/0/0)	19 (1/3/0)
#<data>.L,(bd,PC)	11 (1/0/0)	17 (1/0/0)	21 (1/3/0)
#<data>.W,(d16,B)	6 (1/0/0)	11 (1/0/0)	15 (1/2/0)
#<data>.L,(d16,B)	7 (1/0/0)	13 (1/0/0)	17 (1/2/0)
#<data>.W,(d32,B)	10 (1/0/0)	15 (1/0/0)	19 (1/3/0)
#<data>.L,(d32,B)	11 (1/0/0)	17 (1/0/0)	21 (1/3/0)
#<data>.W,([B],I)	9 (2/0/0)	14 (2/0/0)	16 (2/2/0)
#<data>.L,([B],I)	10 (2/0/0)	16 (2/0/0)	18 (2/2/0)
#<data>.W,([B],I,d16)	11 (2/0/0)	16 (2/0/0)	19 (2/2/0)
#<data>.L,([B],I,d16)	12 (2/0/0)	18 (2/0/0)	21 (2/2/0)
#<data>.W,([B],I,d32)	11 (2/0/0)	16 (2/0/0)	20 (2/3/0)
#<data>.L,([d16,B],I,d32)	12 (2/0/0)	18 (2/0/0)	22 (2/3/0)
#<data>.W,([d16,B],I)	11 (2/0/0)	16 (2/0/0)	19 (2/2/0)
#<data>.L,([d16,B],I)	12 (2/0/0)	18 (2/0/0)	21 (2/2/0)
#<data>.W,([d16,B],I,d16)	13 (2/0/0)	18 (2/0/0)	22 (2/3/0)
#<data>.L,([d16,B],I,d16)	14 (2/0/0)	20 (2/0/0)	24 (2/3/0)
#<data>.W,([d32,B],I)	15 (2/0/0)	20 (2/0/0)	23 (2/2/0)
#<data>.L,([d32,B],I)	16 (2/0/0)	22 (2/0/0)	25 (2/3/0)
#<data>.W,([d32,B],I,d16)	17 (2/0/0)	22 (2/0/0)	25 (2/3/0)
#<data>.L,([d32,B],I,d16)	18 (2/0/0)	24 (2/0/0)	27 (2/3/0)
#<data>.W,([d32,B],I,d32)	17 (2/0/0)	22 (2/0/0)	27 (2/4/0)
#<data>.L,([d32,B],I,d32)	18 (2/0/0)	24 (2/0/0)	29 (2/4/0)

B = Base address; 0, An, PC, Xn, An+Xn, PC+Xn. Form does not affect timing.

I = Index 0, Xn

NOTE: Xn cannot be in B and I at the same time. Scaling and size of Xn does not affect timing.

9.2.3 Calculate Effective Address

The calculate effective address table indicates the number of clock periods needed for the processor to calculate the specified effective address. Fetch time is only included for the first level of indirection on memory indirect addressing modes. The total number of clock cycles is outside the parentheses, the number of read, prefetch, and write cycles are given inside the parentheses as (r/p/w). They are included in the total clock cycle number.

Address Mode	Best Case	Cache Case	Worst Case
Dn	0 (0/0/0)	0 (0/0/0)	0 (0/0/0)
An	0 (0/0/0)	0 (0/0/0)	0 (0/0/0)
(An)	2 (0/0/0)	2 (0/0/0)	2 (0/0/0)
(An)+	2 (0/0/0)	2 (0/0/0)	2 (0/0/0)
−(An)	2 (0/0/0)	2 (0/0/0)	2 (0/0/0)
(d_{16},An) or (d_{16},PC)	2 (0/0/0)	2 (0/0/0)	3 (0/1/0)
<data>.W	2 (0/0/0)	2 (0/0/0)	3 (0/1/0)
<data>.L	1 (0/0/0)	4 (0/0/0)	5 (0/1/0)
(d_8,An,Xn) or (d_8,PC,Xn)	1 (0/0/0)	4 (0/0/0)	5 (0/1/0)
(d_{16},An,Xn) or (d_{16},PC,Xn)	3 (0/0/0)	6 (0/0/0)	7 (0/1/0)
(B)	3 (0/0/0)	6 (0/0/0)	7 (0/1/0)
(d_{16},B)	5 (0/0/0)	8 (0/0/0)	10 (0/1/0)
(d_{32},B)	9 (0/0/0)	12 (0/0/0)	15 (0/2/0)
([B],I)	8 (1/0/0)	11 (1/0/0)	12 (1/1/0)
$([B],I,d_{16})$	10 (1/0/0)	13 (1/0/0)	15 (1/1/0)
$([B],I,d_{32})$	10 (1/0/0)	13 (1/0/0)	16 (1/2/0)
$([d_{16},B],I)$	10 (1/0/0)	13 (1/0/0)	15 (1/1/0)
$([d_{16},B],I,d_{16})$	12 (1/0/0)	15 (1/0/0)	18 (1/2/0)
$([d_{16},B],I,d_{32})$	12 (1/0/0)	15 (1/0/0)	19 (1/2/0)
$([d_{32},B],I)$	14 (1/0/0)	17 (1/0/0)	19 (1/2/0)
$([d_{32},B],I,d_{16})$	16 (1/0/0)	19 (1/0/0)	21 (1/2/0)
$([d_{32},B],I,d_{32})$	16 (1/0/0)	19 (1/0/0)	24 (1/3/0)

B = Base address; 0, An, PC, Xn, An+Xn, PC+Xn. Form does not affect timing.

I = Index; 0, Xn

NOTE: Xn cannot be in D and I at the same time. Scaling and size of Xn does not affect timing.

9.2.4 Calculate Immediate Effective Address

The calculate immediate effective address table indicates the number of clock periods needed for the processor to fetch the immediate source operand and calculate the specified destination effective address. Fetch time is only included for the first level of indirection on memory indirect addressing modes. The total number of clock cycles is outside the parentheses, the number of read, prefetch, and write cycles are given inside the parentheses as (r/p/w). They are included in the total clock cycle number.

9

Address Mode	Best Case	Cache Case	Worst Case
#<data>.W,Dn	0 (0/0/0)	2 (0/0/0)	3 (0/1/0)
#<data>.L,Dn	1 (0/0/0)	4 (0/0/0)	5 (0/1/0)
#<data>.W,(An)	0 (0/0/0)	2 (0/0/0)	3 (0/1/0)
#<data>.L,(An)	1 (0/0/0)	4 (0/0/0)	5 (0/1/0)
#<data>.W,(An)+	2 (0/0/0)	4 (0/0/0)	5 (0/1/0)
#<data>.L,(An)+	3 (0/0/0)	6 (0/0/0)	7 (0/1/0)
#<data>.W,(bd,An)	1 (0/0/0)	4 (0/0/0)	5 (0/1/0)
#<data>.L,(bd,An)	3 (0/0/0)	6 (0/0/0)	8 (0/2/0)
#<data>.W,(xxx).W	1 (0/0/0)	4 (0/0/0)	5 (0/1/0)
#<data>.L,(xxx).W	3 (0/0/0)	6 (0/0/0)	8 (0/2/0)
#<data>.W,(xxx).L	2 (0/0/0)	4 (0/0/0)	6 (0/2/0)
#<data>.L,(xxx).L	3 (0/0/0)	8 (0/0/0)	10 (0/2/0)
#<data>.W,(d_8,An,Xn) or (d_8,PC,Xn)	0 (0/0/0)	6 (0/0/0)	8 (0/2/0)
#<data>.L,(d_8,An,Xn) or (d_8,PC,Xn)	2 (0/0/0)	8 (0/0/0)	10 (0/2/0)
#<data>.W,(d_{16},An,Xn) or (d_{16},PC,Xn)	3 (0/0/0)	8 (0/0/0)	10 (0/2/0)
#<data>.L,(d_{16},An,Xn) or (d_{16},PC,Xn)	4 (0/0/0)	10 (0/0/0)	12 (0/2/0)
#<data>.W,(B)	3 (0/0/0)	8 (0/0/0)	10 (0/2/0)
#<data>.L,(B)	4 (0/0/0)	10 (0/0/0)	12 (0/2/0)
#<data>.W,(bd,PC)	9 (0/0/0)	14 (0/0/0)	18 (0/3/0)
#<data>.L,(bd,PC)	10 (0/0/0)	16 (0/0/0)	20 (0/3/0)
#<data>.W,(d_{16},B)	5 (0/0/0)	10 (0/0/0)	13 (0/2/0)
#<data>.L,(d_{16},B)	6 (0/0/0)	12 (0/0/0)	15 (0/2/0)
#<data>.W,(d_{32},B)	9 (0/0/0)	14 (0/0/0)	18 (0/3/0)
#<data>.L,(d_{32},B)	10 (0/0/0)	16 (0/0/0)	20 (0/3/0)
#<data>.W,([B],I)	8 (1/0/0)	13 (1/0/0)	15 (1/2/0)
#<data>.L,([B],I)	9 (1/0/0)	15 (1/0/0)	17 (1/2/0)
#<data>.W,([B],I,d_{16})	10 (1/0/0)	15 (1/0/0)	18 (1/2/0)
#<data>.L,([B],I,d_{16})	11 (1/0/0)	17 (1/0/0)	20 (1/2/0)
#<data>.W,([B],I,d_{32})	10 (1/0/0)	15 (1/0/0)	19 (1/3/0)
#<data>.L,([B],I,d_{32})	11 (1/0/0)	17 (1/0/0)	21 (1/3/0)
#<data>.W,([d_{16},B],I)	10 (1/0/0)	15 (1/0/0)	18 (1/2/0)
#<data>.L,([d_{16},B],I)	11 (1/0/0)	17 (1/0/0)	20 (1/2/0)
#<data>.W,([d_{16},B],I,d_{16})	12 (1/0/0)	17 (1/0/0)	21 (1/3/0)
#<data>.L,([d_{16},B],I,d_{16})	13 (1/0/0)	19 (1/0/0)	23 (1/3/0)
#<data>.([d_{16},B],I,d_{32})	12 (1/0/0)	17 (1/0/0)	22 (1/3/0)
#<data>.([d_{16},B],I,d_{32})	13 (1/0/0)	19 (1/0/0)	24 (1/3/0)
#<data>.W,([d_{32},B],I)	14 (1/0/0)	19 (1/0/0)	22 (1/3/0)
#<data>.L,([d_{32},B],I)	15 (1/0/0)	21 (1/0/0)	24 (1/3/0)
#<data>.W,([d_{32},B],I,d_{16})	16 (1/0/0)	21 (1/0/0)	24 (1/3/0)
#<data>.L,([d_{32},B],I,d_{16})	17 (1/0/0)	23 (1/0/0)	26 (1/3/0)
#<data>.W,([d_{32},B],I,d_{32})	16 (1/0/0)	21 (1/0/0)	24 (1/3/0)
#<data>.L,([d_{32},B],I,d_{32})	17 (1/0/0)	23 (1/0/0)	29 (1/3/0)

B = Base address; 0, An, PC, Xn, An+Xn, PC+Xn. Form does not affect timing.

I = Index; 0, Xn

NOTE: Xn cannot be in B and I at the same time. Scaling and size of Xn does not affect timing.

9.2.5 Jump Effective Address

The jump effective address table indicates the number of clock periods needed for the processor to calculate and jump to the specified effective address. Fetch time is only included for the first level of indirection on memory indirect addressing modes. The total number of clock cycles is outside the parentheses, the number of read, prefetch, and write cycles are given inside the parentheses as (r/p/w). They are included in the total clock cycle number.

Address Mode	Best Case	Cache Case	Worst Case
(An)	0 (0/0/0)	2 (0/0/0)	2 (0/0/0)
(d_{16},An)	1 (0/0/0)	4 (0/0/0)	4 (0/0/0)
(xxx).W	0 (0/0/0)	2 (0/0/0)	2 (0/0/0)
(xxx).L	0 (0/0/0)	2 (0/0/0)	2 (0/0/0)
(d_8,An,Xn) or (d_8,PC,Xn)	3 (0/0/0)	6 (0/0/0)	6 (0/0/0)
(d_{16},An,Xn) or (d_{16},PC,Xn)	3 (0/0/0)	6 (0/0/0)	6 (0/0/0)
(B)	3 (0/0/0)	6 (0/0/0)	6 (0/0/0)
(B,d_{16})	5 (0/0/0)	8 (0/0/0)	8 (0/1/0)
(B,d_{32})	9 (0/0/0)	12 (0/0/0)	12 (0/1/0)
([B],I)	8 (1/0/0)	11 (1/0/0)	11 (1/1/0)
$([B],I,d_{16})$	10 (1/0/0)	13 (1/0/0)	14 (1/1/0)
$([B],I,d_{32})$	10 (1/0/0)	13 (1/0/0)	14 (1/1/0)
$([d_{16},B],I)$	10 (1/0/0)	13 (1/0/0)	14 (1/1/0)
$([d_{16},B],I,d_{16})$	12 (1/0/0)	15 (1/0/0)	17 (1/1/0)
$([d_{16},B],I,d_{32})$	12 (1/0/0)	15 (1/0/0)	17 (1/1/0)
$([d_{32},B],I)$	14 (1/0/0)	17 (1/0/0)	19 (1/2/0)
$([d_{32},B],I,d_{16})$	16 (1/0/0)	19 (1/0/0)	21 (1/2/0)
$([d_{32},B],I,d_{32})$	16 (1/0/0)	19 (1/0/0)	23 (1/3/0)

B = Base address; 0, An, PC, Xn, An+Xn, PC+Xn. Form does not affect timing.

I = Index; 0, Xn

NOTE: Xn cannot be in B and I at the same time. Scaling and size of Xn does not affect timing.

9.2.6 MOVE Instruction

The MOVE instruction timing table indicates the number of clock periods needed for the processor to fetch, calculate, and perform the MOVE or MOVEA with the specified source and destination effective addresses, including both levels of indirection on memory indirect addressing modes. No additional tables are needed to calculate the total effective execution time for the MOVE or MOVEA instruction. The total number of clock cycles is outside the parentheses, the number of read, prefetch, and write cycles are given inside the parentheses as (r/p/w). They are included in the total clock cycle number.

BEST CASE

Source Address Mode	Destination							
	An	Dn	(An)	(An)+	−(An)	(d_{16},An)	(xxx).W	(xxx).L
Rn	0 (0/0/0)	0 (0/0/0)	3 (0/0/1)	4 (0/0/1)	3 (0/0/1)	3 (0/0/1)	3 (0/0/1)	5 (0/0/1)
#<data>.B,W	0 (0/0/0)	0 (0/0/0)	3 (0/0/1)	4 (0/0/1)	3 (0/0/1)	3 (0/0/1)	3 (0/0/1)	5 (0/0/1)
#<data>.L	0 (0/0/0)	0 (0/0/0)	3 (0/0/1)	4 (0/0/1)	3 (0/0/1)	3 (0/0/1)	3 (0/0/1)	5 (0/0/1)
(An)	3 (1/0/0)	3 (1/0/0)	6 (1/0/1)	6 (1/0/1)	6 (1/0/1)	6 (1/0/1)	6 (1/0/1)	8 (1/0/1)
(An)+	4 (1/0/0)	4 (1/0/0)	7 (1/0/1)	7 (1/0/1)	7 (1/0/1)	7 (1/0/1)	7 (1/0/1)	9 (1/0/1)
−(An)	3 (1/0/0)	3 (1/0/0)	6 (1/0/1)	6 (1/0/1)	6 (1/0/1)	6 (1/0/1)	6 (1/0/1)	8 (1/0/1)
(d_{16},An) or (d_{16},PC)	3 (1/0/0)	3 (1/0/0)	6 (1/0/1)	6 (1/0/1)	6 (1/0/1)	6 (1/0/1)	6 (1/0/1)	8 (1/0/1)
(xxx).W	3 (1/0/0)	3 (1/0/0)	6 (1/0/1)	6 (1/0/1)	6 (1/0/1)	6 (1/0/1)	6 (1/0/1)	8 (1/0/1)
(xxx).L	3 (1/0/0)	3 (1/0/0)	6 (1/0/1)	6 (1/0/1)	6 (1/0/1)	6 (1/0/1)	6 (1/0/1)	8 (1/0/1)
(d_8,An,Xn) or (d_8,PC,Xn)	4 (1/0/0)	4 (1/0/0)	7 (1/0/1)	7 (1/0/1)	7 (1/0/1)	7 (1/0/1)	7 (1/0/1)	9 (1/0/1)
(d_{16},An,Xn) or (d_{16},PC,Xn)	4 (1/0/0)	4 (1/0/0)	7 (1/0/1)	7 (1/0/1)	7 (1/0/1)	7 (1/0/1)	7 (1/0/1)	9 (1/0/1)
(B)	4 (1/0/0)	4 (1/0/0)	7 (1/0/1)	7 (1/0/1)	7 (1/0/1)	7 (1/0/1)	7 (1/0/1)	9 (1/0/1)
(d_{16},B)	6 (1/0/0)	6 (1/0/0)	9 (1/0/1)	9 (1/0/1)	9 (1/0/1)	9 (1/0/1)	9 (1/0/1)	11 (1/0/1)
(d_{32},B)	10 (1/0/0)	10 (1/0/0)	13 (1/0/1)	13 (1/0/1)	13 (1/0/1)	13 (1/0/1)	13 (1/0/1)	15 (1/0/1)
([B],I)	9 (2/0/0)	9 (2/0/0)	12 (2/0/1)	12 (2/0/1)	12 (2/0/1)	12 (2/0/1)	12 (2/0/1)	14 (2/0/1)
$([B],I,d_{16})$	11 (2/0/0)	11 (2/0/0)	14 (2/0/1)	14 (2/0/1)	14 (2/0/1)	14 (2/0/1)	14 (2/0/1)	16 (2/0/1)
$([B],I,d_{32})$	11 (2/0/0)	11 (2/0/0)	14 (2/0/1)	14 (2/0/1)	14 (2/0/1)	14 (2/0/1)	14 (2/0/1)	16 (2/0/1)
$([d_{16},B],I)$	11 (2/0/0)	11 (2/0/0)	14 (2/0/1)	14 (2/0/1)	14 (2/0/1)	14 (2/0/1)	14 (2/0/1)	16 (2/0/1)
$([d_{16},B],I,d_{16})$	13 (2/0/0)	13 (2/0/0)	16 (2/0/1)	16 (2/0/1)	16 (2/0/1)	16 (2/0/1)	16 (2/0/1)	18 (2/0/1)
$([d_{16},B],I,d_{32})$	13 (2/0/0)	13 (2/0/0)	16 (2/0/1)	16 (2/0/1)	16 (2/0/1)	16 (2/0/1)	16 (2/0/1)	18 (2/0/1)
$([d_{32},B],I)$	15 (2/0/0)	15 (2/0/0)	18 (2/0/1)	18 (2/0/1)	18 (2/0/1)	18 (2/0/1)	18 (2/0/1)	20 (2/0/1)
$([d_{32},B],I,d_{16})$	17 (2/0/0)	17 (2/0/0)	20 (2/0/1)	20 (2/0/1)	20 (2/0/1)	20 (2/0/1)	20 (2/0/1)	22 (2/0/1)
$([d_{32},B],I,d_{32})$	17 (2/0/0)	17 (2/0/0)	20 (2/0/1)	20 (2/0/1)	20 (2/0/1)	20 (2/0/1)	20 (2/0/1)	22 (2/0/1)

BEST CASE (Continued)

Source Address Mode	Destination							
	(d_8,An,Xn)	(d_{16},An,Xn)	(B)	(d_{16},B)	(d_{32},B)	([B],I)	$([B],I,d_{16})$	$([B],I,d_{32})$
Rn	4 (0/0/1)	6 (0/0/1)	5 (0/0/1)	7 (0/0/1)	11 (0/0/1)	9 (1/0/1)	11 (1/0/1)	12 (1/0/1)
#<data>.B,W	4 (0/0/1)	6 (0/0/1)	5 (0/0/1)	7 (0/0/1)	11 (0/0/1)	9 (1/0/1)	11 (1/0/1)	12 (1/0/1)
#<data>.L	4 (0/0/1)	6 (0/0/1)	5 (0/0/1)	7 (0/0/1)	11 (0/0/1)	9 (1/0/1)	11 (1/0/1)	12 (1/0/1)
(An)	8 (1/0/1)	10 (1/0/1)	9 (1/0/1)	11 (1/0/1)	15 (1/0/1)	13 (2/0/1)	15 (2/0/1)	16 (2/0/1)
(An)+	9 (1/0/1)	11 (1/0/1)	10 (1/0/1)	12 (1/0/1)	16 (1/0/1)	14 (2/0/1)	16 (2/0/1)	17 (2/0/1)
−(An)	8 (1/0/1)	10 (1/0/1)	9 (1/0/1)	11 (1/0/1)	15 (1/0/1)	13 (2/0/1)	15 (2/0/1)	16 (2/0/1)
(d_{16},An) or (d_{16},PC)	8 (1/0/1)	10 (1/0/1)	9 (1/0/1)	11 (1/0/1)	15 (1/0/1)	13 (2/0/1)	15 (2/0/1)	16 (2/0/1)
(xxx).W	8 (1/0/1)	10 (1/0/1)	9 (1/0/1)	11 (1/0/1)	15 (1/0/1)	13 (2/0/1)	15 (2/0/1)	16 (2/0/1)
(xxx).L	8 (1/0/1)	10 (1/0/1)	9 (1/0/1)	11 (1/0/1)	15 (1/0/1)	13 (2/0/1)	15 (2/0/1)	16 (2/0/1)
(d_8,An,Xn) or (d_8,PC,Xn)	9 (1/0/1)	10 (1/0/1)	10 (1/0/1)	12 (1/0/1)	16 (1/0/1)	14 (2/0/1)	16 (2/0/1)	17 (2/0/1)
(d_{16},An,Xn) or (d_{16},PC,Xn)	9 (1/0/1)	11 (1/0/1)	10 (1/0/1)	12 (1/0/1)	16 (1/0/1)	14 (2/0/1)	16 (2/0/1)	17 (2/0/1)
(B)	9 (1/0/1)	11 (1/0/1)	10 (1/0/1)	12 (1/0/1)	16 (1/0/1)	14 (2/0/1)	16 (2/0/1)	17 (2/0/1)
(d_{16},B)	11 (1/0/1)	13 (1/0/1)	12 (1/0/1)	14 (1/0/1)	18 (1/0/1)	16 (2/0/1)	18 (2/0/1)	19 (2/0/1)
(d_{32},B)	15 (1/0/1)	17 (1/0/1)	18 (1/0/1)	18 (1/0/1)	22 (1/0/1)	20 (2/0/1)	22 (2/0/1)	23 (2/0/1)
([B],I)	14 (2/0/1)	16 (2/0/1)	17 (2/0/1)	17 (2/0/1)	21 (2/0/1)	19 (3/0/1)	21 (3/0/1)	22 (3/0/1)
$([B],I,d_{16})$	16 (2/0/1)	18 (2/0/1)	19 (2/0/1)	19 (2/0/1)	23 (2/0/1)	21 (3/0/1)	23 (3/0/1)	24 (3/0/1)
$([B],I,d_{32})$	16 (2/0/1)	18 (2/0/1)	19 (2/0/1)	19 (2/0/1)	23 (2/0/1)	21 (3/0/1)	23 (3/0/1)	24 (3/0/1)
$([d_{16},B],I)$	16 (2/0/1)	18 (2/0/1)	19 (2/0/1)	19 (2/0/1)	23 (2/0/1)	21 (3/0/1)	23 (3/0/1)	24 (3/0/1)
$([d_{16},B],I,d_{16})$	18 (2/0/1)	20 (2/0/1)	21 (2/0/1)	21 (2/0/1)	25 (2/0/1)	23 (3/0/1)	25 (3/0/1)	26 (3/0/1)
$([d_{16},B],I,d_{32})$	18 (2/0/1)	20 (2/0/1)	21 (2/0/1)	21 (2/0/1)	25 (2/0/1)	23 (3/0/1)	25 (3/0/1)	26 (3/0/1)
$([d_{32},B],I)$	20 (2/0/1)	22 (2/0/1)	23 (2/0/1)	23 (2/0/1)	27 (2/0/1)	25 (3/0/1)	27 (3/0/1)	28 (3/0/1)
$([d_{32},B],I,d_{16})$	22 (2/0/1)	24 (2/0/1)	25 (2/0/1)	25 (2/0/1)	29 (2/0/1)	27 (3/0/1)	29 (3/0/1)	30 (3/0/1)
$([d_{32},B],I,d_{32})$	22 (2/0/1)	24 (2/0/1)	25 (2/0/1)	25 (2/0/1)	29 (2/0/1)	27 (3/0/1)	29 (3/0/1)	30 (3/0/1)

BEST CASE (Concluded)

Source Address Mode	Destination					
	([d16,B],I)	([d16,B],I,d16)	([d16,B],I,d32)	([d32,B],I)	([d32,B],I,d16)	([d32,B],I,d32)
Rn	11 (1/0/1)	13 (1/0/1)	14 (1/0/1)	15 (1/0/1)	17 (1/0/1)	18 (1/0/1)
#<data>.B,W	11 (1/0/1)	13 (1/0/1)	14 (1/0/1)	15 (1/0/1)	17 (1/0/1)	18 (1/0/1)
#<data>.L	11 (1/0/1)	13 (1/0/1)	14 (1/0/1)	15 (1/0/1)	17 (1/0/1)	18 (1/0/1)
(An)	15 (2/0/1)	17 (2/0/1)	18 (2/0/1)	19 (2/0/1)	21 (2/0/1)	22 (2/0/1)
(An)+	16 (2/0/1)	18 (2/0/1)	19 (2/0/1)	20 (2/0/1)	22 (2/0/1)	23 (2/0/1)
−(An)	15 (2/0/1)	17 (2/0/1)	18 (2/0/1)	19 (2/0/1)	21 (2/0/1)	22 (2/0/1)
(d16,An) or (d16,PC)	15 (2/0/1)	17 (2/0/1)	18 (2/0/1)	19 (2/0/1)	21 (2/0/1)	22 (2/0/1)
(xxx).W	15 (2/0/1)	17 (2/0/1)	18 (2/0/1)	19 (2/0/1)	21 (2/0/1)	22 (2/0/1)
(xxx).L	15 (2/0/1)	17 (2/0/1)	18 (2/0/1)	19 (2/0/1)	21 (2/0/1)	22 (2/0/1)
(d8,An,Xn) or (d8,PC,Xn)	16 (2/0/1)	18 (2/0/1)	19 (2/0/1)	20 (2/0/1)	22 (2/0/1)	23 (2/0/1)
(d16,An,Xn) or (d16,PC,Xn)	16 (2/0/1)	18 (2/0/1)	19 (2/0/1)	20 (2/0/1)	22 (2/0/1)	23 (2/0/1)
(B)	16 (2/0/1)	18 (2/0/1)	19 (2/0/1)	20 (2/0/1)	22 (2/0/1)	23 (2/0/1)
(d16,B)	18 (2/0/1)	20 (2/0/1)	21 (2/0/1)	22 (2/0/1)	24 (2/0/1)	25 (2/0/1)
(d32,B)	22 (2/0/1)	24 (2/0/1)	25 (2/0/1)	26 (2/0/1)	28 (2/0/1)	29 (2/0/1)
([B],I)	21 (3/0/1)	23 (3/0/1)	24 (3/0/1)	25 (3/0/1)	27 (3/0/1)	28 (3/0/1)
([B],I,d16)	23 (3/0/1)	25 (3/0/1)	26 (3/0/1)	27 (3/0/1)	29 (3/0/1)	30 (3/0/1)
([B],I,d32)	23 (3/0/1)	25 (3/0/1)	26 (3/0/1)	27 (3/0/1)	29 (3/0/1)	30 (3/0/1)
([d16,B],I)	23 (3/0/1)	25 (3/0/1)	26 (3/0/1)	27 (3/0/1)	29 (3/0/1)	30 (3/0/1)
([d16,B],I,d16)	25 (3/0/1)	27 (3/0/1)	28 (3/0/1)	29 (3/0/1)	31 (3/0/1)	32 (3/0/1)
([d16,B],I,d32)	25 (3/0/1)	27 (3/0/1)	28 (3/0/1)	29 (3/0/1)	31 (3/0/1)	32 (3/0/1)
([d32,B],I)	27 (3/0/1)	29 (3/0/1)	30 (3/0/1)	31 (3/0/1)	33 (3/0/1)	34 (3/0/1)
([d32,B],I,d16)	29 (3/0/1)	31 (3/0/1)	32 (3/0/1)	33 (3/0/1)	35 (3/0/1)	36 (3/0/1)
([d32,B],I,d32)	29 (3/0/1)	31 (3/0/1)	32 (3/0/1)	33 (3/0/1)	35 (3/0/1)	36 (3/0/1)

CACHE CASE

Source Address Mode	Destination							
	An	Dn	(An)	(An)+	−(An)	(d16,An)	(xxx).W	(xxx).L
Rn	2 (0/0/0)	2 (0/0/0)	4 (0/0/1)	4 (0/0/1)	5 (0/0/1)	5 (0/0/1)	4 (0/0/1)	6 (0/0/1)
#<data>.B,W	4 (0/0/0)	4 (0/0/0)	6 (0/0/1)	6 (0/0/1)	7 (0/0/1)	7 (0/0/1)	6 (0/0/1)	8 (0/0/1)
#<data>.L	6 (0/0/0)	6 (0/0/0)	8 (0/0/1)	8 (0/0/1)	9 (0/0/1)	9 (0/0/1)	8 (0/0/1)	10 (0/0/1)
(An)	6 (1/0/0)	6 (1/0/0)	7 (1/0/1)	7 (1/0/1)	7 (1/0/1)	7 (1/0/1)	7 (1/0/1)	9 (1/0/1)
(An)+	6 (1/0/0)	6 (1/0/0)	7 (1/0/1)	7 (1/0/1)	7 (1/0/1)	7 (1/0/1)	7 (1/0/1)	9 (1/0/1)
−(An)	7 (1/0/0)	7 (1/0/0)	8 (1/0/1)	8 (1/0/1)	8 (1/0/1)	8 (1/0/1)	8 (1/0/1)	10 (1/0/1)
(d16,An) or (d16,PC)	7 (1/0/0)	7 (1/0/0)	8 (1/0/1)	8 (1/0/1)	8 (1/0/1)	8 (1/0/1)	8 (1/0/1)	10 (1/0/1)
(xxx).W	6 (1/0/0)	6 (1/0/0)	7 (1/0/1)	7 (1/0/1)	7 (1/0/1)	7 (1/0/1)	7 (1/0/1)	9 (1/0/1)
(xxx).L	6 (1/0/0)	6 (1/0/0)	7 (1/0/1)	7 (1/0/1)	7 (1/0/1)	7 (1/0/1)	7 (1/0/1)	9 (1/0/1)
(d8,An,Xn) or (d8,PC,Xn)	9 (1/0/0)	9 (1/0/0)	10 (1/0/1)	10 (1/0/1)	10 (1/0/1)	10 (1/0/1)	10 (1/0/1)	12 (1/0/1)
(d16,An,Xn) or (d16,PC,Xn)	9 (1/0/0)	9 (1/0/0)	10 (1/0/1)	10 (1/0/1)	10 (1/0/1)	10 (1/0/1)	10 (1/0/1)	12 (1/0/1)
(B)	9 (1/0/0)	9 (1/0/0)	10 (1/0/1)	10 (1/0/1)	10 (1/0/1)	10 (1/0/1)	10 (1/0/1)	12 (1/0/1)
(d16,B)	11 (1/0/0)	11 (1/0/0)	12 (1/0/1)	12 (1/0/1)	12 (1/0/1)	12 (1/0/1)	12 (1/0/1)	14 (1/0/1)
(d32,B)	15 (1/0/0)	15 (1/0/0)	16 (1/0/1)	16 (1/0/1)	16 (1/0/1)	16 (1/0/1)	16 (1/0/1)	18 (1/0/1)
([B],I)	14 (2/0/0)	14 (2/0/0)	15 (2/0/1)	15 (2/0/1)	15 (2/0/1)	15 (2/0/1)	15 (2/0/1)	17 (2/0/1)
([B],I,d16)	16 (2/0/0)	16 (2/0/0)	17 (2/0/1)	17 (2/0/1)	17 (2/0/1)	17 (2/0/1)	17 (2/0/1)	19 (2/0/1)
([B],I,d32)	16 (2/0/0)	16 (2/0/0)	17 (2/0/1)	17 (2/0/1)	17 (2/0/1)	17 (2/0/1)	17 (2/0/1)	19 (2/0/1)
([d16,B],I)	16 (2/0/0)	16 (2/0/0)	17 (2/0/1)	17 (2/0/1)	17 (2/0/1)	17 (2/0/1)	17 (2/0/1)	19 (2/0/1)
([d16,B],I,d16)	18 (2/0/0)	18 (2/0/0)	19 (2/0/1)	19 (2/0/1)	19 (2/0/1)	19 (2/0/1)	19 (2/0/1)	21 (2/0/1)
([d16,B],I,d32)	18 (2/0/0)	18 (2/0/0)	19 (2/0/1)	19 (2/0/1)	19 (2/0/1)	19 (2/0/1)	19 (2/0/1)	21 (2/0/1)
([d32,B],I)	20 (2/0/0)	20 (2/0/0)	21 (2/0/1)	21 (2/0/1)	21 (2/0/1)	21 (2/0/1)	21 (2/0/1)	23 (2/0/1)
([d32,B],I,d16)	22 (2/0/0)	22 (2/0/0)	23 (2/0/1)	23 (2/0/1)	23 (2/0/1)	23 (2/0/1)	23 (2/0/1)	25 (2/0/1)
([d32,B],I,d32)	22 (2/0/0)	22 (2/0/0)	23 (2/0/1)	23 (2/0/1)	23 (2/0/1)	23 (2/0/1)	23 (2/0/1)	25 (2/0/1)

CACHE CASE (Continued)

Source Address Mode	\(d_8,An,Xn\)	\(d_{16},An,Xn\)	(B)	\(d_{16},B\)	\(d_{32},B\)	([B],I)	([B],I,d_{16})	([B],I,d_{32})
Rn	7 (0/0/1)	9 (0/0/1)	8 (0/0/1)	10 (0/0/1)	14 (0/0/1)	12 (1/0/1)	14 (1/0/1)	15 (1/0/1)
#<data>.B,W	7 (0/0/1)	9 (0/0/1)	8 (0/0/1)	10 (0/0/1)	14 (0/0/1)	12 (1/0/1)	14 (1/0/1)	15 (1/0/1)
#<data>.L	9 (0/0/1)	11 (0/0/1)	10 (0/0/1)	12 (0/0/1)	16 (0/0/1)	14 (1/0/1)	16 (1/0/1)	17 (1/0/1)
(An)	9 (1/0/1)	11 (1/0/1)	10 (1/0/1)	12 (1/0/1)	16 (1/0/1)	14 (2/0/1)	16 (2/0/1)	17 (2/0/1)
(An)+	9 (1/0/1)	11 (1/0/1)	10 (1/0/1)	12 (1/0/1)	16 (1/0/1)	14 (2/0/1)	16 (2/0/1)	17 (2/0/1)
−(An)	10 (1/0/1)	12 (1/0/1)	11 (1/0/1)	13 (1/0/1)	17 (1/0/1)	15 (2/0/1)	17 (2/0/1)	18 (2/0/1)
(d_{16},An) or (d_{16},PC)	10 (1/0/1)	12 (2/0/1)	11 (1/0/1)	13 (1/0/1)	17 (1/0/1)	15 (2/0/1)	17 (2/0/1)	18 (2/0/1)
(xxx).W	9 (1/0/1)	11 (1/0/1)	10 (1/0/1)	12 (1/0/1)	16 (1/0/1)	14 (2/0/1)	16 (2/0/1)	17 (2/0/1)
(xxx).L	9 (1/0/1)	11 (1/0/1)	10 (1/0/1)	12 (1/0/1)	16 (1/0/1)	14 (2/0/1)	16 (2/0/1)	17 (2/0/1)
(d_8,An,Xn) or (d_8,PC,Xn)	12 (1/0/1)	14 (1/0/1)	13 (1/0/1)	15 (1/0/1)	19 (1/0/1)	17 (2/0/1)	19 (2/0/1)	20 (2/0/1)
(d_{16},An,Xn) or (d_{16},PC,Xn)	12 (1/0/1)	14 (1/0/1)	13 (1/0/1)	15 (1/0/1)	19 (1/0/1)	17 (2/0/1)	19 (2/0/1)	20 (2/0/1)
(B)	12 (1/0/1)	14 (1/0/1)	13 (1/0/1)	15 (1/0/1)	19 (1/0/1)	17 (2/0/1)	19 (2/0/1)	20 (2/0/1)
(d_{16},B)	14 (1/0/1)	16 (1/0/1)	15 (1/0/1)	17 (1/0/1)	21 (1/0/1)	19 (2/0/1)	21 (2/0/1)	22 (2/0/1)
(d_{32},B)	18 (1/0/1)	20 (1/0/1)	19 (1/0/1)	21 (1/0/1)	25 (1/0/1)	23 (2/0/1)	25 (2/0/1)	26 (2/0/1)
([B],I)	17 (2/0/1)	19 (2/0/1)	18 (2/0/1)	20 (2/0/1)	24 (2/0/1)	22 (3/0/1)	24 (3/0/1)	25 (3/0/1)
([B],I,d_{16})	19 (2/0/1)	21 (2/0/1)	20 (2/0/1)	22 (2/0/1)	26 (2/0/1)	24 (3/0/1)	26 (3/0/1)	27 (3/0/1)
([B],I,d_{32})	19 (2/0/1)	21 (2/0/1)	20 (2/0/1)	22 (2/0/1)	26 (2/0/1)	24 (3/0/1)	26 (3/0/1)	27 (3/0/1)
([d_{16},B],I)	19 (2/0/1)	21 (2/0/1)	20 (2/0/1)	22 (2/0/1)	26 (2/0/1)	24 (3/0/1)	26 (3/0/1)	27 (3/0/1)
([d_{16},B],I,d_{16})	21 (2/0/1)	23 (2/0/1)	22 (2/0/1)	24 (2/0/1)	28 (2/0/1)	26 (3/0/1)	28 (3/0/1)	29 (3/0/1)
([d_{16},B],I,d_{32})	21 (2/0/1)	23 (2/0/1)	22 (2/0/1)	24 (2/0/1)	28 (2/0/1)	26 (3/0/1)	28 (3/0/1)	29 (3/0/1)
([d_{32},B],I)	23 (2/0/1)	25 (2/0/1)	24 (2/0/1)	26 (2/0/1)	30 (2/0/1)	28 (3/0/1)	30 (3/0/1)	31 (3/0/1)
([d_{32},B],I,d_{16})	25 (2/0/1)	27 (2/0/1)	26 (2/0/1)	28 (2/0/1)	32 (2/0/1)	30 (3/0/1)	32 (3/0/1)	33 (3/0/1)
([d_{32},B],I,d_{32})	25 (2/0/1)	27 (2/0/1)	26 (2/0/1)	28 (2/0/1)	32 (2/0/1)	30 (3/0/1)	32 (3/0/1)	33 (3/0/0)

CACHE CASE (Concluded)

Source Address Mode	([d_{16},B],I)	([d_{16},B],I,d_{16})	([d_{16},B],I,d_{32})	([d_{32},B],I)	([d_{32},B],I,d_{16})	([d_{32},B],I,d_{32})
Rn	14 (1/0/1)	16 (1/0/1)	17 (1/0/1)	18 (1/0/1)	20 (1/0/1)	21 (1/0/1)
#<data>.B,W	14 (1/0/1)	16 (1/0/1)	17 (1/0/1)	18 (1/0/1)	20 (1/0/1)	21 (1/0/1)
#<data>.L	16 (1/0/1)	18 (1/0/1)	19 (1/0/1)	20 (1/0/1)	22 (1/0/1)	23 (1/0/1)
(An)	16 (2/0/1)	18 (2/0/1)	19 (2/0/1)	20 (2/0/1)	22 (2/0/1)	23 (2/0/1)
(An)+	16 (2/0/1)	18 (2/0/1)	19 (2/0/1)	20 (2/0/1)	22 (2/0/1)	23 (2/0/1)
−(An)	17 (2/0/1)	19 (2/0/1)	20 (2/0/1)	21 (2/0/1)	23 (2/0/1)	24 (2/0/1)
(d_{16},An) or (d_{16},PC)	17 (2/0/1)	19 (2/0/1)	20 (2/0/1)	21 (2/0/1)	23 (2/0/1)	24 (2/0/1)
(xxx).W	16 (2/0/1)	18 (2/0/1)	19 (2/0/1)	20 (2/0/1)	22 (2/0/1)	23 (2/0/1)
(xxx).L	16 (2/0/1)	18 (2/0/1)	19 (2/0/1)	20 (2/0/1)	22 (2/0/1)	23 (2/0/1)
(d_8,An,Xn) or (d_8,PC,Xn)	19 (2/0/1)	21 (2/0/1)	22 (2/0/1)	23 (2/0/1)	25 (2/0/1)	26 (2/0/1)
(d_{16},An,Xn) or (d_{16},PC,Xn)	19 (2/0/1)	21 (2/0/1)	22 (2/0/1)	23 (2/0/1)	25 (2/0/1)	26 (2/0/1)
(B)	19 (2/0/1)	21 (2/0/1)	22 (2/0/1)	23 (2/0/1)	25 (2/0/1)	26 (2/0/1)
(d_{16},B)	21 (2/0/1)	23 (2/0/1)	24 (2/0/1)	25 (2/0/1)	27 (2/0/1)	28 (2/0/1)
(d_{32},B)	25 (2/0/1)	27 (2/0/1)	28 (2/0/1)	29 (2/0/1)	31 (2/0/1)	32 (2/0/1)
([B],I)	24 (3/0/1)	26 (3/0/1)	27 (3/0/1)	28 (3/0/1)	30 (3/0/1)	31 (3/0/1)
([B],I,d_{16})	26 (3/0/1)	28 (3/0/1)	29 (3/0/1)	30 (3/0/1)	32 (3/0/1)	33 (3/0/1)
([B],I,d_{32})	26 (3/0/1)	28 (3/0/1)	29 (3/0/1)	30 (3/0/1)	32 (3/0/1)	33 (3/0/1)
([d_{16},B],I)	26 (3/0/1)	28 (3/0/1)	29 (3/0/1)	30 (3/0/1)	32 (3/0/1)	33 (3/0/1)
([d_{16},B],I,d_{16})	28 (3/0/1)	30 (3/0/1)	31 (3/0/1)	32 (3/0/1)	34 (3/0/1)	35 (3/0/1)
([d_{16},B],I,d_{32})	28 (3/0/1)	30 (3/0/1)	31 (3/0/1)	32 (3/0/1)	34 (3/0/1)	35 (3/0/1)
([d_{32},B],I)	30 (3/0/1)	32 (3/0/1)	33 (3/0/1)	34 (3/0/1)	36 (3/0/1)	37 (3/0/1)
([d_{32},B],I,d_{16})	32 (3/0/1)	34 (3/0/1)	35 (3/0/1)	36 (3/0/1)	38 (3/0/1)	39 (3/0/1)
([d_{32},B],I,d_{32})	32 (3/0/1)	34 (3/0/1)	35 (3/0/1)	36 (3/0/1)	38 (3/0/1)	39 (3/0/1)

9

WORST CASE

Source Address Mode	An	Dn	(An)	(An)+	−(An)	(d₁₆,An)	(xxx).W	(xxx).L
						(d_{16},An)		
Rn	3 (0/1/0)	3 (0/1/0)	5 (0/1/0)	5 (0/1/0)	6 (0/1/1)	7 (0/1/1)	7 (0/1/1)	9 (0/2/1)
#<data>.B,W	3 (0/1/0)	3 (0/1/0)	5 (0/1/0)	8 (0/1/1)	6 (0/1/1)	7 (0/1/1)	7 (0/1/1)	9 (0/2/1)
#<data>.L	5 (0/1/0)	5 (0/1/0)	7 (0/0/1)	7 (0/1/1)	8 (0/1/1)	9 (0/1/1)	9 (0/1/1)	11 (0/2/1)
(An)	7 (1/1/0)	7 (1/1/0)	9 (1/1/1)	9 (1/1/1)	9 (1/1/1)	11 (1/1/1)	11 (1/1/1)	13 (1/2/1)
(An)+	7 (1/1/0)	7 (1/1/0)	9 (1/1/1)	9 (1/1/1)	9 (1/1/1)	11 (1/1/1)	11 (1/1/1)	13 (1/2/1)
−(An)	8 (1/1/0)	8 (1/1/0)	10 (1/1/1)	10 (1/1/1)	10 (1/1/1)	12 (1/1/1)	12 (1/1/1)	14 (1/2/1)
(d_{16},An) or (d_{16},PC)	9 (1/2/0)	9 (1/2/0)	11 (1/2/1)	11 (1/2/1)	11 (1/2/1)	13 (1/2/1)	13 (1/2/1)	15 (1/3/1)
(xxx).W	8 (1/2/0)	8 (1/2/0)	10 (1/2/1)	10 (1/2/1)	10 (1/2/1)	12 (1/2/1)	12 (1/2/1)	14 (1/3/1)
(xxx).L	10 (1/2/0)	10 (1/2/0)	12 (1/2/1)	12 (1/2/1)	12 (1/2/1)	14 (1/2/1)	14 (1/2/1)	16 (1/3/1)
(d_8,An,Xn) or (d_8,PC,Xn)	11 (1/2/0)	11 (1/2/0)	13 (1/2/1)	13 (1/2/1)	13 (1/2/1)	15 (1/2/1)	15 (1/2/1)	17 (1/3/1)
(d_{16},An,Xn) or (d_{16},PC,Xn)	12 (1/2/0)	12 (1/2/0)	14 (1/2/1)	14 (1/2/1)	14 (1/2/1)	16 (1/2/1)	16 (1/2/1)	18 (1/3/1)
(B)	12 (1/2/0)	12 (1/2/0)	14 (1/2/1)	14 (1/2/1)	14 (1/2/1)	16 (1/2/1)	16 (1/2/1)	18 (1/3/1)
(d_{16},B)	15 (1/2/0)	15 (1/2/0)	17 (1/2/1)	17 (1/2/1)	17 (1/3/1)	19 (1/2/1)	19 (1/2/1)	21 (1/3/1)
(d_{32},B)	19 (1/3/0)	19 (1/3/0)	21 (1/3/1)	21 (1/3/1)	21 (1/3/1)	23 (1/3/1)	23 (1/3/1)	25d(1/4/1)
([B],I)	16 (2/2/0)	16 (2/2/0)	18 (2/2/1)	18 (2/2/1)	18 (2/2/1)	20 (2/2/1)	20 (2/2/1)	22d(2/3/1)
$([B],I,d_{16})$	19 (2/2/0)	19 (2/2/0)	121(2/2/1)	21 (2/2/1)	21 (2/2/1)	23 (2/2/1)	23 (2/2/1)	25 (2/3/1)
$([B],I,d_{32})$	20 (2/3/0)	20 (2/3/0)	22 (2/3/1)	22 (2/3/1)	22 (2/3/1)	24 (2/3/1)	24 (2/3/1)	26 (2/4/1)
$([d_{16},B],I)$	19 (2/2/0)	19 (2/2/0)	21 (2/2/1)	21 (2/2/1)	21 (2/2/1)	23 (2/2/1)	23 (2/2/1)	25 (2/3/1)
$([d_{16},B],I,d_{16})$	22 (2/3/0)	22 (2/3/0)	24 (2/3/1)	24 (2/3/1)	24 (2/3/1)	26 (2/3/1)	26 (2/3/1)	28 (2/4/1)
$([d_{16},B],I,d_{32})$	23 (2/3/0)	23 (2/3/0)	25 (2/3/1)	25 (2/3/1)	25 (2/3/1)	27 (2/3/1)	27 (2/3/1)	29 (2/4/1)
$([d_{32},B],I)$	23 (2/3/0)	23 (2/3/0)	25 (2/3/1)	25 (2/3/1)	25 (2/3/1)	27 (2/3/1)	27 (2/3/1)	29 (2/4/1)
$([d_{32},B],I,d_{16})$	25 (2/3/0)	25 (2/3/0)	27 (2/3/1)	27 (2/3/1)	27 (2/3/1)	29 (2/3/1)	29 (2/3/1)	31 (2/4/1)
$([d_{32},B],I,d_{32})$	27 (2/4/0)	27 (2/4/0)	20 (2/4/1)	29 (2/4/1)	29 (2/4/1)	31 (2/4/1)	31 (2/4/1)	33 (2/5/1)

WORST CASE (Continued)

Source Address Mode	(d_8,An,Xn)	(d_{16},An,Xn)	(B)	(d_{16},B)	(d_{32},B)	([B],I)	$([B],I,d_{16})$	$([R],I,d_{32})$
Rn	9 (0/1/1)	12 (0/2/1)	10 (0/1/1)	14 (0/2/1)	19 (0/2/1)	14 (1/1/1)	17 (1/2/1)	20 (1/2/1)
#<data>.B,W	9 (0/1/1)	12 (0/2/1)	10 (0/1/1)	14 (0/2/1)	19 (0/2/1)	14 (1/1/1)	17 (1/2/1)	20 (1/2/1)
#<data>.L	11 (0/1/1)	14 (0/2/1)	12 (0/1/1)	16 (0/2/1)	21 (0/2/1)	16 (1/1/1)	19 (1/2/1)	22 (1/2/1)
(An)	11 (1/1/1)	14 (1/2/1)	12 (1/1/1)	16 (1/2/1)	21 (1/2/1)	12 (2/1/1)	19 (2/2/1)	22 (2/2/1)
(An)+	11 (1/1/1)	14 (1/2/1)	12 (1/1/1)	16 (1/2/1)	21 (1/2/1)	12 (2/1/1)	19 (2/2/1)	22 (2/2/1)
−(An)	12 (1/1/1)	15 (1/2/1)	13 (1/1/1)	17 (1/2/1)	22 (1/2/1)	13 (2/1/1)	20 (2/2/1)	23 (2/2/1)
(d_{16},An) or (d_{16},PC)	13 (1/2/1)	16 (2/3/1)	14 (1/2/1)	18 (1/3/1)	23 (1/3/1)	14 (2/2/1)	21 (2/3/1)	24 (2/3/1)
(xxx).W	12 (1/2/1)	15 (1/3/1)	13 (1/2/1)	17 (1/3/1)	22 (1/3/1)	13 (2/2/1)	20 (2/3/1)	23 (2/3/1)
(xxx).L	14 (1/2/1)	17 (1/3/1)	15 (1/2/1)	19 (1/3/1)	24 (1/3/1)	15 (2/2/1)	22 (2/3/1)	25 (2/3/1)
(d_8,An,Xn) or (d_8,PC,Xn)	15 (1/2/1)	18 (1/3/1)	16 (1/2/1)	20 (1/3/1)	25 (1/3/1)	16 (2/2/1)	23 (2/3/1)	26 (2/3/1)
(d_{16},An,Xn) or (d_{16},PC,Xn)	16 (1/2/1)	19 (1/3/1)	17 (1/2/1)	21 (1/3/1)	26 (1/3/1)	17 (2/2/1)	24 (2/3/1)	27 (2/3/1)
(B)	16 (1/2/1)	19 (1/3/1)	17 (1/2/1)	21 (1/3/1)	26 (1/3/1)	17 (2/2/1)	24 (2/3/1)	27 (2/3/1)
(d_{16},B)	19 (1/2/1)	22 (1/3/1)	20 (1/2/1)	24 (1/3/1)	29 (1/3/1)	20 (2/2/1)	27 (2/3/1)	30 (2/3/1)
(d_{32},B)	23 (1/3/1)	26 (1/4/1)	24 (1/3/1)	28 (1/4/1)	33 (1/4/1)	24 (2/3/1)	31 (2/4/1)	34 (2/4/1)
([B],I)	20 (2/2/1)	23 (2/3/1)	21 (2/2/1)	25 (2/3/1)	30 (2/3/1)	21 (3/2/1)	28 (3/3/1)	31 (3/3/1)
$([B],I,d_{16})$	23 (2/2/1)	26 (2/3/1)	24 (2/2/1)	28 (2/3/1)	33 (2/3/1)	24 (3/2/1)	31 (3/3/1)	34 (3/3/1)
$([B],I,d_{32})$	24 (2/3/1)	27 (2/4/1)	25 (2/3/1)	29 (2/4/1)	34 (2/4/1)	25 (3/3/1)	32 (3/4/1)	35 (3/4/1)
$([d_{16},B],I)$	23 (2/2/1)	26 (2/3/1)	24 (2/2/1)	28 (2/3/1)	33 (2/3/1)	24 (3/2/1)	31 (3/3/1)	34 (3/3/1)
$([d_{16},B],I,d_{16})$	26 (2/3/1)	29 (2/4/1)	27 (2/3/1)	31 (2/4/1)	36 (2/4/1)	27 (3/3/1)	34 (3/4/1)	37 (3/4/1)
$([d_{16},B],I,d_{32})$	27 (2/3/1)	30 (2/4/1)	28 (2/3/1)	32 (2/4/1)	37 (2/4/1)	28 (3/3/1)	35 (3/4/1)	38 (3/4/1)
$([d_{32},B],I)$	27 (2/3/1)	30 (2/4/1)	28 (2/3/1)	32 (2/4/1)	37 (2/4/1)	28 (3/3/1)	35 (3/4/1)	38 (3/4/1)
$([d_{32},B],I,d_{16})$	29 (2/3/1)	32 (2/4/1)	30 (2/3/1)	34 (2/4/1)	39 (2/4/1)	30 (3/3/1)	37 (3/4/1)	40 (3/4/1)
$([d_{32},B],I,d_{32})$	31 (2/4/1)	34 (2/5/1)	32 (2/4/1)	36 (2/5/1)	41 (2/5/1)	32 (3/4/1)	39 (3/5/1)	42 (3/5/1)

9

WORST CASE (Concluded)

Source Address Mode	Destination					
	([d16,B],I)	([d16,B],I,d16)	([d16,B],I,d32)	([d32,B],I)	([d32,B],I,d16)	([d32,B],I,d32)
Rn	17 (1/2/1)	20 (1/2/1)	23 (1/3/1)	22 (1/2/1)	25 (1/3/1)	27 (1/3/1)
#<data>.B,W	17 (1/2/1)	20 (1/2/1)	23 (1/3/1)	22 (1/2/1)	25 (1/3/1)	27 (1/3/1)
#<data>.L	19 (1/2/1)	22 (1/2/1)	25 (1/3/1)	24 (1/2/1)	27 (1/3/1)	29 (1/3/1)
(An)	19 (2/2/1)	22 (2/2/1)	25 (2/3/1)	24 (2/2/1)	27 (2/3/1)	29 (2/3/1)
(An)+	19 (2/2/1)	22 (2/2/1)	25 (2/3/1)	24 (2/2/1)	27 (2/3/1)	29 (2/3/1)
−(An)	20 (2/2/1)	23 (2/2/1)	26 (2/3/1)	25 (2/2/1)	28 (2/3/1)	30 (2/3/1)
(d16,An) or (d16,PC)	21 (2/3/1)	24 (2/3/1)	27 (2/4/1)	26 (2/3/1)	29 (2/4/1)	31 (2/4/1)
(xxx).W	20 (2/3/1)	23 (2/3/1)	26 (2/4/1)	27 (2/3/1)	28 (2/4/1)	30 (2/4/1)
(xxx).L	22 (2/3/1)	25 (2/3/1)	28 (2/4/1)	29 (2/3/1)	30 (2/4/1)	32 (2/4/1)
(d8,An,Xn) or (d8,PC,Xn)	23 (2/3/1)	26 (2/3/1)	29 (2/4/1)	30 (2/3/1)	31 (2/4/1)	33 (2/4/1)
(d16,An,Xn) or (d16,PC,Xn)	24 (2/3/1)	27 (2/3/1)	30 (2/4/1)	31 (2/3/1)	32 (2/4/1)	34 (2/4/1)
(B)	24 (2/3/1)	27 (2/3/1)	30 (2/4/1)	31 (2/3/1)	32 (2/4/1)	34 (2/4/1)
(d16,B)	27 (2/3/1)	30 (2/3/1)	33 (2/4/1)	34 (2/3/1)	35 (2/4/1)	37 (2/4/1)
(d32,B)	31 (2/4/1)	34 (2/4/1)	37 (2/5/1)	38 (2/4/1)	39 (2/5/1)	41 (2/5/1)
([B],I)	28 (3/3/1)	31 (3/3/1)	34 (3/4/1)	35 (3/3/1)	36 (3/4/1)	38 (3/4/1)
([B],I,d16)	31 (3/3/1)	34 (3/3/1)	37 (3/4/1)	38 (3/3/1)	39 (3/4/1)	41 (3/4/1)
([B],I,d32)	32 (3/4/1)	35 (3/4/1)	38 (3/5/1)	39 (3/4/1)	40 (3/5/1)	42 (3/5/1)
([d16,B],I)	31 (3/3/1)	34 (3/3/1)	37 (3/4/1)	38 (3/3/1)	39 (3/4/1)	41 (3/4/1)
([d16,B],I,d16)	34 (3/4/1)	37 (3/4/1)	40 (3/5/1)	41 (3/4/1)	42 (3/5/1)	44 (3/5/1)
([d16,B],I,d32)	35 (3/4/1)	38 (3/4/1)	41 (3/5/1)	42 (3/4/1)	43 (3/5/1)	45 (3/5/1)
([d32,B],I)	35 (3/4/1)	38 (3/4/1)	41 (3/5/1)	42 (3/4/1)	43 (3/5/1)	45 (3/5/1)
([d32,B],I,d16)	37 (3/4/1)	40 (3/4/1)	43 (3/5/1)	44 (3/4/1)	45 (3/5/1)	47 (3/5/1)
([d32,B],I,d32)	39 (3/5/1)	42 (3/5/1)	45 (3/6/1)	46 (3/5/1)	47 (3/6/1)	49 (3/6/1)

9

9.2.7 Special Purpose MOVE Instruction

The special purpose MOVE timing table indicates the number of clock periods needed for the processor to fetch, calculate, and perform the special purpose MOVE operation on the control registers or specified effective address. The total number of clock cycles is outside the parentheses, the number of read, prefetch, and write cycles are given inside the parentheses as (r/p/w). They are included in the total clock cycle number.

	Instruction		Best Case	Cache Case	Worst Case
	EXG	Ry,Rx	0 (0/0/0)	2 (0/0/0)	3 (0/1/0)
	MOVEC	Cr,Rn	3 (0/0/0)	6 (0/0/0)	7 (0/1/0)
	MOVEC	Rn,Cr	9 (0/0/0)	12 (0/0/0)	13 (0/1/0)
	MOVE	PSW,Rn	1 (0/0/0)	4 (0/0/0)	5 (0/1/0)
#	MOVE	PSW,Mem	5 (0/0/1)	5 (0/0/1)	7 (0/1/1)
*	MOVE	EA,CCR	4 (0/0/0)	4 (0/0/0)	5 (0/1/0)
*	MOVE	EA,SR	8 (0/0/0)	8 (0/0/0)	11 (0/2/0)
#*	MOVEM	EA,RL	8+4n (n/0/0)	8+4n (n/0/0)	9+4n (n/1/0)
#*	MOVEM	RL,EA	4+3n (0/0/n)	4+3n (0/0/n)	5+3n (0/1/n)
	MOVEP.W	Dn,(d_{16},An)	8 (0/0/2)	11 (0/0/2)	11 (0/1/2)
	MOVEP.L	Dn,(d_{16},An)	14 (0/0/4)	17 (0/0/4)	17 (0/1/4)
	MOVEP.W	(d_{16},An),Dn	10 (2/0/0)	12 (2/0/0)	12 (2/1/0)
	MOVEP.L	(d_{16},An),Dn	18 (4/0/0)	18 (4/0/0)	18 (4/1/0)
#*	MOVES	EA,Rn	7 (1/0/0)	7 (1/0/0)	8 (1/1/0)
#*	MOVES	Rn,EA	5 (0/0/1)	5 (0/0/1)	7 (0/1/1)
	MOVE	USP	0 (0/0/0)	2 (0/0/0)	3 (0/1/0)
	SWAP	Rx,Ry	1 (0/0/0)	4 (0/0/0)	4 (0/1/0)

n = number of registers to transfer
RL = Register List
* Add Fetch Effective Address time
# Add Calculate Effective Address time
#* Add Calculate Immediate Address time

9

9.2.8 Arithmetic/Logical Operations

The arithmetic/logical operations timing table indicates the number of clock periods needed for the processor to perform the specified arithmetic/logical operation using the specified addressing mode. It also includes, in worst case, the amount of time needed to prefetch the instruction. Footnotes specify when to add either fetch address or fetch immediate effective address time. This sum gives the total effective execution time for the operation using the specified addressing mode. The total number of clock cycles is outside the parentheses, the number of read, prefetch, and write cycles are given inside the parentheses as (r/p/w). They are included in the total clock cycle number.

	Instruction		Best Case	Cache Case	Worst Case
*	ADD	EA,Dn	0 (0/0/0)	2 (0/0/0)	3 (0/1/0)
*	ADD	EA,An	0 (0/0/0)	2 (0/0/0)	3 (0/1/0)
*	ADD	Dn,EA	3 (0/0/1)	4 (0/0/1)	6 (0/1/1)
*	AND	EA,Dn	0 (0/0/0)	2 (0/0/0)	3 (0/1/0)
*	AND	Dn,EA	3 (0/0/1)	4 (0/0/1)	6 (0/1/1)
*	EOR	Dn,Dn	0 (0/0/0)	2 (0/0/0)	3 (0/1/0)
*	EOR	Dn,Mem	3 (0/0/1)	4 (0/0/1)	6 (0/1/1)
*	OR	EA,Dn	0 (0/0/0)	2 (0/0/0)	3 (0/1/0)
*	OR	Dn,EA	3 (0/0/1)	4 (0/0/1)	6 (0/1/1)
*	SUB	EA,Dn	0 (0/0/0)	2 (0/0/0)	3 (0/1/0)
*	SUB	EA,An	0 (0/0/0)	2 (0/0/0)	3 (0/1/0)
*	SUB	Dn,EA	3 (0/0/1)	4 (0/0/1)	6 (0/1/1)
*	CMP	EA,Dn	0 (0/0/0)	2 (0/0/0)	3 (0/1/0)
*	CMP	EA,An	1 (0/0/0)	4 (0/0/0)	4 (0/1/0)
**	CMP2	EA,Rn	16 (1/0/0)	18 (1/0/0)	18 (1/1/0)
*	MUL.W	EA,Dn	25 (0/0/0)	27 (0/0/0)	28 (0/1/0)
**	MUL.L	EA,Dn	41 (0/0/0)	43 (0/0/0)	44 (0/1/0)
*	DIVU.W	EA,Dn	42 (0/0/0)	44 (0/0/0)	44 (0/1/0)
**	DIVU.L	EA,Dn	76 (0/0/0)	78 (0/0/0)	78 (0/1/0)
*	DIVS.W	EA,Dn	54 (0/0/0)	56 (0/0/0)	56 (0/1/0)
**	DIVS.L	EA,Dn	88 (0/0/0)	90 (0/0/0)	90 (0/1/0)

*   Add Fetch Effective Address time
** Add Fetch Immediate Address time

9.2.9 Immediate Arithmetic/Logical Operations

The immediate arithmetic/logical operations timing table indicates the number of clock periods needed for the processor to fetch the source immediate data value, and perform the specified arithmetic/logical operation using the specified destination addressing mode. Footnotes indicate when to add appropriate fetch effective or fetch immediate effective address times. This computation will give the total execution time needed to perform the appropriate immediate arithmetic/logical operation. The total number of clock cycles is outside the parentheses, the number of read, prefetch, and write cycles are given inside the parentheses as (r/p/w). They are included in the total clock cycle number.

	Instruction	Best Case	Cache Case	Worst Case
	MOVEQ #<data>,Dn	0 (0/0/0)	2 (0/0/0)	3 (0/1/0)
	ADDQ #<data>,Rn	0 (0/0/0)	2 (0/0/0)	3 (0/1/0)
*	ADDQ #<data>,Mem	3 (0/0/1)	4 (0/0/1)	6 (0/1/1)
	SUBQ #<data>,Rn	0 (0/0/0)	2 (0/0/0)	3 (0/1/0)
*	SUBQ #<data>,Mem	3 (0/0/1)	4 (0/0/1)	6 (0/1/1)
**	ADDI #<data>,Dn	0 (0/0/0)	2 (0/0/0)	3 (0/1/0)
**	ADDI #<data>,Mem	3 (0/0/1)	4 (0/0/1)	6 (0/1/1)
**	ANDI #<data>,Dn	0 (0/0/0)	2 (0/0/0)	3 (0/1/0)
**	ANDI #<data>,Mem	3 (0/0/1)	4 (0/0/1)	6 (0/1/1)
**	EORI #<data>,Dn	0 (0/0/0)	2 (0/0/0)	3 (0/1/0)
**	EORI #<data>,Mem	3 (0/0/1)	4 (0/0/1)	6 (0/1/1)
**	ORI #<data>,Dn	0 (0/0/0)	2 (0/0/0)	3 (0/1/0)
**	ORI #<data>,Mem	3 (0/0/1)	4 (0/0/1)	6 (0/1/1)
**	SUBI #<data>,Dn	0 (0/0/0)	2 (0/0/0)	3 (0/1/0)
**	SUBI #<data>,Mem	3 (0/0/1)	4 (0/0/1)	6 (0/1/1)
**	CMPI #<data>,EA	0 (0/0/0)	2 (0/0/0)	3 (0/1/0)

* Add Fetch Effective Address time
** Add Fetch Immediate Address time

9.2.10 Binary Coded Decimal Operations

The binary coded decimal operations table indicates the number of clock periods needed for the processor to perform the specified operation using the given addressing modes, with complete execution times given. No additional tables are needed to calculate total effective execution time for these instructions. The total number of clock cycles is outside the parentheses, the number of read, prefetch, and write cycles are given inside the parentheses as (r/p/w). They are included in the total clock cycle number.

Instruction	Best Case	Cache Case	Worst Case
ABCD Dn,Dn	4 (0/0/0)	4 (0/0/0)	5 (0/1/0)
ABCD −(An),−(An)	14 (2/0/1)	16 (2/0/1)	17 (2/1/1)
SBCD Dn,Dn	4 (0/0/0)	4 (0/0/0)	5 (0/1/0)
SBCD −(An),−(An)	14 (2/0/1)	16 (2/0/1)	17 (2/1/1)
ADDX Dn,Dn	2 (0/0/0)	2 (0/0/0)	3 (0/1/0)
ADDX −(An),−(An)	10 (2/0/1)	12 (2/0/1)	13 (2/1/1)
SUBX Dn,Dn	2 (0/0/0)	2 (0/0/0)	3 (0/1/0)
SUBX −(An),−(An)	10 (2/0/1)	12 (2/0/1)	13 (2/1/1)
CMPM (An)+,(An)+	8 (2/0/0)	9 (2/0/0)	10 (2/1/0)
PACK Dn,Dn,#<data>	3 (0/0/0)	6 (0/0/0)	7 (0/1/0)
PACK −(An),−(An),#<data>	11 (1/0/1)	13 (1/0/1)	13 (1/1/1)
UNPK Dn,Dn,#<data>	5 (0/0/0)	8 (0/0/0)	9 (0/1/0)
UNPK −(An),−(An),#<data>	11 (1/0/1)	13 (1/0/1)	13 (1/1/1)

9

9.2.11 Single Operand Instructions

The single operand instructions table indicates the number of clock periods needed for the processor to perform the specified operation on the given addressing mode. Footnotes indicate when it is necessary to add another table entry to calculate the total effective execution time for the instruction. The total number of clock cycles is outside the parentheses, the number of read, prefetch, and write cycles are given inside the parentheses as (r/p/w). They are included in the total clock cycle number.

	Instruction		Best Case	Cache Case	Worst Case
	CLR	Dn	0 (0/0/0)	2 (0/0/0)	3 (0/1/0)
#	CLR	Mem	3 (0/0/1)	4 (0/0/1)	6 (0/1/1)
	NEG	Dn	0 (0/0/0)	2 (0/0/0)	3 (0/1/0)
*	NEG	Mem	3 (0/0/1)	4 (0/0/1)	6 (0/1/1)
	NEGX	Dn	0 (0/0/0)	2 (0/0/0)	3 (0/1/0)
*	NEGX	Mem	3 (0/0/1)	4 (0/0/1)	6 (0/1/1)
	NOT	Dn	0 (0/0/0)	2 (0/0/0)	3 (0/1/0)
*	NOT	Mem	3 (0/0/1)	4 (0/0/1)	6 (0/1/1)
	EXT	Dn	1 (0/0/0)	4 (0/0/0)	4 (0/1/0)
	NBCD	Dn	6 (0/0/0)	6 (0/0/0)	6 (0/1/0)
	Scc	Dn	1 (0/0/0)	4 (0/0/0)	4 (0/1/0)
#	Scc	Mem	6 (0/0/1)	6 (0/0/1)	6 (0/1/1)
	TAS	Dn	1 (0/0/0)	4 (0/0/0)	4 (0/1/0)
#	TAS	Mem	12 (1/0/1)	12 (1/0/1)	13 (1/1/1)
*	TST	EA	0 (0/0/0)	2 (0/0/0)	3 (0/1/0)

* Add Fetch Effective Address time
# Add Calculate Effective Address time

9.2.12 Shift/Rotate Instructions

The shift/rotate instructions table indicates the number of clock periods needed for the processor to perform the specified operation on the given addressing mode. Footnotes indicate when it is necessary to add another table entry to calculate the total effective execution time for the instruction. The number of bits shifted does not affect execution time. The total number of clock cycles is outside the parentheses, the number of read, prefetch, and write cycles are given inside the parentheses as (r/p/w). They are included in the total clock cycle number.

	Instruction	Best Case	Cache Case	Worst Case
	LSL	Dn (Static)	1 (0/0/0)	4 (0/0/0)	4 (0/1/0)
	LSR	Dn (Static)	1 (0/0/0)	4 (0/0/0)	4 (0/1/0)
	LSL	Dn (Dynamic)	3 (0/0/0)	6 (0/0/0)	6 (0/1/0)
	LSR	Dn (Dynamic)	3 (0/0/0)	6 (0/0/0)	6 (0/1/0)
*	LSL	Mem by 1	5 (0/0/1)	5 (0/0/1)	6 (0/1/1)
*	LSR	Mem by 1	5 (0/0/1)	5 (0/0/1)	6 (0/1/1)
	ASL	Dn	5 (0/0/0)	8 (0/0/0)	8 (0/1/0)
	ASR	Dn	3 (0/0/0)	6 (0/0/0)	6 (0/1/0)
*	ASL	Mem by 1	6 (0/0/1)	6 (0/0/1)	7 (0/1/1)
*	ASR	Mem by 1	5 (0/0/1)	5 (0/0/1)	6 (0/1/1)
	ROL	Dn	5 (0/0/0)	8 (0/0/0)	8 (0/1/0)
	ROR	Dn	5 (0/0/0)	8 (0/0/0)	8 (0/1/0)
*	ROL	Mem by 1	7 (0/0/1)	7 (0/0/1)	7 (0/1/1)
*	ROR	Mem by 1	7 (0/0/1)	7 (0/0/1)	7 (0/1/1)
	ROXL	Dn	9 (0/0/0)	12 (0/0/0)	12 (0/1/0)
	ROXR	Dn	9 (0/0/0)	12 (0/0/0)	12 (0/1/0)
*	ROXd	Mem by 1	5 (0/0/1)	5 (0/0/1)	6 (0/1/1)

*   Add Fetch Effective Address time
d   Is direction of shift/rotate; L or R

9.2.13 Bit Manipulation Instructions

The bit manipulation instructions table indicates the number of clock periods needed for the processor to perform the specified bit operation on the given addressing mode. Footnotes indicate when it is necessary to add another table entry to calculate the total effective execution time for the instruction. The total number of clock cycles is outside the parentheses, the number of read, prefetch, and write cycles are given inside the parentheses as (r/p/w). They are included in the total clock cycle number.

	Instruction	Best Case	Cache Case	Worst Case
	BTST	#<data>,Dn	1 (0/0/0)	4 (0/0/0)	5 (0/1/0)
	BTST	Dn,Dn	1 (0/0/0)	4 (0/0/0)	5 (0/1/0)
**	BTST	#<data>,Mem	4 (0/0/0)	4 (0/0/0)	5 (0/1/0)
*	BTST	Dn,Mem	4 (0/0/0)	4 (0/0/0)	5 (0/1/0)
	BCHG	#<data>,Dn	1 (0/0/0)	4 (0/0/0)	5 (0/1/0)
	BCHG	Dn,Dn	1 (0/0/0)	4 (0/0/0)	5 (0/1/0)
**	BCHG	#<data>,Mem	4 (0/0/1)	4 (0/0/1)	5 (0/1/1)
*	BCHG	Dn,Mem	4 (0/0/1)	4 (0/0/1)	5 (0/1/1)
	BCLR	#<data>,Dn	1 (0/0/0)	4 (0/0/0)	5 (0/1/0)
	BCLR	Dn,Dn	1 (0/0/0)	4 (0/0/0)	5 (0/1/0)
**	BCLR	#<data>,Mem	4 (0/0/1)	4 (0/0/1)	5 (0/1/1)
*	BCLR	Dn,Mem	4 (0/0/1)	4 (0/0/1)	5 (0/1/1)
	BSET	#<data>,Dn	1 (0/0/0)	4 (0/0/0)	5 (0/1/0)
	BSET	Dn,Dn	1 (0/0/0)	4 (0/0/0)	5 (0/1/0)
**	BSET	#<data>,Mem	4 (0/0/1)	4 (0/0/1)	5 (0/1/1)
*	BSET	Dn,Mem	4 (0/0/1)	4 (0/0/1)	5 (0/1/1)

*   Add Fetch Effective Address time
**   Add Fetch Immediate Address time

9.2.14 Bit Field Manipulation Instructions

The bit field manipulation instructions table indicates the number of clock periods needed for the processor to perform the specified bit field operation using the given addressing mode. Footnotes indicate when it is necessary to add another table entry to calculate the total effective execution time for the instruction. The total number of clock cycles is outside the parentheses, the number of read, prefetch, and write cycles are given inside the parentheses as (r/p/w). They are included in the total clock cycle number.

	Instruction		Best Case	Cache Case	Worst Case
	BFTST	Dn	3 (0/0/0)	6 (0/0/0)	7 (0/1/0)
#*	BFTST	Mem (<5 bytes)	11 (1/0/0)	11 (1/0/0)	12 (1/1/0)
#*	BFTST	Mem (5 bytes)	15 (2/0/0)	15 (2/0/0)	16 (2/1/0)
	BFCHG	Dn	9 (0/0/0)	12 (0/0/0)	12 (0/1/0)
#*	BFCHG	Mem (<5 bytes)	16 (1/0/1)	16 (1/0/1)	16 (1/1/1)
#*	BFCHG	Mem (5 bytes)	24 (2/0/2)	24 (2/0/2)	24 (2/0/2)
	BFCLR	Dn	9 (0/0/0)	12 (0/0/0)	12 (0/1/0)
#*	BFCLR	Mem (<5 bytes)	16 (1/0/1)	16 (1/0/1)	16 (1/1/1)
#*	BFCLR	Mem (5 bytes)	24 (2/0/2)	24 (2/0/2)	24 (2/0/2)
	BFSET	Dn	9 (0/0/0)	12 (0/0/0)	12 (0/1/0)
#*	BFSET	Mem (<5 bytes)	16 (1/0/1)	16 (1/0/1)	16 (1/1/1)
#*	BFSET	Mem (5 bytes)	24 (2/0/2)	24 (2/0/2)	24 (2/0/2)
	BFEXTS	Dn	5 (0/0/0)	8 (0/0/0)	8 (0/1/0)
	BFEXTS	Mem (<5 Bytes)	13 (1/0/0)	13 (1/0/0)	13 (1/1/0)
	BFEXTS	MEM (5 Bytes)	18 (2/0/0)	18 (2/0/0)	18 (2/1/0)
	BFEXTU	Dn	5 (0/0/0)	8 (0/0/0)	8 (0/1/0)
	BFEXTU	Mem (<5 Bytes)	13 (1/0/0)	13 (1/0/0)	13 (1/1/0)
	BFEXTU	Mem (5 Bytes)	18 (2/0/0)	18 (2/0/0)	18 (2/1/0)
	BFINS	Dn	7 (0/0/0)	10 (0/0/0)	10 (0/1/0)
	BFINS	Mem (<5 Bytes)	14 (1/0/1)	14 (1/0/1)	15 (1/1/1)
	BFINS	Mem (5 Bytes)	20 (2/0/2)	20 (2/0/2)	21 (2/1/2)
	BFFFO	Dn	15 (0/0/0)	18 (0/0/0)	18 (0/1/0)
	BFFFO	Mem (<5 Bytes)	24 (1/0/0)	24 (1/0/0)	24 (1/1/0)
	BFFFO	Mem (5 Bytes)	32 (2/0/0)	32 (2/0/0)	32 (2/1/0)

#* Add Calculate Immediate Address time

NOTE: A bit field of 32 bits may span 5 bytes that requires two operand cycles to access, or may span 4 bytes that requires only one operand cycle to access.

9.2.15 Conditional Branch Instructions

The conditional branch instructions table indicates the number of clock periods needed for the processor to perform the specified branch on the given branch size, with complete execution times given. No additional tables are needed to calculate total effective execution time for these instructions. The total number of clock cycles is outside the parentheses, the number of read, prefetch, and write cycles are given inside the parentheses as (r/p/w). They are included in the total clock cycle number.

Instruction	Best Case	Cache Case	Worst Case
Bcc (taken)	3 (0/0/0)	6 (0/0/0)	9 (0/0/0)
Bcc.B (not taken)	1 (0/0/0)	4 (0/0/0)	5 (0/1/0)
Bcc.W (not taken)	3 (0/0/0)	6 (0/0/0)	7 (0/1/0)
Bcc.L (not taken)	3 (0/0/0)	6 (0/0/0)	9 (0/0/0)
DBcc (cc=false, count not expired)	3 (0/0/0)	6 (0/0/0)	9 (0/2/0)
DBcc (cc=false, count expired)	7 (0/0/0)	10 (0/0/0)	10 (0/3/0)
DBcc (cc=true)	3 (0/0/0)	6 (0/0/0)	7 (0/1/0)

9.2.16 Control Instructions

The control instructions table indicates the number of clock periods needed for the processor to perform the specified operation. Footnotes specify when it is necessary to add an entry from another table to calculate the total effective execution time for the given instruction. The total number of clock cycles is outside the parentheses, the number of read, prefetch, and write cycles are given inside the parentheses as (r/p/w). They are included in the total clock cycle number.

	Instruction	Best Case	Cache Case	Worst Case
	ANDI to SR	9 (0/0/0)	12 (0/0/0)	15 (0/2/0)
	EORI to SR	9 (0/0/0)	12 (0/0/0)	15 (0/2/0)
	ORI to SR	9 (0/0/0)	12 (0/0/0)	15 (0/2/0)
	ANDI to CCR	9 (0/0/0)	12 (0/0/0)	15 (0/2/0)
	EORI to CCR	9 (0/0/0)	12 (0/0/0)	15 (0/2/0)
	ORI to CCR	9 (0/0/0)	12 (0/0/0)	15 (0/2/0)
	BSR	5 (0/0/1)	7 (0/0/1)	13 (0/2/1)
**	CALLM (type 0)	28 (2/0/6)	30 (2/0/6)	36 (2/2/6)
**	CALLM (type 1) — no stack copy —	48 (5/0/8)	50 (5/0/8)	56 (5/2/8)
**	CALLM (type 1) — no stack copy —	55 (6/0/8)	57 (6/0/8)	64 (6/2/8)
**	CALLM (type 1) — stack copy —	$63+6n$ $(7+n/0/8+n)$	$65+6n$ $(7+n/0/8+n)$	$71+6n$ $(7+n/2/8+n)$
#*	CAS (successful compare)	15 (1/0/1)	15 (1/0/1)	16 (1/1/1)
	CAS (unsuccessful compare)	12 (1/0/0)	12 (1/0/0)	13 (1/1/0)
	CAS2 (successful compare)	23 (2/0/2)	25 (2/0/2)	28 (2/2/2)
	CAS2 (unsuccessful compare)	19 (2/0/0)	22 (2/0/0)	25 (2/2/0)
*	CHK	8 (0/0/0)	8 (0/0/0)	8 (0/1/0)
**	CHK2 FA,Rn	16 (2/0/0)	18 (2/0/0)	18 (2/1/0)
%	JMP	1 (0/0/0)	4 (0/0/0)	7 (0/2/0)
%	JSR	3 (0/0/1)	5 (0/0/1)	11 (0/2/1)
//	LEA	2 (0/0/0)	2 (0/0/0)	3 (0/1/0)
	LINK.W	3 (0/0/1)	5 (0/0/1)	7 (0/1/1)
	LINK.L	4 (0/0/1)	6 (0/0/1)	10 (0/2/1)
	NOP	2 (0/0/0)	2 (0/0/0)	3 (0/1/0)
#	PEA	3 (0/0/1)	5 (0/0/1)	6 (0/1/1)
	RTD	9 (1/0/0)	10 (1/0/0)	12 (1/2/0)
	RTM (type 0)	18 (4/0/0)	19 (4/0/0)	22 (4/2/0)
	RTM (type 1)	31 (6/0/1)	32 (6/0/1)	35 (6/2/1)
	RTR	13 (2/0/0)	14 (2/0/0)	15 (2/2/0)
	RTS	9 (1/0/0)	10 (1/0/0)	12 (1/2/0)
	UNLK	5 (1/0/0)	6 (1/0/0)	7 (1/1/0)

n   number of operand transfers required
*   Add Fetch Effective Address time
#   Add Calculate Effective Address time
%   Add Jump Effective Address time
**   Add Fetch Immediate Address time
#*   Add Calculate Immediate Address time

9.2.17 Exception Related Instructions

The exception related instructions table indicates the number of clock periods needed for the processor to perform the specified exception related action. Footnotes specify when it is necessary to add the entry from another table to calculate the total effective execution time for the given instruction. The total number of clock cycles is outside the parentheses, the number of read, prefetch, and write cycles are given inside the parentheses as (r/p/w). They are included in the total clock cycle number.

Instruction	Best Case	Cache Case	Worst Case
BKPT	9 (1/0/0)	10 (1/0/0)	10 (1/0/0)
Interrupt (I-stack)	26 (2/0/4)	26 (2/0/4)	33 (2/2/4)
Interrupt (M-stack)	41 (2/0/8)	41 (2/0/8)	48 (2/2/8)
RESET Instruction	518 (0/0/0)	518 (0/0/0)	519 (0/1/0)
STOP	8 (0/0/0)	8 (0/0/0)	8 (0/0/0)
Trace	25 (1/0/5)	25 (1/0/5)	32 (1/2/5)
TRAP #n	20 (1/0/4)	20 (1/0/4)	27 (1/2/4)
Illegal Instruction	20 (1/0/4)	20 (1/0/4)	27 (1/2/4)
A-Line Trap	20 (1/0/4)	20 (1/0/4)	27 (1/2/4)
F-Line Trap	20 (1/0/4)	20 (1/0/4)	27 (1/2/4)
Privilege Violation	20 (1/0/4)	20 (1/0/4)	27 (1/2/4)
TRAPcc (trap)	23 (1/0/5)	25 (1/0/5)	32 (1/2/5)
TRAPcc (no trap)	1 (0/0/0)	4 (0/0/0)	5 (0/1/0)
TRAPcc.W (trap)	23 (1/0/5)	25 (1/0/5)	33 (1/3/5)
TRAPcc.W (no trap)	3 (0/0/0)	6 (0/0/0)	7 (0/1/0)
TRAPcc.L (trap)	23 (1/0/5)	25 (1/0/5)	33 (1/3/5)
TRAPcc.L (no trap)	5 (0/0/0)	8 (0/0/0)	10 (0/2/0)
TRAPV (trap)	23 (1/0/5)	25 (1/0/5)	32 (1/2/5)
TRAPV (no trap)	1 (0/0/0)	4 (0/0/0)	5 (0/1/0)

9.2.18 Save and Restore Operations

The save and restore operations table indicates the number of clock periods needed for the processor to perform the specified state save, or return from exception, with complete execution times and stack length given. No additional tables are needed to calculate total effective execution time for these operations. The total number of clock cycles is outside the parentheses, the number of read, prefetch, and write cycles are given inside the parentheses as (r/p/w). They are included in the total clock cycle number.

Operation	Best Case	Cache Case	Worst Case
Bus Cycle Fault (Short)	42 (1/0/10)	43 (1/0/10)	50 (1/2/10)
Bus Cycle Fault (Long)	79 (1/0/24)	79 (1/0/24)	86 (1/2/24)
RTE (Normal)	20 (4/0/0)	21 (4/0/0)	24 (4/2/0)
RTE (Six-Word)	20 (4/0/0)	21 (4/0/0)	24 (4/2/0)
RTE (Throwaway) *	15 (4/0/0)	16 (4/0/0)	39 (4/0/0)
RTE (Coprocessor)	31 (7/0/0)	32 (7/0/0)	33 (7/1/0)
RTE (Short Fault)	42 (10/0/0)	43 (10/0/0)	45 (10/2/0)
RTE (Long Fault)	91 (24/0/0)	92 (24/0/0)	94 (24/2/0)

*Add the time for RTE on second stack frame.

SECTION 10
ELECTRICAL SPECIFICATIONS

This section contains electrical specifications and associated timing information for the MC68020.

10.1 MAXIMUM RATINGS

Rating	Symbol	Value	Unit
Supply Voltage	V_{CC}	−0.3 to +7.0	V
Input Voltage	V_{in}	−0.3 to +7.0	V
Operating Temperature Range	T_A	0 to 70	°C
Storage Temperature Range	T_{stg}	−55 to 150	°C

This device contains protective circuitry against damage due to high static voltages or electrical fields; however, it is advised that normal precautions be taken to avoid application of any voltages higher than maximum-rated voltages to this high-impedance circuit. Reliability of operation is enhanced if unused inputs are tied to an appropriate logic voltage level (e.g., either GND or V_{CC}).

10.2 THERMAL CHARACTERISTICS – PGA PACKAGE

Characteristic	Symbol	Value	Rating
Thermal Resistance — Ceramic			°C/W
Junction to Ambient	θ_{JA}	30*	
Junction to Case	θ_{JC}	15*	

*Estimated

10.3 POWER CONSIDERATIONS

The average chip-junction temperature, T_J, in °C can be obtained from:

$$T_J = T_A + (P_D \bullet \theta_{JA}) \qquad (1)$$

Where:

T_A = Ambient Temperature, °C

θ_{JA} = Package Thermal Resistance, Junction-to-Ambient, °C/W

$P_D = P_{INT} + P_{I/O}$

$P_{INT} = I_{CC} \times V_{CC}$, Watts — Chip Internal Power

$P_{I/O}$ = Power Dissipation on Input and Output Pins — User Determined

For most applications $P_{I/O} < P_{INT}$ and can be neglected.

An approximate relationship between P_D and T_J (if $P_{I/O}$ is neglected) is:

$$P_D = K \div (T_J + 273°C) \qquad (2)$$

Solving equations 1 and 2 for K gives:

$$K = P_D \bullet (T_A + 273°C) + \theta_{JA} \bullet P_D{}^2 \qquad (3)$$

Where K is a constant pertaining to the particular part. K can be determined from equation 3 by measuring P_D (at equilibrium) for a known T_A. Using this value of K the values of P_D and T_J can be obtained by solving equations (1) and (2) iteratively for any value of T_A.

The total thermal resistance of a package (θ_{JA}) can be separated into two components, θ_{JC} and θ_{CA}, representing the barrier to heat flow from the semiconductor junction to the package (case) surface (θ_{JC}) and from the case to the outside ambient (θ_{CA}). These terms are related by the equation:

$$\theta_{JA} = \theta_{JC} + \theta_{CA} \qquad\qquad (4)$$

θ_{JC} is device related and cannot be influenced by the user. However, θ_{CA} is user dependent and can be minimized by such thermal management techniques as heat sinks, ambient air cooling and thermal convention. Thus, good thermal management on the part of the user can significantly reduce θ_{CA} so that θ_{JA} approximately equals θ_{JC}. Substitution of θ_{JC} for θ_{JA} in equation (1) will result in a lower semiconductor junction temperature.

Values for thermal resistance presented in this data sheet, unless estimated, were derived using the procedure described in Motorola Reliability Report 7843, "Thermal Resistance Measurement Method for MC68XX Microcomponent Devices," and are provided for design purposes only. Thermal measurements are complex and dependent on procedure and setup. User derived values for thermal resistance may differ.

10.4 DC ELECTRICAL CHARACTERISTICS
($V_{CC} = 5.0$ Vdc $\pm 5\%$; $V_{SS} = 0$ Vdc, $T_A = 0$ to 70°C; see Figures 10-1, 10-2, and 10-3)

Characteristic		Symbol	Min	Max	Unit
Input High Voltage		V_{IH}	2.0	V_{CC}	V
Input Low Voltage		V_{IL}	−0.5	0.8	V
Input Leakage Current $V_{SS} \leq V_{in} \leq V_{CC}$	$\overline{BERR}$, $\overline{BR}$, $\overline{BGACK}$, CLK, $\overline{IPL0}$-$\overline{IPL2}$, $\overline{AVEC}$, $\overline{CDIS}$, $\overline{DSACK0}$, $\overline{DSACK1}$ $\overline{HALT}$, $\overline{RESET}$	I_{in}	−2.5 −20	2.5 20	µA µA
Hi-Z (Off-State) Leakage Current @ 2.4 V/0.5 V	A0-A31, $\overline{AS}$, $\overline{DBEN}$, $\overline{DS}$, D0-D31, FC0-FC2, R/$\overline{W}$, $\overline{RMC}$, SIZ0-SIZ1	I_{TSI}	−20	20	µA
Output High Voltage $I_{OH} = -400$ µA	A0-A31, $\overline{AS}$, $\overline{BG}$, D0-D31, $\overline{DBEN}$, $\overline{DS}$, $\overline{ECS}$, R/$\overline{W}$, $\overline{IPEND}$, $\overline{OCS}$, $\overline{RMC}$, SIZ0-SIZ1, FC0-FC2	V_{OH}	2.4	−	V
Output Low Voltage $I_{OL} = 3.2$ mA $I_{OL} = 5.3$ mA $I_{OL} = 2.0$ mA $I_{OL} = 10.7$ mA	A0-A31, FC0-FC2, SIZ0-SIZ1, $\overline{BG}$, D0-D31 $\overline{AS}$, $\overline{DS}$, R/$\overline{W}$, $\overline{RMC}$, $\overline{DBEN}$, $\overline{IPEND}$ $\overline{ECS}$, $\overline{OCS}$ $\overline{HALT}$, $\overline{RESET}$	V_{OL}	− − − −	0.5 0.5 0.5 0.5	V V V V
Power Dissipation ($T_A = 0$°C)		P_D	−	1.75	W
Capacitance (see Note 1) $V_{in} = 0$ V, $T_A = 25$°C, f = 1 MHz		C_{in}	−	20.0	pF

NOTE:
1. Capacitance is periodically sampled rather than 100% tested.

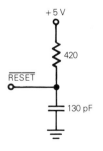

Figure 10-1. $\overline{\text{RESET}}$ Test Load

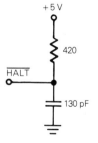

Figure 10-2. $\overline{\text{HALT}}$ Test Load

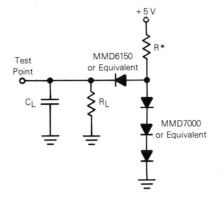

$C_L = 50$ pF for $\overline{ECS}$ and $\overline{OCS}$
$C_L = 130$ pF for All Other (Includes all Parasitics)
$R_L = 6.0$ kΩ

* $R = 1.22$ kΩ for A0-A31, D0-D31, $\overline{BG}$, FC0-FC2, SIZ0-SIZ1
  $R = 2$ kΩ for $\overline{ECS}$, $\overline{OCS}$
  $R = 740$ Ω for $\overline{AS}$, $\overline{DS}$, R/$\overline{W}$, $\overline{RMC}$, $\overline{DBEN}$, $\overline{IPEND}$

Figure 10-3. Test Loads

10.5 AC ELECTRICAL SPECIFICATIONS – CLOCK INPUT (See Figure 10-4)

Num	Characteristic	Symbol	MC68020RC12		MC68020RC16		Unit
			Min	Max	Min	Max	
	Frequency of Operation	f	8	12.5	8	16.7	MHz
1	Cycle Time	t_{cyc}	80	125	60	125	ns
2, 3	Clock Pulse Width	t_{CL}, t_{CH}	32	125	24	95	ns
4, 5	Rise and Fall Times	t_{Cr}, t_{Cf}	—	5	—	5	ns

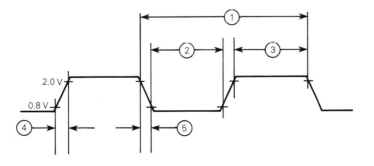

NOTE:
   Timing measurements are referenced to and from a low voltage of 0.8 volt and a high voltage of 2.0 volts, unless otherwise noted. The voltage swing through this range should start outside, and pass through, the range such that the rise or fall will be linear between 0.8 volt and 2.0 volts.

Figure 10-4. Clock Input Timing Diagram

10.6 AC ELECTRICAL SPECIFICATIONS – READ AND WRITE CYCLES

(V_{CC} = 5.0 Vdc $\pm$ 5%; GND = 0 Vdc; T_A = 0 to 70°C; see Figures 10-5, 10-6, and 10-7)

Num	Characteristic	Symbol	MC68020RC12		MC68020RC16		Unit
			Min	Max	Min	Max	
6	Clock High to Address/FC/Size/$\overline{RMC}$ Valid	t_{CHAV}	0	40	0	30	ns
6A	Clock High to $\overline{ECS}$, $\overline{OCS}$ Asserted	t_{CHEV}	0	30	0	20	ns
7	Clock High to Address, Data, FC, $\overline{RMC}$, Size High Impedance	t_{CHAZx}	0	80	0	60	ns
8	Clock High to Address/FC/Size/$\overline{RMC}$ Invalid	t_{CHAZn}	0	—	0	—	ns
9	Clock Low to $\overline{AS}$, $\overline{DS}$ Asserted	t_{CLSA}	3	40	3	30	ns
9A[1]	$\overline{AS}$ to $\overline{DS}$ Assertion (Read) (Skew)	t_{STSA}	– 20	20	– 15	15	ns
10	$\overline{ECS}$ Width Asserted	t_{ECSA}	25	—	20	—	ns
10A	$\overline{OCS}$ Width Asserted	t_{OCSA}	25	—	20	—	ns
11[6]	Address/FC/Size/$\overline{RMC}$ Valid to $\overline{AS}$ (and $\overline{DS}$ Asserted Read)	t_{AVSA}	20	—	15	—	ns
12	Clock Low to $\overline{AS}$, $\overline{DS}$ Negated	t_{CLSN}	0	40	0	30	ns
12A	Clock Low to $\overline{ECS}/\overline{OCS}$ Negated	t_{CLEN}	0	40	0	30	ns
13	$\overline{AS}$, $\overline{DS}$ Negated to Address, FC, Size Invalid	t_{SNAI}	20	—	15	—	ns
14	$\overline{AS}$ (and $\overline{DS}$ Read) Width Asserted	t_{SWA}	120	—	100	—	ns
14A	$\overline{DS}$ Width Asserted Write	t_{SWAW}	50	—	40	—	ns
15	$\overline{AS}$, $\overline{DS}$ Width Negated	t_{SN}	50	—	40	—	ns
16	Clock High to $\overline{AS}$, $\overline{DS}$, R/$\overline{W}$, $\overline{DBEN}$ High Impedance	t_{CSZ}	—	80	—	60	ns
17[6]	$\overline{AS}$, $\overline{DS}$ Negated to R/$\overline{W}$ High	t_{SNRN}	20	—	15	—	ns
18	Clock High to R/$\overline{W}$ High	t_{CHRH}	0	40	0	30	ns
20	Clock High to R/$\overline{W}$ Low	t_{CHRL}	0	40	0	30	ns
21[6]	R/$\overline{W}$ High to $\overline{AS}$ Asserted	t_{RAAA}	20	—	15	—	ns
22[6]	R/$\overline{W}$ Low to $\overline{DS}$ Asserted (Write)	t_{RASA}	90	—	70	—	ns
23	Clock High to Data Out Valid	t_{CHDO}	—	40	—	30	ns
25[6]	$\overline{DS}$ Negated to Data Out Invalid	t_{SNDI}	20	—	15	—	ns
26[6]	Data Out Valid to $\overline{DS}$ Asserted (Write)	t_{DVSA}	20	—	15	—	ns
27	Data-In Valid to Clock Low (Data Setup)	t_{DICL}	10	—	5	—	ns
27A	Late $\overline{BERR}/\overline{HALT}$ Asserted to Clock Low Setup Time	t_{BELCL}	25	—	20	—	ns
28	$\overline{AS}$, $\overline{DS}$ Negated to $\overline{DSACKx}$, $\overline{BERR}$, $\overline{HALT}$, $\overline{AVEC}$ Negated	t_{SNDN}	0	110	0	80	ns
29	$\overline{DS}$ Negated to Data-In Invalid (Data-In Hold Time)	t_{SNDI}	0	—	0	—	ns
29A	$\overline{DS}$ Negated to Data-In (High Impedance)	t_{SNDI}	—	80	—	60	ns
31[2]	$\overline{DSACKx}$ Asserted to Data-In Valid	t_{DADI}	—	60	—	50	ns
31A[3]	$\overline{DSACKx}$ Asserted to $\overline{DSACKx}$ Valid ($\overline{DSACK}$ Asserted Skew)	t_{DADV}	—	20	—	15	ns
32	$\overline{RESET}$ Input Transition Time	t_{HRrf}	—	2.5	—	2.5	Clk Per
33	Clock Low to $\overline{BG}$ Asserted	t_{CLBA}	0	40	0	30	ns
34	Clock Low to $\overline{BG}$ Negated	t_{CLBN}	0	40	0	30	ns
35	$\overline{BR}$ Asserted to $\overline{BG}$ Asserted ($\overline{RMC}$ Not Asserted)	t_{BRAGA}	1.5	3.5	1.5	3.5	Clk Per
37	$\overline{BGACK}$ Asserted to $\overline{BG}$ Negated	t_{GAGN}	1.5	3.5	1.5	3.5	Clk Per
39	$\overline{BG}$ Width Negated	t_{GN}	120	—	90	—	ns
39A	$\overline{BG}$ Width Asserted	t_{GA}	120	—	90	—	ns
40	Clock High to $\overline{DBEN}$ Asserted (Read)	t_{CHDAR}	0	40	0	30	ns

10

10.6 AC ELECTRICAL SPECIFICATIONS – READ AND WRITE CYCLES (Continued)
(V$_{CC}$ = 5.0 Vdc ± 5%; GND = 0 Vdc; T$_A$ = 0 to 70°C; see Figures 10-5, 10-6, and 10-7)

Num	Characteristic		Symbol	MC68020RC12		MC68020RC16		Unit
				Min	Max	Min	Max	
41	Clock Low to DBEN Negated (Read)		t$_{CLDNR}$	0	40	0	30	ns
42	Clock Low to DBEN Asserted (Write)		t$_{CLDAW}$	0	40	0	30	ns
43	Clock High to DBEN Negated (Write)		t$_{CHDNW}$	0	40	0	30	ns
44[6]	R/W̄ Low to DBEN Asserted (Write)		t$_{RADA}$	20	—	15	—	ns
45[5]	DBEN Width Asserted	Read	t$_{DA}$	80	—	60	—	ns
		Write		160	—	120	—	ns
46	R/W̄ Width Asserted (Write or Read)		t$_{RWA}$	180	—	150	—	ns
47a	Asynchronous Input Setup Time		t$_{AIST}$	10	—	5	—	ns
47b	Asynchronous Input Hold Time		t$_{AIHT}$	20	—	15	—	ns
48[4]	DSACKx Asserted to BERR, HALT Asserted		t$_{DABA}$	—	35	—	30	ns
53	Data Out Hold from Clock High		t$_{DOCH}$	0	—	0	—	ns
55	R/W̄ Asserted to Data Bus Impedance Change		t$_{RADC}$	40	—	40	—	ns
56	RESET Pulse Width (Reset Instruction)		t$_{HRPW}$	512	—	512	—	Clks
57	BERR Negated to HALT Negated (Rerun)		t$_{BNHN}$	0	—	0	—	ns

NOTES:
1. This number can be reduced to 5 nanoseconds if strobes have equal loads.
2. If the asynchronous setup time (#47) requirements are satisfied, the DSACKx low to data setup time (#31) and DSACKx low to BERR low setup time (#48) can be ignored. The data must only satisfy the data-in to clock low setup time (#27) for the following clock cycle, BERR must only satisfy the late BERR low to clock low setup time (#27A) for the following clock cycle.
3. This parameter specifies the maximum allowable skew between DSACK0 to DSACK1 asserted or DSACK1 to DSACK0 asserted, specification #47 must be met by DSACK0 or DSACK1.
4. In the absence of DSACKx, BERR is an asynchronous input using the asynchronous input setup time (#47).
5. DBEN may stay asserted on consecutive write cycles.
6. Actual value depends on the clock input waveform.

Timing Diagrams (Figures 10-5, 10-6, and 10-7) are located on foldout pages at the end of this document.

10

10.7 AC ELECTRICAL CHARACTERISTICS – TYPICAL CAPACITANCE DERATING CURVES

Figures 10-8 through 10-13 provide the capacitance derating curves for the MC68020. These graphs may not be linear outside of range shown. Capacitance includes stray capacitance.

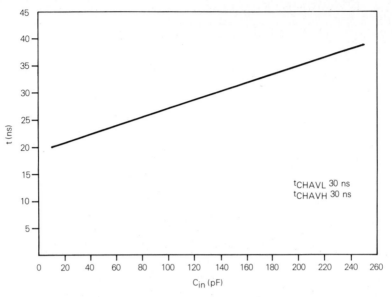

Figure 10-8. Address Capacitance Derating Curve

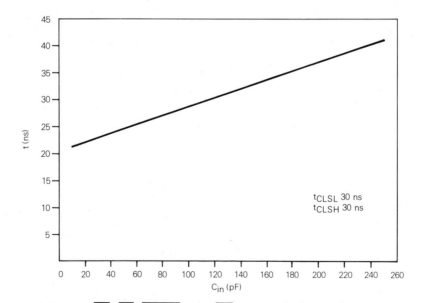

Figure 10-9. $\overline{DS}$, $\overline{AS}$, $\overline{IPEND}$, and $\overline{BG}$ Capacitance Derating Curve

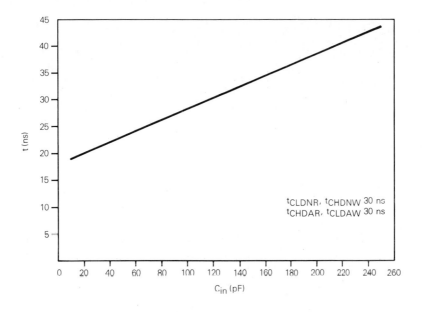

Figure 10-10. $\overline{DBEN}$ Capacitance Derating Curve

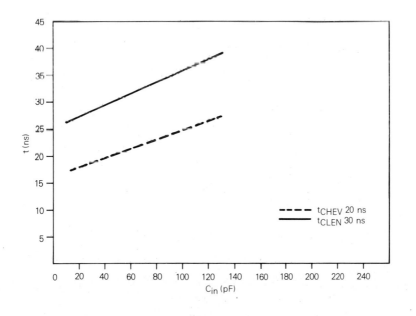

Figure 10-11. $\overline{ECS}$ and $\overline{OCS}$ Capacitance Derating Curve

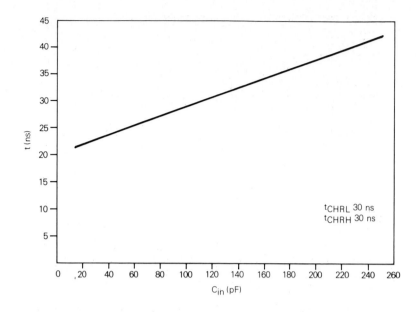

Figure 10-12. R/$\overline{\text{W}}$, FC, SIZ0-SIZ1, and $\overline{\text{RMC}}$ Capacitance Derating Curve

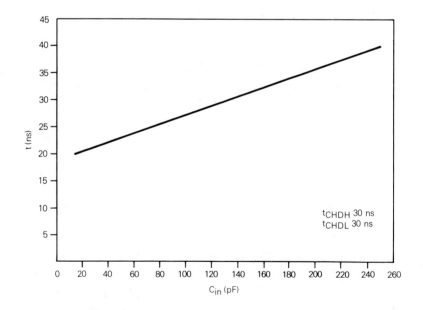

Figure 10-13. Data Capacitance Derating Curve

SECTION 11
ORDERING INFORMATION AND MECHANICAL DATA

This section contains the pin assignments and package dimensions of the MC68020. In addition, detailed information is provided to be used as a guide when ordering.

11.1 STANDARD MC68020 ORDERING INFORMATION

Package Type	Frequency (MHz)	Temperature	Order Number
Pin Grid Array	12.5	0°C to 70°C	MC68020RC12
RC Suffix	16.7	0°C to 70°C	MC68020RC16

11

11.2 PACKAGE DIMENSIONS AND PIN ASSIGNMENT

MC68020
RC Suffix Package
Preliminary
Mechanical
Detail

DIM	MILLIMETERS		INCHES	
	MIN	MAX	MIN	MAX
A	34.18	34.90	1.345	1.375
B	34.18	34.90	1.345	1.375
C	2.67	3.17	.100	.150
D0	.46	.51	.017	.019
G	2.54 BSC		.100 BSC	
K	4.32	4.82	.170	.190
V	1.74	2.28	.065	.095

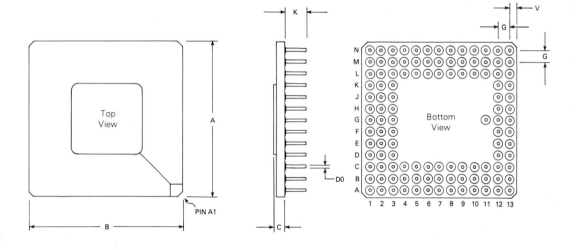

11

Pin Number	Function
A1	$\overline{BGACK}$
A2	A1
A3	A31
A4	A28
A5	A26
A6	A23
A7	A22
A8	A19
A9	V_{CC}
A10	GND
A11	A14
A12	A11
A13	A8
B1	GND
B2	$\overline{BG}$
B3	$\overline{BR}$
B4	A30
B5	A27
B6	A24
B7	A20
B8	A18
B9	GND
B10	A15
B11	A13
B12	A10
B13	A6
C1	RESET
C2	CLOCK
C3	GND
C4	A0
C5	A29
C6	A25
C7	A21
C8	A17
C9	A16
C10	A12
C11	A9
C12	A7
C13	A5

Pin Number	Function
D1	V_{CC}
D2	V_{CC}
D3	V_{CC}
D4-D11	—
D12	A4
D13	A3
E1	FC0
E2	$\overline{RMC}$
E3	V_{CC}
E12	A2
E13	$\overline{OCS}$
F1	SIZ0
F2	FC2
F3	FC1
F12	GND
F13	$\overline{IPEND}$
G1	$\overline{ECS}$
G2	SIZ1
G3	$\overline{DBEN}$
G11	V_{CC}
G12	GND
G13	V_{CC}
H1	$\overline{CDIS}$
H2	$\overline{AVEC}$
H3	$\overline{DSACK0}$
H12	IPL2
H13	GND
J1	$\overline{DSACK1}$
J2	$\overline{BERR}$
J3	GND
J12	$\overline{IPL0}$
J13	$\overline{IPL1}$

Pin Number	Function
K1	GND
K2	$\overline{HALT}$
K3	GND
K12	D1
K13	D0
L1	$\overline{AS}$
L2	$R/\overline{W}$
L3	D30
L4	D27
L5	D23
L6	D19
L7	GND
L8	D15
L9	D11
L10	D7
L11	GND
L12	D3
L13	D2
M1	$\overline{DS}$
M2	D29
M3	D26
M4	D24
M5	D21
M6	D18
M7	D16
M8	V_{CC}
M9	D13
M10	D10
M11	D6
M12	D5
M13	D4
N1	D31
N2	D28
N3	D25
N4	D22
N5	D20
N6	D17
N7	GND
N8	V_{CC}
N9	D14
N10	D12
N11	D9
N12	D8
N13	V_{CC}

The V_{CC} and GND pins are separated into three groups to provide individual power supply connections for the address bus buffers, data bus buffers, and all other output buffers and internal logic.

Group	V_{CC}	GND
Address Bus	A9, D3	A10, B9, C3, F12
Data Bus	M8, N8, N13	L7, L11, N7, K3
Logic	D1, D2, E3, G11, G13	G12, H13, J3, K1
Clock		B1

11

11

APPENDIX A
CONDITION CODES COMPUTATION

A.1 INTRODUCTION

This appendix provides a discussion of how the condition codes were developed, the meanings of each bit, how they are computed, and how they are represented in the instruction set details.

Two criteria were used in developing the condition codes:
- Consistency — across instruction, uses, and instances
- Meaningful Results — no change unless it provides useful information

The consistency across instructions means that instructions which are special cases of more general instructions affect the condition codes in the same way. Consistency across instances means that if an instruction ever affects a condition code, it will always affect that condition code. Consistency across uses means that whether the condition codes were set by a compare, test, or move instruction, the conditional instructions test the same situation. The tests used for the conditional instructions and the code computations are given in paragraph A.5.

A.2 CONDITION CODE REGISTER

The condition code register portion of the status register contains five bits:
    N — Negative
    Z — Zero
    V — Overflow
    C — Carry
    X — Extend

The first four bits are true condition code bits in that they reflect the condition of the result of a processor operation. The X bit is an operand for multiprecision computations. The carry bit (C) and the multiprecision operand extend bit (X) are separate in the M68000 Family to simplify the programming model.

A.3 CONDITION CODE REGISTER NOTATION

In the instruction set details given in **APPENDIX B,** the description of the effect on the condition codes is given in the following form:

Condition Codes: X   N   Z   V   C

A

where:

N (negative)	Set if the most significant bit of the result is set. Cleared otherwise.
Z (zero)	Set if the result equals zero. Cleared otherwise.
V (overflow)	Set if there was an arithmetic overflow. This implies that the result is not representable in the operand size. Cleared otherwise.
C (carry)	Set if a carry is generated out of the most significant bit of the operands for an addition. Also, set if a borrow is generated in a subtraction. Cleared otherwise.
X (extend)	Transparent to data movement. When affected, by arithmetic operations, it is set the same as the C bit.

The convention for the notation that is used in the condition code register representation is:

* set according to the result of the operation
– not affected by the operation
0 cleared
1 set
U undefined after the operation

A.4 CONDITION CODE COMPUTATION

Most operations take a source operand and a destination operand, compute, and store the result in the destination location. Unary operations take a destination operand, compute, and store the result in the destination location. Table A-1 details how each instruction sets the condition codes.

A.5 CONDITION TESTS

Table A-2 lists the condition names, encodings, and tests for the condition branch and set instructions. The test associated with each condition is a logical formula based on the current state of the condition codes. If this formula evaluates to one, the condition succeeds, or is true. If the formula evaluates to zero, the condition is unsuccessful, or false. For example, the T condition always succeeds, while the EQ condition succeeds only if the Z bit is currently set in the condition codes.

A

Table A-1. Condition Code Computations

Operations	X	N	Z	V	C	Special Definition
ABCD	*	U	?	U	?	C = Decimal Carry $Z = Z \wedge \overline{Rm} \wedge \ldots \wedge \overline{R0}$
ADD, ADDI, ADDQ	*	*	*	?	?	$V = Sm \wedge Dm \wedge \overline{Rm} \vee \overline{Sm} \wedge \overline{Dm} \wedge Rm$ $C = Sm \wedge Dm \vee \overline{Rm} \wedge Dm \vee Sm \wedge \overline{Rm}$
ADDX	*	*	?	?	?	$V = Sm \wedge Dm \wedge \overline{Rm} \vee \overline{Sm} \wedge \overline{Dm} \wedge Rm$ $C = Sm \wedge Dm \vee \overline{Rm} \wedge Dm \vee Sm \wedge \overline{Rm}$ $Z = Z \wedge \overline{Rm} \wedge \ldots \wedge \overline{R0}$
AND, ANDI, EOR, EORI, MOVEQ, MOVE, OR, ORI, CLR, EXT, NOT, TAS, TST	—	*	*	0	0	
CHK	—	*	U	U	U	
CHK2, CMP2	—	U	?	U	?	$Z = (R = LB) \vee (R = UB)$ $C = (LB < = UB) \wedge ((R < LB) \vee (R > UB)) \vee$ $(UB < LB) \wedge (R > UB) \wedge (R < LB)$
SUB, SUBI, SUBQ	*	*	*	?	?	$V = \overline{Sm} \wedge Dm \wedge \overline{Rm} \vee Sm \wedge \overline{Dm} \wedge Rm$ $C = Sm \wedge \overline{Dm} \vee Rm \wedge \overline{Dm} \vee Sm \wedge Rm$
SUBX	*	*	?	?	?	$V = \overline{Sm} \wedge Dm \wedge \overline{Rm} \vee Sm \wedge \overline{Dm} \wedge Rm$ $C = Sm \wedge \overline{Dm} \vee Rm \wedge \overline{Dm} \vee Sm \wedge Rm$ $Z = Z \wedge \overline{Rm} \wedge \ldots \wedge \overline{R0}$
CAS, CAS2, CMP, CMPI, CMPM	—	*	*	?	?	$V = \overline{Sm} \wedge Dm \wedge \overline{Rm} \vee Sm \wedge \overline{Dm} \wedge Rm$ $C = Sm \wedge \overline{Dm} \vee Rm \wedge \overline{Dm} \vee Sm \wedge Rm$
DIVS, DIVU	—	*	*	?	0	V = Division Overflow
MULS, MULU	—	*	*	?	0	V = Multiplication Overflow
SBCD, NBCD	*	U	?	U	?	C = Decimal Borrow $Z = Z \wedge \overline{Rm} \wedge \ldots \wedge \overline{R0}$
NEG	*	*	*	?	?	$V = Dm \wedge Rm$, $C = Dm \vee Rm$
NEGX	*	*	?	?	?	$V = Dm \wedge Rm$, $C = Dm \vee Rm$ $Z = Z \wedge \overline{Rm} \wedge \ldots \wedge \overline{R0}$
BTST, BCHG, BSET, BCLR	—	—	?	—	—	$Z = \overline{Dn}$
BFTST, BFCHG, BFSET, BFCLR	—	?	?	0	0	N = Dm $Z = \overline{Dm} \wedge \overline{Dm-1} \wedge \ldots \wedge \overline{D0}$
BFEXTS, BFEXTU, BFFFO	—	?	?	0	0	N = Sm $Z = \overline{Sm} \wedge \overline{Sm-1} \wedge \ldots \wedge \overline{S0}$
BFINS	—	?	?	0	0	N = Dm $Z = \overline{Dm} \wedge \overline{Dm-1} \wedge \ldots \wedge \overline{D0}$
ASL	*	*	*	?	?	$V = Dm \wedge (\overline{Dm-1} \vee \ldots \vee \overline{Dm-r}) \vee \overline{Dm} \wedge (Dm-1 \vee \ldots + Dm-r)$ $C = \overline{Dm-r+1}$
ASL (r = 0)	—	*	*	0	0	
LSL, ROXL	*	*	*	0	?	$C = Dm-r+1$
LSR (r = 0)	—	*	*	0	0	
ROXL (r = 0)		*	*	0	?	C = X
ROL	—	*	*	0	?	$C = Dm-r+1$
ROL (r = 0)	—	*	*	0	0	
ASR, LSR, ROXR	*	*	*	0	?	$C = Dr-1$
ASR, LSR (r = 0)	—	*	*	0	0	
ROXR (r = 0)	—	*	*	0	?	C = X
ROR	—	*	*	0	?	$C = Dr-1$
ROR (r = 0)	—	*	*	0	0	

—	= Not Affected	Rm	= Result Operand — most significant bit
U	= Undefined, result meaningless	R	= Register Tested
?	= Other — See Special Definition	n	= Bit Number
*	= General Case	r	= Shift Count
	$\quad X = C$	LB	= Lower Bound
	$\quad N = Rm$	UB	= Upper Bound
	$\quad Z = \overline{Rm} \wedge \ldots \wedge \overline{R0}$	$\wedge$	= Boolean AND
Sm	= Source Operand — most significant bit	$\vee$	= Boolean OR
Dm	= Destination Operand — most significant bit	$\overline{Rm}$	= NOT Rm

Table A-2. Conditional Tests

Mnemonic	Condition	Encoding	Test
T*	True	0000	1
F*	False	0001	0
HI	High	0010	$\overline{C} \cdot \overline{Z}$
LS	Low or Same	0011	$C + Z$
CC(HS)	Carry Clear	0100	$\overline{C}$
CS(LO)	Carry Set	0101	C
NE	Not Equal	0110	$\overline{Z}$
EQ	Equal	0111	Z
VC	Overflow Clear	1000	$\overline{V}$
VS	Overflow Set	1001	V
PL	Plus	1010	$\overline{N}$
MI	Minus	1011	N
GE	Greater or Equal	1100	$N \cdot V + \overline{N} \cdot \overline{V}$
LT	Less Than	1101	$N \cdot \overline{V} + \overline{N} \cdot V$
GT	Greater Than	1110	$N \cdot V \cdot \overline{Z} + \overline{N} \cdot \overline{V} \cdot \overline{Z}$
LE	Less or Equal	1111	$Z + N \cdot \overline{V} + \overline{N} \cdot V$

• = Boolean AND
+ = Boolean OR
$\overline{N}$ = Boolean NOT N

*Not available for the Bcc instruction

APPENDIX B
INSTRUCTION SET DETAILS

B.1 INTRODUCTION

This appendix contains detailed information about each instruction in the MC68020 instruction set. They are arranged in alphabetical order with the mnemonic heading set in large bold type for easy reference.

B.2 ADDRESSING CATEGORIES

Effective address modes may be categorized by the ways in which they may be used. The following classifications will be used In the instruction definitions.

Data
: If an effective address mode may be used to refer to data operands, it is considered a data addressing effective address mode.

Memory
: If an effective address mode may be used to refer to memory operands, It is considered a memory addressing effective address mode.

Alterable
: If an effective address mode may be used to refer to alterable (writeable) operands, it is considered an alterable addressing effective address mode.

Control
: If an effective address mode may be used to refer to memory operands without an associated size, it is considered a control addressing effective address mode.

Table B-1 shows the various categories to which each of the effective address modes belong.

B

Table B-1. Effective Addressing Mode Categories

Address Modes	Mode	Register	Data	Memory	Control	Alterable	Assembler Syntax
Data Register Direct	000	reg. no.	X	—	—	X	Dn
Address Register Direct	001	reg. no.	—	—	—	X	An
Address Register Indirect	010	reg. no.	X	X	X	X	(An)
Address Register Indirect with Postincrement	011	reg. no.	X	X	—	X	(An)+
Address Register Indirect with Predecrement	100	reg. no.	X	X	—	X	−(An)
Address Register Indirect with Displacement	101	reg. no	X	X	X	X	(d_{16},An)
Address Register Indirect with Index (8-Bit Displacement)	110	reg. no.	X	X	X	X	(d_8,An,Xn)
Address Register Indirect with Index (Base Displacement)	110	reg. no.	X	X	X	X	(bd,An,Xn)
Memory Indirect Post-Indexed	110	reg. no.	X	X	X	X	([bd,An],Xn,od)
Memory Indirect Pre-Indexed	110	reg. no.	X	X	X	X	([bd,An,Xn],od)
Absolute Short	111	000	X	X	X	X	(xxx).W
Absolute Long	111	001	X	X	X	X	(xxx).L
Program Counter Indirect with Displacement	111	010	X	X	X	—	(d_{16},PC)
Program Counter Indirect with Index (8-Bit Displacement)	111	011	X	X	X	—	(d_8,PC,Xn)
Program Counter Indirect with Index (Base Displacement)	111	011	X	X	X	—	(bd,PC,Xn)
PC Memory Indirect Post-Indexed	111	011	X	X	X	—	([bd,PC],Xn,od)
PC Memory Indirect Pre-Indexed	111	011	X	X	X	—	([bd,PC,Xn],od)
Immediate	111	100	X	X	—	—	#<data>

These categories may be combined so that additional, more restrictive, classifications may be defined. For example, the instruction descriptions use such classifications as alterable memory or data alterable. The former refers to those addressing modes which are both alterable and memory addresses, and the latter refers to addressing modes which are both data and alterable.

B

B.3 INSTRUCTION DESCRIPTION

The formats of each instruction are given in the following pages. Figure B-1 illustrates what information is given.

Instruction Name ———————————————————→ **ABCD**   Add

Operation Description ———————————————————→ **Operation:** Source₁₀ + Destinatior
       (see paragraph B.4)

Assembler Syntax for this Instruction ———————→ **Assembler** ABCD Dy,Dx
        Syntax: ABCD – (Ay), – (Ax)

Attributes: Size = (Byte)

Text Description of Instruction Operation   **Description:** Add the source operar
       bit, and store the result in the d
       binary coded decimal arithmeti
       ways:
       1. Data register to data registe
         specified in the instruction.
       2. Memory to memory: The oper
         ing mode using the address ı
       This operation is a byte operati

Condition Code Effects (see **Appendix A**) ——————→ **Condition Codes:**

X	N	Z	V	C
*	U	*	U	*

N Undefined.
Z Cleared if the result is n
V Undefined.
C Set if a carry (decimal) w
X Set the same as the carı

Instruction Format — Specifies the bit pattern
and fields of the operation word and any other
words which are part of the instruction. The effective address extensions are not explicitly illustrated. The extensions (if there are any) would
follow the illustrated portions of the instructions.
For the MOVE instruction, the source effective
address extension is the first, followed by the
destination effective address extension.

Normally the Z conditior
an operation. This allows
multiple-precision opera

Instruction Format:

15	14	13	12	11	10	9
ı	1	0	0	Register Rx		

Instruction Fields:
Register Rx field — Specifies t
If R/M = 0, specifies a data re
If R/M = 1, specifies an addre
R/M field — Specifies the oper
0 — The operation is data re
1 — The operation is memor

Meanings and allowed values of the various
fields required by the instruction format.

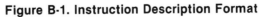

B

Figure B-1. Instruction Description Format

B.4 OPERATION DESCRIPTION DEFINITIONS

The following definitions are used for the operation description in the details of the instruction set.

OPERANDS:

An	— address register
Dn	— data register
Rn	— any data or address register
PC	— program counter
SR	— status register
CCR	— condition codes (lower order byte of status register)
SSP	— supervisor stack pointer
USP	— user stack pointer
SP	— active stack pointer (equivalent to A7)
X	— extend operand (from condition codes)
Z	— zero condition code
V	— overflow condition code
Immediate Data	— immediate data from the instruction
d	— address displacement
Source	— source contents
Destination	— destination contents
Vector	— location of exception vector
ea	— any valid effective address

SUBFIELDS AND QUALIFIERS:

<bit>OF<operand>	selects a single bit of the operand
<ea>{offset:width}	selects a bit field
(<operand>)	the contents of the referenced location
<operand>$_{10}$	the operand is binary coded decimal; operations are to be performed in decimal.
(<address register>) −(<address register>) (<address register>)+	the register indirect operator which indicates that the operand register points to the memory location of the instruction operand. The optional mode qualifiers are −, +, (d) and (d, ix); these are explained in **SECTION 2 DATA ORGANIZATION AND ADDRESSING CAPABILITIES.**
#xxx or #<data>	immediate data located with the instruction is the operand.

OPERATIONS: Operations are grouped into binary, unary, and other.

Binary—These operations are written <operand> <op> <operand> where <op> is one of the following:

→	the left operand is moved to the right operand
↔	the two operands are exchanged
+	the operands are added
−	the right operand is subtracted from the left operand
*	the operands are multiplied
/	the first operand is divided by the second operand
∧	the operands are logically ANDed
∨	the operands are logically ORed
⊕	the operands are logically exclusively ORed
<	relational test, true if left operand is less than right operand
>	relational test, true if left operand is greater than right operand
shifted by	the left operand is shifted or rotated by the number of positions
rotated by	specified by the right operand

Unary:

· <operand>	the operand is logically complemented
<operand> sign-extended	the operand is sign extended, all bits of the upper portion are made equal to high order bit of the lower portion
<operand> tested	the operand is compared to 0, the results are used to set the condition codes

Other:

TRAP   equivalent to Format/Offset Word→(SSP); SSP−2→SSP; PC→(SSP); SSP−4→SSP; SR→(SSP); SSP−2→SSP; (vector)→PC

STOP   enter the stopped state, waiting for interrupts

If <condition> then <operations> else <operations>. The condition is tested. If true, the operations after the "then" are performed. If the condition is false and the optional "else" clause is present, the operations after the "else" are performed. If the condition is false and the optional "else" clause is absent, the instruction performs no operation.

B

ABCD

Operation: Source$_{10}$ + Destination$_{10}$ + X → Destination

Assembler   ABCD Dy,Dx
Syntax: ABCD − (Ay), − (Ax)

Attributes: Size = (Byte)

Description: Add the source operand to the destination operand along with the extend bit, and store the result in the destination location. The addition is performed using binary coded decimal arithmetic. The operands may be addressed in two different ways:
1. Data register to data register: The operands are contained in the data registers specified in the instruction.
2. Memory to memory: The operands are addressed with the predecrement addressing mode using the address registers specified in the instruction.

This operation is a byte operation only.

Condition Codes:

X	N	Z	V	C
*	U	*	U	*

N   Undefined.
Z   Cleared if the result is non-zero. Unchanged otherwise.
V   Undefined.
C   Set if a carry (decimal) was generated. Cleared otherwise.
X   Set the same as the carry bit.

NOTE

Normally the Z condition code bit is set via programming before the start of an operation. This allows successful tests for zero results upon completion of multiple-precision operations.

Instruction Format:

15	14	13	12	11	10	9	8	7	6	5	4	3	2	1	0
1	1	0	0	Register Rx			1	0	0	0	0	R/M	Register Ry		

Instruction Fields:

Register Rx field — Specifies the destination register:
    If R/M = 0, specifies a data register
    If R/M = 1, specifies an address register for the predecrement addressing mode
R/M field — Specifies the operand addressing mode:
    0 — The operation is data register to data register
    1 — The operation is memory to memory
Register Ry field — Specifies the source register:
    If R/M = 0, specifies a data register
    If R/M = 1, specifies an address register for the predecrement addressing mode

B

ADD

ADD **Add** ADD

Operation: Source + Destination → Destination

Assembler ADD <ea>,Dn
Syntax: ADD Dn,<ea>

Attributes: Size = (Byte, Word, Long)

Description: Add the source operand to the destination operand using binary addition, and store the result in the destination location. The size of the operation may be specified to be byte, word, or long. The mode of the instruction indicates which operand is the source and which is the destination as well as the operand size.

Condition Codes:

X	N	Z	V	C
*	*	*	*	*

N   Set if the result is negative. Cleared otherwise.
Z   Set if the result is zero. Cleared otherwise.
V   Set if an overflow is generated. Cleared otherwise.
C   Set if a carry is generated. Cleared otherwise.
X   Set the same as the carry bit.

Instruction Format:

15	14	13	12	11	10	9	8	7	6	5	4	3	2	1	0
1	1	0	1	Register Dn			Op-Mode			Effective Address					
										Mode			Register		

Instruction Fields:

Register field — Specifies any of the eight data registers.

Op-Mode field —

Byte	Word	Long	Operation
000	001	010	<ea> + <Dn> → <Dn>
100	101	110	<Dn> + <ea> → <ea>

Effective Address Field — Determines addressing mode:
a. If the location specified in a source operand, the all addressing modes are allowed as shown:

B

Addr. Mode	Mode	Register
Dn	000	reg. number:Dn
An*	001	reg. number:An
(An)	010	reg. number:An
(An)+	011	reg. number:An
−(An)	100	reg. number:An
(d$_{16}$,An)	101	reg. number:An
(d$_8$,An,Xn)	110	reg. number:An
(bd,An,Xn)	110	reg. number:An
([bd,An,Xn],od)	110	reg. number:An
([bd,An],Xn,od)	110	reg. number:An

Addr. Mode	Mode	Register
(xxx).W	111	000
(xxx).L	111	001
#<data>	111	100
(d$_{16}$,PC)	111	010
(d$_8$,PC,Xn)	111	011
(bd,PC,Xn)	111	011
([bd,PC,Xn],od)	111	011
([bd,PC],Xn,od)	111	011

*Word and Long only.

b. If the location specified is a destination operand, then only alterable memory addressing modes are allowed as shown:

Addr. Mode	Mode	Register
Dn	—	—
An	—	—
(An)	010	reg. number:An
(An)+	011	reg. number:An
−(An)	100	reg. number:An
(d$_{16}$,An)	101	reg. number:An
(d$_8$,An,Xn)	110	reg. number:An
(bd,An,Xn)	110	reg. number:An
([bd,An,Xn],od)	110	reg. number:An
([bd,An],Xn,od)	110	reg. number:An

Addr. Mode	Mode	Register
(xxx).W	111	000
(xxx).L	111	001
#<data>	—	—
(d$_{16}$,PC)	—	—
(d$_8$,PC,Xn)	—	—
(bd,PC,Xn)	—	—
([bd,PC,Xn],od)	—	—
([bd,PC],Xn,od)	—	—

Notes: 1. If the destination is a data register, then it cannot be specified by using the destination <ea> mode, but must use the destination Dn mode instead.
2. ADDA is used when the destination is an address register. ADDI and ADDQ are used when the source is immediate data. Most assemblers automatically make this distinction.

B

ADDA

Add Address

ADDA

Operation: Source + Destination → Destination

**Assembler
Syntax:** ADDA <ea>,An

Attributes: Size = (Word, Long)

Description: Add the source operand to the destination address register, and store the result in the address register. The size of the operation may be specified to be word or long. The entire destination address register is used regardless of the operation size.

Condition Codes: Not affected.

Instruction Format:

15	14	13	12	11	10	9	8	7	6	5	4	3	2	1	0
1	1	0	1	Register An			Op-Mode			Effective Address					
										Mode			Register		

Instruction Fields:

Register field — Specifies any of the eight address registers. This is always the destination.

Op-Mode field — Specifies the size of the operation:

011— word operation. The source operand is sign-extended to a long operand and the operation is performed on the address register using all 32 bits.

111—long operation.

Effective Address field — Specifies the source operand. All addressing modes are allowed as shown:

Addr. Mode	Mode	Register
Dn	000	reg. number:Dn
An	001	reg. number:An
(An)	010	reg. number:An
(An) +	011	reg. number:An
− (An)	100	reg. number:An
(d_{16},An)	101	reg. number:An
(d_8,An,Xn)	110	reg. number:An
(bd,An,Xn)	110	reg. number:An
([bd,An,Xn],od)	110	reg. number:An
([bd,An],Xn,od)	110	reg. number:An

Addr. Mode	Mode	Register
(xxx).W	111	000
(xxx).L	111	001
#<data>	111	100
(d_{16},PC)	111	010
(d_8,PC,Xn)	111	011
(bd,PC,Xn)	111	011
([bd,PC,Xn],od)	111	011
([bd,PC],Xn,od)	111	011

B

ADDI

Add Immediate

ADDI

Operation: Immediate Data + Destination → Destination

**Assembler
Syntax:** ADDI #<data>,<ea>

Attributes: Size = (Byte, Word, Long)

Description: Add the immediate data to the destination operand, and store the result in the destination location. The size of the operation may be specified to be byte, word, or long. The size of the immediate data matches the operation size.

Condition Codes:

X	N	Z	V	C
*	*	*	*	*

N Set if the result is negative. Cleared otherwise.
Z Set if the result is zero. Cleared otherwise.
V Set if an overflow is generated. Cleared otherwise.
C Set if a carry is generated. Cleared otherwise.
X Set the same as the carry bit.

Instruction Format:

15	14	13	12	11	10	9	8	7	6	5	4	3	2	1	0
0	0	0	0	0	1	1	0	Size		Effective Address Mode			Register		

Word Data								Byte Data							
Long Data (Includes Previous Word)															

Instruction Fields:

Size field — Specifies the size of the operation:
00—byte operation.
01—word operation.
10—long operation.
Effective Address field — Specifies the destination operand. Only data alterable addressing modes are allowed as shown:

B

B-10

Add Immediate

Addr. Mode	Mode	Register		Addr. Mode	Mode	Register
Dn	000	reg. number:Dn		(xxx).W	111	000
An	—	—		(xxx).L	111	001
(An)	010	reg. number:An		#<data>	—	—
(An)+	011	reg. number:An				
−(An)	100	reg. number:An				
(d_{16},An)	101	reg. number:An		(d_{16},PC)	—	—
(d_8,An,Xn)	110	reg. number:An		(d_8,PC,Xn)	—	—
(bd,An,Xn)	110	reg. number:An		(bd,PC,Xn)	—	—
([bd,An,Xn],od)	110	reg. number:An		([bd,PC,Xn],od)	—	—
([bd,An],Xn,od)	110	reg. number:An		([bd,PC],Xn,od)	—	—

Immediate field — (Data immediately following the instruction):

If size = 00, then the data is the low order byte of the immediate word.

If size = 01, then the data Is the entire immediate word.

If size = 10, then the data is the next two immediate words.

B

ADDQ   Add Quick   ADDQ

Operation: Immediate Data + Destination → Destination

Assembler
Syntax: ADDQ #<data>,<ea>

Attributes: Size = (Byte, Word, Long)

Description: Add the immediate data to the operand at the destination location. The data range is from 1 to 8. The size of the operation may be specified to be byte, word, or long. Word and long operations are also allowed on the address registers, in which case the condition codes are not affected. When adding to address registers, the entire destination address register is used, regardless of the operation size.

Condition Codes:

X	N	Z	V	C
*	*	*	*	*

N   Set if the result is negative. Cleared otherwise.
Z   Set if the result is zero. Cleared otherwise.
V   Set if an overflow is generated. Cleared otherwise.
C   Set if a carry is generated. Cleared otherwise.
X   Set the same as the carry bit.

The condition codes are not affected if the destination is an address register.

Instruction Format:

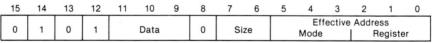

15	14	13	12	11 10 9	8	7 6	5 4 3	2 1 0
0	1	0	1	Data	0	Size	Effective Address Mode	Register

Instruction Fields:

Data field — Three bits of immediate data, 0, 1-7 representing a range of 8, 1 to 7 respectively.
Size field — Specifies the size of the operation:
  00—byte operation.
  01—word operation.
  10—long operation.
Effective Address field — Specifies the destination location. Only alterable addressing modes are allowed as shown:

B

ADDQ

ADDQ

Addr. Mode	Mode	Register
Dn	000	reg. number:Dn
An*	001	reg. number:An
(An)	010	reg. number:An
(An)+	011	reg. number:An
−(An)	100	reg. number:An
(d_{16},An)	101	reg. number:An
(d_8,An,Xn)	110	reg. number:An
(bd,An,Xn)	110	reg. number:An
([bd,An,Xn],od)	110	reg. number:An
([bd,An],Xn,od)	110	reg. number:An

Addr. Mode	Mode	Register
(xxx).W	111	000
(xxx).L	111	001
#<data>	—	—
(d_{16},PC)	—	—
(d_8,PC,Xn)	—	—
(bd,PC,Xn)	—	—
([bd,PC,Xn],od)	—	—
([bd,PC],Xn,od)	—	—

*Word and Long Only.

B

ADDX
Add Extended
ADDX

Operation: Source + Destination + X → Destination

Assembler ADDX Dy,Dx
Syntax: ADDX − (Ay), − (Ax)

Attributes: Size = (Byte, Word, Long)

Description: Add the source operand to the destination operand along with the extend bit and store the result in the destination location. The operands may be addressed in two different ways:
1. Data register to data register: the operands are contained in data registers specified in the instruction.
2. Memory to memory: the operands are addressed with the predecrement addressing mode using the address registers specified in the instruction.
The size of the operation may be specified to be byte, word, or long.

Condition Codes:

X	N	Z	V	C
*	*	*	*	*

N   Set if the result is negative. Cleared otherwise.
Z   Cleared if the result is non-zero. Unchanged otherwise.
V   Set if an overflow is generated. Cleared otherwise.
C   Set if a carry is generated. Cleared otherwise.
X   Set the same as the carry bit.

NOTE
Normally the Z condition code bit is set via programming before the start of an operation. This allows successful tests for zero results upon completion of multiple-precision operations.

Instruction Format:

15	14	13	12	11	10	9	8	7	6	5	4	3	2	1	0
1	1	0	1	Register Rx			1	Size		0	0	R/M	Register Ry		

Instruction Fields:

Register Rx field — Specifies the destination register:

If R/M = 0, specifies a data register.

If R/M = 1, specifies an address register for the predecrement addressing mode.

Size field — Specifies the size of the operation:

00—byte operation.

01—word operation.

10—long operation.

R/M field — Specifies the operand address mode:

0—The operation is data register to data register.

1—The operation is memory to memory.

Register Ry field — Specifies the source register:

If R/M = 0, specifies a data register.

If R/M = 1, specifies an address register for the predecrement addressing mode.

B

AND

AND

Operation: Source∧Destination → Destination

Assembler   AND <ea>,Dn
Syntax: AND Dn,<ea>

Attributes: Size = (Byte, Word, Long)

Description: AND the source operand to the destination operand and store the result in the destination location. The size of the operation may be specified to be byte, word, or long. The contents of an address register may not be used as an operand.

Condition Codes:

X	N	Z	V	C
—	*	*	0	0

N   Set if the most significant bit of the result is set. Cleared otherwise.
Z   Set if the result is zero. Cleared otherwise.
V   Always cleared.
C   Always cleared.
X   Not affected.

Instruction Format:

15	14	13	12	11	10	9	8	7	6	5	4	3	2	1	0
1	1	0	0	Register Dn			Op-Mode			Effective Address Mode			Register		

Instruction Fields:

Register field — Specifies any of the eight data registers.
Op-Mode field —

Byte	Word	Long	Operation
000	001	010	(<ea>)∧(<Dn>) → Dn
100	101	110	(<Dn>)∧(<ea>) → ea

Effective Address field — Determines addressing mode:
If the location specified is a source operand then only data addressing modes are allowed as shown:

B

Addr. Mode	Mode	Register
Dn	000	reg. number:Dn
An	—	—
(An)	010	reg. number:An
(An)+	011	reg. number:An
−(An)	100	reg. number:An
(d16,An)	101	reg. number:An
(d8,An,Xn)	110	reg. number:An
(bd,An,Xn)	110	reg. number:An
([bd,An,Xn],od)	110	reg. number:An
([bd,An],Xn,od)	110	reg. number:An

Addr. Mode	Mode	Register
(xxx).W	111	000
(xxx).L	111	001
#<data>	111	100
(d16,PC)	111	010
(d8,PC,Xn)	111	011
(bd,PC,Xn)	111	011
([bd,PC,Xn],od)	111	011
([bd,PC],Xn,od)	111	011

If the location specified is a destination operand then only alterable memory addressing modes are allowed as shown:

Addr. Mode	Mode	Register
Dn	—	—
An	—	—
(An)	010	reg. number:An
(An)+	011	reg. number:An
−(An)	100	reg. number:An
(d16,An)	101	reg. number:An
(d8,An,Xn)	110	reg. number:An
(bd,An,Xn)	110	reg. number:An
([bd,An,Xn],od)	110	reg. number:An
([bd,An],Xn,od)	110	reg. number:An

Addr. Mode	Mode	Register
(xxx).W	111	000
(xxx).L	111	001
#<data>	—	—
(d16,PC)	—	—
(d8,PC,Xn)	—	—
(bd,PC,Xn)	—	—
([bd,PC,Xn],od)	—	—
([bd,PC],Xn,od)	—	—

Notes: 1. If the destination is a data register, then it cannot be specified by using the destination <ea> mode, but must use the destination Dn mode instead.

2. ANDI is used when the source is immediate data. Most assemblers automatically make this distinction.

ANDI
AND Immediate
ANDI

Operation: Immediate Data ∧ Destination → Destination

Assembler
Syntax: ANDI #<data>,<ea>

Attributes: Size = (Byte, Word, Long)

Description: AND the immediate data to the destination operand and store the result in the destination location. The size of the operation may be specified to be byte, word, or long. The size of the immediate data matches the operation size.

Condition Codes:

X	N	Z	V	C
—	*	*	0	0

    N   Set if the most significant bit of the result is set. Cleared otherwise.
    Z   Set if the result is zero. Cleared otherwise.
    V   Always cleared.
    C   Always cleared.
    X   Not affected.

Instruction Format:

15	14	13	12	11	10	9	8	7	6	5	4	3	2	1	0
0	0	0	0	0	0	1	0	Size		Effective Address Mode			Register		
Word Data								Byte Data							
Long Data (Includes Previous Word)															

Instruction Fields:
    Size field — Specifies the size of the operation:
        00—byte operation.
        01—word operation.
        10—long operation.
    Effective Address field — Specifies the destination operand. Only data alterable addressing modes are allowed as shown:

B

AND Immediate

Addr. Mode	Mode	Register
Dn	000	reg. number:Dn
An	—	—
(An)	010	reg. number:An
(An)+	011	reg. number:An
−(An)	100	reg. number:An
(d$_{16}$,An)	101	reg. number:An
(d$_8$,An,Xn)	110	reg. number:An
(bd,An,Xn)	110	reg. number:An
([bd,An,Xn],od)	110	reg. number:An
([bd,An],Xn,od)	110	reg. number:An

Addr. Mode	Mode	Register
(xxx).W	111	000
(xxx).L	111	001
#>data>	—	—
(d$_{16}$,PC)	—	—
(d$_8$,PC,Xn)	—	—
(bd,PC,Xn)	—	—
([bd,PC,Xn],od)	—	—
([bd,PC].Xn,od)	—	—

Immediate field — (Data immediately following the Instruction):
  If size = 00, then the data is the low order byte of the immediate word.
  If size = 01, then the data is the entire Immediate word.
  If size = 10, then the data is the next two immediate words.

B

AND Immediate to Condition Codes

Operation: Source ∧ CCR → CCR

**Assembler
Syntax:** ANDI #<data>,CCR

Attributes: Size = (Byte)

Description: AND the immediate operand with the condition codes and store the result in the low-order byte of the status register.

Condition Codes:

X	N	Z	V	C
*	*	*	*	*

N   Cleared if bit 3 of immediate operand is zero. Unchanged otherwise.
Z   Cleared if bit 2 of immediate operand is zero. Unchanged otherwise.
V   Cleared if bit 1 of immediate operand is zero. Unchanged otherwise.
C   Cleared if bit 0 of immediate operand is zero. Unchanged otherwise.
X   Cleared if bit 4 of immediate operand is zero. Unchanged otherwise.

Instruction Format:

15	14	13	12	11	10	9	8	7	6	5	4	3	2	1	0
0	0	0	0	0	0	1	0	0	0	1	1	1	1	0	0
0	0	0	0	0	0	0	0	Byte Data (8 Bits)							

B

ANDI
to SR

AND Immediate to the Status Register
(Privileged Instruction)

Operation: If supervisor state
then Source ∧ SR → SR
else TRAP

Assembler
Syntax: ANDI #<data>,SR

Attributes: Size = (Word)

Description: AND the immediate operand with the contents of the status register and store the result in the status register. All bits of the status register are affected.

Condition Codes:

X	N	Z	V	C
*	*	*	*	*

N Cleared if bit 3 of immediate operand is zero. Unchanged otherwise.
Z Cleared if bit 2 of immediate operand is zero. Unchanged otherwise.
V Cleared if bit 1 of immediate operand is zero. Unchanged otherwise.
C Cleared if bit 0 of immediate operand is zero. Unchanged otherwise.
X Cleared if bit 4 of immediate operand is zero. Unchanged otherwise.

Instruction Format:

15	14	13	12	11	10	9	8	7	6	5	4	3	2	1	0
0	0	0	0	0	0	1	0	0	1	1	1	1	1	0	0
Word Data (16 Bits)															

B

Arithmetic Shift

Operation: Destination Shifted by < count > → Destination

Assembler   ASd Dx,Dy
Syntax: ASd # < data >,Dy
              ASd < ea >
              where d is direction, L or R

Attributes: Size = (Byte, Word, Long)

Description: Arithmetically shift the bits of the operand in the direction (L or R) specified. The carry bit receives the last bit shifted out of the operand. The shift count for the shifting of a register may be specified in two different ways:
1. Immediate: the shift count is specified in the instruction (shift range, 1-8).
2. Register: the shift count is contained in a data register specified in the instruction (shift count is modulo 64).
The size of the operation may be specified to be byte, word, or long. The content of memory may be shifted one bit only, and the operand size is restricted to a word.

For ASL, the operand is shifted left; the number of positions shifted is the shift count. Bits shifted out of the high order bit go to both the carry and the extend bits; zeroes are shifted into the low order bit. The overflow bit indicates if any sign changes occur during the shift.

ASL:

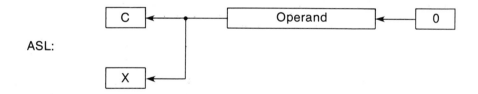

For ASR, the operand is shifted right; the number of positions shifted is the shift count. Bits shifted out of the low order bit go to both the carry and the extend bits; the sign bit (MSB) is replicated into the high order bit.

ASR:

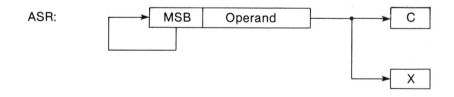

Condition Codes:

X	N	Z	V	X
*	*	*	*	*

N   Set if the most significant bit of the result is set. Cleared otherwise.

Z   Set if the result is zero. Cleared otherwise.

V   Set if the most significant bit is changed at any time during the shift operation. Cleared otherwise.

C   Set according to the last bit shifted out of the operand. Cleared for a shift count of zero.

X   Set according to the last bit shifted out of the operand. Unaffected for a shift count of zero.

Instruction Format (Register Shifts):

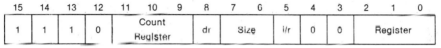

15	14	13	12	11	10	9	8	7	6	5	4	3	2	1	0
1	1	1	0	Count Register			dr	Size		i/r	0	0	Register		

Instruction Fields (Register Shifts):

Count/Register field — Specifies shift count or register where count is located:

If i/r = 0, the shift count is specified in this field. The values 0, 1-7 represent a range of 8, 1 to 7 respectively.

If i/r = 1, the shift count (modulo 64) is contained in the data register specified in this field.

dr field — Specifies the direction of the shift:

0—shift right.

1—shift left.

Size field — Specifies the size of the operation:

00—byte operation.

01—word operation.

10—long operation.

i/r field —

If i/r = 0, specifies immediate shift count.

If i/r = 1, specifies register shift count.

Register field — Specifies a data register whose content is to be shifted.

B

ASL, ASR   Arithmetic Shift   ASL, ASR

Instruction Format (Memory Shifts):

15	14	13	12	11	10	9	8	7	6	5	4	3	2	1	0
1	1	1	0	0	0	0	dr	1	1	Effective Address Mode			Register		

Instruction Fields (Memory Shifts):

dr field — Specifies the direction of the shift:

0—shift right

1—shift left

Effective Address field — Specifies the operand to be shifted. Only memory alterable addressing modes are allowed as shown:

Addr. Mode	Mode	Register		Addr. Mode	Mode	Register
Dn	—	—		(xxx).W	111	000
An	—	—		(xxx).L	111	001
(An)	010	reg. number:An		#<data>	—	—
(An)+	011	reg. number:An				
−(An)	100	reg. number:An				
(d$_{16}$,An)	101	reg. number:An		(d$_{16}$,PC)	—	—
(d$_8$,An,Xn)	110	reg. number:An		(d$_8$,PC,Xn)	—	—
(bd,An,Xn)	110	reg. number:An		(bd,PC,Xn)	—	—
([bd,An,Xn],od)	110	reg. number:An		([bd,PC,Xn],od)	—	—
([bd,An],Xn,od)	110	reg. number:An		([bd,PC],Xn,od)	—	—

Branch Conditionally

Operation: If (condition true) then PC + d → PC

**Assembler
Syntax:**   Bcc <label>

Attributes: Size = (Byte, Word, Long)

Description: If the specified condition is met, program execution continues at location (PC) + displacement. The displacement is a twos complement integer which counts the relative distance in bytes. The value in the PC is the sign-extended instruction location plus two. If the 8-bit displacement in the instruction word is zero, then the 16-bit displacement (word immediately following the instruction) is used. If the 8-bit displacement in the instruction word is all ones ($FF), then the 32-bit displacement (long word immediately following the instruction) is used. "cc" may specify the following conditions:

CC	carry clear	0100	$\overline{C}$		LS	low or same	0011	$C + Z$
CS	carry set	0101	C		LT	less than	1101	$N \cdot \overline{V} + \overline{N} \cdot V$
EQ	equal	0111	Z		MI	minus	1011	N
GE	greater or equal	1100	$N \cdot V + \overline{N} \cdot \overline{V}$		NE	not equal	0110	$\overline{Z}$
GT	greater than	1110	$N \cdot V \cdot \overline{Z} + \overline{N} \cdot \overline{V} \cdot \overline{Z}$		PL	plus	1010	$\overline{N}$
HI	high	0010	$\overline{C} \cdot \overline{Z}$		VC	overflow clear	1000	$\overline{V}$
LE	less or equal	1111	$Z + N \cdot \overline{V} + \overline{N} \cdot V$		VS	overflow set	1001	V

Condition Codes: Not affected.

Instruction Format:

15	14	13	12	11	10	9	8	7	6	5	4	3	2	1	0
0	1	1	0	Condition				8-Bit Displacement							
16-Bit Displacement if 8-Bit Displacement = $00															
32-Bit Displacement If 8-Bit Displacement = $FF															

Instruction Fields:

Condition field — One of fourteen conditions discussed in description.

8-Bit Displacement field — Twos complement integer specifying the relative distance (in bytes) between the branch instruction and the next instruction to be executed if the condition is met.

16-Bit Displacement field — Allows a larger displacement than 8 bits. Used only if the 8-bit displacement is equal to $00.

32-Bit Displacement field — Allows a larger displacement than 16 bits. Used only If the 8-bit displacement is equal to $FF.

Note: A short branch to the immediately following instruction cannot be generated, because it would result in a zero offset, which forces a word branch instruction definition.

B

BCHG Test a Bit and Change BCHG

Operation: ~(<bit number> of Destination)→Z;
~(<bit number> of Destination)→<bit number> of Destination

Assembler BCHG Dn,<ea>
Syntax: BCHG #<data>,<ea>

Attributes: Size = (Byte, Long)

Description: A bit in the destination operand is tested and the state of the specified bit is reflected in the Z condition code. After the test, the state of the specified bit is changed in the destination. If a data register is the destination, then the bit numbering is modulo 32 allowing bit manipulation on all bits in a data register. If a memory location is the destination, a byte is read from that location, the bit operation is performed using the bit number, modulo 8, and the byte is written back to the location. In all cases, bit zero refers to the least significant bit. The bit number for this operation may be specified in two different ways:
1. Immediate — the bit number is specified in a second word of the instruction.
2. Register — the bit number is contained in a data register specified in the instruction.

Condition Codes:

X	N	Z	V	C
—	—	*	—	—

N   Not affected.
Z   Set if the bit tested is zero. Cleared otherwise.
V   Not affected.
C   Not affected.
X   Not affected.

Instruction Format (Bit Number Dynamic specified by a register):

15	14	13	12	11	10	9	8	7	6	5	4	3	2	1	0
0	0	0	0	Register Dn			1	0	1	Effective Address Mode			Register		

Instruction Fields (Bit Number Dynamic):
Register field — Specifies the data register whose content is the bit number.
Effective Address field — Specifies the destination location. Only data alterable addressing modes are allowed as shown:

Test a Bit and Change

Addr. Mode	Mode	Register		Addr. Mode	Mode	Register
Dn*	000	reg. number:Dn		(xxx).W	111	000
An	—	—		(xxx).L	111	001
(An)	010	reg. number:An		#<data>	—	—
(An)+	011	reg. number:An				
−(An)	100	reg. number:An				
(d$_{16}$,An)	101	reg. number:An		(d$_{16}$,PC)	—	—
(d$_8$,An,Xn)	110	reg. number:An		(d$_8$PC,Xn)	—	—
(bd,An,Xn)	110	reg. number:An		(bd,PC,Xn)	—	—
([bd,An,Xn],od)	110	reg. number:An		([bd,PC,Xn],od)	—	—
([bd,An],Xn,od)	110	reg. number:An		([bd,PC],Xn,od)	—	—

*Long only; all others are byte only.

Instruction Format (Bit Number Static, specified as immediate data):

15	14	13	12	11	10	9	8	7	6	5	4	3	2	1	0
0	0	0	0	1	0	0	0	0	1	Effective Address					
										Mode		Register			
0	0	0	0	0	0	0	0	Bit Number							

Instruction Fields (Bit Number Static):

Effective Address field — Specifies the destination location. Only data alterable addressing modes are allowed as shown:

Addr. Mode	Mode	Register		Addr. Mode	Mode	Register
Dn*	000	reg. number:Dn		(xxx).W	111	000
An	—	—		(xxx).L	111	001
(An)	010	reg. number:An		#<data>	—	—
(An)+	011	reg. number:An				
−(An)	100	reg. number:An				
(d$_{16}$,An)	101	reg. number:An		(d$_{16}$,PC)	—	—
(d$_8$,An,Xn)	110	reg. number:An		(d$_8$,PC,Xn)	—	—
(bd,An,Xn)	110	reg. number:An		(bd,PC,Xn)	—	—
([bd,An,Xn],od)	110	reg. number:An		([bd,PC,Xn],od)	—	—
([bd,An],Xn,od)	110	reg. number:An		([bd,PC],Xn,od)	—	—

*Long only; all others are byte only.

Bit Number field — Specifies the bit number.

B

BCLR　　　　Test a Bit and Clear　　　　BCLR

Operation:　　~(<bit number> of Destination)→Z;
　　　　　　　　0→<bit number> of Destination

Assembler　　BCLR Dn,<ea>
Syntax:　　　 BCLR #<data>,<ea>

Attributes:　 Size = (Byte, Long)

Description: A bit in the destination operand is tested and the state of the specified bit is reflected in the Z condition code. After the test, the specified bit is cleared in the destination. If a data register is the destination, then the bit numbering is modulo 32 allowing bit manipulation on all bits in a data register. If a memory location is the destination, a byte is read from that location, the bit operation performed using the bit number, modulo 8, and the byte written back to the location. In all cases, bit zero refers to the least significant bit. The bit number for this operation may be specified in two different ways:
1. Immediate — the bit number is specified in a second word of the instruction.
2. Register — the bit number is contained in a data register specified in the instruction.

Condition Codes:

X	N	Z	V	C
—	—	*	—	—

　　N　Not affected.
　　Z　Set if the bit tested is zero. Cleared otherwise.
　　V　Not affected.
　　C　Not affected.
　　X　Not affected.

Instruction Format (Bit Number Dynamic, specified in a register):

15	14	13	12	11	10	9	8	7	6	5	4	3	2	1	0
0	0	0	0	Register Dn			1	1	0	Effective Address Mode			Register		

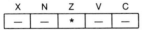

Instruction Fields (Bit Number Dynamic):
Register field — Specifies the data register whose content is the bit number.
Effective Address field — Specifies the destination location. Only data alterable addressing modes are allowed as shown:

Addr. Mode	Mode	Register
Dn*	000	reg. number:Dn
An	—	—
(An)	010	reg. number:An
(An)+	011	reg. number:An
−(An)	100	reg. number:An
(d$_{16}$,An)	101	reg. number:An
(d$_8$,An,Xn)	110	reg. number:An
(bd,An,Xn)	110	reg. number:An
([bd,An,Xn],od)	110	reg. number:An
([bd,An],Xn,od)	110	reg. number:An

Addr. Mode	Mode	Register
(xxx).W	111	000
(xxx).L	111	001
#<data>	—	—
(d$_{16}$,PC)	—	—
(d$_8$,PC,Xn)	—	—
(bd,PC,Xn)	—	—
([bd,PC,Xn],od)	—	—
([bd,PC],Xn,od)	—	—

*Long only; all others are byte only

Instruction Format (Bit Number Static, specified as immediate data):

15	14	13	12	11	10	0	8	7	6	5	4	3	2	1	0
0	0	0	0	1	0	0	0	1	0	Effective Address Mode			Register		
0	0	0	0	0	0	0	0	Bit Number							

Instruction Fields (Bit Number Static):

Effective Address field — Specifies the destination location. Only data alterable addressing modes are allowed as shown:

Addr. Mode	Mode	Register
Dn*	000	reg. number:Dn
An	—	—
(An)	010	reg. number:An
(An)+	011	reg. number:An
−(An)	100	reg. number:An
(d$_{16}$,An)	101	reg. number:An
(d$_8$,An,Xn)	110	reg. number:An
(bd,An,Xn)	110	reg. number:An
([bd,An,Xn],od)	110	reg. number:An
([bd,An],Xn,od)	110	reg. number:An

Addr. Mode	Mode	Register
(xxx).W	111	000
(xxx).L	000	001
#<data>	—	—
(d$_{16}$,PC)	—	—
(d$_8$,PC,Xn)	—	—
(bd,PC,Xn)	—	—
([bd,PC,Xn],od)	—	—
([bd,PC],Xn,od)	—	—

*Long only; all others are byte only.

Bit Number field — Specifies the bit number.

B

Operation: ~(<bit field> of Destination) → <bit field> of Destination

**Assembler
Syntax:** BFCHG <ea> {offset:width}

Attributes: Unsized

Description: Complement a bit field at the specified effective address location. The condition codes are set according to the value in the field before it is changed.

The field selection is specified by a field offset and field width. The field offset denotes the starting bit of the field. The field width determines the number of bits to be included in the field.

Condition Codes:

X	N	Z	V	C
—	*	*	0	0

N   Set if the most significant bit of the field is set. Cleared otherwise.
Z   Set if all bits of the field are zero. Cleared otherwise.
V   Always cleared.
C   Always cleared.
X   Not affected.

Instruction Format:

15	14	13	12	11	10	9	8	7	6	5	4	3	2	1	0
1	1	1	0	1	0	1	0	1	1		Effective Address Mode			Register	
0	0	0	0	Do			Offset			Dw			Width		

Instruction Fields:

Effective Address field — Specifies the base location for the bit field. Only data register direct or alterable control addressing modes are allowed, as shown below:

Do field — Determines how the field offset is specified.
   0—the field offset is in the Offset field.
   1—bits [8:6] of the extension word specify a data register which contains the off-set; bits [10:9] are 0.

Offset field — Specifies the field offset, depending on Do.
   If Do = 0—the Offset field is an immediate operand; the operand value is in the range 0-31, specifying a field offset of 0-31.
   If Do = 1—the Offset field specifies a data register which contains the offset. The value is in the range -2^{31} to $2^{31} - 1$.

Dw field — Determines how the field width is specified.

0—the field width is in the Width field.

1—bits [2:0] of the extension word specify a data register which contains the width; bits [3:4] are 0.

Width field — Specifies the field width, depending on Dw.

If Dw = 0—the Width field is an immediate operand; the operand value is in the range 0, 1-31 specifying a field width of 32, 1-31 respectively.

If Dw = 1—the Width field specifies a data register which contains the width. The operand value is taken modulo 32, with values 0, 1-31 specifying a field width of 32, 1-31.

Addr. Mode	Mode	Register
Dn	000	reg. number:Dn
An	—	—
(An)	010	reg. number:An
(An)+	—	—
−(An)	—	—
(d₁₆,An)	101	reg. number:An
(d₈,An,Xn)	110	reg. number:An
(bd,An,Xn)	110	reg. number:An
([bd,An,Xn],od)	110	reg. number:An
([bd,An],Xn,od)	110	reg. number:An

Addr. Mode	Mode	Register
(xxx).W	111	000
(xxx).L	111	001
#<data>	—	—
(d₁₆,PC)	—	—
(d₈,PC,Xn)	—	—
(bd,PC,Xn)	—	—
([bd,PC,Xn],od)	—	—
([bd,PC],Xn,od)	—	—

B

BFCLR

BFCLR

Operation: $0 \rightarrow$ <bit field> of Destination

**Assembler
Syntax:** BFCLR <ea> {offset:width}

Attributes: Unsized

Description: Clear a bit field at the specific effective address location. The condition codes are set according to the value in the field before it is cleared.

The field selection is specified by a field offset and field width. The field offset denotes the starting bit of the field. The field width determines the number of bits to be included in the field.

Condition Codes:

X	N	Z	V	C
—	*	*	0	0

N   Set if the most significant bit of the field is set. Cleared otherwise.
Z   Set if all bits of the field are zero. Cleared otherwise.
V   Always cleared.
C   Always cleared.
X   Not affected.

Instruction Format:

15	14	13	12	11	10	9	8	7	6	5	4	3	2	1	0
1	1	1	0	1	1	0	0	1	1	Effective Address Mode			Register		
0	0	0	0	Do	Offset					Dw	Width				

Instruction Fields:

Effective Address field — Specifies the base location for the bit field. Only data register direct or alterable control addressing modes are allowed, as shown below:

Do field — Determines how the field offset is specified.

　0—the field offset is in the Offset field.

　1—bits [8:6] of the extension word specify a data register which contains the offset; bits [10:9] are 0.

Offset field — Specifies the field offset, depending on Do.

　If Do = 0—the Offset field is an immediate operand; the operand value is in the range 0-31, specifying a field offset of 0-31.

　If Do = 1—the Offset field specifies a data register which contains the offset. The value is in the range -2^{31} to $2^{31} - 1$.

B

B-32

Dw field — Determines how the field width is specified.

    0—the field width is in the Width field.

    1—bits [2:0] of the extension word specify a data register which contains the width; bits [4:3] are 0.

Width field — Specifies the field width, depending on Dw.

    If Dw = 0—the Width field is an immediate operand; the operand value is in the range 0, 1-31 specifying a field width of 32, 1-31.

    If Dw = 1—the Width field specifies a data register which contains the width. The operand value is taken modulo 32, with values 0, 1-31 specifying a field width of 32, 1-31.

Addr. Mode	Mode	Register
Dn	000	reg. number:Dn
An	—	—
(An)	010	reg. number:An
(An)+	—	—
–(An)	—	—
(d16,An)	101	reg. number:An
(d8,An,Xn)	110	reg. number:An
(bd,An,Xn)	110	reg. number:An
([bd,An,Xn],od)	110	reg. number:An
([bd,An],Xn,od)	110	reg. number:An

Addr. Mode	Mode	Register
(xxx).W	111	000
(xxx).L	111	001
#<data>	—	—
(d16,PC)	—	—
(d8,PC,Xn)	—	—
(bd,PC,Xn)	—	—
([bd,PC,Xn],od)	—	—
([bd,PC],Xn,od)	—	—

B

BFEXTS   Extract Bit Field Signed   BFEXTS

Operation: < bit field > of Source → Dn

**Assembler
Syntax:**   BFEXTS <ea> {offset:width},Dn

Attributes: Unsized

Description: Extract a bit field from the specified effective address location, sign extend to 32 bits, and load the result into the destination data register.

The field selection is specified by a field offset and field width. The field offset denotes the starting bit of the field. The field width determines the number of bits to be included in the field.

Condition Codes:

X	N	Z	V	C
—	*	*	0	0

N   Set if the most significant bit of the field is set. Cleared otherwise.
Z   Set if all bits of the field are zero. Cleared otherwise.
V   Always cleared.
C   Always cleared.
X   Not affected.

Instruction Format:

15	14	13	12	11	10	9	8	7	6	5	4	3	2	1	0
1	1	1	0	1	0	1	1	1	1	Effective Address Mode		Register			
0	Register		Do	Offset						Dw	Width				

Instruction Fields:

Effective Address field — Specifies the base location for the bit field. Only data register direct or control addressing modes are allowed as shown below:
Register field — Specifies the destination register.
Do field — Determines how the field offset is specified.
   0—the field offset is in the Offset field.
   1—bits [8:6] of the extension word specify a data register which contains the offset; bits [10:9] are 0.
Offset field — Specifies the field offset, depending on Do.
   If Do = 0—the Offset field is an immediate operand; the operand value is in the range 0-31, specifying a field offset of 0-31.
   If Do = 1—the Offset field specifies a data-register which contains the offset. The value is in the range -2^{31} to $2^{31} - 1$.

Dw field — Determines how the field width is specified.

   0—the field width is in the Width field.

   1—bits [2:0] of the extension word specify a data register which contains the width; bits [4:3] are 0.

Width field — Specifies the field width, depending on Dw.

   If Dw = 0—the Width field is an immediate operand; the operand value is in the range 0, 1-31, specifying a field width of 32, 1-31.

   If Dw = 1—the Width field specifies a data register which contains the width. The operand value is taken modulo 32, with values 0, 1-31 specifying a field width of 32, 1-31.

Addr. Mode	Mode	Register
Dn	000	reg. number:Dn
An	—	—
(An)	010	reg. number:An
(An) +	—	—
– (An)	—	—
(d$_{16}$,An)	101	reg. number:An
(d$_8$,An,Xn)	110	reg. number:An
(bd,An,Xn)	110	reg. number:An
([bd,An,Xn],od)	110	reg. number:An
([bd,An],Xn,od)	110	reg. number:An

Addr. Mode	Mode	Register
(xxx).W	111	000
(xxx).L	111	001
#<data>		—
(d$_{16}$,PC)	111	010
(d$_8$,PC,Xn)	111	011
(bd,PC,Xn)	111	011
([bd,PC,Xn],od)	111	011
([bd,PC],Xn,od)	111	011

B

Operation: < bit field > of Source → Dn

**Assembler
Syntax:**   BFEXTU <ea> {offset:width},Dn

Attributes: Unsized

Description: Extract a bit field from the specified effective address location, zero extend to 32 bits, and load the results into the destination data register.

The field selection is specified by a field offset and field width. The field offset denotes the starting bit of the field. The field width determines the number of bits to be included in the field.

Condition Codes:

X	N	Z	V	C
—	*	*	0	0

N   Set if the most significant bit of the source field is set. Cleared otherwise.
Z   Set if all bits of the field are zero. Cleared otherwise.
V   Always cleared.
C   Always cleared.
X   Not affected.

Instruction Format:

15	14	13	12	11	10	9	8	7	6	5	4	3	2	1	0
1	1	1	0	1	0	0	1	1	1	Effective Address Mode / Register					
0	Register			Do	Offset				Dw	Width				

Instruction Fields:
Effective Address field — Specifies the base location for the bit field. Only data register direct or control addressing modes are allowed as shown below:
Register field — Specifies the destination data register.
Do field — Determines how the field offset is specified.
　0—the field offset is in the Offset field.
　1—bits [8:6] of the extension word specify a data register which contains the offset; bits [10:9] are 0.
Offset field — Specifies the field offset, depending on Do.
　If Do = 0—the Offset field is an immediate operand; the operand value is in the range 0-31, specifying a field offset of 0-31.
　If Do = 1—the Offset field specifies a data register which contains the offset. The value is in the range -2^{31} to $2^{31} - 1$.

Extract Bit Field Unsigned

Dw field — Determines how the field width is specified.
> 0—the field width is in the Width field.
> 1—bits [2:0] of the extension word specify a data register which contains the width; bits [4:3] are 0.

Width field — Specifies the field width, depending on Dw.
> If Dw = 0—the Width field is an immediate operand; the operand value is in the range 0, 1-31, specifying a field width of 32, 1-31.
> If Dw = 1—the Width field specifies a data register which contains the width. The operand value is taken modulo 32, with values 0, 1-31 specifying a field width of 32, 1-31.

Addr. Mode	Mode	Register
Dn	000	reg. number:Dn
An	—	—
(An)	010	reg. number:An
(An) +	—	—
− (An)	—	—
(d_{16},An)	101	reg. number:An
(d_8,An,Xn)	110	reg. number:An
(bd,An,Xn)	110	reg. number:An
([bd,An,Xn],od)	110	reg. number:An
([bd,An],Xn,od)	110	reg. number:An

Addr. Mode	Mode	Register
(xxx).W	111	000
(xxx).L	111	001
#<data>	—	—
(d_{16},PC)	111	010
(d_8,PC,Xn)	111	011
(bd,PC,Xn)	111	011
([bd,PC,Xn],od)	111	011
([bd,PC],Xn,od)	111	011

B

BFFFO

Find First One in Bit Field

BFFFO

Operation: < bit field > of Source Bit Scan → Dn

Assembler
Syntax: BFFFO <ea> {offset:width},Dn

Attributes: Unsized

Description: The source operand is searched for the most significant bit position that contains a set bit. The bit offset (the original bit offset plus the offset of the first set bit) of that bit is then placed in Dn. If no bit of the bit field is set, the value placed in Dn is the field offset plus field width. The condition codes are set according to the bit field operand.

The field selection is specified by a field offset and field width. The field offset denotes the starting bit of the field. The field width determines the number of bits to be included in the field.

Condition Codes:

X	N	Z	V	C
—	*	*	0	0

N   Set if the most significant bit of the field is set. Cleared otherwise.
Z   Set if all bits of the field are zero. Cleared otherwise.
V   Always cleared.
C   Always cleared.
X   Not affected.

Instruction Format:

15	14	13	12	11	10	9	8	7	6	5	4	3	2	1	0
1	1	1	0	1	1	0	1	1	1	Mode			Register		

0	Register		Do	Offset			Dw	Width		

Effective Address: Mode / Register (bits 5-0)

Instruction Fields:

Effective Address field — Specifies the base location for the bit field. Only data register direct or control addressing modes are allowed as shown below:

Register field — Specifies the destination data register operand.

Do field — Determines how the field offset is specified.

   0—the field offset is in the Offset field.

   1—bits [8:6] of the extension word specify a data register which contains the offset; bits [10:9] are 0.

Offset field — Specifies the field offset, depending on Do.

   If Do = 0—the Offset field is an immediate operand; the operand value is in the range 0-31, specifying a field offset of 0-31.

   If Do = 1—the Offset field specifies a data register which contains the offset. The value is in the range -2^{31} to $2^{31} - 1$.

Dw field — Determines how the field width is specified.

0—the field width is in the Width field.

1—bits [2:0] of the extension word specify a data register which contains the width; bits [4:3] are 0.

Width field — Specifies the field width, depending on Dw.

If Dw = 0—the Width field is an immediate operand; the operand value is in the range 0, 1-31, specifying a field width of 32, 1-31.

If Dw = 1—the Width field specifies a data register which contains the width. The operand value is taken modulo 32, with values 0, 1-31 specifying a field width of 32, 1-31.

Addr. Mode	Mode	Register
Dn	000	reg. number:Dn
An	—	—
(An)	010	reg. number:An
(An)+		—
−(An)	—	—
(d$_{16}$,An)	101	reg. number:An
(d$_8$,An,Xn)	110	reg. number:An
(bd,An,Xn)	110	reg. number.An
([bd,An,Xn],od)	110	reg. number:An
([bd,An],Xn,od)	110	reg. number:An

Addr. Mode	Mode	Register
(xxx).W	111	000
(xxx).L	111	001
#<data>		—
(d$_{16}$,PC)	111	010
(d$_8$,PC,Xn)	111	011
(bd,PC,Xn)	111	011
([bd,PC,Xn],od)	111	011
([bd,PC],Xn,od)	111	011

B

Insert Bit Field

Operation: Dn → <bit field> of Destination

**Assembler
Syntax:** BFINS Dn,<ea> {offset:width}

Attributes: Unsized

Description: Move a bit field from the low-order bits of the specified data register to a bit field at the specified effective address location. The condition codes are set according to the inserted value.

The field selection is specified by a field offset and field width. The field offset denotes the starting bit of the field. The field width determines the number of bits to be included in the field.

Condition Codes:

X	N	Z	V	C
—	*	*	0	0

N   Set if the most significant bit of the field is set. Cleared otherwise.
Z   Set if all bits of the field are zero. Cleared otherwise.
V   Always cleared.
C   Always cleared.
X   Not affected.

Instruction Format:

15	14	13	12	11	10	9	8	7	6	5	4	3	2	1	0
										Effective Address					
1	1	1	0	1	1	1	1	1	1	Mode			Register		
0	Register		Do	Offset						Dw	Width				

Instruction Fields:
　　Effective Address field — Specifies the base location for the bit field. Only data register direct or alterable control addressing modes are allowed as shown below:
　　Register field — Specifies the source data register operand.
　　Do field — Determines how the field offset is specified.
　　　　0—the field offset is in the Offset field.
　　　　1—bits [8:6] of the extension word specify a data register which contains the offset; bits [10:9] are 0.
　　Offset field — Specifies the field offset, depending on Do.
　　　　If Do = 0—the Offset field is an immediate operand; the operand value is in the range 0-31, specifying a field offset of 0-31.
　　　　If Do = 1—the Offset field specifies a data register which contains the offset. The value is in the range -2^{31} to $2^{31} - 1$.

B

Dw field — Determines how the field width is specified.

0—the field width is in the Width field.

1—bits [2:0] of the extension word specify a data register which contains the width; bits [4:3] are 0.

Width field — Specifies the field width, depending on Dw.

If Dw = 0—the Width field is an immediate operand; the operand value is in the range 0, 1-31, specifying a field width of 32, 1-31.

If Dw = 1—the Width field specifies a data register which contains the width. The operand value is taken modulo 32, with values 0, 1-31 specifying a field width of 32, 1-31.

Addr. Mode	Mode	Register
Dn	000	reg. number:Dn
An	—	—
(An)	010	reg. number:An
(An) +	—	—
− (An)	—	—
(d$_{16}$,An)	101	reg. number:An
(d$_8$,An,Xn)	110	reg. number:An
(bd,An,Xn)	110	reg. number:An
([bd,An,Xn],od)	110	reg. number:An
([bd,An],Xn,od)	110	reg. number:An

Addr. Mode	Mode	Register
(xxx).W	111	000
(xxx).L	111	001
# < data >	—	—
(d$_{16}$,PC)	—	—
(d$_8$,PC,Xn)	—	—
(bd,PC,Xn)	—	—
([bd,PC,Xn],od)	—	—
([bd,PC],Xn,od)	—	—

B

BFSET

Set Bit Field

BFSET

Operation: $1s \rightarrow$ <bit field> of Destination

**Assembler
Syntax:** BFSET <ea> {offset:width}

Attributes: Unsized

Description: Set all bits of a bit field at the specified effective address location. The condition codes are set according to the value in the field before it is set.

The field selection is specified by a field offset and field width. The field offset denotes the starting bit of the field. The field width determines the number of bits to be included in the field.

Condition Codes:

X	N	Z	V	C
—	*	*	0	0

N   Set if the most significant bit of the field is set. Cleared otherwise.
Z   Set if all bits of the field are zero. Cleared otherwise.
V   Always cleared.
C   Always cleared.
X   Not affected.

Instruction Format:

15	14	13	12	11	10	9	8	7	6	5	4	3	2	1	0
1	1	1	0	1	1	1	0	1	1	Effective Address					
										Mode			Register		
0	0	0	0	Do	Offset				Dw	Width				

Instruction Fields:

Effective Address field — Specifies the base location for the bit field. Only data register direct or alterable control addressing modes are allowed as shown below:

Do field — Determines how the field offset is specified.

0—the field offset is in the Offset field.

1—bits [8:6] of the extension word specify a data register which contains the offset; bits [10:9] are 0.

Offset field — Specifies the field offset, depending on Do.

If Do = 0—the Offset field is an immediate operand; the operand value is in the range 0-31, specifying a field offset of 0-31.

If Do = 1—the Offset field specifies a data register which contains the offset. The value is in the range -2^{31} to $2^{31} - 1$.

Dw field — Determines how the field width is specified.

0—the field width is in the Width field.

1—bits [2:0] of the extension word specify a data register which contains the width; bits [4:3] are 0.

Width field — Specifies the field width, depending on Dw.

If Dw = 0—the Width field is an immediate operand; the operand value is in the range 0, 1-31, specifying a field width of 32, 1-31.

If Dw = 1—the Width field specifies a data register which contains the width. The operand value is taken modulo 32, with values 0, 1-31 specifying a field width of 32, 1-31.

Addr. Mode	Mode	Register
Dn	000	reg. number:Dn
An		—
(An)	010	reg. number:An
(An) +	—	—
– (An)	—	—
(d_{16},An)	101	reg. number:An
(d_8,An,Xn)	110	reg. number:An
(bd,An,Xn)	110	reg. number:An
([bd,An,Xn],od)	110	reg. number:An
([bd,An],Xn,od)	110	reg. number:An

Addr. Mode	Mode	Register
(xxx).W	111	000
(xxx).L	111	001
#<data>	—	—
(d_{16},PC)	—	—
(d_8,PC,Xn)	—	—
(bd,PC,Xn)	—	—
([bd,PC,Xn],od)	—	—
([bd,PC],Xn,od)	—	—

BFTST   Test Bit Field   BFTST

Operation: < bit field > of Destination

**Assembler
Syntax:**   BFTST <ea> {offset:width}

Attributes: Unsized

Description: Extract a bit field from the specified effective address location, and set the condition codes according to the value in the field.

The field selection is specified by a field offset and field width. The field offset denotes the starting bit of the field. The field width determines the number of bits to be included in the field.

Condition Codes:

X	N	Z	V	C
—	*	*	0	0

N   Set if the most significant bit of the field is set. Cleared otherwise.
Z   Set if all bits of the field are zero. Cleared otherwise.
V   Always cleared.
C   Always cleared.
X   Not affected.

Instruction Format:

15	14	13	12	11	10	9	8	7	6	5	4	3	2	1	0
1	1	1	0	1	0	0	0	1	1	Effective Address Mode			Register		
0	0	0	0	Do		Offset				Dw		Width			

Instruction Fields:
Effective Address field — Specifies the base location for the bit field. Only data register direct or control addressing modes are allowed as shown below:
Do field — Determines how the field offset is specified.
   0—the field offset is in the Offset field.
   1—bits [8:6] of the extension word specify a data register which contains the offset; bits [10:9] are 0.
Offset field — Specifies the field offset, depending on Do.
   If Do = 0—the Offset field is an immediate operand; the operand value is in the range 0-31, specifying a field offset of 0-31.
   If Do = 1—the Offset field specifies a data register which contains the offset. The value is in the range -2^{31} to $2^{31} - 1$.

B

Test Bit Field

Dw field — Determines how the field width is specified.

0—the field width is in the Width field.

1—bits [2:0] of the extension word specify a data register which contains the width; bits [4:3] are 0.

Width field — Specifies the field width, depending on Dw.

If Dw = 0—the Width field is an immediate operand; the operand value is in the range 0, 1-31, specifying a field width of 32, 1-31.

If Dw = 1—the Width field specifies a data register which contains the width. The operand value is taken modulo 32, with values 0, 1-31 specifying a field width of 32, 1-31.

Addr. Mode	Mode	Register
Dn	000	reg. number:Dn
An	—	—
(An)	010	reg. number:An
(An) +	—	—
– (An)	—	—
(d_{16},An)	101	reg. number:An
(d_8,An,Xn)	110	reg. number:An
(bd,An,Xn)	110	reg. number:An
([bd,An,Xn],od)	110	reg. number:An
([bd,An],Xn,od)	110	reg. number:An

Addr. Mode	Mode	Register
(xxx).W	111	000
(xxx).L	111	001
#< data >	—	—
(d_{16},PC)	111	010
(d_8,PC,Xn)	111	011
(bd,PC,Xn)	111	011
([bd,PC,Xn],od)	111	011
([bd,PC],Xn,od)	111	011

B

BKPT

Breakpoint

BKPT

BKPT

Operation: If breakpoint vector acknowledged
then execute returned operation word
else Trap as Illegal instruction

**Assembler
Syntax:** BKPT #<data>

Attributes: Unsized

Description: This instruction is used to support the program breakpoint function for debug monitors and real-time hardware emulators, and the operation will be dependent on the implementation. Execution of this instruction will cause the MC68020 to run a breakpoint acknowledge bus cycle, with the immediate data (value 0-7) presented on address lines A2, A3, and A4, and zeros on address lines A0 and A1. Two responses are permitted: normal and exception.

The normal response to the MC68020 is an operation word (typically an instruction, originally replaced by the breakpoint instruction) on the data lines with the $\overline{\text{DSACKx}}$ signal asserted. This operation word will then be executed in place of the breakpoint instruction.

For the exception response, a bus error signal will cause the MC68020 to take an illegal instruction exception.

Condition Codes: Not affected.

Instruction Format:

15	14	13	12	11	10	9	8	7	6	5	4	3	2	1	0
0	1	0	0	1	0	0	0	0	1	0	0	1		Vector	

Instruction Fields:

Vector field — Specifies the breakpoint for which the processor is to request the corresponding operation word.

B

BRA

Branch Always

BRA

Operation: PC + d → PC

Assembler
Syntax: BRA < label >

Attributes: Size = (Byte, Word, Long)

Description: Program execution continues at location (PC) + displacement. The displacement is a twos complement integer, which counts the relative distance in bytes. The value in the PC is the instruction location plus two. If the 8-bit displacement in the instruction word is zero, then the 16-bit displacement (word immediately following the instruction) is used. If the 8-bit displacement in the instruction word is all ones ($FF), then the 32-bit displacement (long word immediately following the instruction) is used.

Condition Codes: Not affected.

Instruction Format:

15	14	13	12	11	10	9	8	7	6	5	4	3	2	1	0
0	1	1	0	0	0	0	0				8-Bit Displacement				
16-Bit Displacement if 8-Bit Displacement = $00															
32-Bit Displacement if 8-Bit Displacement = $FF															

Instruction Fields:

8-Bit Displacement field — Two complement integer specifying the relative distance (in bytes) between the branch instruction and the next instruction to be executed.

16-Bit Displacement field — Allows a larger displacement than 8 bits. Used only if the 8-bit displacement is equal to $00.

32-Bit Displacement field — Allows a larger displacement than 8 bits. Used only if the 8-bit displacement is equal to $FF.

Note: A short branch to the immediately following instruction cannot be generated because it would result in a zero offset, which forces a word branch instruction definition.

B

BSET

Test a Bit and Set

Operation: ~(<bit number> of Destination)→Z;
1→<bit number> of Destination

Assembler BSET Dn,<ea>
Syntax: BSET #<data>,<ea>

Attributes: Size = (Byte, Long)

Description: A bit in the destination operand is tested, and the state of the specified bit is reflected in the Z condition code. After the test, the specified bit is set in the destination. If a data register is the destination, then the bit numbering is modulo 32, allowing bit manipulation on all bits in a data register. If a memory location is the destination, a byte is read from that location, the bit operation performed using the bit number, modulo 8, and the byte written back to the location. Bit zero refers to the least significant bit. The bit number for this operation may be specified in two different ways:
1. Immediate — the bit number is specified in a second word of the instruction.
2. Register — the bit number is contained in a data register specified in the instruction.

Condition Codes:

X	N	Z	V	C
—	—	*	—	—

N   Not affected.
Z   Set if the bit tested is zero. Cleared otherwise.
V   Not affected.
C   Not affected.
X   Not affected.

Instruction Format (Bit Number Dynamic, specified in a register):

15	14	13	12	11	10	9	8	7	6	5	4	3	2	1	0
0	0	0	0	Register			1	1	1	Effective Address					
										Mode			Register		

Instruction Fields (Bit Number Dynamic):
Register field — Specifies the data register whose content is the bit number.
Effective Address field — Specifies the destination location. Only data alterable addressing modes are allowed as shown:

Test a Bit and Set

Addr. Mode	Mode	Register
Dn *	000	reg. number:Dn
An	—	—
(An)	010	reg. number:An
(An) +	011	reg. number:An
– (An)	100	reg. number:An
(d$_{16}$,An)	101	reg. number:An
(d$_8$,An,Xn)	110	reg. number:An
(bd,An,Xn)	110	reg. number:An
([bd,An,Xn],od)	110	reg. number:An
([bd,An],Xn,od)	110	reg. number:An

Addr. Mode	Mode	Register
(xxx).W	111	000
(xxx).L	111	001
#<data>	—	—
(d$_{16}$,PC)	—	—
(d$_8$PC,Xn)	—	—
(bd,PC,Xn)	—	—
([bd,PC,Xn],od)	—	—
([bd,PC],Xn,od)	—	—

*Long only; all others are byte only.

Instruction Format (Bit Number Static, specified as immediate data):

15	14	13	12	11	10	9	8	7	6	5	4	3	2	1	0
0	0	0	0	1	0	0	0	1	1	Effective Address Mode			Register		
0	0	0	0	0	0	0	0	Bit Number							

Instruction Fields (Bit Number Static):

Effective Address field — Specifies the destination location. Only data alterable addressing modes are allowed as shown:

Addr. Mode	Mode	Register
Dn *	000	reg. number:Dn
An	—	—
(An)	010	reg. number:An
(An) +	011	reg. number:An
– (An)	100	reg. number:An
(d$_{16}$,An)	101	reg. number:An
(d$_8$,An,Xn)	110	reg. number:An
(bd,An,Xn)	110	reg. number:An
([bd,An,Xn],od)	110	reg. number:An
([bd,An],Xn,od)	110	reg. number:An

Addr. Mode	Mode	Register
(xxx).W	111	000
(xxx).L	111	001
#<data>	—	—
(d$_{16}$,PC)	—	—
(d$_8$,PC,Xn)	—	—
(bd,PC,Xn)	—	—
([bd,PC,Xn],od)	—	—
([bd,PC],Xn,od)	—	—

*Long only; all others are byte only.

Bit Number field — Specifies the bit number.

Branch to Subroutine

Operation: SP − 4 → SP; PC → (SP); PC + d → PC

**Assembler
Syntax:**   BSR < label >

Attributes: Size = (Byte, Word, Long)

Description: The long word address of the instruction immediately following the BSR instruction is pushed onto the system stack. Program execution then continues at location (PC) + displacement. The displacement in a twos complement integer which counts the relative distances in the bytes. The value in the PC is the instruction location plus two. If the 8-bit displacement in the instruction word is zero, then the 16-bit displacement (word immediately following the instruction) is used. If the 8-bit displacement in the instruction word is all ones ($FF), then the 32-bit displacement (long word immediately following the instruction) is used.

Condition Codes: Not affected.

Instruction Format:

15	14	13	12	11	10	9	8	7	6	5	4	3	2	1	0
0	1	1	0	0	0	0	1	8-Bit Displacement							
16-Bit Displacement if 8-Bit Displacement = $00															
32-Bit Displacement if 8-Bit Displacement = $FF															

Instruction Fields:

8-Bit Displacement field — Twos complement integer specifying the relative distance (in bytes) between the branch instruction and the next instruction to be executed.

16-Bit Displacement field — Allows a larger displacement than 8 bits. Used only if the 8-bit displacement is equal to $00.

32-Bit Displacement field — Allows a larger displacement than 8 bits. Used only if the 8-bit displacement is equal to $FF.

Note: A short subroutine branch to the immediately following instruction cannot be generated because it would result in a zero offset, which forces a word branch instruction definition.

B

Operation: ~(<bit number> of Destination)→Z;

Assembler   BTST Dn,<ea>
Syntax: BTST #<data>,<ea>

Attributes: Size = (Byte, Long)

Description: A bit in the destination operand is tested, and the state of the specified bit is reflected in the Z condition code. If a data register is the destination, then the bit numbering is modulo 32, allowing bit manipulation on all bits in a data register. If a memory location is the destination, a byte is read from that location, and the bit operation performed using the bit number, modulo 8, with zero referring to the least significant bit. The bit number for this operation may be specified in two different ways:
1. Immediate — the bit number is specified in a second word of the instruction.
2. Register — the bit number is contained in a data register specified in the instruction.

Condition Codes:

X	N	Z	V	C
—	—	*	—	—

N   Not affected.
Z   Set if the bit tested is zero. Cleared otherwise.
V   Not affected.
C   Not affected.
X   Not affected.

Instruction Format (Bit Number Dynamic, specified in a register):

15	14	13	12	11	10	9	8	7	6	5	4	3	2	1	0
0	0	0	0	Register Dn			1	0	0	Effective Address					

| 0 | 0 | 0 | 0 | Register Dn | | | 1 | 0 | 0 | Mode | | | Register | | |

Instruction Fields (Bit Number Dynamic):
   Register field — Specifies the data register whose content is the bit number.
   Effective Address field — Specifies the destination location. Only data addressing modes are allowed as shown:

B

BTST

Test a Bit

BTST

Addr. Mode	Mode	Register
Dn*	000	reg. number:Dn
An	—	—
(An)	010	reg. number:An
(An)+	011	reg. number:An
−(An)	100	reg. number:An
(d_{16},An)	101	reg. number:An
(d_8,An,Xn)	110	reg. number:An
(bd,An,Xn)	110	reg. number:An
([bd,An,Xn],od)	110	reg. number:An
([bd,An],Xn,od)	110	reg. number:An

Addr. Mode	Mode	Register
(xxx).W	111	000
(xxx).L	111	001
#<data>	111	100
(d_{16},PC)	111	010
(d_8PC,Xn)	111	011
(bd,PC,Xn)	111	011
([bd,PC,Xn],od)	111	011
([bd,PC],Xn,od)	111	011

*Long only; all others are byte only.

Instruction Format (Bit Number Static, specified as immediate data):

15	14	13	12	11	10	9	8	7	6	5	4	3	2	1	0
0	0	0	0	1	0	0	0	0	0	\multicolumn{6}{c}{Effective Address}
										Mode			Register		
0	0	0	0	0	0	0	0	\multicolumn{8}{c}{Bit Number}

Instruction Fields (Bit Number Static):

Effective Address field — Specifies the destination location. Only data addressing modes are allowed as shown:

Addr. Mode	Mode	Register
Dn*	000	reg. number:Dn
An	—	—
(An)	010	reg. number:An
(An)+	011	reg. number:An
−(An)	100	reg. number:An
(d_{16},An)	101	reg. number:An
(d_8,An,Xn)	110	reg. number:An
(bd,An,Xn)	110	reg. number:An
([bd,An,Xn],od)	110	reg. number:An
([bd,An],Xn,od)	110	reg. number:An

Addr. Mode	Mode	Register
(xxx).W	111	000
(xxx).L	111	001
#<data>	—	—
(d_{16},PC)	111	010
(d_8,PC,Xn)	111	011
(bd,PC,Xn)	111	011
([bd,PC,Xn],od)	111	011
([bd,PC],Xn,od)	111	011

*Long only; all others are byte only.

B

Bit Number field — Specifies the bit number.

CALLM

CALL Module

CALLM

Operation: Save current module state on stack;
Load new module state from destination

**Assembler
Syntax:** CALLM #<data>,<ea>

Attributes: Unsized

Description: The effective address of the instruction is the location of an external module descriptor. A module frame is created on the top of the stack, and the current module state is saved in the frame. The Immediate operand specifies the number of bytes of arguments to be passed to the called module. A new module state is loaded from the descriptor addressed by the effective address. Additional information is presented in Appendix D.

Condition Codes: Not affected

Instruction Format:

15	14	13	12	11	10	9	8	7	6	5	4	3	2	1	0
U	U	U	U	U	1	1	0	1	1	Effective Address					
										Mode			Register		
0	0	0	0	0	0	0	0	Argument Count							

Instruction Fields:

Effective Address field — Specifies the address of the module descriptor. Only control addressing modes are allowed as shown:

Addr. Mode	Mode	Register
Dn	—	—
An	—	—
(An)	010	reg. number:An
(An)+	—	—
−(An)	—	—
(d$_{16}$,An)	101	reg. number:An
(d$_8$,An,Xn)	110	reg. number:An
(bd,An,Xn)	110	reg. number:An
([bd,An,Xn],od)	110	reg. number:An
([bd,An],Xn,od)	110	reg. number:An

Addr. Mode	Mode	Register
(xxx).W	111	000
(xxx).L	111	001
#<data>	—	—
(d$_{16}$,PC)	111	010
(d$_8$,PC,Xn)	111	011
(bd,PC,Xn)	111	011
([bd,PC,Xn],od)	111	011
([bd,PC],Xn,od)	111	011

Agrument Count field — Specifies the number of bytes of arguments to be passed to the called module. The 8-bit field can specify from 0 to 255 bytes of arguments. The same number of bytes is removed from the stack by the RTM instruction.

CAS
CAS2

Compare and Swap with Operand

Operation: CAS Destination — Compare Operand → cc;
if Z, Update__Operand → Destination
else Destination → Compare__Operand

CAS2 Destination 1 — Compare 1 → cc;
if Z, Destination 2 — Compare 2 → cc
if Z, Update 1 → Destination 1 Update 2 → Destination 2
else Destination 1 → Compare 1 Destination 2 → Compare 2

Assembler CAS Dc,Du,<ea>
Syntax: CAS2 Dc1:Dc2,Du1:Du2,(Rn1):(Rn2)

Attributes: Size = (Byte*, Word, Long)

Description: The Effective Address operand(s) is fetched and compared to the compare operand data register(s). If the operands match, the update operand data register(s) is (are) written to the destination location(s); otherwise, the memory operand location is left unchanged and the compare operand is loaded with the memory operand. The operation is indivisible (using a read-modify-write memory cycle) to allow synchronization of several processors. Additional information is presented in Appendix D.

Condition Codes:

X	N	Z	V	C
—	*	*	*	*

N Set if the result is negative. Cleared otherwise.
Z Set if the result is zero. Cleared otherwise.
V Set if an overflow is generated. Cleared otherwise.
C Set if a carry is generated. Cleared otherwise.
X Not affected.

Instruction Format: (Single Operand):

15	14	13	12	11	10	9	8	7	6	5	4	3	2	1	0
0	0	0	0	1	Size		0	1	1	Effective Address					
										Mode			Register		
0	0	0	0	0	0	0	Du			0	0	0	Dc		

Instruction Fields:
Size field — Specifies the size of the operation.
01—byte operation.
10—word operation.
11—long operation.
Effective Address field — Specifies the location of the tested operand. Only alterable memory addressing modes are allowed as shown below:
Du field — Specifies the data register which holds the update value to be written to the memory operand location if the comparison is successful.

*Single Operand Form Only

B

Dc field — Specifies the data register which contains the test value to be compared against the memory operand.

Addr. Mode	Mode	Register
Dn	—	—
An	—	—
(An)	010	reg. number:An
(An) +	011	reg. number:An
– (An)	100	reg. number:An
(d$_{16}$,An)	101	reg. number:An
(d$_8$,An,Xn)	110	reg. number:An
(bd,An,Xn)	110	reg. number:An
([bd,An,Xn],od)	110	reg. number:An
([bd,An],Xn,od)	110	reg. number:An

Addr. Mode	Mode	Register
(xxx).W	111	000
(xxx).L	111	001
#<data>	—	—
(d$_{16}$,PC)	—	—
(d$_8$,PC,Xn)	—	—
(bd,PC,Xn)	—	
([bd,PC,Xn],od)	—	—
([bd,PC],Xn,od)	—	—

Instruction Format (Dual Operand):

15	14	13	12	11	10	9	8	7	6	5	4	3	2	1	0
0	0	0	0	1	Size		0	1	1	1	1	1	1	0	0
D/A1	Rn1			0	0	0		Du1		0	0	0		Dc1	
D/A2	Rn2			0	0	0		Du2		0	0	0		Du2	

Instruction Fields:

Size field — Specifies the size of the operation.

10—word operation.

11—long operation.

D/A1,D/A2 fields — Specify whether Rn1 and Rn2 reference data or address registers, respectively.

0—The corresponding register is a data register.

1—The corresponding register is an address register.

Rn1,Rn2 fields — Specify the numbers of the registers which contain the address of the first and second tested operands, respectively. If the operands overlap in memory, the results of any memory update are undefined.

Du1,Du2 fields — Specify the data registers which hold the update values to be written to the first and second memory operand locations if the comparison is successful.

Dc1,Dc2 fields — Specify the data registers which contain the test values to be compared against the first and second memory operands, respectively. If Dc1 and Dc2 specify the same data register and the comparison fails, the data register is loaded from the first memory operand.

Programming Note: The CAS and CAS2 instructions may be used to perform secure update operations on system control data structures in a multiprocessing environment.

B

CHK

Operation: If Dn <0 or Dn> Source then TRAP

**Assembler
Syntax:**   CHK <ea>,Dn

Attributes: Size = (Word, Long)

Description: The content of the data register specified in the instruction is examined and compared to the upper bound. The upper bound is a twos complement integer. If the register value is less than zero or greater than the upper bound, then the processor initiates exception processing. The vector number is generated to reference the CHK instruction exception vector.

Condition Codes:

X	N	Z	V	C
—	*	U	U	U

N   Set if Dn< 0; cleared if Dn> Source. Undefined otherwise.
Z   Undefined.
V   Undefined.
C   Undefined.
X   Not affected.

Instruction Format:

15	14	13	12	11	10	9	8	7	6	5	4	3	2	1	0
0	1	0	0	Register Dn			Size			Effective Address					
										Mode			Register		

Instruction Fields:

Register field — Specifies the data register whose content is checked.
Size field — Specifies the size of the operation.
   110—word operation.
   100—long operation.
Effective Address field — Specifies the upper bound operand word. Only data addressing modes are allowed as shown:

CHK

Check Register Against Bounds

CHK

Addr. Mode	Mode	Register
Dn*	000	reg. number:Dn
An	—	—
(An)	010	reg. number:An
(An)+	011	reg. number:An
−(An)	100	reg. number:An
(d$_{16}$,An)	101	reg. number:An
(d$_8$,An,Xn)	110	reg. number:An
(bd,An,Xn)	110	reg. number:An
([bd,An,Xn],od)	110	reg. number:An
([bd,An],Xn,od)	110	reg. number:An

Addr. Mode	Mode	Register
(xxx).W	111	000
(xxx).L	111	001
#<data>	111	100
(d$_{16}$,PC)	111	010
(d$_8$PC,Xn)	111	011
(bd,PC,Xn)	111	011
([bd,PC,Xn],od)	111	011
([bd,PC],Xn,od)	111	011

B

CHK2　　　　Check Register Against Bounds　　　　**CHK2**

Operation:　　If Rn < Source—lower-bound or
　　　　　　　　　　Rn > Source—upper-bound
　　　　　　　　Then TRAP

**Assembler
Syntax:**　　　　CHK2 <ea>,Rn

Attributes:　　Size = (Byte, Word, Long)

Description:　Check the value in Rn against the bounds pair at the effective address location. The lower bound is at the address specified by the effective address, with the upper bound at that address plus the operand length. For signed comparisons, the arithmetically smaller value should be the lower bound, while for unsigned comparison, the logically smaller value should be the lower bound.

The size of the data to be checked, and the bounds to be used, may be specified as byte, word, or long. If the checked register is a data register and the operation size is byte or word, only the appropriate low-order part of Rn is checked. If the checked register is an address register and the operation size is byte or word, the bounds operands are sign-extended to 32 bits and the resultant operands compared against the full 32 bits of An.

If the upper bound equals the lower bound, then the valid range is a single value. If the register operand is out of bounds, the processor initiates exception processing. The vector number is generated to reference the CHK instruction exception vector. Otherwise, the next instruction is executed.

Condition Codes:

X	N	Z	V	C
—	U	*	U	*

N　Undefined.
Z　Set if Rn is equal to either bound. Cleared otherwise.
V　Undefined.
C　Set if Rn is out of bounds. Cleared otherwise.
X　Not affected.

B

Instruction Format:

15	14	13	12	11	10	9	8	7	6	5	4	3	2	1	0
0	0	0	0	0	Size		0	1	1	Effective Address					
										Mode			Register		
D/A	Register			1	0	0	0	0	0	0	0	0	0	0	0

Check Register Against Bounds

Instruction Fields:

Size field — Specifies the size of the operation.

00—byte operation.

01—word operation.

10—long operation.

Effective Address field — Specifies the location of the bounds operands. Only control addressing modes are allowed as shown below:

D/A field — Specifies whether an address register or data register is to be checked.

0—Data register.

1—Address register.

Register field — Specifies the address or data register whose content is to be checked.

Addr. Mode	Mode	Register
Dn	—	—
An	—	—
(An)	010	reg. number:An
(An)+	—	—
−(An)	—	—
(d$_{16}$,An)	101	reg. number:An
(d$_8$,An,Xn)	110	reg. number:An
(bd,An,Xn)	110	reg. number:An
([bd,An,Xn],od)	110	reg. number:An
([bd,An],Xn,od)	110	reg. number:An

Addr. Mode	Mode	Register
(xxx).W	111	000
(xxx).L	111	001
#<data>	—	—
(d$_{16}$,PC)	111	010
(d$_8$,PC,Xn)	111	011
(bd,PC,Xn)	111	011
([bd,PC,Xn],od)	111	011
([bd,PC],Xn,od)	111	011

CLR

Clear an Operand

CLR

Operation: 0 → Destination

**Assembler
Syntax:** CLR <ea>

Attributes: Size = (Byte, Word, Long)

Description: The destination is cleared to all zero. The size of the operation may be specified to be byte, word, or long.

Condition Codes:

X	N	X	V	C
—	0	1	0	0

N Always cleared.
Z Always set.
V Always cleared.
C Always cleared.
X Not affected.

Instruction Format:

15	14	13	12	11	10	9	8	7	6	5	4	3	2	1	0
0	1	0	0	0	0	1	0	Size		Effective Address					
										Mode			Register		

Instruction Fields:

Size field — Specifies the size of the operation.
00—byte operation.
01—word operation.
10—long operation.

Effective Address field — Specifies the destination location. Only data alterable addressing modes are allowed as shown:

Addr. Mode	Mode	Register
Dn *	000	reg. number:Dn
An	—	—
(An)	010	reg. number:An
(An) +	011	reg. number:An
− (An)	100	reg. number:An
(d$_{16}$,An)	101	reg. number:An
(d$_8$,An,Xn)	110	reg. number:An
(bd,An,Xn)	110	reg. number:An
([bd,An,Xn],od)	110	reg. number:An
([bd,An],Xn,od)	110	reg. number:An

Addr. Mode	Mode	Register
(xxx).W	111	000
(xxx).L	111	001
#<data>	—	—
(d$_{16}$,PC)	—	—
(d$_8$,PC,Xn)	—	—
(bd,PC,Xn)	—	—
([bd,PC,Xn],od)	—	—
([bd,PC],Xn,od)	—	—

CMP

Compare

CMP

Operation: Destination — Source

Assembler
Syntax: CMP <ea>,Dn

Attributes: Size = (Byte, Word, Long)

Description: Subtract the source operand from the specified data register and set the condition codes according to the result; the data register is not changed. The size of the operation may be byte, word, or long.

Condition Codes:

X	N	Z	V	C
—	*	*	*	*

N   Set if the result is negative. Cleared otherwise.
Z   Set if the result is zero. Cleared otherwise.
V   Set if an overflow is generated. Cleared otherwise.
C   Set if a borrow is generated. Cleared otherwise.
X   Not affected.

Instruction Format:

15	14	13	12	11	10	9	8	7	6	5	4	3	2	1	0
1	0	1	1	Register Dn			Op-Mode			Effective Address Mode			Register		

Instruction Fields:

Register field — Specifies the destination data register.
Op-Mode field —

Byte	Word	Long	Operation
000	001	010	Dn – (<ea>)

Effective Address field — Specifies the source operand. All addressing modes are allowed as shown:

CMP

CMP

Addr. Mode	Mode	Register
Dn	000	reg. number:Dn
An*	001	reg. number:An
(An)	010	reg. number:An
(An)+	011	reg. number:An
−(An)	100	reg. number:An
(d$_{16}$,An)	101	reg. number:An
(d$_8$,An,Xn)	110	reg. number:An
(bd,An,Xn)	110	reg. number:An
([bd,An,Xn],od)	110	reg. number:An
([bd,An],Xn,od)	110	reg. number:An

Addr. Mode	Mode	Register
(xxx).W	111	000
(xxx).L	111	001
#<data>	111	100
(d$_{16}$,PC)	111	010
(d$_8$,PC,Xn)	111	011
(bd,PC,Xn)	111	011
([bd,PC,Xn],od)	111	011
([bd,PC],Xn,od)	111	011

*Word and Long only.

Note: CMPA is used when the destination is an address register. CMPI is used when the source is immediate data. CMPM is used for memory to memory compares. Most assemblers automatically make this distinction.

CMPA

Compare Address

CMPA

Operation: Destination − Source

**Assembler
Syntax:** CMPA <ea>,An

Attributes: Size = (Word, Long)

Description: Subtract the source operand from the destination address register and set the condition codes according to the result; the address register is not changed. The size of the operation may be specified to be word or long. Word length source operands are sign extended to 32-bit quantities before the operation is done.

Condition Codes:

X	N	Z	V	C
—	*	*	*	*

N   Set if the result is negative. Cleared otherwise.
Z   Set if the result is zero. Cleared otherwise.
V   Set if an overflow is generated. Cleared otherwise.
C   Set if a borrow is generated. Cleared otherwise.
X   Not affected.

Instruction Format:

15	14	13	12	11	10	9	8	7	6	5	4	3	2	1	0
1	0	1	1	Register An			Op-Mode			Effective Address Mode			Register		

Instruction Fields:

Register field — Specifies the destination data register.
Op-Mode field — Specifies the size of the operation:
   011—word operation. The source operand is sign-extended to a long operand and the operation is performed on the address register using all 32 bits.
   111—long operation.
Effective Address field — Specifies the source operand. All addressing modes are allowed as shown:

Compare Address

Addr. Mode	Mode	Register
Dn	000	reg. number:Dn
An	001	reg. number:An
(An)	010	reg. number:An
(An)+	011	reg. number:An
−(An)	100	reg. number:An
(d_{16},An)	101	reg. number:An
(d_8,An,Xn)	110	reg. number:An
(bd,An,Xn)	110	reg. number:An
([bd,An,Xn],od)	110	reg. number:An
([bd,An],Xn,od)	110	reg. number:An

Addr. Mode	Mode	Register
(xxx).W	111	000
(xxx).L	111	001
#<data>	111	100
(d_{16},PC)	111	010
(d_8,PC,Xn)	111	011
(bd,PC,Xn)	111	011
([bd,PC,Xn],od)	111	011
([bd,PC],Xn,od)	111	011

B

Operation: Destination − Immediate Data

**Assembler
Syntax:**   CMPI #<data>,<ea>

Attributes: Size = (Byte, Word, Long)

Description: Subtract the immediate data from the destination operand and set the condition codes according to the result; the destination location is not changed. The size of the operation may be specified to be byte, word, or long. The size of the immediate data matches the operation size.

Condition Codes:

X	N	Z	V	C
—	*	*	*	*

N   Set if the result is negative. Cleared otherwise.
Z   Set if the result is zero. Cleared otherwise.
V   Set if an overflow is generated. Cleared otherwise.
C   Set if a borrow is generated. Cleared otherwise.
X   Not affected.

Instruction Format:

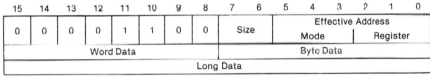

15	14	13	12	11	10	9	8	7 6	5 4 3	2 1 0
0	0	0	0	1	1	0	0	Size	Mode	Register

Effective Address (Mode / Register)

| Word Data | Byte Data |
| Long Data |

Instruction Fields:

   Size field — Specifies the size of the operation:
   00—byte operation.
   01—word operation.
   10—long operation.
   Effective Address field — Specifies the destination operand. Only data addressing modes are allowed as shown:

B

Addr. Mode	Mode	Register		Addr. Mode	Mode	Register
Dn	000	reg. number:Dn		(xxx).W	111	000
An	—	—		(xxx).L	111	001
(An)	010	reg. number:An		#<data>	—	—
(An)+	011	reg. number:An				
−(An)	100	reg. number:An				
(d$_{16}$,An)	101	reg. number:An		(d$_{16}$,PC)	111	010
(d$_8$,An,Xn)	110	reg. number:An		(d$_8$,PC,Xn)	111	011
(bd,An,Xn)	110	reg. number:An		(bd,PC,Xn)	111	011
([bd,An,Xn],od)	110	reg. number:An		([bd,PC,Xn],od)	111	011
([bd,An],Xn,od)	110	reg. number:An		([bd,PC],Xn,od)	111	011

Immediate field — (Data immediately following the instruction):
  If size = 00, then the data is the low order byte of the immediate word.
  If size = 01, then the data is the entire immediate word.
  If size = 10, then the data is the next two immediate words.

B

Compare Memory

Operation: Destination – Source

**Assembler
Syntax:** CMPM (Ay) + ,(Ax) +

Attributes: Size = (Byte, Word, Long)

Description: Subtract the source operand from the destination operand, and set the condition codes according to the results; the destination location is not changed. The operands are always addressed with the postincrement addressing mode, using the address registers specified in the instruction. The size of the operation may be specified to be byte, word, or long.

Condition Codes:

X	N	Z	V	C
—	*	*	*	*

N   Set if the result is negative. Cleared otherwise.
Z   Set if the result is zero. Cleared otherwise.
V   Set if an overflow is generated. Cleared otherwise.
C   Set if a borrow is generated. Cleared otherwise.
X   Not affected.

Instruction Format:

15	14	13	12	11	10	9	8	7	6	5	4	3	2	1	0
1	0	1	1	Register Ax			1	Size		0	0	1	Register Ay		

Instruction Fields:

Register Ax field — (always the destination) Specifies an address register for the postincrement addressing mode.
Size field — Specifies the size of the operation:
   00—byte operation.
   01—word operation.
   10—long operation.
Register Ay field — (always the source) Specifies an address register for the postincrement addressing mode.

B

B-67

CMP2

Operation: Compare Rn < Source—lower-bound or
Rn > Source—upper-bound
and Set Condition Codes

**Assembler
Syntax:** CMP2 < ea >,Rn

Attributes: Size = (Byte, Word, Long)

Description: Compare the value in Rn against the bounds pair at the effective address location and set the condition codes accordingly. The lower bound is at the address specified by the effective address, with the upper bound at that address plus the operand length. For signed comparisons, the arithmetically smaller value should be the lower bound, while for unsigned comparison, the logically smaller value should be the lower bound.

The size of the data to be compared, and the bounds to be used, may be specified as byte, word, or long. If the compared register is a data register and the operation size is byte or word, only the appropriate low-order part of Dn is checked. If the checked register is an address register and the operation size is byte or word, the bounds operands are sign-extended to 32 bits and the resultant operands compared against the full 32 bits of An.

If the upper bound equals the lower bound, then the valid range is a single value.

NOTE: This instruction is analougous to CHK2, but avoids causing exception processing to handle the out-of-bounds case.

Condition Codes:

X	N	Z	V	C
—	U	*	U	*

N   Undefined.
Z   Set if Rn is equal to either bound. Cleared otherwise.
V   Undefined.
C   Set if Rn is out of bounds. Cleared otherwise.
X   Not affected.

Instruction Format:

15	14	13	12	11	10	9	8	7	6	5	4	3	2	1	0
0	0	0	0	0	Size		0	1	1	Effective Address					
										Mode			Register		
D/A	Register			0	0	0	0	0	0	0	0	0	0	0	0

CMP2

Instruction Fields:

Size field — Specifies the size of the operation.

    00—byte operation.

    01—word operation.

    10—long operation.

Effective Address field — Specifies the location of the bounds pair. Only control addressing modes are allowed as shown:

Addr. Mode	Mode	Register
Dn	—	—
An	—	—
(An)	010	reg. number:An
(An)+	—	—
−(An)	—	—
(d$_{16}$,An)	101	reg. number:An
(d$_8$,An,Xn)	110	reg. number:An
(bd,An,Xn)	110	reg. number:An
([bd,An,Xn],od)	110	reg. number:An
([bd,An],Xn,od)	110	reg. number:An

Addr. Mode	Mode	Register
(xxx).W	111	000
(xxx).L	111	001
#<data>	—	—
(d$_{16}$,PC)	111	010
(d$_8$,PC,Xn)	111	011
(bd,PC,Xn)	111	011
([bd,PC,Xn],od)	111	011
([bd,PC],Xn,od)	111	011

D/A field — Specifies whether an address register or data register is to be compared.

    0—Data register.

    1—Address register.

Register field — Specifies the address or data register whose content is to be checked.

B

Operation: If cpcc true then PC + d → PC

**Assembler
Syntax:**   cpBcc <label>

Attributes: Size = (Word, Long)

Description: If the specified coprocessor condition is met, program execution continues at location (PC) + displacement. The displacement is a twos complement integer which counts the relative distance in bytes. The value in the PC is the address of the displacement word(s). The displacement may be either 16 bits or 32 bits. The coprocessor determines the specific condition from the condition field in the operation word.

Condition Codes: Not affected.

Instruction Format:

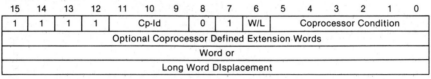

15	14	13	12	11	10	9	8	7	6	5	4	3	2	1	0
1	1	1	1	Cp-Id			0	1	W/L	Coprocessor Condition					
Optional Coprocessor Defined Extension Words															
Word or															
Long Word Displacement															

Instruction Fields:

Cp-Id field — Identifies the coprocessor that is to process this operation.

W/L field — Specifies the size of the displacement.

    0—the displacement is 16 bits.

    1—the displacement is 32 bits.

Coprocessor Condition field — Specifies the coprocessor condition to be tested. This field is passed to the coprocessor, which provides directives to the main processor for processing this instruction.

16-Bit Displacement field — The shortest displacement form for coprocessor branches is 16 bits.

32-Bit Displacement field — Allows a displacement larger than 16 bits.

B

cpDBcc Test Coprocessor Condition Decrement and Branch cpDBcc

Operation: If cpcc false then (Dn − 1 → Dn; If Dn ≠ − 1 then PC + d → PC)

Assembler
Syntax: cpDBcc Dn, < label >

Attributes: Size = (Word)

Description: If the specified coprocessor condition is met, execution continues with the next instruction. Otherwise, the low order word in the specified data register is decremented by one. If the result is equal to − 1, execution continues with the next instruction. If the result is not equal to − 1, execution continues at the location indicated by the current value of PC plus the sign extended 16-bit displacement. The value in the PC is the address of the displacement word. The coprocessor determines the specific condition from the condition word which follows the operation word.

Condition Codes: Not affected.

Instruction Format:

15	14	13	12	11	10	9	8	7	6	5	4	3	2	1	0
1	1	1	1	Cp-Id			0	0	1	0	0	1	Register		
0	0	0	0	0	0	0	0	0	0	Coprocessor Condition					
Optional Coprocessor Defined Extension Words															
Displacement															

Instruction Fields:

Cp-Id field — Identifies the coprocessor that is to process this operation.

Register field — Specifies the data register which is the counter.

Coprocessor Condition field — Specifies the coprocessor condition to be tested. This field is passed to the coprocessor, which provides directives to the main processor for processing this instruction.

Displacement field — Specifies the distance of the branch (in bytes).

B

Operation: Pass Command Word to Coprocessor

**Assembler
Syntax:**   cpGEN <parameters as defined by coprocessor>

Attributes: Unsized

Description: This instruction is the form used by coprocessors to specify the general data processing and movement operations. The coprocessor determines the specific operation from the command word which follows the operation word. Usually a coprocessor defines specific instances of this instruction to provide its instruction set.

Condition Codes: May be modified by coprocessor. Unchanged otherwise.

Instruction Format:

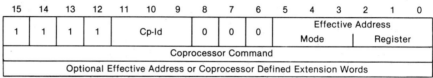

15	14	13	12	11	10	9	8	7	6	5	4	3	2	1	0
1	1	1	1	Cp-Id			0	0	0	Effective Address Mode			Register		

Coprocessor Command

Optional Effective Address or Coprocessor Defined Extension Words

Instruction Fields:

Cp-Id field — Identifies the coprocessor that is to process this operation.

Effective Address field — Specifies the location of any operand outside the coprocessor. The allowable addressing modes are determined by the operation to be performed.

Coprocessor Command field — Specifies the coprocessor operation to be performed. This word is passed to the coprocessor, which provides directives to the main processor for processing this instruction.

cpRESTORE Coprocessor Restore Functions cpRESTORE
(Privileged Instruction)

Operation: Restore Internal State of Coprocessor

Assembler
Syntax: cpRESTORE <ea>

Attributes: Unsized

Description: This instruction is used to restore the internal state of a coprocessor.

Condition Codes: Not affected.

Instruction Format:

15	14	13	12	11	10	9	8	7	6	5	4	3	2	1	0
1	1	1	1	Cp-Id			1	0	1	Effective Address					
										Mode			Register		

Instruction Field:

Cp-Id field — Identifies the coprocessor that is to be restored.

Effective Address field — Specifies the location where the internal state of the co-processor is located. Only postincrement or control addressing modes are allowed as shown:

Addr. Mode	Mode	Register
Dn	—	—
An	—	—
(An)	010	reg. number:An
(An) +	011	reg. number:An
− (An)	—	—
(d₁₆,An)	101	reg. number:An
(d₈,An,Xn)	110	reg. number:An
(bd,An,Xn)	110	reg. number:An
([bd,An,Xn],od)	110	reg. number:An
([bd,An],Xn,od)	110	reg. number:An

Addr. Mode	Mode	Register
(xxx).W	111	000
(xxx).L	111	001
#<data>	—	—
(d₁₆,PC)	111	010
(d₈,PC,Xn)	111	011
(bd,PC,Xn)	111	011
([bd,PC,Xn],od)	111	011
([bd,PC],Xn,od)	111	011

Programmer's Note: If the format word returned by the coprocessor indicates "come again", pending interrupts are not serviced.

B

cpSAVE

**Coprocessor Save Function
(Privileged Instruction)**

Operation: Save Internal State of Coprocessor

**Assembler
Syntax:** cpSAVE <ea>

Attributes: Unsized

Description: This instruction is used to save the internal state of a coprocessor.

Condition Codes: Not affected.

Instruction Format:

15	14	13	12	11	10	9	8	7	6	5	4	3	2	1	0
1	1	1	1		Cp-Id		1	0	0		Effective Address				
										Mode			Register		

Instruction Fields:

Cp-Id field — Identifies the coprocessor that is to save its state.

Effective Address field — Specifies the location where the internal state of the coprocessor is to be saved. Only predecrement or alterable control addressing modes are allowed as shown:

Addr. Mode	Mode	Register
Dn	—	—
An	—	—
(An)	010	reg. number:An
(An) +	—	—
– (An)	100	reg. number:An
(d$_{16}$,An)	101	reg. number:An
(d$_8$,An,Xn)	110	reg. number:An
(bd,An,Xn)	110	reg. number:An
([bd,An,Xn],od)	110	reg. number:An
([bd,An],Xn,od)	110	reg. number:An

Addr. Mode	Mode	Register
(xxx).W	111	000
(xxx).L	111	001
#<data>	—	—
(d$_{16}$,PC)	—	—
(d$_8$,PC,Xn)	—	—
(bd,PC,Xn)	—	—
([bd,PC,Xn],od)	—	—
([bd,PC],Xn,od)	—	—

B

Operation: If cpcc true then 1s → Destination
                   else 0s → Destination

**Assembler
Syntax:**   cpScc <ea>

Attributes: Size = (Byte)

Description: The specified coprocessor condition code is tested; if the condition is true, the byte specified by the effective address is set to TRUE (all ones), otherwise that byte is set to FALSE (all zeros). The coprocessor determines the specific condition from the condition word which follows the operation word.

Condition Codes: Not affected.

Instruction Format:

15	14	13	12	11	10	9	8	7	6	5	4	3	2	1	0
1	1	1	1	Cp-Id			0	0	1	Effective Address Mode | Register					
0	0	0	0	0	0	0	0	0	0	Coprocessor Condition					
Optional Effective Address or Coprocessor Defined Extension Words															

Instruction Fields:

Cp-Id field — Identifies the coprocessor that is to process this operation.

Effective Address field — Specifies the destination location. Only data alterable addressing modes are allowed as shown:

Addr. Mode	Mode	Register		Addr. Mode	Mode	Register
Dn	000	reg. number:Dn		(xxx).W	111	000
An	—	—		(xxx).L	111	001
(An)	010	reg. number:An		#<data>	—	—
(An)+	011	reg. number:An				
−(An)	100	reg. number:An				
(d16,An)	101	reg. number:An		(d16,PC)	—	—
(d8,An,Xn)	110	reg. number:An		(d8,PC,Xn)	—	—
(bd,An,Xn)	110	reg. number:An		(bd,PC,Xn)	—	—
([bd,An,Xn],od)	110	reg. number:An		([bd,PC,Xn],od)	—	—
([bd,An],Xn,od)	110	reg. number:An		([bd,PC],Xn,od)	—	—

B

Coprocessor Condition field — Specifies the coprocessor condition to be tested. This field is passed to the coprocessor, which provides directives to the main processor for processing this instruction.

cpTRAPcc   Trap on Coprocessor Condition   cpTRAPcc

Operation: If cpcc true then TRAP

Assembler   cpTRAPcc
Syntax: cpTRAPcc #<data>

Attributes: Unsized or Size = (Word, Long)

Description: If the selected coprocessor condition is true, the processor initiates exception processing. The vector number is generated to reference the cpTRAPcc exception vector, the stacked program counter is the address of the next instruction. If the selected condition is not true, no operation is performed, and execution continues with the next instruction. The coprocessor determines the specific condition from the condition word which follows the operation word. Following the condition word is a user-defined data operand specified as immediate data data, to be used by the trap handler.

Condition Codes: Not affected.

Instruction Format:

15	14	13	12	11	10	9	8	7	6	5	4	3	2	1	0
1	1	1	1	Cp-Id			0	0	1	1	1	1	Op-Mode		
0	0	0	0	0	0	0	0	0	0	Coprocessor Condition					
Optional Coprocessor Defined Extension Words															
Optional Word															
or Long Word Operand															

Instruction Fields:

Cp-Id field — Identifies the coprocessor that is to process this operation.

Op-Mode field — Selects the instruction form.

010—Instruction is followed by one operand word.

011—Instruction is followed by two operand words.

100—Instruction has no following operand words.

Coprocessor Condition field — Specifies the coprocessor condition to be tested. This field is passed to the coprocessor, which provides directives to the main processor for processing this instruction.

B

Test Condition, Decrement, and Branch

Operation: If condition false then $(Dn - 1 \rightarrow Dn$; If $Dn \neq -1$ then $PC + d \rightarrow PC)$

**Assembler
Syntax:** DBcc Dn,< label >

Attributes: Size = (Word)

Description: This instruction is a looping primitive of three parameters: a condition, a counter (data register), and a displacement. The instruction first tests the condition to determine if the termination condition for the loop has been met, and if so, no operation is performed. If the termination condition is not true, the low order 16 bits of the counter data register are decremented by one. If the result is -1, the counter is exhausted and execution continues with the next instruction. If the result is not equal to -1, execution continues at the location indicated by the current value of the PC plus the sign-extended 16-bit displacement. The value in the PC is the current instruction location plus two.

"cc" may specify the following conditions:

CC	carry clear	0100	$\overline{C}$		LS	low or same	0011	$C+Z$
CS	carry set	0101	C		LI	less than	1101	$N \cdot \overline{V} + \overline{N} \cdot V$
EQ	equal	0111	Z		MI	minus	1011	N
F	never true	0001	0		NE	not equal	0110	$\overline{Z}$
GE	greater or equal	1100	$N \cdot V + \overline{N} \cdot \overline{V}$		PL	plus	1010	$\overline{N}$
GT	greater than	1110	$N \cdot V \cdot \overline{Z} + \overline{N} \cdot \overline{V} \cdot \overline{Z}$		T	always true	0000	1
HI	high	0010	$\overline{C} \cdot \overline{Z}$		VC	overflow clear	1000	$\overline{V}$
LE	less or equal	1111	$Z + N \cdot \overline{V} + \overline{N} \cdot V$		VS	overflow set	1001	V

Condition Codes: Not affected.

Instruction Format:

15	14	13	12	11	10	9	8	7	6	5	4	3	2	1	0
0	1	0	1		Condition			1	1	0	0	1		Register	
Displacement															

Instruction Fields:
Condition field — One of the sixteen conditions discussed in description.
Register field — Specifies the data register which is the counter.
Displacement field — Specifies the distance of the branch (in bytes).

Notes: 1. The terminating condition is like that defined by the UNTIL loop constructs of high-level languages. For example: DBMI can be stated as "decrement and branch until minus".

B

2. Most assemblers accept DBRA for DBF for use when no condition is required for termination of a loop.

3. There are two basic ways of entering a loop: at the beginning or by branching to the trailing DBcc instruction. If a loop structure terminated with DBcc is entered at the beginning, the control index count must be one less than the number of loop executions desired. This count is useful for indexed addressing modes and dynamically specified bit operations. However, when entering a loop by branching directly to the trailing DBcc instruction, the control index should equal the loop execution count. In this case, if a zero count occurs, the DBcc instruction will not branch, causing a complete bypass of the main loop.

B

DIVS
DIVSL

Signed Divide

Operation: Destination/Source → Destination

Assembler	DIVS.W<ea>,Dn	32/16 → 16r:16q
Syntax:	DIVS.L<ea>,Dq	32/32 → 32q
	DIVS.L<ea>,Dr:Dq	64/32 → 32r:32q
	DIVSL.L<ea>,Dr:Dq	32/32 → 32r:32q

Attributes: Size = (Word, Long)

Description: Divide the destination operand by the source and store the result in the destination. The operation is performed using signed arithmetic.

The instruction has a word form and three long forms. For the word form, the destination operand is a long word and the source operand is a word. The result is 32-bits, such that the quotient is in the lower word (least significant 16 bits) of the destination and the remainder is in the upper word (most significant 16 bits) of the destination. Note that the sign of the remainder is the same as the sign of the dividend.

For the first long form, the destination operand is a long word and the source operand is a long word. The result is a long quotient, and the remainder is discarded.

For the second long form, the destination operand is a quad word, contained in any two data registers, and the source operand is a long word. The result is a long word quotient and a long word remainder.

For the third long form, the destination operand is a long word and the source operand is a long word. The result is a long word quotient and a long word remainder.

Two special conditions may arise during the operation:
1. Division by zero causes a trap.
2. Overflow may be detected and set before completion of the instruction. If overflow is detected, the condition is flagged but the operands are unaffected.

Condition Codes:

X	N	Z	V	C
—	*	*	*	0

N   Set if the quotient is negative. Cleared otherwise. Undefined if overflow or divide by zero.

Z   Set if the quotient is zero. Cleared otherwise. Undefined if overflow or divide by zero.

V   Set if division overflow is detected. Cleared otherwise.

C   Always cleared.

X   Not affected.

B

DIVS
DIVSL

Signed Divide

Instruction Format (word form):

15	14	13	12	11	10	9	8	7	6	5	4	3	2	1	0
1	0	0	0	Register Dn			1	1	1	Effective Address					
										Mode			Register		

Instruction Fields:

Register field — Specifies any of the eight data registers. This field always specifies the destination operand.

Effective Address field — Specifies the source operand. Only data addressing modes are allowed as shown:

Addr. Mode	Mode	Register
Dn	000	reg. number:Dn
An	—	—
(An)	010	reg. number:An
(An)+	011	reg. number:An
−(An)	100	reg. number:An
(d_{16},An)	101	reg. number:An
(d_8,An,Xn)	110	reg. number:An
(bd,An,Xn)	110	reg. number:An
([bd,An,Xn],od)	110	reg. number:An
([bd,An],Xn,od)	110	reg. number:An

Addr. Mode	Mode	Register
(xxx).W	111	000
(xxx).L	111	001
#<data>	111	100
(d_{16},PC)	111	010
(d_8,PC,Xn)	111	011
(bd,PC,Xn)	111	011
([bd,PC,Xn],od)	111	011
([bd,PC],Xn,od)	111	011

Note: Overflow occurs if the quotient is larger than a 16-bit signed integer.

Instruction Format (long form):

15	14	13	12	11	10	9	8	7	6	5	4	3	2	1	0
0	1	0	0	1	1	0	0	0	1	Effective Address					
										Mode			Register		
0	Register Dq			1	Sz	0	0	0	0	0	0	0	Register Dr		

Instruction Fields:

Effective Address field — Specifies the source operand. Only data addressing modes are allowed as shown:

DIVS
DIVSL

Signed Divide

Addr. Mode	Mode	Register
Dn	000	reg. number:Dn
An	—	—
(An)	010	reg. number:An
(An) +	011	reg. number:An
– (An)	100	reg. number:An
(d_{16},An)	101	reg. number:An
(d_8,An,Xn)	110	reg. number:An
(bd,An,Xn)	110	reg. number:An
([bd,An,Xn],od)	110	reg. number:An
([bd,An],Xn,od)	110	reg. number:An

Addr. Mode	Mode	Register
(xxx).W	111	000
(xxx).L	111	001
#<data>	111	100
(d_{16},PC)	111	010
(d_8,PC,Xn)	111	011
(bd,PC,Xn)	111	011
([bd,PC,Xn],od)	111	011
([bd,PC],Xn,od)	111	011

Register Dq field — Specifies a data register for the destination operand. The low order 32 bits of the dividend comes from this register, and the 32-bit quotient is loaded into this register.

Sz field — Selects a 32 or 64 bit division operation.

    0—32-bit dividend is in Register Dq.

    1—64-bit dividend is in Dr:Dq.

Register Dr field — After the division, the 32-bit remainder is loaded into this register. If Dr = Dq, only the quotient is returned. If Sz is 1, this field also specifies the data register in which the high order 32 bits of the dividend is located.

Note: Overflow occurs if the quotient is larger than a 32-bit signed integer.

B

DIVU
DIVUL

Unsigned Divide

Operation: Destination/Source → Destination

Assembler DIVU.W <ea>,Dn $\qquad$ 32/16 → 16r:16q
Syntax: DIVU.L <ea>,Dq $\qquad$ 32/32 → 32q
$\qquad$ DIVU.L <ea>,Dr:Dq $\qquad$ 64/32 → 32r:32q
$\qquad$ DIVUL.L <ea>,Dr:Dq $\qquad$ 32/32 → 32r:32q

Attributes: Size = (Word, Long)

Description: Divide the destination operand by the source and store the result in the destination. The operation is performed using unsigned arithmetic.

The instruction has a word from and three long forms. For the word form, the destination operand is a long word and the source operand is a word. The result is 32-bits, such that the quotient is in the lower word (least significant 16 bits) of the destination and the remainder is in the upper word (most significant 16 bits) of the destination. Note that the sign of the remainder is the same as the sign of the dividend.

For the first long form, the destination operand is a long word and the source operand is a long word. The result is a long word quotient, and the remainder is discarded.

For the second long form, the destination operand is a quad word, contained in any two data registers, and the source operand is a long word. The result is a long word quotient and a long word remainder.

For the third long form, the destination operand is a long word and the source operand is a long word. The result is a long word quotient and a long word remainder.

Two special conditions may arise:
1. Division by zero causes a trap.
2. Overflow may be detected and set before completion of the instruction. If overflow is detected, the condition is flagged but the operands are unaffected.

Condition Codes:

X	N	Z	V	C
—	*	*	*	0

N $\quad$ Set if the quotient is negative. Cleared otherwise. Undefined if overflow or divide by zero.
Z $\quad$ Set if the quotient is zero. Cleared otherwise. Undefined if overflow or divide by zero.
V $\quad$ Set if division overflow is detected. Cleared otherwise.
C $\quad$ Always cleared.
X $\quad$ Not affected.

DIVU
DIVUL

Unsigned Divide

Instruction Format (word form):

15	14	13	12	11	10	9	8	7	6	5	4	3	2	1	0
1	0	0	0	Register Dn			0	1	1	Effective Address Mode			Register		

Instruction Fields:

Register field — Specifies any of the eight data registers. This field always specifies the destination operand.

Effective Address field — Specifies the source operand. Only data addressing modes are allowed as shown:

Addr. Mode	Mode	Register
Dn	000	reg. number:Dn
An	—	—
(An)	010	reg. number:An
(An)+	011	reg. number:An
−(An)	100	reg. number:An
(d$_{16}$,An)	101	reg. number:An
(d$_8$,An,Xn)	110	reg. number:An
(bd,An,Xn)	110	reg. number:An
([bd,An,Xn],od)	110	reg. number:An
([bd,An],Xn,od)	110	reg. number:An

Addr. Mode	Mode	Register
(xxx).W	111	000
(xxx).L	111	001
#<data>	111	100
(d$_{16}$,PC)	111	010
(d$_8$,PC,Xn)	111	011
(bd,PC,Xn)	111	011
([bd,PC,Xn],od)	111	011
([bd,PC],Xn,od)	111	011

Note: Overflow occurs if the quotient is larger than a 16-bit unsigned integer.

Instruction Format (long form):

15	14	13	12	11	10	9	8	7	6	5	4	3	2	1	0
0	1	0	0	1	1	0	0	0	1	Effective Address Mode			Register		
0	Register Dq		0	Sz	0	0	0	0	0	0	0	Register Dr			

Instruction Fields:

Effective Address field — Specifies the source operand. Only data addressing modes are allowed as shown:

B

Unsigned Divide

Addr. Mode	Mode	Register
Dn	000	reg. number:Dn
An	—	—
(An)	010	reg. number:An
(An) +	011	reg. number:An
– (An)	100	reg. number:An
(d_{16},An)	101	reg. number:An
(d_8,An,Xn)	110	reg. number:An
(bd,An,Xn)	110	reg. number:An
([bd,An,Xn],od)	110	reg. number:An
([bd,An],Xn,od)	110	reg. number:An

Addr. Mode	Mode	Register
(xxx).W	111	000
(xxx).L	111	001
#<data>	111	100
(d_{16},PC)	111	010
(d_8,PC,Xn)	111	011
(bd,PC,Xn)	111	011
([bd,PC,Xn],od)	111	011
([bd,PC],Xn,od)	111	011

Register Dq field — Specifies a data register for the destination operand. The low order 32 bits of the dividend come from this register, and the 32-bit quotient is loaded into this register.

Sz field — Selects a 32 or 64 bit division operation.

0—32-bit dividend is in Register Dq.

1—64-bit dividend is in Dr:Dq.

Register Dr field — After the division, the 32-bit remainder is loaded into this register. If Dr = Dq, only the quotient is returned. If Sz is 1, this field also specifies the data register in which the high order 32 bits of the dividend are located.

Note: Overflow occurs if the quotient is larger than a 32-bit unsigned integer.

B

EOR

Exclusive OR Logical

EOR

Operation: Source $\oplus$ Destination $\rightarrow$ Destination

Assembler Syntax: EOR Dn, <ea>

Attributes: Size = (Byte, Word, Long)

Description: Exclusive OR the source operand to the destination operand and store the result in the destination location. The size of the operation may be specified to be byte, word, or long. This operation is restricted to data registers as the source operand. The destination operand is specified in the effective address field.

Condition Codes:

X	N	Z	V	C
—	*	*	0	0

N   Set if the most significant bit of the result is set. Cleared otherwise.
Z   Set if the result is zero. Cleared otherwise.
V   Always cleared.
C   Always cleared.
X   Not affected.

Instruction Format (word form):

15	14	13	12	11	10	9	8	7	6	5	4	3	2	1	0
1	0	1	1	Register Dn			Op-Mode			Effective Address					
										Mode			Register		

Instruction Fields:

Register field — Specifies any of the eight data registers.

Op-Mode field —

Byte	Word	Long	Operation
100	101	110	<ea> $\oplus$ <Dx> $\rightarrow$ <ea>

Effective Address field — Specifies the destination operand. Only data alterable addressing modes are allowed as shown:

B

EOR

Exclusive OR Logical

EOR

Addr. Mode	Mode	Register
Dn	000	reg. number:Dn
An	—	—
(An)	010	reg. number:An
(An)+	011	reg. number:An
−(An)	100	reg. number:An
(d_{16},An)	101	reg. number:An
(d_8,An,Xn)	110	reg. number:An
(bd,An,Xn)	110	reg. number:An
([bd,An,Xn],od)	110	reg. number:An
([bd,An],Xn,od)	110	reg. number:An

Addr. Mode	Mode	Register
(xxx).W	111	000
(xxx).L	111	001
#<data>	—	—
(d_{16},PC)	—	—
(d_8,PC,Xn)	—	—
(bd,PC,Xn)	—	—
([bd,PC,Xn],od)	—	—
([bd,PC],Xn,od)	—	—

Note: Memory to data register operations are not allowed. EORI is used when the source is immediate data. Most assemblers automatically make this distinction.

EORI

Exclusive OR Immediate

Operation: Immediate Data $\oplus$ Destination $\rightarrow$ Destination

Assembler Syntax: EORI #<data>,<ea>

Attributes: Size = (Byte, Word, Long)

Description: Exclusive OR the immediate data to the destination operand and store the result in the destination location. The size of the operation may be specified to be byte, word, or long. The immediate data matches the operation size.

Condition Codes:

X	N	Z	V	C
—	*	*	0	0

N   Set if the most significant bit of the result is set. Cleared otherwise.
Z   Set if the result is zero. Cleared otherwise.
V   Always cleared.
C   Always cleared.
X   Not affected.

Instruction Format:

15	14	13	12	11	10	9	8	7	6	5	4	3	2	1	0
0	0	0	0	1	0	1	0	Size		Effective Address Mode			Register		

0	0	0	0	1	0	1	0	Size		Effective Address — Mode			Register		
Word Data (10 Bits)								Byte Data (8 Bits)							
Long Data (32 Bits, including Previous Word)															

Instruction Fields:

Size field — Specifies the size of the operation:
　　00—byte operation.
　　01—word operation.
　　10—long operation.
Effective Address field — Specifies the destination operand. Only data alterable addressing modes are allowed as shown:

B

Exclusive OR Immediate

Addr. Mode	Mode	Register
Dn	000	reg. number:Dn
An	—	—
(An)	010	reg. number:An
(An)+	011	reg. number:An
−(An)	100	reg. number:An
(d$_{16}$,An)	101	reg. number:An
(d$_8$,An,Xn)	110	reg. number:An
(bd,An,Xn)	110	reg. number:An
([bd,An,Xn],od)	110	reg. number:An
([bd,An],Xn,od)	110	reg. number:An

Addr. Mode	Mode	Register
(xxx).W	111	000
(xxx).L	111	001
#<data>	—	—
(d$_{16}$,PC)	—	—
(d$_8$,PC,Xn)	—	—
(bd,PC,Xn)	—	—
([bd,PC,Xn],od)	—	—
([bd,PC],Xn,od)	—	—

Immediate field — (Data immediately following the instruction):
   If size = 00, then the data is the low order byte of the immediate word.
   If size = 01, then the data is the entire immediate word.
   If size = 10, then the data is next two immediate words.

B

Exclusive OR Immediate to Condition Code

EORI
to CCR

Operation: Source $\oplus$ CCR $\rightarrow$ CCR

**Assembler
Syntax:** EORI #<data>,CCR

Attributes: Size = (Byte)

Description: Exclusive OR the immediate operand with the condition codes and store the result in the low-order byte of the status register.

Condition Codes:

X	N	Z	V	C
*	*	*	*	*

N   Changed if bit 3 of immediate operand is one. Unchanged otherwise.
Z   Changed if bit 2 of immediate operand is one. Unchanged otherwise.
V   Changed if bit 1 of immediate operand is one. Unchanged otherwise.
C   Changed if bit 0 of immediate operand is one. Unchanged otherwise.
X   Changed if bit 4 of immediate operand is one. Unchanged otherwise.

Instruction Format:

15	14	13	12	11	10	9	8	7	6	5	4	3	2	1	0
0	0	0	0	1	0	1	0	0	0	1	1	1	1	0	0
0	0	0	0	0	0	0	0	Byte Data (8 Bits)							

B

**Exclusive OR Immediate to the Status Register
(Privileged Instruction)**

Operation: If supervisor state
then Source $\oplus$ SR $\rightarrow$ SR
else TRAP

**Assembler
Syntax:**   EORI #<data>,SR

Attributes: Size = (Word)

Description: Exclusive OR the immediate operand with the contents of the status register and store the result in the status register. All bits of the status register are affected.

Condition Codes:

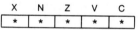

X	N	Z	V	C
*	*	*	*	*

N   Changed if bit 3 of immediate operand is one. Unchanged otherwise.
Z   Changed if bit 2 of immediate operand is one. Unchanged otherwise.
V   Changed if bit 1 of immediate operand is one. Unchanged otherwise.
C   Changed if bit 0 of immediate operand is one. Unchanged otherwise.
X   Changed if bit 4 of immediate operand is one. Unchanged otherwise.

Instruction Format:

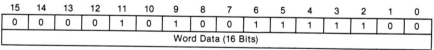

15	14	13	12	11	10	9	8	7	6	5	4	3	2	1	0
0	0	0	0	1	0	1	0	0	1	1	1	1	1	0	0
Word Data (16 Bits)															

B

EXG

EXG

Operation: Rx ↔ Ry

Assembler EXG Dx,Dy
Syntax: EXG Ax,Ay
EXG Dx,Ay

Attributes: Size = (Long)

Description: Exchange the contents of two registers. This exchange is always a long (32 bit) operation. Exchange works in three modes:
1. Exchange data registers.
2. Exchange address registers.
3. Exchange a data register and an address register.

Condition Codes: Not affected.

Instruction Format:

15	14	13	12	11	10	9	8	7	6	5	4	3	2	1	0
1	1	0	0	Register Rx			1	Op-Mode					Register Ry		

Instruction Fields:

Register Rx field — Specifies either a data register or an address register depending on the mode. If the exchange is between data and address registers, this field always specifies the data register.

Op-Mode field — Specifies whether exchanging:

01000—data registers.

01001—address registers.

10001—data register and address register.

Register Ry field — Specifies either a data register or an address register depending on the mode. If the exchange is between data and address registers, this field always specifies the address register.

Sign Extend

Operation: Destination Sign-extended → Destination

Assembler   EXT.W Dn   extend byte to word
Syntax: EXT.L Dn   extend word to long word
                 EXTB.L Dn   extend byte to long word

Attributes: Size = (Word, Long)

Description: Extend the sign bit of a data register from a byte to a word, from a word to a long word, or from a byte to a long word operand, depending on the size selected. If the operation is word, bit [7] of the designated data register is copied to bits [15:8] of that data register. If the operation is long, bit [15] of the designated data register is copied to bits [31:16] of the data register. The EXTB form copies bit [7] of the designated register to bits [31:8] of the data register.

Condition Codes:

X	N	Z	V	C
—	*	*	0	0

N   Set if the result is negative. Cleared otherwise.
Z   Set if the result is zero. Cleared otherwise.
V   Always cleared.
C   Always cleared.
X   Not affected.

Instruction Format:

15	14	13	12	11	10	9	8	7	6	5	4	3	2	1	0
0	1	0	0	1	0	0		Op-Mode		0	0	0		Register Dn	

Instruction Fields:

Op-Mode field — Specifies the size of the sign-extension operation:
   010—Sign-extend low order byte of data register to word.
   011—Sign-extend low order word of data register to long.
   111—Sign-extend low order byte of data register to long.
Register field — Specifies the data register whose content is to be sign-extended.

ILLEGAL

Take Illegal Instruction Trap

ILLEGAL

Operation: SSP − 2 → SSP; Vector Offset → (SSP);
SSP − 4 → SSP; PC → (SSP);
SSP − 2 → SSP; SR → (SSP);
Illegal Instruction Vector Address → PC

**Assembler
Syntax:** ILLEGAL

Attributes: Unsized

Description: This bit pattern causes an illegal instruction exception. All other illegal instruction bit patterns are reserved for future extension of the instruction set.

Condition Codes: Not affected.

Instruction Format:

15	14	13	12	11	10	9	8	7	6	5	4	3	2	1	0
0	1	0	0	1	0	1	0	1	1	1	1	1	1	0	0

B

JMP

Operation: Destination Address → PC

**Assembler
Syntax:**   JMP <ea>

Attributes: Unsized

Description: Program execution continues at the effective address specified by the instruction. The address is specified by the control addressing modes.

Condition Codes: Not affected.

Instruction Format:

15	14	13	12	11	10	9	8	7	6	5	4	3	2	1	0
0	1	0	0	1	1	1	0	1	1	Effective Address					
										Mode			Register		

Instruction Fields:

Effective Address field — Specifies the address of the next instruction. Only control addressing modes are allowed as shown:

Addr. Mode	Mode	Register
Dn	—	—
An	—	—
(An)	010	reg. number:An
(An)+	—	—
−(An)	—	—
(d$_{16}$,An)	101	reg. number:An
(d$_8$,An,Xn)	110	reg. number:An
(bd,An,Xn)	110	reg. number:An
([bd,An,Xn],od)	110	reg. number:An
([bd,An],Xn,od)	110	reg. number:An

Addr. Mode	Mode	Register
(xxx).W	111	000
(xxx).L	111	001
#<data>	—	—
(d$_{16}$,PC)	111	010
(d$_8$,PC,Xn)	111	011
(bd,PC,Xn)	111	011
([bd,PC,Xn],od)	111	011
([bd,PC],Xn,od)	111	011

B

JSR

JSR

Operation: $SP - 4 \rightarrow SP$; $PC \rightarrow (SP)$
Destination Address $\rightarrow PC$

**Assembler
Syntax:** JSR $<$ea$>$

Attributes: Unsized

Description: The long word address of the instruction immediately following the JSR instruction is pushed onto the system stack. Program execution then continues at the address specified in the instruction.

Condition Codes: Not affected.

Instruction Format:

15	14	13	12	11	10	9	8	7	6	5	4	3	2	1	0
0	1	0	0	1	1	1	0	1	0		Effective Address				
											Mode		Register		

Instruction Fields:

Effective Address field — Specifies the address of the next instruction. Only control addressing modes are allowed as shown:

Addr. Mode	Mode	Register
Dn	—	—
An	—	—
(An)	010	reg. number:An
(An)+	—	—
−(An)	—	—
(d_{16},An)	101	reg. number:An
(d_8,An,Xn)	110	reg. number:An
(bd,An,Xn)	110	reg. number:An
([bd,An,Xn],od)	110	reg. number:An
([bd,An],Xn,od)	110	reg. number:An

Addr. Mode	Mode	Register
(xxx).W	111	000
(xxx).I	111	001
#$<$data$>$	—	—
(d_{16},PC)	111	010
(d_8,PC,Xn)	111	011
(bd,PC,Xn)	111	011
([bd,PC,Xn],od)	111	011
([bd,PC],Xn,od)	111	011

B

LEA

Load Effective Address

LEA

Operation: $<ea> \to An$

**Assembler
Syntax:** LEA $<ea>$,An

Attributes: Size = (Long)

Description: The effective address is loaded into the specified address register. All 32 bits of the address register are affected by this instruction.

Condition Codes: Not affected.

Instruction Format:

15	14	13	12	11	10	9	8	7	6	5	4	3	2	1	0
0	1	0	0	Register An			1	1	1	Effective Address Mode			Register		

Instruction Fields:

Register field — Specifies the address register which is to be loaded with the effective address.

Effective Address field — Specifies the address to be loaded into the address register. Only control addressing modes are allowed as shown:

Addr. Mode	Mode	Register
Dn	—	—
An	—	—
(An)	010	reg. number:An
(An) +	—	—
– (An)	—	—
(d_{16},An)	101	reg. number:An
(d_8,An,Xn)	110	reg. number:An
(bd,An,Xn)	110	reg. number:An
([bd,An,Xn],od)	110	reg. number:An
([bd,An],Xn,od)	110	reg. number:An

Addr. Mode	Mode	Register
(xxx).W	111	000
(xxx).L	111	001
#$<data>$	—	—
(d_{16},PC)	111	010
(d_8,PC,Xn)	111	011
(bd,PC,Xn)	111	011
([bd,PC,Xn],od)	111	011
([bd,PC],Xn,od)	111	011

B

Link and Allocate

Operation: SP − 4 → SP; An → (SP);
SP → An; SP + d → SP

**Assembler
Syntax:** LINK An, #<displacement>

Attributes: Size = (Word, Long)

Description: The current content of the specified address register is pushed onto the stack. After the push, the address register is loaded from the updated stack pointer. Finally, the displacement operand is added to the stack pointer. For word size operation, the displacement is the sign-extended word following the operation word. For long size operation, the displacement is the long word following the operation word. The content of the address register occupies one long word on the stack. A negative displacement is specified to allocate stack area.

Condition Codes: Not affected.

Instruction Format:

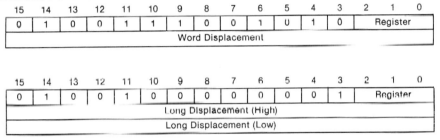

15	14	13	12	11	10	9	8	7	6	5	4	3	2	1	0
0	1	0	0	1	1	1	0	0	1	0	1	0	Register		
Word Displacement															

15	14	13	12	11	10	9	8	7	6	5	4	3	2	1	0
0	1	0	0	1	0	0	0	0	0	0	0	1	Register		
Long Displacement (High)															
Long Displacement (Low)															

Instruction Fields:

Register field — Specifies the address register through which the link is to be constructed.

Displacement field — Specifies the twos complement integer which is to be added to the stack pointer.

Note: LINK and UNLK can be used to maintain a linked list of local data and parameter areas on the stack for nested subroutine calls.

B

LSL, LSR　　　Logical Shift　　　LSL,LSR

Operation:　Destination Shifted by <count> → Destination

Assembler　LSd Dx,Dy
Syntax:　　LSd #<data>,Dy
　　　　　　　LSd <ea>
　　　　　　　where d is direction, L or R

Attributes:　Size = (Byte, Word, Long)

Description: Shift the bits of the operand in the direction (L or R) specified. The carry bit receives the last bit shifted out of the operand. The shift count for the shifting of a register may be specified in two different ways:
1. Immediate — the shift count is specified in the instruction (shift range 1-8).
2. Register — the shift count is contained in a data register specified in the instruction (shift count modulo 64).

The size of the operation may be specified to be byte, word, or long. The content of memory may be shifted one bit only, and the operand size is restricted to a word.

For LSL, the operand is shifted left; the number of positions shifted is the shift count. Bits shifted out of the high order bit go to both the carry and the extend bits; zeroes are shifted into the low order bit.

LSL:

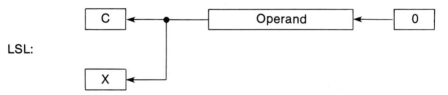

For LSR, the operand is shifted right; the number of positions shifted is the shift count. Bits shifted out of the low order bit go to both the carry and the extend bits; zeroes are shifted into the high order bit.

LSR:

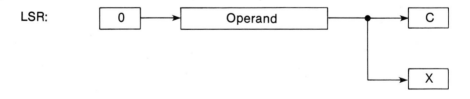

— Continued —

Condition Codes:

X	N	Z	V	C
*	*	*	0	*

N   Set if the result is negative. Cleared otherwise.
Z   Set if the result is zero. Cleared otherwise.
V   Always cleared.
C   Set according to the last bit shifted out of the operand. Cleared for a shift count of zero.
X   Set according to the last bit shifted out of the operand. Unaffected for a shift count of zero.

Instruction Format (Register Shifts):

15	14	13	12	11 10 9	8	7 6	5	4	3	2 1 0
1	1	1	0	Count/Register	dr	Size	i/r	0	1	Register

Instruction Field (Register Shifts):

Count/Register field —
   If i/r = 0, the shift count is specified in this field. The values 0, 1-7 represent a range of 8, 1 to 7 respectively.
   If i/r = 1, the shift count (modulo 64) is contained in the data register specified in this field.
dr field — Specifies the direction of the shift:
   0— shift right.
   1—shift left.
Size field — Specifies the size of the operation:
   00—byte operation.
   01—word operation.
   10—long operation.
i/r field —
   If i/r = 0, Specifies immediate shift count.
   If i/r = 1, Specifies register shift count.
Register field — Specifies a data register whose content is to be shifted.

Instruction Format (Memory Shifts):

15	14	13	12	11	10	9	8	7	6	5 4 3	2 1 0
1	1	1	0	0	0	1	dr	1	1	Effective Address Mode	Register

Instruction Fields (Memory Shifts):

dr field — Specifies the direction of the shift:
   0—shift right.
   1—shift left.
Effective Address field — Specifies the operand to be shifted. Only memory alterable addressing modes are allowed as shown:

B

Addr. Mode	Mode	Register
Dn	—	—
An	—	—
(An)	010	reg. number:An
(An) +	011	reg. number:An
– (An)	100	reg. number:An
(d$_{16}$,An)	101	reg. number:An
(d$_8$,An,Xn)	110	reg. number:An
(bd,An,Xn)	110	reg. number:An
([bd,An,Xn],od)	110	reg. number:An
([bd,An],Xn,od)	110	reg. number:An

Addr. Mode	Mode	Register
(xxx).W	111	000
(xxx).L	111	001
#<data>	—	—
(d$_{16}$,PC)	—	—
(d$_8$,PC,Xn)	—	—
(bd,PC,Xn)	—	—
([bd,PC,Xn],od)	—	—
([bd,PC],Xn,od)	—	—

B

MOVE   Move Data from Source to Destination   **MOVE**

Operation: Source → Destination

Assembler
Syntax: MOVE <ea>,<ea>

Attributes: Size = (Byte, Word, Long)

Description: Move the content of the source to the destination location. The data is examined as it is moved, and the condition codes set accordingly. The size of the operation may be specified to be byte, word, or long.

Condition Codes:

X	N	Z	V	C
—	*	*	0	0

N   Set if the result is negative. Cleared otherwise.
Z   Set if the result is zero. Cleared otherwise.
V   Always cleared.
C   Always cleared.
X   Not affected.

Instruction Format:

15	14	13	12	11	10	9	8	7	6	5	4	3	2	1	0
0	0	Size		Destination						Source					
				Register			Mode			Mode			Register		

Instruction Fields:

Size field — Specifies the size of the operand to be moved:
01—byte operation.
11—word operation.
10—long operation.

Destination Effective Address field — Specifies the destination location. Only data alterable addressing modes are allowed as shown:

Addr. Mode	Mode	Register		Addr. Mode	Mode	Register
Dn	000	reg. number:An		(xxx).W	111	000
An	—	—		(xxx).L	111	001
(An)	010	reg. number:An		#<data>	—	—
(An)+	011	reg. number:An				
−(An)	100	reg. number:An				
(d_{16},An)	101	reg. number:An		(d_{16},PC)	—	—
(d_8,An,Xn)	110	reg. number:An		(d_8,PC,Xn)	—	—
(bd,An,Xn)	110	reg. number:An		(bd,PC,Xn)	—	—
([bd,An,Xn],od)	110	reg. number:An		([bd,PC,Xn],od)	—	—
([bd,An],Xn,od)	110	reg. number:An		([bd,PC],Xn,od)	—	—

MOVE

MOVE

Source Effective Address field — Specifies the source operand. All addressing modes are allowed as shown:

Addr. Mode	Mode	Register
Dn	000	reg. number:Dn
An*	001	reg. number:An
(An)	010	reg. number:An
(An)+	011	reg. number:An
-(An)	100	reg. number:An
(d_{16},An)	101	reg. number:An
(d_8,An,Xn)	110	reg. number:An
(bd,An,Xn)	110	reg. number:An
([bd,An,Xn],od)	110	reg. number:An
([bd,An],Xn,od)	110	reg. number:An

Addr. Mode	Mode	Register
(xxx).W	111	000
(xxx).L	111	001
#<data>	111	100
(d_{16},PC)	111	010
(d_8,PC,Xn)	111	011
(bd,PC,Xn)	111	011
([bd,PC,Xn],od)	111	011
([bd,PC],Xn,od)	111	011

*For byte size operation, address register direct is not allowed.

Notes: 1. MOVEA is used when the destination is an address register. Most assemblers automatically make this distinction.
2. MOVEQ can also be used for certain operations on data registers.

MOVEA   Move Address   MOVEA

Operation: Source → Destination

**Assembler
Syntax:**   MOVEA <ea>,An

Attributes: Size = (Word, Long)

Description: Move the content of the source to the destination address register. The size of the operation may be specified to be word or long. Word size source operands are sign extended to 32 bit quantities before the operation is done.

Condition Codes: Not affected.

Instruction Format:

15	14	13 12	11 10 9	8	7	6	5 4 3	2 1 0
0	0	Size	Destination Register	0	0	1	Source Mode	Register

Instruction Fields:

Size field — Specifies the size of the operand to be moved:
    11—Word operation. The source operand is sign-extended to a long operand and all 32 bits are loaded into the address register.
    10—Long operation.
Destination Register field — Specifies the destination address register.
Source Effective Address field — Specifies the location of source operand. All addressing modes are allowed as shown:

Addr. Mode	Mode	Register
Dn	000	reg. number:Dn
An	001	reg. number:An
(An)	010	reg. number:An
(An)+	011	reg. number:An
−(An)	100	reg. number:An
(d$_{16}$,An)	101	reg. number:An
(d$_8$,An,Xn)	110	reg. number:An
(bd,An,Xn)	110	reg. number:An
([bd,An,Xn],od)	110	reg. number:An
([bd,An],Xn,od)	110	reg. number:An

Addr. Mode	Mode	Register
(xxx).W	111	000
(xxx).L	111	001
#<data>	111	100
(d$_{16}$,PC)	111	010
(d$_8$,PC,Xn)	111	011
(bd,PC,Xn)	111	011
([bd,PC,Xn],od)	111	011
([bd,PC],Xn,od)	111	011

B

MOVE
from CCR

MOVE
from CCR

Move from the
Condition Code Register

Operation: CCR → Destination

Assembler
Syntax: MOVE CCR, < ea >

Attributes: Size = (Word)

Description: The content of the status register is moved to the destination location. The source operand is a word, but only the low order byte contains the condition codes. The upper byte is all zeroes.

Condition Codes: Not affected.

Instruction Format:

15	14	13	12	11	10	9	8	7	6	5	4	3	2	1	0
0	1	0	0	0	0	1	0	1	1	Effective Address					

Effective Address	
Mode	Register

Instruction Fields:

Effective Address field — Specifies the destination location. Only data alterable addressing modes are allowed as shown:

Addr. Mode	Mode	Register
Dn	000	reg. number:Dn
An	—	—
(An)	010	reg. number:An
(An) +	011	reg. number:An
– (An)	100	reg. number:An
(d$_{16}$,An)	101	reg. number:An
(d$_8$,An,Xn)	110	reg. number:An
(bd,An,Xn)	110	reg. number:An
([bd,An,Xn],od)	110	reg. number:An
([bd,An],Xn,od)	110	reg. number:An

Addr. Mode	Mode	Register
(xxx).W	111	000
(xxx).L	111	001
#<data>	—	—
(d$_{16}$,PC)	—	—
(d$_8$,PC,Xn)	—	—
(bd,PC,Xn)	—	—
([bd,PC,Xn],od)	—	—
([bd,PC],Xn,od)	—	—

Note: MOVE from CCR is a word operation. ANDI, ORI, and EORI to CCR are byte operations.

Operation: Source → CCR

Assembler
Syntax: MOVE <ea>,CCR

Attributes: Size = (Word)

Description: The content of the source operand is moved to the condition codes. The source operand is a word, but only the low order byte is used to update the condition codes. The upper byte is ignored.

Condition Codes:

X	N	Z	V	C
*	*	*	*	*

N   Set the same as bit 3 of the source operand.
Z   Set the same as bit 2 of the source operand.
V   Set the same as bit 1 of the source operand.
C   Set the same as bit 0 of the source operand.
X   Set the same as bit 4 of the source operand.

Instruction Format:

15	14	13	12	11	10	9	8	7	6	5	4	3	2	1	0
0	1	0	0	0	1	0	0	1	1	Effective Address					
										Mode			Register		

Instruction Fields:

Effective Address field — Specifies the location of the source operand. Only data addressing modes are allowed as shown:

Addr. Mode	Mode	Register	Addr. Mode	Mode	Register
Dn	000	reg. number:Dn	(xxx).W	111	000
An	—	—	(xxx).L	111	001
(An)	010	reg. number:An	#<data>	111	100
(An)+	011	reg. number:An			
−(An)	100	reg. number:An			
(d$_{16}$,An)	101	reg. number:An	(d$_{16}$,PC)	111	010
(d$_8$,An,Xn)	110	reg. number:An	(d$_8$,PC,Xn)	111	011
(bd,An,Xn)	110	reg. number:An	(bd,PC,Xn)	111	011
([bd,An,Xn],od)	110	reg. number:An	([bd,PC,Xn],od)	111	011
([bd,An],Xn,od)	110	reg. number:An	([bd,PC],Xn,od)	111	011

Note: MOVE to CCR is a word operation. ANDI, ORI, and EORI to CCR are byte operations.

MOVE
from SR

**Move from the Status Register
(Privileged Instruction)**

Operation: If supervisor state
   then SR → Destination
   else TRAP

**Assembler
Syntax:** MOVE SR,< ea >

Attributes: Size = (Word)

Description: The content of the status register is moved to the destination location. The operand size is a word.

Condition Codes: Not affected.

Instruction Format:

15	14	13	12	11	10	9	8	7	6	5	4	3	2	1	0
0	1	0	0	0	0	0	0	1	1	Effective Address					

15	14	13	12	11	10	9	8	7	6	5	4	3	2	1	0
0	1	0	0	0	0	0	0	1	1	Mode			Register		

Instruction Fields:
   Effective Address field — Specifies the destination location. Only data alterable addressing modes are allowed as shown:

Addr. Mode	Mode	Register		Addr. Mode	Mode	Register
Dn	000	reg. number:Dn		(xxx).W	111	000
An	—	—		(xxx).L	111	001
(An)	010	reg. number:An		#< data >	—	—
(An) +	011	reg. number:An				
– (An)	100	reg. number:An				
(d$_{16}$,An)	101	reg. number:An		(d$_{16}$,PC)	—	—
(d$_8$,An,Xn)	110	reg. number:An		(d$_8$,PC,Xn)	—	—
(bd,An,Xn)	110	reg. number:An		(bd,PC,Xn)	—	—
([bd,An,Xn],od)	110	reg. number:An		([bd,PC,Xn],od)	—	—
([bd,An],Xn,od)	110	reg. number:An		([bd,PC],Xn,od)	—	—

Note: Use the MOVE from CCR instruction to access only the condition codes.

Move to the Status Register
(Privileged Instruction)

Operation: If supervisor state
                    then Source → SR
                    else TRAP

Assembler
Syntax: MOVE <ea>,SR

Attributes: Size = (Word)

Description: The content of the source operand is moved to the status register. The source operand is a word and all bits of the status register are affected.

Condition Codes: Set according to the source operand.

Instruction Format:

15	14	13	12	11	10	9	8	7	6	5	4	3	2	1	0
0	1	0	0	0	1	1	0	1	1	Effective Address					

										Effective Address					
0	1	0	0	0	1	1	0	1	1	Mode			Register		

Instruction Fields:

Effective Address field — Specifies the location of the source operand. Only data addressing modes are allowed as shown:

Addr. Mode	Mode	Register
Dn	000	reg. number:Dn
An	—	—
(An)	010	reg. number:An
(An)+	011	reg. number:An
−(An)	100	reg. number:An
(d$_{16}$,An)	101	reg. number:An
(d$_8$,An,Xn)	110	reg. number:An
(bd,An,Xn)	110	reg. number:An
([bd,An,Xn],od)	110	reg. number:An
([bd,An],Xn,od)	110	reg. number:An

Addr. Mode	Mode	Register
(xxx).W	111	000
(xxx).L	111	001
#<data>	111	100
(d$_{16}$,PC)	111	010
(d$_8$,PC,Xn)	111	011
(bd,PC,Xn)	111	011
([bd,PC,Xn],od)	111	011
([bd,PC],Xn,od)	111	011

B

**Move User Stack Pointer
(Privileged Instruction)**

Operation: If supervisor state
then USP → An or An → USP
else TRAP

Assembler MOVE USP,An
Syntax: Move An,USP

Attributes: Size = (Long)

Description: The contents of the user stack pointer are transferred to or from the specified address register.

Condition Codes: Not affected.

Instruction Format:

15	14	13	12	11	10	9	8	7	6	5	4	3	2	1	0
0	1	0	0	1	1	1	0	0	1	1	0	dr		Register	

Instruction Fields:

dr field — Specifies the direction of transfer:
0—transfer the address register to the USP.
1—transfer the USP to the address register.
Register field — Specifies the address register to or from which the user stack pointer is to be transferred.

**Move Control Register
(Privileged Instruction)**

Operation: If supervisor state
        then Rc → Rn or Rn → Rc
        else TRAP

Assembler   MOVEC Rc,Rn
Syntax: MOVEC Rn,Rc

Attributes: Size = (Long)

Description: Copy the contents of the specified control register (Rc) to the specified general register or copy the contents of the specified general register to the specified control register. This is always a 32-bit transfer even though the control register may be implemented with fewer bits. Unimplemented bits are read as zeros.

Condition Codes: Not affected.

Instruction Format:

15	14	13	12	11	10	9	8	7	6	5	4	3	2	1	0
0	1	0	0	1	1	1	0	0	1	1	1	1	0	1	dr
A/D	Register			Control Register											

Instruction Fields:

    dr field — Specifies the direction of the transfer:
        0—control register to general register.
        1—general register to control register.
    A/D field   Specifies the type of general register:
        0—data register.
        1—address register.
    Register field — Specifies the register number.
    Control Register field — Specifies the control register.

    Hex   **Control Register**
    000   Source Function Code (SFC) register.

    001   Destination Function Code (DFC) register.
    002   Cache Control Register (CACR).
    800   User Stack Pointer (USP).
    801   Vector Base Register (VBR).
    802   Cache Address Register (CAAR).
    803   Master Stack Pointer (MSP).
    804   Interrupt Stack Pointer (ISP).

    All other codes cause an illegal instruction exception.

B

MOVEM   Move Multiple Registers   MOVEM

Operation: Registers → Destination
                 Source → Registers

Assembler   MOVEM register list,<ea>
Syntax: MOVEM <ea>,register list

Attributes: Size = (Word, Long)

Description: Selected registers are transferred to or from consecutive memory locations starting at the location specified by the effective address. A register is transferred if the bit corresponding to that register is set in the mask field. The instruction selects how much of each register is transferred; either the entire long word can be moved or just the low order word. In the case of a word transfer to the registers, each word is sign-extended to 32 bits (including data registers) and the resulting long word loaded into the associated register.

MOVEM allows three forms of address modes: the control modes, the predecrement mode, or the postincrement mode. If the effective address is in one of the control modes, the registers are transferred starting at the specified address and up through higher addresses. The order of transfer is from data register 0 to data register 7, then from address register 0 to address register 7.

If the effective address is the predecrement mode, only a register to memory operation is allowed. The registers are stored starting at the specified address minus the operand length (2 or 4) and down through lower addresses. The order of storing is from address register 7 to address register 0, then from data register 7 to data register 0. The decremented address register is updated to contain the address of the last word stored.

If the effective address is the postincrement mode, only a memory to register operation is allowed. The registers are loaded starting at the specified address and up through higher addresses. The order of loading is the same as for the control mode addressing. The incremented address register is updated to contain the address of the last word loaded plus the operand length (2 or 4).

Condition Codes: Not affected.

Instruction Format:

15	14	13	12	11	10	9	8	7	6	5	4	3	2	1	0
0	1	0	0	1	dr	0	0	1	Sz	Effective Address					
										Mode			Register		
Register List Mask															

— Continued —

Instruction Fields:

dr field — Specifies the direction of the transfer:

0—register to memory.

1—memory to register.

Sz field — Specifies the size of the registers being transferred:

0—word transfer.

1—long transfer.

Effective Address field — Specifies the memory address to or from which the registers are to be moved.

For register to memory transfers, only control alterable addressing modes or the predecrement addressing mode are allowed as shown:

Addr. Mode	Mode	Register
Dn	—	—
An	—	—
(An)	010	reg. number:An
(An)+	011	—
−(An)	100	reg. number:An
(d$_{16}$,An)	101	reg. number:An
(d$_8$,An,Xn)	110	reg. number:An
(bd,An,Xn)	110	reg. number:An
([bd,An,Xn],od)	110	reg. number:An
([bd,An],Xn,od)	110	reg. number:An

Addr. Mode	Mode	Register
(xxx).W	111	000
(xxx).L	111	001
#<data>	—	—
(d$_{16}$,PC)	—	—
(d$_8$,PC,Xn)	—	—
(bd,PC,Xn)	—	—
([bd,PC,Xn],od)	—	—
([bd,PC],Xn,od)	—	—

For memory to register transfers, only control addressing modes or the post-increment addressing mode are allowed as shown:

Addr. Mode	Mode	Register
Dn		
An	—	—
(An)	010	reg. number:An
(An)+	011	reg. number:An
−(An)	—	—
(d$_{16}$,An)	101	reg. number:An
(d$_8$,An,Xn)	110	reg. number:An
(bd,An,Xn)	110	reg. number:An
([bd,An,Xn],od)	110	reg. number:An
([bd,An],Xn,od)	110	reg. number:An

Addr. Mode	Mode	Register
(xxx).W	111	000
(xxx).L	111	001
#<data>	—	—
(d$_{16}$,PC)	111	010
(d$_8$,PC,Xn)	111	011
(bd,PC,Xn)	111	011
([bd,PC,Xn],od)	111	011
([bd,PC],Xn,od)	111	011

Register List Mask field — Specifies which registers are to be transferred. The low order bit corresponds to the first register to be transferred; the high bit corresponds to the last register to be transferred. Thus, both for control modes and for the postincrement mode addresses, the mask correspondence is

15	14	13	12	11	10	9	8	7	6	5	4	3	2	1	0
A7	A6	A5	A4	A3	A2	A1	A0	D7	D6	D5	D4	D3	D2	D1	D0

while for the predecrement mode addresses, the mask correspondence is

15	14	13	12	11	10	9	8	7	6	5	4	3	2	1	0
D0	D1	D2	D3	D4	D5	D6	D7	A0	A1	A2	A3	A4	A5	A6	A7

Note: An extra read bus cycle occurs for memory operands. This accesses an operand at one address higher than the last register image required.

MOVEP Move Peripheral Data MOVEP

Operation: Source → Destination

Assembler MOVEP Dx,(d,Ay)
Syntax: MOVEP (d,Ay)Dx

Attributes: Size = (Word, Long)

Description: Data is transferred between a data register and alternate bytes of memory, starting at the location specified and incrementing by two. The high order byte of the data register is transferred first and the low order byte is transferred last. The memory address is specified using the address register indirect plus 16-bit displacement addressing mode. This instruction is designed to work with 8-bit peripherals on a 16-bit data bus. If the address is even, all the transfers are made on the high order half of the data bus; if the address is odd, all the transfers are made on the low order half of the data bus. On an 8- or 32-bit bus, the instruction still accesses every other byte.

Example: Long transfer to/from an even address.

Byte organization in register

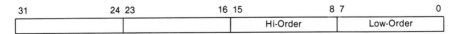

31	24 23	16 15	8 7	0
Hi-Order	Mid-Upper	Mid-Lower	Low-Order	

Byte organization in memory (low address at top)

15	8	7	0
Hi-Order			
Mid-Upper			
Mid-Lower			
Low-Order			

Example: Word transfer to/from an odd address.

Byte organization in register

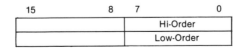

31	24 23	16 15	8 7	0
		Hi-Order	Low-Order	

Byte organization in memory (low address at top)

15	8	7	0
		Hi-Order	
		Low-Order	

— Continued —

B

MOVEP

Move Peripheral Data

Condition Codes: Not affected.

Instruction Format:

15	14	13	12	11	10	9	8	7	6	5	4	3	2	1	0
0	0	0	0	Data Register			Op-Mode			0	0	1	Address Register		
Displacement															

Instruction Fields:

Data Register field — Specifies the data register to or from which the data is to be transferred.

Op-Mode field — Specifies the direction and size of the operation:

100—transfer word from memory to register.

101—transfer long from memory to register.

110—transfer word from register to memory.

111—transfer long from register to memory.

Address Register field — Specifies the address register which is used in the address register indirect plus displacement addressing mode.

Displacement field — Specifies the displacement which is used in calculating the operand address.

B

MOVEQ

Operation: Immediate Data → Destination

**Assembler
Syntax:**   MOVEQ #<data>,Dn

Attributes: Size = (Long)

Description: Move immediate data to a data register. The data is contained in an 8-bit field within the operation word. The data is sign-extended to a long operand and all 32 bits are transferred to the data register.

Condition Codes:

X	N	Z	V	C
—	*	*	0	0

N   Set if the result is negative. Cleared otherwise.
Z   Set if the result is zero. Cleared otherwise.
V   Always cleared.
C   Always cleared.
X   Not affected.

Instruction Format:

15	14	13	12	11	10	9	8	7	6	5	4	3	2	1	0
0	1	1	1		Register		0				Data				

Instruction Fields:
  Register field — Specifies the data register to be loaded.
  Data field — 8 bits of data which are sign extended to a long operand.

MOVES

Move Address Space
(Privileged Instruction)

Operation: If supervisor state
then Rn → Destination [DFC] or Source [SFC] → Rn
else TRAP

Assembler MOVES Rn, < ea >
Syntax: MOVES < ea >, Rn

Attributes: Size = (Byte, Word, Long)

Description: Move the byte, word, or long operand from the specified general register to a location within the address space specified by the destination function code (DFC) register. Or, move the byte, word, or long operand from a location within the address space specified by the source function code (SFC) register to the specified general register.

If the destination is a data register, the source operand replaces the corresponding low-order bits of that data register. If the destination is an address register, the source operand is sign-extended to 32 bits and then loaded into that address register.

Condition Codes: Not affected.

Instruction Format:

15	14	13	12	11	10	9	8	7	6	5	4	3	2	1	0
											Effective Address				
0	0	0	0	1	1	1	0	Size		Mode			Register		
A/D	Register			dr	0	0	0	0	0	0	0	0	0	0	0

Instruction Fields:

Size field — Specifies the size of the operation:
00—byte operation.
01—word operation.
10—long operation.

Effective Address field — Specifies the source or destination location within the alternate address space. Only alterable memory addressing modes are allowed as shown:

— Continued —

B

Addr. Mode	Mode	Register
Dn	—	—
An	—	—
(An)	010	reg. number:An
(An) +	011	reg. number:An
– (An)	100	reg. number:An
(d$_{16}$,An)	101	reg. number:An
(d$_8$,An,Xn)	110	reg. number:An
(bd,An,Xn)	110	reg. number:An
([bd,An,Xn],od)	110	reg. number:An
([bd,An],Xn,od)	110	reg. number:An

Addr. Mode	Mode	Register
(xxx).W	111	000
(xxx).L	111	001
#<data>	—	—
(d$_{16}$,PC)	—	—
(d$_8$,PC,Xn)	—	—
(bd,PC,Xn)	—	—
([bd,PC,Xn],od)	—	—
([bd,PC],Xn,od)	—	—

A/D field — Specifies the type of general register:
   0—data register.
   1—address register.
Register field — Specifies the register number.
dr field — Specifies the direction of the transfer:
   0—from <ea> to general register.
   1—from general register to <ea>.

MOVES.x An(An)+
   or
MOVES.x An, – (An)

where An is the same address register for both source and destination and is an undefined operation. The value stored in memory is undefined.

NOTE

On the MC68010 and MC68020 implementations, the value stored is the increment or the decrement value of An. This implementation may not appear on future devices.

B

MULS

Operation: Source*Destination → Destination

Assembler   MULS.W<ea>,Dn $16 \times 16 \rightarrow 32$
Syntax: MULS.L<ea>,Dl $32 \times 32 \rightarrow 32$
              MULS.L<ea>,Dh:Dl $32 \times 32 \rightarrow 64$

Attributes: Size = (Word, Long)

Description: Multiply two signed operands yielding a signed result. The operation is per-formed using signed arithmetic.

The instruction has a word form and a long form. For the word form, the multiplier and multiplicand are both word operands and the result is long word operand. A register operand is taken from the low order word, the upper word is unused. All 32 bits of the product are saved in the destination data register.

For the long form, the multiplier and multiplicand are both long word operands and the result is either a long word or a quad word. The long word result is the low order 32 bits of the quad word result.

Condition Codes:

X	N	Z	V	C
—	*	*	*	0

N   Set if the result is negative. Cleared otherwise.
Z   Set if the result is zero. Cleared otherwise.
V   Set if overflow. Cleared otherwise.
C   Always cleared.
X   Not affected.

Note: Overflow (V = 1) can occur only in the case of multiplying 32-bit operands to yield a 32-bit result. Overflow occurs if the high-order 32 bits of the quad word pro-duct are not the sign-extension of the low order 32 bits.

Instruction Format (word form):

15	14	13	12	11	10	9	8	7	6	5	4	3	2	1	0
1	1	0	0	Register Dn			1	1	1	Effective Address Mode			Register		

Instruction Fields:

Register field — Specifies one of the data registers. This field always specifies the destination.

Effective Address field — Specifies the source operand. Only data addressing modes are allowed as shown:

B

Addr. Mode	Mode	Register		Addr. Mode	Mode	Register
Dn	000	reg. number:Dn		(xxx).W	111	000
An	—	—		(xxx).L	111	001
(An)	010	reg. number:An		#<data>	111	100
(An)+	011	reg. number:An				
−(An)	100	reg. number:An				
(d$_{16}$,An)	101	reg. number:An		(d$_{16}$,PC)	111	010
(d$_8$,An,Xn)	110	reg. number:An		(d$_8$,PC,Xn)	111	011
(bd,An,Xn)	110	reg. number:An		(bd,PC,Xn)	111	011
([bd,An,Xn],od)	110	reg. number:An		([bd,PC,Xn],od)	111	011
([bd,An],Xn,od)	110	reg. number:An		([bd,PC],Xn,od)	111	011

Instruction Format (long form):

15	14	13	12	11	10	9	8	7	6	5	4	3	2	1	0
0	1	0	0	1	1	0	0	0	0	Effective Address					

15	14	13	12	11	10	9	8	7	6	5	4	3	2	1	0
0	1	0	0	1	1	0	0	0	0	Mode			Register		
0	Register Dl			1	Sz	0	0	0	0	0	0	0	Register Dh		

Instruction Fields:

Effective Address field — Specifies the source operand. Only data addressing modes are allowed as shown:

Addr. Mode	Mode	Register		Addr. Mode	Mode	Register
Dn	000	reg. number:Dn		(xxx).W	111	000
An	—	—		(xxx).L	111	001
(An)	010	reg. number:An		#<data>	111	100
(An)+	011	reg. number:An				
−(An)	100	reg. number:An				
(d$_{16}$,An)	101	reg. number:An		(d$_{16}$,PC)	111	010
(d$_8$,An,Xn)	110	reg. number:An		(d$_8$,PC,Xn)	111	011
(bd,An,Xn)	110	reg. number:An		(bd,PC,Xn)	111	011
([bd,An,Xn],od)	110	reg. number:An		([bd,PC,Xn],od)	111	011
([bd,An],Xn,od)	110	reg. number:An		([bd,PC],Xn,od)	111	011

Register Dl field — Specifies a data register for the destination operand. The 32-bit multiplicand comes from this register, and the low order 32 bits of the product is loaded into this register.

Sz field — Selects a 32- or 64-bit product result.

0—32-bit product to be returned to Register Dl.

1—64-bit product to be returned to Dh:Dl.

Register Dh field — If Sz is 1, specifies the data register into which the high order 32 bits of the product is loaded. If Dh = Dl and Sz is 1, the results of the operation are undefined. Otherwise, this field is unused.

B

MULU

Operation: Source*Destination → Destination

Assembler   MULU.W<ea>,Dn $16 \times 16 \to 32$
Syntax: MULU.L<ea>,Dl $32 \times 32 \to 32$
                MULU.L<ea>,Dh:Dl $32 \times 32 \to 64$

Attributes: Size = (Word, Long)

Description: Multiply two unsigned operands yielding a unsigned result. The operation is performed using unsigned arithmetic.

The instruction has a word form and a long form. For the word form, the multiplier and multiplicand are both word operands and the result is a long word operand. A register operand is taken from the low order word, the upper word is unused. All 32 bits of the product are saved in the destination data register.

For the long form, the multiplier and multiplicand are both long word operands and the result is either a long word or a quad word. The long word result is the low order 32 bits of the quad word result.

Condition Codes:

X	N	Z	V	C
—	*	*	*	0

N   Set if the result is negative. Cleared otherwise.
Z   Set if the result is zero. Cleared otherwise.
V   Set if overflow. Cleared otherwise.
C   Always cleared.
X   Not affected.

Note: Overflow (V = 1) can occur only in the case of multiplying 32-bit operands to yield a 32-bit result. Overflow occurs if the high-order 32 bits of the quad word product are non-zero.

Instruction Format (word form):

15	14	13	12	11	10	9	8	7	6	5	4	3	2	1	0
1	1	0	0	Register Dn			0	1	1	Effective Address Mode			Register		

Instruction Fields:

Register field — Specifies one of the data registers. This field always specifies the destination.

Effective Address field — Specifies the source operand. Only data addressing modes are allowed as shown:

MULU   Unsigned Multiply   MULU

Addr. Mode	Mode	Register
Dn	000	reg. number:Dn
An	—	—
(An)	010	reg. number:An
(An)+	011	reg. number:An
−(An)	100	reg. number:An
(d$_{16}$,An)	101	reg. number:An
(d$_8$,An,Xn)	110	reg. number:An
(bd,An,Xn)	110	reg. number:An
([bd,An,Xn],od)	110	reg. number:An
([bd,An],Xn,od)	110	reg. number:An

Addr. Mode	Mode	Register
(xxx).W	111	000
(xxx).L	111	001
#<data>	111	100
(d$_{16}$,PC)	111	010
(d$_8$,PC,Xn)	111	011
(bd,PC,Xn)	111	011
([bd,PC,Xn],od)	111	011
([bd,PC],Xn,od)	111	011

Instruction Format (long form):

15	14	13	12	11	10	9	8	7	6	5	4	3	2	1	0
0	1	0	0	1	1	0	0	0	0	Effective Address Mode			Register		
0	Register DI		0	Sz	0	0	0	0	0	0	0	Register Dh			

Instruction Fields:

Effective Address field — Specifies the source operand. Only data addressing modes are allowed as shown:

Addr. Mode	Mode	Register
Dn	000	reg. number:Dn
An	—	—
(An)	010	reg. number:An
(An)+	011	reg. number:An
−(An)	100	reg. number:An
(d$_{16}$,An)	101	reg. number:An
(d$_8$,An,Xn)	110	reg. number:An
(bd,An,Xn)	110	reg. number:An
([bd,An,Xn],od)	110	reg. number:An
([bd,An],Xn,od)	110	reg. number:An

Addr. Mode	Mode	Register
(xxx).W	111	000
(xxx).L	111	001
#<data>	111	100
(d$_{16}$,PC)	111	010
(d$_8$,PC,Xn)	111	011
(bd,PC,Xn)	111	011
([bd,PC,Xn],od)	111	011
([bd,PC],Xn,od)	111	011

Register DI field — Specifies a data register for the destination operand. The 32-bit multiplicand comes from this register, and the low order 32 bits of the product are loaded into this register.

Sz field — Selects a 32- or 64-bit product result.

   0—32-bit product to be returned to Register DI.

   1—64-bit product to be returned to Dh:DI.

Register Dh field — If Sz is 1, specifies the data register into which the high order 32 bits of the product are loaded. If Dh = DI and Sz is 1, the results of the operation are undefined. Otherwise, this field is unused.

Negate Decimal with Extend

Operation: $0 - \text{Destination}_{10} - X \rightarrow \text{Destination}$

**Assembler
Syntax:**   NBCD $<$ea$>$

Attributes: Size = (Byte)

Description: The operand addressed as the destination and the extend bit are subtracted from zero. The operation is performed using decimal arithmetic. The result is saved in the destination location. This instruction produces the tens complement of the destination if the extend bit is clear, the nines complement if the extend bit is set. This is a byte operation only.

Condition Codes:

X	N	Z	V	C
*	U	*	U	*

N   Undefined.
Z   Cleared if the result is non-zero. Unchanged otherwise.
V   Undefined.
C   Set if a borrow (decimal) was generated. Cleared otherwise.
X   Set the same as the carry bit.

NOTE

Normally the Z condition code bit is set via programming before the start of an operation. This allows successful tests for zero results upon completion of multiple precision operations.

Instruction Format:

15	14	13	12	11	10	9	8	7	6	5	4	3	2	1	0
0	1	0	0	1	0	0	0	0	0	Effective Address					

Effective Address: Mode | Register

Instruction Fields:

Effective Address field — Specifies the destination operand. Only data alterable addressing modes are allowed as shown:

B

Negate Decimal with Extend

Addr. Mode	Mode	Register
Dn	000	reg. number:Dn
An	—	—
(An)	010	reg. number:An
(An)+	011	reg. number:An
−(An)	100	reg. number:An
(d_{16},An)	101	reg. number:An
(d_8,An,Xn)	110	reg. number:An
(bd,An,Xn)	110	reg. number:An
([bd,An,Xn],od)	110	reg. number:An
([bd,An],Xn,od)	110	reg. number:An

Addr. Mode	Mode	Register
(xxx).W	111	000
(xxx).L	111	001
#<data>	—	—
(d_{16},PC)	—	—
(d_8,PC,Xn)	—	—
(bd,PC,Xn)	—	—
([bd,PC,Xn],od)	—	—
([bd,PC],Xn,od)	—	—

B

NEG

Negate

NEG

Operation: 0 − Destination → Destination

**Assembler
Syntax:** NEG <ea>

Attributes: Size = (Byte, Word, Long)

Description: The operand addressed as the destination is subtracted from zero. The result is stored in the destination location. The size of the operation may be specified to be byte, word, or long.

Condition Codes:

X	N	Z	V	C
*	*	*	*	*

N   Set if the result is negative. Cleared otherwise.
Z   Set if the result is zero. Cleared otherwise.
V   Set if an overflow is generated. Cleared otherwise.
C   Cleared if the result is zero. Set otherwise.
X   Set the same as the carry bit.

Instruction Format:

15	14	13	12	11	10	9	8	7	6	5	4	3	2	1	0
0	1	0	0	0	1	0	0	Size		Effective Address					
										Mode			Register		

Instruction Fields:

Size field — Specifies the size of the operation.
  00—byte operation.
  01—word operation.
  10—long operation.
Effective Address field — Specifies the destination operand. Only data alterable addressing modes are allowed as shown:

Addr. Mode	Mode	Register
Dn	000	reg. number:Dn
An	—	—
(An)	010	reg. number:An
(An)+	011	reg. number:An
−(An)	100	reg. number:An
(d₁₆,An)	101	reg. number:An
(d₈,An,Xn)	110	reg. number:An
(bd,An,Xn)	110	reg. number:An
([bd,An,Xn],od)	110	reg. number:An
([bd,An],Xn,od)	110	reg. number:An

Addr. Mode	Mode	Register
(xxx).W	111	000
(xxx).L	111	001
#<data>	—	—
(d₁₆,PC)	—	—
(d₈,PC,Xn)	—	—
(bd,PC,Xn)	—	—
([bd,PC,Xn],od)	—	—
([bd,PC],Xn,od)	—	—

Negate with Extend

Operation: 0 − (Destination) − X → Destination

**Assembler
Syntax:**   NEGX <ea>

Attributes: Size = (Byte, Word, Long)

Description: The operand addressed as the destination and the extend bit are subtracted from zero. The result is stored in the destination location. The size of the operation may be specified to be byte, word, or long.

Condition Codes:

X	N	Z	V	C
*	*	*	*	*

- N   Set if the result is negative. Cleared otherwise.
- Z   Cleared if the result is non-zero. Unchanged otherwise.
- V   Set if an overflow is generated. Cleared otherwise.
- C   Set if a borrow is generated. Cleared otherwise.
- X   Set the same as the carry bit.

NOTE

Normally the Z condition code bit is set via programming before the start of an operation. This allows successful tests for zero results upon completion of multiple-precision operations.

Instruction Format:

15	14	13	12	11	10	9	8	7	6	5	4	3	2	1	0
0	1	0	0	0	0	0	0	Size		Effective Address					
										Mode			Register		

Instruction Fields:

Size field — Specifies the size of the operation.

     00—byte operation.

     01—word operation.

     10—long operation.

Effective Address field — Specifies the destination operand. Only data alterable addressing modes are allowed as shown:

B

Negate with Extend

Addr. Mode	Mode	Register
Dn	000	reg. number:Dn
An	—	—
(An)	010	reg. number:An
(An)+	011	reg. number:An
−(An)	100	reg. number:An
(d$_{16}$,An)	101	reg. number:An
(d$_8$,An,Xn)	110	reg. number:An
(bd,An,Xn)	110	reg. number:An
([bd,An,Xn],od)	110	reg. number:An
([bd,An],Xn,od)	110	reg. number:An

Addr. Mode	Mode	Register
(xxx).W	111	000
(xxx).L	111	001
#<data>	—	—
(d$_{16}$,PC)	—	—
(d$_8$,PC,Xn)	—	—
(bd,PC,Xn)	—	—
([bd,PC,Xn],od)	—	—
([bd,PC],Xn,od)	—	—

NOP

No Operation

NOP

Operation: None

Assembler Syntax: NOP

Attributes: Unsized

Description: No operation occurs. The processor state, other than the program counter, is unaffected. Execution continues with the instruction following the NOP instruction. The NOP instruction does not complete execution until all pending bus cycles are completed. This allows synchronization of the pipeline to be accomplished, and prevents instruction overlap.

Condition Codes: Not affected.

Instruction Format:

15	14	13	12	11	10	9	8	7	6	5	4	3	2	1	0
0	1	0	0	1	1	1	0	0	1	1	1	0	0	0	1

Logical Complement

Operation: ~ Destination → Destination

Assembler
Syntax: NOT <ea>

Attributes: Size = (Byte, Word, Long)

Description: The ones complements of the destination operand is taken and the result is stored in the destination location. The size of the operation may be specified to be byte, word, or long.

Condition Codes:

X	N	Z	V	C
—	*	*	0	0

N Set if the result is negative. Cleared otherwise.
Z Set if the result is zero. Cleared otherwise.
V Always cleared.
C Always cleared.
X Not affected.

Instruction Format:

15	14	13	12	11	10	9	8	7	6	5	4	3	2	1	0
0	1	0	0	0	1	1	0	Size		Effective Address					
										Mode			Register		

Instruction Fields:

Size field — Specifies the size of the operation.
  00—byte operation.
  01—word operation.
  10—long operation.
Effective Address field — Specifies the destination operand. Only data alterable addressing modes are allowed as shown:

Addr. Mode	Mode	Register
Dn	000	reg. number:Dn
An	—	—
(An)	010	reg. number:An
(An)+	011	reg. number:An
−(An)	100	reg. number:An
(d$_{16}$,An)	101	reg. number:An
(d$_8$,An,Xn)	110	reg. number:An
(bd,An,Xn)	110	reg. number:An
([bd,An,Xn],od)	110	reg. number:An
([bd,An],Xn,od)	110	reg. number:An

Addr. Mode	Mode	Register
(xxx).W	111	000
(xxx).L	111	001
#<data>	—	—
(d$_{16}$,PC)	—	—
(d$_8$,PC,Xn)	—	—
(bd,PC,Xn)	—	—
([bd,PC,Xn],od)	—	—
([bd,PC],Xn,od)	—	—

Inclusive OR Logical

Operation: Source v Destination → Destination

Assembler   OR <ea>,Dn
Syntax: OR Dn,<ea>

Attributes: Size = (Byte, Word, Long)

Description: Inclusive OR the source operand to the destination operand and store the result in the destination location. The size of the operation may be specified to be byte, word, or long. The contents of an address register may not be used as an operand.

Condition Codes:

X	N	Z	V	C
—	*	*	0	0

N   Set if the most significant bit of the result is set. Cleared otherwise.
Z   Set if the result is zero. Cleared otherwise.
V   Always cleared.
C   Always cleared.
X   Not affected.

Instruction Format:

15	14	13	12	11	10	9	8	7	6	5	4	3	2	1	0
1	0	0	0		Register			Op-Mode			Effective Address Mode			Register	

Instruction Fields:

Register field — Specifies any of the eight data registers.

Op-Mode field —

Byte	Word	Long	Operation
000	001	010	(<ea>)v(<Dn>)→<Dn>
100	101	110	(<Dn>)v(<ea>)→<ea>

Effective Address field —

If the location specified is a source operand then only data addressing modes are allowed as shown:

Inclusive OR Logical

Addr. Mode	Mode	Register
Dn	000	reg. number:Dn
An	—	—
(An)	010	reg. number:An
(An)+	011	reg. number:An
−(An)	100	reg. number:An
(d_{16},An)	101	reg. number:An
(d_8,An,Xn)	110	reg. number:An
(bd,An,Xn)	110	reg. number:An
([bd,An,Xn],od)	110	reg. number:An
([bd,An],Xn,od)	110	reg. number:An

Addr. Mode	Mode	Register
(xxx).W	111	000
(xxx).L	111	001
#<data>	111	100
(d_{16},PC)	111	010
(d_8,PC,Xn)	111	011
(bd,PC,Xn)	111	011
([bd,PC,Xn],od)	111	011
([bd,PC],Xn,od)	111	011

If the location specified is a destination operand then only memory alterable addressing modes are allowed as shown:

Addr. Mode	Mode	Register
Dn	—	—
An	—	—
(An)	010	reg. number:An
(An)+	011	reg. number:An
−(An)	100	reg. number:An
(d_{16},An)	101	reg. number:An
(d_8,An,Xn)	110	reg. number:An
(bd,An,Xn)	110	reg. number:An
([bd,An,Xn],od)	110	reg. number:An
([bd,An],Xn,od)	110	reg. number:An

Addr. Mode	Mode	Register
(xxx).W	111	000
(xxx).L	111	001
#<data>	—	—
(d_{16},PC)	—	—
(d_8,PC,Xn)	—	—
(bd,PC,Xn)	—	—
([bd,PC,Xn],od)	—	—
([bd,PC],Xn,od)	—	—

Notes: 1. If the destination is a data register, then it cannot be specified by using the destination <ea> mode, but must use the destination Dn mode instead.
2. ORI is used when the source is immediate data. Most assemblers automatically make this distinction.

B

ORI

ORI

Operation: Immediate Data v Destination → Destination

**Assembler
Syntax:**   ORI #<data>,<ea>

Attributes: Size = (Byte, Word, Long)

Description: Inclusive OR the immediate data to the destination operand and store the result in the destination location. The size of the operation may be specified to be byte, word, or long. The size of the immediate data matches the operation size.

Condition Codes:

X	N	Z	V	C
—	*	*	0	0

N   Set if the most significant bit of the result is set. Cleared otherwise.
Z   Set if the result is zero. Cleared otherwise.
V   Always cleared.
C   Always cleared.
X   Not affected.

Instruction Format:

15	14	13	12	11	10	9	8	7	6	5	4	3	2	1	0
0	0	0	0	0	0	0	0	Size		Effective Address Mode			Register		
Word Data								Byte Data							
Long Data															

Instruction Fields:

Size field — Specifies the size of the operation.
   00—byte operation.
   01—word operation.
   10—long operation.
Effective Address field — Specifies the destination operand. Only data alterable addressing modes are allowed as shown:

B

Addr. Mode	Mode	Register
Dn	000	reg. number:Dn
An	—	—
(An)	010	reg. number:An
(An)+	011	reg. number:An
−(An)	100	reg. number:An
(d$_{16}$,An)	101	reg. number:An
(d$_8$,An,Xn)	110	reg. number:An
(bd,An,Xn)	110	reg. number:An
([bd,An,Xn],od)	110	reg. number:An
([bd,An],Xn,od)	110	reg. number:An

Addr. Mode	Mode	Register
(xxx).W	111	000
(xxx).L	111	001
#<data>	—	—
(d$_{16}$,PC)	—	—
(d$_8$,PC,Xn)	—	—
(bd,PC,Xn)	—	—
([bd,PC,Xn],od)	—	—
([bd,PC],Xn,od)	—	—

Immediate field — (Data immediately following the instruction):
    If size = 00, then the data is the low order byte of the immediate word.
    If size = 01, then the data is the entire immediate word.
    If size = 10, then the data is the next two immediate words.

B

ORI
to CCR

Operation: Source v CCR → CCR

**Assembler
Syntax:**   ORI #<data>,CCR

Attributes: Size = (Byte)

Description: Inclusive OR the immediate operand with the condition codes and store the result in the low-order byte of the status register.

Condition Codes:

X	N	Z	V	C
*	*	*	*	*

N   Set if bit 3 of immediate operand is one. Unchanged otherwise.
Z   Set if bit 2 of immediate operand is one. Unchanged otherwise.
V   Set if bit 1 of immediate operand is one. Unchanged otherwise.
C   Set if bit 0 of immediate operand is one. Unchanged otherwise.
X   Set if bit 4 of immediate operand is one. Unchanged otherwise.

Instruction Format:

15	14	13	12	11	10	9	8	7	6	5	4	3	2	1	0
0	0	0	0	0	0	0	0	0	0	1	1	1	1	0	0
0	0	0	0	0	0	0	0	Byte Data (8 Bits)							

B

ORI
to SR

Inclusive OR Immediate to the Status Register
(Privileged Instruction)

ORI
to SR

Operation: If supervisor state
then Source v SR → SR
else TRAP

Assembler
Syntax: ORI #<data>,SR

Attributes: Size = (Word)

Description: Inclusive OR the immediate operand with the contents of the status register and store the result in the status register. All bits of the status register are affected.

Condition Codes:

X	N	Z	V	C
*	*	*	*	*

N   Set if bit 3 of immediate operand is one. Unchanged otherwise.
Z   Set if bit 2 of immediate operand is one. Unchanged otherwise.
V   Set if bit 1 of immediate operand is one. Unchanged otherwise.
C   Set if bit 0 of immediate operand is one. Unchanged otherwise.
X   Set if bit 4 of immediate operand is one. Unchanged otherwise.

Instruction Format:

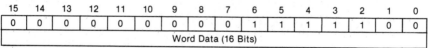

15	14	13	12	11	10	9	8	7	6	5	4	3	2	1	0
0	0	0	0	0	0	0	0	0	1	1	1	1	1	0	0
Word Data (16 Bits)															

B

Operation: Source (Unpacked BCD) + adjustment → Destination (Packed BCD)

Assembler PACK − (Ax), − (Ay),#<adjustment>
Syntax: PACK Dx,Dy,#<adjustment>

Attributes: Unsized

Description: The low four bits of each of two bytes are adjusted and packed into a single byte.

When both operands are data registers, the adjustment is added to the value contained in the source register. Bits [11:8] and [3:0] of the intermediate result are concatenated and placed in bits [7:0] of the destination register. The remainder of the destination register is unaffected.

Source:

	15	14	13	12	11	10	9	8	7	6	5	4	3	2	1	0
Dx	x	x	x	x	a	b	c	d	x	x	x	x	e	f	g	h

Add Adjustment Word:

15	14	13	12	11	10	9	8	7	6	5	4	3	2	1	0
							16-Bit Extension								

Resulting in:

15	14	13	12	11	10	9	8	7	6	5	4	3	2	1	0
x′	x′	x′	x′	a′	b′	c′	d′	x′	x′	x′	x′	e′	f′	g′	h′

Destination:

	15	14	13	12	11	10	9	8	7	6	5	4	3	2	1	0
Dy	u	u	u	u	u	u	u	u	a′	b′	c′	d′	e′	f′	g′	h′

When the addressing mode specified is predecrement, two bytes from the source are fetched, adjusted, and concatenated. The extension word is added to the concatenated bytes. Bits [3:0] of each byte are extracted. These eight bits are concatenated to form a new byte which is then written to the destination.

Source:

	7	6	5	4	3	2	1	0
	x	x	x	x	a	b	c	d
	x	x	x	x	e	f	g	h
(Ax)								

Concatenated Word:

15	14	13	12	11	10	9	8	7	6	5	4	3	2	1	0
x	x	x	x	a	b	c	d	x	x	x	x	e	f	g	h

B

Add Adjustment Word:

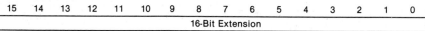

Destination:

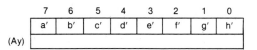

Condition Codes: Not affected.

Instruction Format:

15	14	13	12	11	10	9	8	7	6	5	4	3	2	1	0
1	0	0	0	Register Dy/Ay			1	0	1	0	0	R/M	Register Dx/Ax		
Adjustment															

Instruction Fields:

Register Dy/Ay field — Specifies the destination register.

If R/M = 0, specifies a data register.

If R/M = 1, specifies an address register for the predecrement addressing mode.

R/M field — Specifies the operand addressing mode.

0—The operation is data register to data register.

1—The operation is memory to memory.

Register Dx/Ax field — Specifies the source register.

If R/M = 0, specifies a data register.

If R/M = 1, specifies an address register for the predecrement addressing mode.

Adjustment field — Immediate data word which is added to the source operand.

Appropriate constants can be used to translate from ASCII or EBCDIC to BCD.

B

PEA

PEA

Operation: $SP - 4 \rightarrow SP; EA \rightarrow (SP)$

**Assembler
Syntax:**   PEA <ea>

Attributes: Size = (Long)

Description: The effective address is computed and pushed onto the stack. A long word address is pushed onto the stack.

Condition Codes: Not affected.

Instruction Format:

15	14	13	12	11	10	9	8	7	6	5	4	3	2	1	0
											Effective Address				
0	1	0	0	1	0	0	0	0	1		Mode			Register	

Instruction Fields:

Effective Address field — Specifies the address to be pushed onto the stack. Only control addressing modes are allowed as shown:

Addr. Mode	Mode	Register
Dn	—	—
An	—	—
(An)	010	reg. number:An
(An) +	—	—
− (An)	—	—
(d_{16},An)	101	reg. number:An
(d_8,An,Xn)	110	reg. number:An
(bd,An,Xn)	110	reg. number:An
([bd,An,Xn],od)	110	reg. number:An
([bd,An],Xn,od)	110	reg. number:An

Addr. Mode	Mode	Register
(xxx).W	111	000
(xxx).L	111	001
#<data>	—	—
(d_{16},PC)	111	010
(d_8,PC,Xn)	111	011
(bd,PC,Xn)	111	011
([bd,PC,Xn],od)	111	011
([bd,PC],Xn,od)	111	011

B

RESET

Operation: If supervisor state
    then Assert RESET Line
    else TRAP

Assembler
Syntax: RESET

Attributes: Unsized

Description: The reset line is asserted, causing all external devices to be reset. The processor state, other than the program counter, is unaffected and execution continues with the next instruction.

Condition Codes: Not affected.

Instruction Format:

15	14	13	12	11	10	9	8	7	6	5	4	3	2	1	0
0	1	0	0	1	1	1	0	0	1	1	1	0	0	0	0

B

Rotate (Without Extend)

Operation: Destination Rotated by <count> → Destination

Assembler   ROd Dx,Dy
Syntax: ROd #<data>,Dy
ROd <ea>
where d is direction, L or R

Attributes: Size = (Byte, Word, Long)

Description: Rotate the bits of the operand in the direction (L or R) specified. The extend
bit is not included in the rotation. The rotate count for the rotation of a register may
be specified in two different ways:
1. Immediate — the rotate count is specified in the instruction (rotate range, 1-8).
2. Register — the rotate count is contained in a data register specified in the instruction.
The size of the operation may be specified to be byte, word, or long. The content of
memory may be rotated by one bit only and the operand size is restricted to a word.

For ROL, the operand is rotated left; the number of positions rotated is the rotate
count. Bits rotated out of the high order bit go to both the carry bit and back into the
low order bit. The extend bit is not modified or used.

ROL:

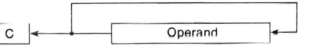

For ROR, the operand is rotated right; the number of positions rotated is the rotate
count. Bits shifted out of the low order bit go to both the carry bit and back into high
order bit. The extend bit is not modified or used.

ROR:

— Continued —

B

Condition Codes:

X	N	Z	V	C
—	*	*	0	*

N   Set if the most significant bit of the result is set. Cleared otherwise.
Z   Set if the result is zero. Cleared otherwise.
V   Always cleared.
C   Set according to the last bit rotated out of the operand. Cleared for a rotate count of zero.
X   Not affected.

Instruction Format (Register Rotate):

15	14	13	12	11	10	9	8	7	6	5	4	3	2	1	0
1	1	1	0	Rotate/ Register			dr	Size		i/r	1	1	Register		

Instruction Fields (Register Rotate):

Rotate/Register field —
   If i/r = 0, the rotate count is specified in this field. The values 0, 1-7 represent a range of 8, 1 to 7 respectively.
   If i/r = 1, the rotate count (modulo 64) is contained in the data register specified in this field.
dr field — Specifies the direction of the rotate:
   0—rotate right.
   1—rotate left.
Size field — Specifies the size of the operation:
   00—byte operation.
   01—word operation.
   10—long operation.
i/r field —
   If i/r = 0, specifies immediate rotate count.
   If i/r = 1, specifies register rotate count.
Register field — Specifies a data register whose content is to be rotated.

Instruction Format (Memory Rotate):

15	14	13	12	11	10	9	8	7	6	5	4	3	2	1	0
1	1	1	0	0	1	1	dr	1	1	Effective Address Mode			Register		

— Continued —

ROL
ROR

Rotate (without Extend)

ROL
ROR

Instruction Fields (Memory Rotate):

dr field — Specifies the direction of the rotate:

0—rotate right.

1—rotate left.

Effective Address field — Specifies the operand to be rotated. Only memory alterable addressing modes are allowed as shown:

Addr. Mode	Mode	Register
Dn	—	—
An	—	—
(An)	010	reg. number:An
(An)+	011	reg. number:An
−(An)	100	reg. number:An
(d_{16},An)	101	reg. number:An
(d_8,An,Xn)	110	reg. number:An
(bd,An,Xn)	110	reg. number:An
([bd,An,Xn],od)	110	reg. number:An
([bd,An],Xn,od)	110	reg. number:An

Addr. Mode	Mode	Register
(xxx).W	111	000
(xxx).L	111	001
#<data>	—	—
(d_{16},PC)	—	—
(d_8,PC,Xn)	—	—
(bd,PC,Xn)	—	—
([bd,PC,Xn],od)	—	—
([bd,PC],Xn,od)	—	—

Operation: Destination Rotated with X by <count> → Destination

Assembler   ROXd Dx,Dy
Syntax: ROXd #<data>,Dy
ROXd <ea>

Attributes: Size = (Byte, Word, Long)

Description: Rotate the bits of the destination operand in the direction specified. The extend bit (X) is included in the rotation. The rotate count for the rotation of a register may be specified in two different ways:
1. Immediate — the rotate count is specified in the instruction (rotate range, 1-8).
2. Register — the rotate count (modulo 64) is contained in a data register specified in the instruction.
The size of the operation may be specified to be byte, word, or long. The content of memory may be rotated one bit only and the operand size is restricted to a word.

For ROXL, the operand is rotated left; the number of positions rotated is the rotate count. Bits rotated out of the high order bit go to both the carry and extend bits; the previous value of the extend bit is rotated into the low order bit.

ROXL:

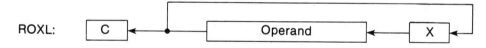

For ROXR, the operand is rotated right; the number of positions shifted is the rotate count. Bits rotated out of the low order bit go to both the carry and extend bits; the previous value of the extend bit is rotated into the high order bit.

ROXR:

Condition Codes:

X	N	Z	V	C
*	*	*	0	*

N   Set if the most significant bit of the result is set. Cleared otherwise.
Z   Set if the result is zero. Cleared otherwise.
V   Always cleared.
C   Set according to the last bit rotated out of the operand. Set to the value of the extend bit for a rotate count of zero.
X   Set according to the last bit rotated out of the operand. Unaffected for a rotate count of zero.

ROXL
ROXR

Rotate with Extend

Instruction Format (Register Rotate):

15	14	13	12	11	10	9	8	7	6	5	4	3	2	1	0
1	1	1	0	Rotate/ Register			dr	Size		i/r	1	0	Register		

Instruction Fields (Register Rotate):

Count/Register field —
  If i/r = 0, the rotate count is specified in this field. The values 0, 1-7 represent a
    range of 8, 1 to 7 respectively.
  If i/r = 1, the rotate count (modulo 64) is contained in the data register specified
    in this field.
dr field — Specifies the direction of the rotate:
  0—rotate right.
  1—rotate left.
Size field — Specifies the size of the operation:
  00—byte operation.
  01—word operation.
  10—long operation.
i/r field —
  If I/r = 0, specifies immediate rotate count.
  If i/r = 1, specifies register rotate count.
Register field — Specifies a data register whose content is to be rotated.

Instruction Format (Memory Rotate):

15	14	13	12	11	10	9	8	7	6	5	4	3	2	1	0
1	1	1	0	0	1	0	dr	1	1	Effective Address					
										Mode			Register		

Instruction Fields (Memory Rotate):

dr field — Specifies the direction of the rotate:
  0—rotate right.
  1—rotate left.
Effective Address field — Specifies the operand to be rotated. Only memory
  alterable addressing modes are allowed as shown:

B

Addr. Mode	Mode	Register
Dn	—	—
An	—	—
(An)	010	reg. number:An
(An)+	011	reg. number:An
−(An)	100	reg. number:An
(d$_{16}$,An)	101	reg. number:An
(d$_8$,An,Xn)	110	reg. number:An
(bd,An,Xn)	110	reg. number:An
([bd,An,Xn],od)	110	reg. number:An
([bd,An],Xn,od)	110	reg. number:An

Addr. Mode	Mode	Register
(xxx).W	111	000
(xxx).L	111	001
#<data>	—	—
(d$_{16}$,PC)	—	—
(d$_8$,PC,Xn)	—	—
(bd,PC,Xn)	—	—
([bd,PC,Xn],od)	—	—
([bd,PC],Xn,od)	—	—

B

Return and Deallocate Parameters

Operation: $(SP) \rightarrow PC; SP + 4 + d \rightarrow SP$

Assembler
Syntax: RTD #<displacement>

Attributes: Unsized

Description: The program counter is pulled from the stack. The previous program counter value is lost. After the program counter is read from the stack, the displacement value (16 bits) is sign-extended to 32 bits and added to the stack pointer.

Condition Codes: Not affected.

Instruction Format:

15	14	13	12	11	10	9	8	7	6	5	4	3	2	1	0
0	1	0	0	1	1	1	0	0	1	1	1	0	1	0	0
Displacement															

Instruction Field:
Displacement field — Specifies the twos complement integer which is to be sign-extended and added to the stack pointer.

Operation: If supervisor state
then (SP) → SR; SP + 2 → SP; (SP) → PC; SP + 4 → SP;
restore state and deallocate
stack according to (SP)
else TRAP

**Assembler
Syntax:**   RTE

Attributes: Unsized

Description: The processor state information in the exception stack frame on top of the
stack is loaded into the processor. The stack format field in the format/offset word is
examined to determine how much information must be restored.

Condition Codes: Set according to the content of the word on the stack.

Instruction Format:

15	14	13	12	11	10	9	8	7	6	5	4	3	2	1	0
0	1	0	0	1	1	1	0	0	1	1	1	0	0	1	1

Format/Offset Word (in stack frame):

15	14	13	12	11	10	9	8	7	6	5	4	3	2	1	0
Format				0	0	Vector Offset									

Instruction Fields:

Format field — This 4-bit field defines the amount of information to be restored.

0000—Short Format, only four words are to be removed from the top of the
stack. The status register and program counter are loaded from the
stack frame.

0001—Throwaway Format, four words are removed from the top of stack. Only the
status register is loaded, after which, the processor begins executing the
RTE from the top of the active system stack. This format is used to mark
the bottom of the interrupt stack.

0010—Instruction Error Format, six words are removed from the top of the
stack. The first four words are used as in the Short Format and the remaining two words are thrown away.

1000—MC68010 Long Format, the MC68020 takes a format error exception.

1001—Coprocessor Mid-Instruction Format, 10 words are removed from the top
of stack. Resumes coprocessor instruction execution.

1010—MC68020 Short Format, 16 words are removed from the top of the
stack. Resumes instruction execution.

1011—MC68020 Long Format, 46 words are removed from the top of the stack.
Resumes instruction execution.

Any others — the processor takes a format error exception.

Return from Module

Operation: Reload Saved Module State from Stack

**Assembler
Syntax:**   RTM Rn

Attributes: Unsized

Description: A previously saved module state is reloaded from the top of stack. After the module state is retrieved from the top of the stack, the caller's stack pointer is incremented by the argument count value in the module state.

Condition Codes: Set according to the content of the word on the stack.

Instruction Format:

15	14	13	12	11	10	9	8	7	6	5	4	3	2	1	0
0	0	0	0	0	1	1	0	1	1	0	0	D/A	Register		

Instruction Fields:

D/A field — Specifies whether the module data pointer is in a data or an address register.

0—the register is a data register.

1— the register is an address register.

Register field — Specifies the register number for the module data area pointer which is to be restored from the saved module state. If the register specified Is A7 (SP), the updated value of the register reflects the stack pointer operatlons, and the saved module data area pointer is lost.

B

RTR

RTR

Operation: (SP)→CCR; SP + 2→SP;
(SP)→PC; SP + 4→SP

**Assembler
Syntax:** RTR

Attributes: Unsized

Description: The condition codes and program counter are pulled from the stack. The previous condition codes and program counter are lost. The supervisor portion of the status register is unaffected.

Condition Codes: Set according to the content of the word on the stack.

Instruction Format:

15	14	13	12	11	10	9	8	7	6	5	4	3	2	1	0
0	1	0	0	1	1	1	0	0	1	1	1	0	1	1	1

RTS

Operation: $(SP) \rightarrow PC; SP + 4 \rightarrow SP$

Assembler
Syntax: RTS

Attributes: Unsized

Description: The program counter is pulled from the stack. The previous program counter is lost.

Condition Codes: Not affected.

Instruction Format:

15	14	13	12	11	10	9	8	7	6	5	4	3	2	1	0
0	1	0	0	1	1	1	0	0	1	1	1	0	1	0	1

B

Subtract Decimal with Extend

Operation: $Destination_{10} - Source_{10} - X \rightarrow Destination$

Assembler SBCD Dx,Dy
Syntax: SBCD $-(Ax), -(Ay)$

Attributes: Size = (Byte)

Description: Subtract the source operand from the destination operand with the extend bit and store the result in the destination location. The subtraction is performed using decimal arithmetic. The operands may be addressed in two different ways:
1. Data register to data register: The operands are contained in the data registers specified in the instruction.
2. Memory to memory: The operands are addressed with the predecrement addressing mode using the address registers specified in the instruction.
This operation is a byte operation only.

Condition Codes:

X	N	Z	V	C
*	U	*	U	*

N   Undefined.
Z   Cleared if the result is non-zero. Unchanged otherwise.
V   Undefined.
C   Set if a borrow (decimal) is generated. Cleared otherwise.
X   Set the same as the carry bit.

NOTE
Normally the Z condition code bit is set via programming before the start of an operation. This allows successful tests for zero results upon completion of multiple-precision operations.

Instruction Format:

15	14	13	12	11	10	9	8	7	6	5	4	3	2	1	0
1	0	0	0	Register Dy/Ay			1	0	0	0	0	R/M	Register Dx/Ax		

Instruction Fields:
Register Dy/Ay field — Specifies the destination register.
If R/M = 0, specifies a data register.
If R/M = 1, specifies an address register for the predecrement addressing mode.
R/M field — Specifies the operand addressing mode:
0—The operation is data register to data register.
1—The operation is memory to memory.
Register Dx/Ax field — Specifies the source register:
If R/M = 0, specifies a data register.
If R/M = 1, specifies an address register for the predecrement addressing mode.

B

Set According to Condition

Operation: If Condition True
then 1s → Destination
else 0s → Destination

**Assembler
Syntax:** Scc <ea>

Attributes: Size = (Byte)

Description: The specified condition code is tested; if the condition is true, the byte specified by the effective address is set to TRUE (all ones), otherwise that byte is set to FALSE (all zeroes). "cc" may specify the following conditions:

CC	carry clear	0100	$\overline{C}$
CS	carry set	0101	C
EQ	equal	0111	Z
F	never true	0001	0
GE	greater or equal	1100	$N \cdot V + \overline{N} \cdot \overline{V}$
GT	greater than	1110	$N \cdot V \cdot \overline{Z} + \overline{N} \cdot \overline{V} \cdot \overline{Z}$
HI	high	0010	$C \cdot \overline{Z}$
LE	less or equal	1111	$Z + N \cdot \overline{V} + \overline{N} \cdot V$

LS	low or same	0011	$C + Z$
LT	less than	1101	$N \cdot \overline{V} + \overline{N} \cdot V$
MI	minus	1011	N
NE	not equal	0110	$\overline{Z}$
PL	plus	1010	$\overline{N}$
T	always true	0000	1
VC	overflow clear	1000	$\overline{V}$
VS	overflow set	1001	V

Condition Codes: Not affected.

Instruction Format:

15	14	13	12	11	10	9	8	7	6	5	4	3	2	1	0
0	1	0	1		Condition			1	1		Effective Address				
											Mode			Register	

Instruction Fields:
Condition field — One of sixteen conditions discussed in description.
Effective Address field — Specifies the location in which the true/false byte is to be stored. Only data alterable addressing modes are allowed as shown:

Addr. Mode	Mode	Register
Dn	000	reg. number:Dn
An	—	—
(An)	010	reg. number:An
(An)+	011	reg. number:An
−(An)	100	reg. number:An
(d_{16},An)	101	reg. number:An
(d_8,An,Xn)	110	reg. number:An
(bd,An,Xn)	110	reg. number:An
([bd,An,Xn],od)	110	reg. number:An
([bd,An],Xn,od)	110	reg. number:An

Addr. Mode	Mode	Register
(xxx).W	111	000
(xxx).L	111	001
#<data>	—	—
(d_{16},PC)	—	—
(d_8,PC,Xn)	—	—
(bd,PC,Xn)	—	—
([bd,PC,Xn],od)	—	—
([bd,PC],Xn,od)	—	—

Note: 1. An arithmetic one and zero result may be generated by following the Scc instruction with a NEG instruction.

Load Status Register and Stop
(Privileged Instruction)

Operation: If supervisor state
                 then Immediate Data → SR; STOP
                 else TRAP

Assembler
Syntax: STOP #<data>

Attributes: Unsized

Description: The immediate operand is moved into the entire status register; the program counter is advanced to point to the next instruction and the processor stops fetching and executing instructions. Execution of instructions resumes when a trace, interrupt, or reset exception occurs. A trace exception will occur if the trace state is on when the STOP instruction begins execution. If an interrupt request is asserted with a priority higher than the priority level set by the immediate data, an interrupt exception occurs, otherwise, the interrupt request has no effect. If the bit of the immediate data corresponding to the S-bit is off, execution of the instruction will cause a privilege violation. External reset will always initiate reset exception processing.

Condition Codes: Set according to the immediate operand.

Instruction Format:

15	14	13	12	11	10	9	8	7	6	5	4	3	2	1	0
0	1	0	0	1	1	1	0	0	1	1	1	0	0	1	0
Immediate Data															

Instruction Fields:
Immediate field — Specifies the data to be loaded into the status register.

B

SUB

SUB

Operation: Destination − Source → Destination

Assembler SUB <ea>,Dn
Syntax: SUB Dn,<ea>

Attributes: Size = (Byte, Word, Long)

Description: Subtract the source operand from the destination operand and store the result in the destination. The size of the operation may be specified to be byte, word, or long. The mode of the instruction indicates which operand is the source and which is the destination as well as the operand size.

Condition Codes:

X	N	Z	V	C
*	*	*	*	*

N   Set if the result is negative. Cleared otherwise.
Z   Set if the result is zero. Cleared otherwise.
V   Set if an overflow is generated. Cleared otherwise.
C   Set if a borrow is generated. Cleared otherwise.
X   Set the same as the carry bit.

Instruction Format:

15	14	13	12	11	10	9	8	7	6	5	4	3	2	1	0
1	0	0	1	Register			Op-Mode			Effective Address					
										Mode			Register		

Instruction Fields:

Register field — Specifies any of the eight data registers.
Op-Mode field —

Byte	Word	Long	Operation
000	001	010	<Dn> − <ea> → <Dn>
100	101	110	<ea> − <Dn> → <ea>

Effective Address field — Determines addressing mode:
   If the location specified is a source operand, then all addressing modes are allowed as shown:

Addr. Mode	Mode	Register
Dn	000	reg. number:Dn
An*	001	reg. number:An
(An)	010	reg. number:An
(An)+	011	reg. number:An
−(An)	100	reg. number:An
(d_{16},An)	101	reg. number:An
(d_8,An,Xn)	110	reg. number:An
(bd,An,Xn)	110	reg. number:An
([bd,An,Xn],od)	110	reg. number:An
([bd,An],Xn,od)	110	reg. number:An

Addr. Mode	Mode	Register
(xxx).W	111	000
(xxx).L	111	001
#<data>	111	100
(d_{16},PC)	111	010
(d_8,PC,Xn)	111	011
(bd,PC,Xn)	111	011
([bd,PC,Xn],od)	111	011
([bd,PC],Xn,od)	111	011

*For byte size operation, address register direct is not allowed.

If the location specified is a destination operand, then only alterable memory addressing modes are allowed as shown:

Addr. Mode	Mode	Register
Dn	—	—
An	—	—
(An)	010	reg. number:An
(An)+	011	reg. number:An
−(An)	100	reg. number:An
(d_{16},An)	101	reg. number:An
(d_8,An,Xn)	110	reg. number:An
(bd,An,Xn)	110	reg. number:An
([bd,An,Xn],od)	110	reg. number:An
([bd,An],Xn,od)	110	reg. number:An

Addr. Mode	Mode	Register
(xxx).W	111	000
(xxx).L	111	001
#<data>	—	—
(d_{16},PC)	—	—
(d_8,PC,Xn)	—	—
(bd,PC,Xn)	—	—
([bd,PC,Xn],od)	—	—
([bd,PC],Xn,od)	—	—

Notes: 1. If the destination is a data register, then it cannot be specified by using the destination <ea> mode, but must use the destination Dn mode instead.
2. SUBA is used when the destination is an address register. SUBI and SUBQ are used when the source is immediate data. Most assemblers automatically make this distinction.

SUBA

Subtract Address

Operation: Destination − Source → Destination

**Assembler
Syntax:** SUBA <ea>,An

Attributes: Size = (Word, Long)

Description: Subtract the source operand from the destination address register and store the result in the address register. The size of the operation may be specified to be word or long. Word size source operands are sign extended to 32 bit quantities before the operation is done.

Condition Codes: Not affected.

Instruction Format:

15	14	13	12	11	10	9	8	7	6	5	4	3	2	1	0
1	0	0	1	Register			Op-Mode			Effective Address					
										Mode			Register		

Instruction Fields:

Register field — Specifies any of the eight address registers. This is always the destination.

Op-Mode field — Specifies the size of the operation:

011—Word operation. The source operand is sign-extended to a long operand and the operation is performed on the address register using all 32 bits.

111—Long operations.

Effective Address field — Specifies the source operand. All addressing modes are allowed as shown:

Addr. Mode	Mode	Register
Dn	000	reg. number:Dn
An	001	reg. number:An
(An)	010	reg. number:An
(An) +	011	reg. number:An
− (An)	100	reg. number:An
(d$_{16}$,An)	101	reg. number:An
(d$_8$,An,Xn)	110	reg. number:An
(bd,An,Xn)	110	reg. number:An
([bd,An,Xn],od)	110	reg. number:An
([bd,An],Xn,od)	110	reg. number:An

Addr. Mode	Mode	Register
(xxx).W	111	000
(xxx).L	111	001
#<data>	111	100
(d$_{16}$,PC)	111	010
(d$_8$,PC,Xn)	111	011
(bd,PC,Xn)	111	011
([bd,PC,Xn],od)	111	011
([bd,PC],Xn,od)	111	011

B

SUBI

Subtract Immediate

SUBI

Operation: Destination − Immediate Data → Destination

**Assembler
Syntax:** SUBI #<data>,<ea>

Attributes: Size = (Byte, Word, Long)

Description: Subtract the immediate data from the destination operand and store the result in the destination location. The size of the operation may be specified to be byte, word, or long. The size of the immediate data matches the operation size.

Condition Codes:

X	N	Z	V	C
*	*	*	*	*

N   Set if the result is negative. Cleared otherwise.
Z   Set if the result is zero. Cleared otherwise.
V   Set if an overflow is generated. Cleared otherwise.
C   Set if a borrow is generated. Cleared otherwise.
X   Set the same as the carry bit.

Instruction Format:

15	14	13	12	11	10	9	8	7	6	5	4	3	2	1	0
0	0	0	0	0	1	0	0	Size		Effective Address					
										Mode			Register		
Word Data								Byte Data							
Long Data															

Instruction Fields:

Size field — Specifies the size of the operation.
   00—byte operation.
   01—word operation.
   10—long operation.
Effective Address field — Specifies the destination operand. Only data alterable addressing modes are allowed as shown:

B

Addr. Mode	Mode	Register
Dn	000	reg. number:Dn
An	—	—
(An)	010	reg. number:An
(An)+	011	reg. number:An
−(An)	100	reg. number:An
(d_{16},An)	101	reg. number:An
(d_8,An,Xn)	110	reg. number:An
(bd,An,Xn)	110	reg. number:An
([bd,An,Xn],od)	110	reg. number:An
([bd,An],Xn,od)	110	reg. number:An

Addr. Mode	Mode	Register
(xxx).W	111	000
(xxx).L	111	001
#<data>	—	—
(d_{16},PC)	—	—
(d_8,PC,Xn)	—	—
(bd,PC,Xn)	—	—
([bd,PC,Xn],od)	—	—
([bd,PC],Xn,od)	—	—

Immediate field — (Data immediately following the instruction)

If size = 00, then the data is the low order byte of the immediate word.

If size = 01, then the data is the entire immediate word.

If size = 10, then the data is the next two immediate words.

B

SUBQ
Subtract Quick
SUBQ

Operation: Destination − Immediate Data → Destination

Assembler
Syntax: SUBQ #<data>,<ea>

Attributes: Size = (Byte, Word, Long)

Description: Subtract the immediate data from the destination operand. The data range is from 1-8. The size of the operation may be specified to be byte, word, or long. Word and long operations are also allowed on the address registers and the condition codes are not affected. When subtracting from address registers, the entire destination address register is used, regardless of the operation size.

Condition Codes:

X	N	Z	V	C
*	*	*	*	*

N Set if the result is negative. Cleared otherwise.
Z Set if the result is zero. Cleared otherwise.
V Set if an overflow is generated. Cleared otherwise.
C Set if a borrow is generated. Cleared otherwise.
X Set the same as the carry bit.

Instruction Format:

15	14	13	12	11	10	9	8	7	6	5	4	3	2	1	0
0	1	0	1		Data		1		Size		Effective Address				
											Mode			Register	

Instruction Fields:

Data field — Three bits of immediate data, 0, 1-7 representing a range of 8, 1 to 7 respectively.

Size field — Specifies the size of the operation:
    00—byte operation.
    01—word operation.
    10—long operation.

Effective Address field — Specifies the destination location. Only alterable addressing modes are allowed as shown:

B

SUBQ

Subtract Quick

SUBQ

Addr. Mode	Mode	Register
Dn	000	reg. number:Dn
An*	001	reg. number:An
(An)	010	reg. number:An
(An) +	011	reg. number:An
– (An)	100	reg. number:An
(d16,An)	101	reg. number:An
(d8,An,Xn)	110	reg. number:An
(bd,An,Xn)	110	reg. number:An
([bd,An,Xn],od)	110	reg. number:An
([bd,An],Xn,od)	110	reg. number:An

*Word and long only.

Addr. Mode	Mode	Register
(xxx).W	111	000
(xxx).L	111	001
#<data>	—	—
(d16,PC)	—	—
(d8,PC,Xn)	—	—
(bd,PC,Xn)	—	—
([bd,PC,Xn],od)	—	—
([bd,PC],Xn,od)	—	—

B

SUBX

Subtract with Extend

SUBX

Operation: Destination − Source − X → Destination

Assembler SUBX Dx,Dy
Syntax: SUBX − (Ax), − (Ay)

Attributes: Size = (Byte, Word, Long)

Description: Subtract the source operand from the destination operand along with the extend bit and store the result in the destination location. The operands may be ad-dressed in two different ways:
1. Data register to data register: The operands are contained in data registers specified in the instruction.
2. Memory to memory. The operands are contained in memory and addressed with the predecrement addressing mode using the address registers specified in the instruction.
The size of the operand may be specified to be byte, word, or long.

Condition Codes:

X	N	Z	V	C
*	*	*	*	*

N Set if the result is negative. Cleared otherwise.
Z Cleared if the result is non-zero. Unchanged otherwise.
V Set if an overflow is generated. Cleared otherwise.
C Set if a carry is generated. Cleared otherwise.
X Set the same as the carry bit.

NOTE
Normally the Z condition code bit is set via programming before the start of an operation. This allows successful tests for zero results upon completion of multiple-precision operations.

Instruction Format:

15	14	13	12	11	10	9	8	7	6	5	4	3	2	1	0
1	0	0	1	Register Dy/Ay			1	Size		0	0	R/M	Register Dx/Ax		

Instruction Fields:

Register Dy/Ay field — Specifies the destination register:
If R/M = 0, specifies a data register.
If R/M = 1, specifies an address register for the predecrement addressing mode.
Size field — Specifies the size of the operation:
00—byte operation.
01—word operation.
10—long operation.

B

R/M field — Specifies the operand addressing mode:

   0—The operation is data register to data register.

   1—The operation is memory to memory.

Register Dx/Ax field — Specifies the source register:

   If R/M = 0, specifies a data register.

   If R/M = 1, specifies an address register for the predecrement addressing mode.

B

SWAP

Swap Register Halves

SWAP

Operation: Register [31:16] ↔ Register [15:0]

**Assembler
Syntax:**   SWAP Dn

Attributes: Size = (Word)

Description: Exchange the 16-bit halves of a data register.

Condition Codes:

X	N	Z	V	C
—	*	*	0	0

N   Set if the most significant bit of the 32-bit result is set. Cleared otherwise.
Z   Set if the 32-bit result is zero. Cleared otherwise.
V   Always cleared.
C   Always cleared.
X   Not affected.

Instruction Format:

15	14	13	12	11	10	9	8	7	6	5	4	3	2	1	0
0	1	0	0	1	0	0	0	0	1	0	0	0	Register		

Instruction Fields:
Register field — Specifies the data register to swap.

B

Operation: Destination Tested → Condition Codes; 1 → bit 7 of Destination

**Assembler
Syntax:**   TAS <ea>

Attributes: Size = (Byte)

Description: Test and set the byte operand addressed by the effective address field. The current value of the operand is tested and N and Z are set accordingly. The high order bit of the operand is set. The operation is indivisible (using a read-modify-write memory cycle) to allow synchronization of several processors.

Condition Codes:

X	N	Z	V	C
—	*	*	0	0

N   Set if the most significant bit of the operand was set. Cleared otherwise.
Z   Set if the operand was zero. Cleared otherwise.
V   Always cleared.
C   Always cleared.
X   Not affected.

Instruction Format:

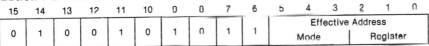

15	14	13	12	11	10	9	8	7	6	5	4	3	2	1	0
0	1	0	0	1	0	1	0	1	1		Effective Address				
											Mode		Register		

Instruction Fields:

Effective Address field — Specifies the location of the tested operand. Only data alterable addressing modes are allowed as shown:

Addr. Mode	Mode	Register
Dn	000	reg. number:Dn
An	—	—
(An)	010	reg. number:An
(An)+	011	reg. number:An
−(An)	100	reg. number:An
(d$_{16}$,An)	101	reg. number:An
(d$_8$,An,Xn)	110	reg. number:An
(bd,An,Xn)	110	reg. number:An
([bd,An,Xn],od)	110	reg. number:An
([bd,An],Xn,od)	110	reg. number:An

Addr. Mode	Mode	Register
(xxx).W	111	000
(xxx).L	111	001
#<data>	—	—
(d$_{16}$,PC)	—	—
(d$_8$,PC,Xn)	—	—
(bd,PC,Xn)	—	—
([bd,PC,Xn],od)	—	—
([bd,PC],Xn,od)	—	—

B

Operation: SSP – 2 → SSP; Format/Offset → (SSP);
SSP – 4 → SSP; PC → (SSP); SSP – 2 → SSP;
SR → (SSP); Vector Address → PC

**Assembler
Syntax:** TRAP # <vector>

Attributes: Unsized

Description: The processor initiates exception processing. The vector number is generated to reference the TRAP instruction exception vector specified by the low order four bits of the instruction. Sixteen TRAP instruction vectors (0-15) are available.

Condition Codes: Not affected.

Instruction Format:

15	14	13	12	11	10	9	8	7	6	5	4	3	2	1	0
0	1	0	0	1	1	1	0	0	1	0	0	Vector			

Instruction Fields:

Vector field — Specifies which trap vector contains the new program counter to be loaded.

B

TRAPcc

Trap on Condition

TRAPcc

Operation: If cc then TRAP

Assembler TRAPcc
Syntax: TRAPcc.W #<data>
TRAPcc.L #<data>

Attributes: Unsized or Size = (Word, Long)

Description: If the selected condition is true, the processor initiates exception processing. The vector number is generated to reference the TRAPcc exception vector. The
stacked program counter points to the next instruction. If the selected condition is
not true, no operation is performed, and execution continues with the next instruction in sequence. The immediate data operand(s) is placed in the next word(s) following the operation word and is (are) available for user definition for use within the
trap handler. "cc" may specify the following conditions.

CC	carry clear	0100	$\overline{C}$
CS	carry set	0101	C
EQ	equal	0111	Z
F	never true	0001	0
GE	greater or equal	1100	$N \cdot V + \overline{N} \cdot \overline{V}$
GT	greater than	1110	$N \cdot V \cdot \overline{Z} + \overline{N} \cdot \overline{V} \cdot \overline{Z}$
HI	high	0010	$\overline{C} \cdot \overline{Z}$
LE	less or equal	1111	$Z + N \cdot \overline{V} + \overline{N} \cdot V$

LS	low or same	0011	$C + Z$
LT	less than	1101	$N \cdot \overline{V} + \overline{N} \cdot V$
MI	minus	1011	N
NE	not equal	0110	$\overline{Z}$
PL	plus	1010	$\overline{N}$
T	always true	0000	1
VC	overflow clear	1000	$\overline{V}$
VS	overflow set	1001	V

Condition Codes: Not affected.

Instruction Format:

15	14	13	12	11	10	9	8	7	6	5	4	3	2	1	0
0	1	0	1	Condition				1	1	1	1	1	Op-Mode		
Optional Word															
or Long Word															

Instruction Fields:

Condition field — One of sixteen conditions discussed previously.
Op-Mode field — Selects the instruction form.
010—Instruction is followed by one operand word.
011—Instruction is followed by two operands words.
100—Instruction has no following operand words.

B

TRAPV

Trap on Overflow

TRAPV

Operation: If V then TRAP

**Assembler
Syntax:** TRAPV

Attributes: Unsized

Description: If the overflow condition is set, the processor initiates exception processing. The vector number is generated to reference the TRAPV exception vector. If the overflow condition is clear, no operation is performed and execution continues with the next instruction in sequence.

Condition Codes: Not affected.

Instruction Format:

15	14	13	12	11	10	9	8	7	6	5	4	3	2	1	0
0	1	0	0	1	1	1	0	0	1	1	1	0	1	1	0

B

Operation: Destination Tested → Condition Codes

Assembler
Syntax: TST <ea>

Attributes: Size = (Byte, Word, Long)

Description: Compare the operand with zero. No results are saved; however, the condition codes are set according to results of the test. The size of the operation may be specified to be byte, word, or long.

Condition Codes:

X	N	Z	V	C
—	*	*	0	0

N   Set if the operand is negative. Cleared otherwise.
Z   Set if the operand is zero. Cleared otherwise.
V   Always cleared.
C   Always cleared.
X   Not affected.

Instruction Format:

15	14	13	12	11	10	9	8	7	6	5	4	3	2	1	0
0	1	0	0	1	0	1	0	Size		Effective Address					
										Mode			Register		

Instruction Fields:

Size field — Specifies the size of the operation:
00—byte operation.
01—word operation.
10—long operation.
Effective Address field — Specifies the destination operand. If the operation size is word or long, all addressing modes are allowed. If the operation size is byte, only data addressing modes are allowed as shown:

Addr. Mode	Mode	Register
Dn	000	reg. number:Dn
An	—	—
(An)	010	reg. number:An
(An)+	011	reg. number:An
–(An)	100	reg. number:An
(d_{16},An)	101	reg. number:An
(d_8,An,Xn)	110	reg. number:An
(bd,An,Xn)	110	reg. number:An
([bd,An,Xn],od)	110	reg. number:An
([bd,An],Xn,od)	110	reg. number:An

Addr. Mode	Mode	Register
(xxx).W	111	000
(xxx).L	111	001
#<data>	—	—
(d_{16},PC)	111	010
(d_8,PC,Xn)	111	011
(bd,PC,Xn)	111	011
([bd,PC,Xn],od)	111	011
([bd,PC],Xn,od)	111	011

B

Operation: An → SP; (SP) → An; SP + 4 → SP

**Assembler
Syntax:** UNLK An

Attributes: Unsized

Description: The stack pointer is loaded from the specified address register. The address register is then loaded with the long word pulled from the top of the stack.

Condition Codes: Not affected.

Instruction Format:

15	14	13	12	11	10	9	8	7	6	5	4	3	2	1	0
0	1	0	0	1	1	1	0	0	1	0	1	1	Register		

Instruction Fields:
Register field — Specifies the address register through which the unlinking is to be
done.

Unpack BCD

Operation: Source (Packed BCD) + adjustment → Destination (Unpacked BCD)

Assembler   UNPACK – (Ax), – (Ay),#<adjustment>
Syntax: UNPK Dx,Dy,#<adjustment>

Attributes: Unsized

Description: In the unpack operation, two BCD digits within the byte source operand are separated into two bytes with the BCD digit residing in the lower nibble and 0 in the upper nibble. The adjustment is then added to this unpacked value without affecting the condition codes.

When both operands are data registers, the source register contents are unpacked, the extension word is added, and the result is placed in the destination register. The high word of the destination register is unaffected.

Source:

	15	14	13	12	11	10	9	8	7	6	5	4	3	2	1	0
Dx	u	u	u	u	u	u	u	u	a	b	c	d	e	f	g	h

Intermediate Expansion:

15	14	13	12	11	10	9	8	7	6	5	4	3	2	1	0
0	0	0	0	a	b	c	d	0	0	0	0	e	f	g	h

Add Adjustment Word:

15	14	13	12	11	10	9	8	7	6	5	4	3	2	1	0
						16-Bit Extension									

Destination:

	15	14	13	12	11	10	9	8	7	6	5	4	3	2	1	0
Dy	v	v	v	v	a'	b'	c'	d'	w	w	w	w	e'	f'	g'	h'

When the addressing mode specified is predecrement, two BCD digits are extracted from a byte at the source address. After adding the extension word, two bytes are then written to the destination address.

Source:

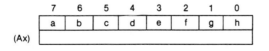

— Continued —

Unpack BCD

Intermediate Expansion:

15	14	13	12	11	10	9	8	7	6	5	4	3	2	1	0
0	0	0	0	a	b	c	d	0	0	0	0	e	f	g	h

Add Adjustment Word:

15	14	13	12	11	10	9	8	7	6	5	4	3	2	1	0
16-Bit Extension															

Destination:

	7	6	5	4	3	2	1	0
	v	v	v	v	a'	b'	c'	d'
	w	w	w	w	e'	f'	g'	h'
(Ay)								

Condition Codes: Not affected.

Instruction Format:

15	14	13	12	11	10	9	8	7	6	5	4	3	2	1	0
1	0	0	0	Register Dy/Ay			1	1	0	0	0	R/M	Register Dx/Ax		
Adjustment															

Instruction Fields:

Register Dy/Ay field — Specifies the destination register.
   If R/M = 0, specifies a data register.
   If R/M = 1, specifies an address register for the predecrement addressing mode.
R/M field — Specifies the operand addressing mode.
   0—The operation is data register to data register.
   1—The operation is memory to memory.
Register Dx/Ax field — Specifies the data register.
   If R/M = 0, specifies a data register.
   If R/M = 1, specifies an address register for the predecrement addressing mode.
Adjustment field — Immediate data word which is added to the source operand.
   Appropriate constants can be used to translate from BCD to ASCII or EBCDIC.

B

APPENDIX C
INSTRUCTION FORMAT SUMMARY

This appendix provides a summary of the primary words in each instruction of the instruction set. The complete instruction definition consists of the primary words followed by the addressing mode operands such as immediate data fields, displacements, and index operands. Table C-1 is an operation code (opcode) map which illustrates how bits 15 through 12 are used to specify the operations. The first section groups the standard instructions according to the opcode map. Distinctions are made as to processor model support. Later processors support all earlier model instructions and addressing modes. The next section documents coprocessor instruction forms. The last shows coprocessor primitives which themselves are not instructions but are command formats used across the coprocessor interface.

Table C-1. Operation Code Map

Bits 15 through 12	Operation
0000	Bit Manipulation/MOVEP/Immediate
0001	Move Byte
0010	Move Long
0011	Move Word
0100	Miscellaneous
0101	ADDQ/SUBQ/Scc/DBcc/TRAPcc
0110	Bcc/BSR/BRA
0111	MOVEQ
1000	OR/DIV/SBCD
1001	SUB/SUBX
1010	(Unassigned, Reserved)
1011	CMP/EOR
1100	AND/MUL/ABCD/EXG
1101	ADD/ADDX
1110	Shift/Rotate/Bit Field
1111	Coprocessor Interface

C

Table C-2. Effective Addressing Mode Categories

Address Modes	Mode	Register	Data	Memory	Control	Alterable	Assembler Syntax
Data Register Direct	000	reg. no.	X	—	—	X	Dn
Address Register Direct	001	reg. no.	—	—	—	X	An
Address Register Indirect	010	reg. no.	X	X	X	X	(An)
Address Register Indirect with Postincrement	011	reg. no.	X	X	—	X	(An) +
Address Register Indirect with Predecrement	100	reg. no.	X	X	—	X	− (An)
Address Register Indirect with Displacement	101	reg. no	X	X	X	X	(d$_{16}$,An)
Address Register Indirect with Index (8-Bit Displacement)	110	reg. no.	X	X	X	X	(d$_8$,An,Xn)
Address Register Indirect with Index (Base Displacement)	110	reg. no.	X	X	X	X	(bd,An,Xn)
Memory Indirect Post-Indexed	110	reg. no.	X	X	X	X	([bd,An],Xn,od)
Memory Indirect Pre-Indexed	110	reg. no.	X	X	X	X	([bd,An,Xn],od)
Absolute Short	111	000	X	X	X	X	(xxx).W
Absolute Long	111	001	X	X	X	X	(xxx).L
Program Counter Indirect with Displacement	111	101	X	X	X	—	(d$_{16}$,PC)
Program Counter Indirect with Index (8-Bit Displacement)	111	011	X	X	X	—	(d$_8$,PC,Xn)
Program Counter Indirect with Index (Base Displacement)	111	011	X	X	X	—	(bd,PC,Xn)
PC Memory Indirect Post-Indexed	111	011	X	X	X	—	([bd,PC],Xn,od)
PC Memory Indirect Pre-Indexed	111	011	X	X	X	—	([bd,PC,Xn],od)
Immediate	111	100	X	X	—	—	#<data>

Table C-3. Conditional Tests

Mnemonic	Condition	Encoding	Test
T*	True	0000	1
F*	False	0001	0
HI	High	0010	$\overline{C} \cdot \overline{Z}$
LS	Low or Same	0011	$C + Z$
CC(HS)	Carry Clear	0100	$\overline{C}$
CS(LO)	Carry Set	0101	C
NE	Not Equal	0110	$\overline{Z}$
EQ	Equal	0111	Z
VC	Overflow Clear	1000	$\overline{V}$
VS	Overflow Set	1001	V
PL	Plus	1010	$\overline{N}$
MI	Minus	1011	N
GE	Greater or Equal	1100	$N \cdot V + \overline{N} \cdot \overline{V}$
LT	Less Than	1101	$N \cdot \overline{V} + \overline{N} \cdot V$
GT	Greater Than	1110	$N \cdot V \cdot \overline{Z} + \overline{N} \cdot \overline{V} \cdot \overline{Z}$
LE	Less or Equal	1111	$Z + N \cdot \overline{V} + \overline{N} \cdot V$

• = Boolean AND
+ = Boolean OR
$\overline{N}$ = Boolean NOT N

*Not available for the Bcc and cpBcc instructions

OR Immediate

15	14	13	12	11	10	9	8	7	6	5	4	3	2	1	0
0	0	0	0	0	0	0	0	Size		Effective Address					
										Mode			Register		

Size field: 00 = byte   01 = word   10 = long

OR Immediate to CCR

15	14	13	12	11	10	9	8	7	6	5	4	3	2	1	0
0	0	0	0	0	0	0	0	0	0	1	1	1	1	0	0
0	0	0	0	0	0	0	0	Byte Data							

OR Immediate to SR

15	14	13	12	11	10	9	8	7	6	5	4	3	2	1	0
0	0	0	0	0	0	0	0	0	1	1	1	1	1	0	0
Word Data															

CMP2 (MC68020)

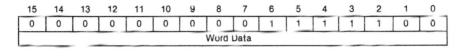

15	14	13	12	11	10	9	8	7	6	5	4	3	2	1	0
0	0	0	0	0	Size		0	1	1	Effective Address					
										Mode			Register		
A/D	Register		0	0	0	0	0	0	0	0	0	0	0	0	0

Size field: 00 = byte   01 = word   10 = long

CHK2 (MC68020)

15	14	13	12	11	10	9	8	7	6	5	4	3	2	1	0
0	0	0	0	0	Size		0	1	1	Effective Address					
										Mode			Register		
A/D	Register		1	0	0	0	0	0	0	0	0	0	0	0	0

Size field: 00 = byte   01 = word   10 = long

Dynamic Bit

15	14	13	12	11	10	9	8	7	6	5	4	3	2	1	0
0	0	0	0	Data Register			1	Type		Effective Address					
										Mode			Register		

Type field: 00 = TST   10 = CLR
01 = CHG 11 = SET

C

MOVEP

15	14	13	12	11 10 9	8 7 6	5	4	3	2 1 0
0	0	0	0	Data Register	Op-Mode	0	0	1	Address Register

Op-Mode field: 100 = transfer word from memory to register
101 = transfer long from memory to register
110 = transfer word from register to memory
111 = transfer long from register to memory

AND Immediate

15	14	13	12	11	10	9	8	7 6	5 4 3	2 1 0
0	0	0	0	0	0	1	0	Size	Effective Address Mode	Register

Size field: 00 = byte 01 = word 10 = long

AND Immediate to CCR

15	14	13	12	11	10	9	8	7	6	5	4	3	2	1	0
0	0	0	0	0	0	1	0	0	0	1	1	1	1	0	0
0	0	0	0	0	0	0	0	Byte Data							

AND Immediate to SR

15	14	13	12	11	10	9	8	7	6	5	4	3	2	1	0
0	0	0	0	0	0	1	0	0	1	1	1	1	1	0	0
Word Data															

SUB Immediate

15	14	13	12	11	10	9	8	7 6	5 4 3	2 1 0
0	0	0	0	0	1	0	0	Size	Effective Address Mode	Register

Size field: 00 = byte 01 = word 10 = long

ADD Immediate

15	14	13	12	11	10	9	8	7 6	5 4 3	2 1 0
0	0	0	0	0	1	1	0	Size	Effective Address Mode	Register

Size field: 00 = byte 01 = word 10 = long

RTM (MC68020)

15	14	13	12	11	10	9	8	7	6	5	4	3	2	1	0
0	0	0	0	0	1	1	0	1	1	0	0	D/A	Register		

CALLM (MC68020)

15	14	13	12	11	10	9	8	7	6	5	4	3	2	1	0
0	0	0	0	0	1	1	0	1	1	Effective Address					
										Mode			Register		
0	0	0	0	0	0	0	0	Argument Count							

CAS (MC68020)

15	14	13	12	11	10	9	8	7	6	5	4	3	2	1	0
0	0	0	0	1	Size		0	1	1	Effective Address					
										Mode			Register		
0	0	0	0	0	0	0	Du			0	0	0	Dc		

Size field: 01 = byte 10 = word 11 = long

CAS2 (MC68020)

15	14	13	12	11	10	9	8	7	6	5	4	3	2	1	0
0	0	0	0	1	Size		0	1	1	1	1	1	1	0	0
D/A1	Register 1		0	0	0	Du1			0	0	0	Dc1			
D/A2	Register 2		0	0	0	Du2			0	0	0	Dc2			

Size field: 01 = byte 10 = word 11 = long

Static Bit

15	14	13	12	11	10	9	8	7	6	5	4	3	2	1	0
0	0	0	0	1	0	0	0	Type		Effective Address					
										Mode			Register		
0	0	0	0	0	0	0	Bit Number								

Type field: 00 = TST 10 = CLR
01 = CHG 11 = SET

EOR Immediate

15	14	13	12	11	10	9	8	7	6	5	4	3	2	1	0
0	0	0	0	1	0	1	0	Size		Effective Address					
										Mode			Register		

Size field: 00 = byte 01 = word 10 = long

C

EOR Immediate to CCR

15	14	13	12	11	10	9	8	7	6	5	4	3	2	1	0
0	0	0	0	1	0	1	0	0	0	1	1	1	1	0	0
0	0	0	0	0	0	0	0	Byte Data							

EOR Immediate to SR

15	14	13	12	11	10	9	8	7	6	5	4	3	2	1	0
0	0	0	0	1	0	1	0	0	1	1	1	1	1	0	0
Word Data															

CMP Immediate

15	14	13	12	11	10	9	8	7	6	5	4	3	2	1	0
0	0	0	0	1	1	0	0	Size		Effective Address					
										Mode			Register		

Size field: 00 = byte 01 = word 10 = long

MOVES (MC68010)

15	14	13	12	11	10	9	8	7	6	5	4	3	2	1	0
0	0	0	0	1	1	1	0	Size		Effective Address					
										Mode			Register		
A/D	Register			dr	0	0	0	0	0	0	0	0	0	0	0

dr field: 0 = EA to register
1 = register to EA

MOVE Byte

15	14	13	12	11	10	9	8	7	6	5	4	3	2	1	0
0	0	0	1	Destination						Source					
				Register			Mode			Mode			Register		

Note register and mode locations

MOVEA Long

15	14	13	12	11	10	9	8	7	6	5	4	3	2	1	0
0	0	1	0	Destination			0	0	1	Source					
				Register						Mode			Register		

C

MOVE Long

15	14	13	12	11	10	0	0	7	6	5	4	3	2	1	0
0	0	1	0	Destination						Source					
				Register			Mode			Mode			Register		

Note register and mode locations

MOVEA Word

15	14	13	12	11	10	9	8	7	6	5	4	3	2	1	0
0	0	1	1	Destination			0	0	1	Source					
				Register						Mode			Register		

MOVE Word

15	14	13	12	11	10	9	8	7	6	5	4	3	2	1	0
0	0	1	1	Destination						Source					
				Register			Mode			Mode			Register		

Note register and mode locations

NEGX

15	14	13	12	11	10	9	8	7	6	5	4	3	2	1	0
0	1	0	0	0	0	0	0	Size		Effective Address					
										Mode			Register		

Size field: 00 = byte 01 = word 10 = long

MOVE from SR

15	14	13	12	11	10	9	8	7	6	5	4	3	2	1	0
0	1	0	0	0	0	0	0	1	1	Effective Address					
										Mode			Register		

CHK

15	14	13	12	11	10	9	8	7	6	5	4	3	2	1	0
0	1	0	0	Data			Size		0	Effective Address					
				Register						Mode			Register		

Size field: 10 = Longword (MC68020)
            11 = Word

C

LEA

15	14	13	12	11	10	9	8	7	6	5	4	3	2	1	0
0	1	0	0	Address Register			1	1	1	Effective Address					
										Mode			Register		

CLR

15	14	13	12	11	10	9	8	7	6	5	4	3	2	1	0
0	1	0	0	0	0	1	0	Size		Effective Address					
										Mode			Register		

Size field: 00 = byte   01 = word   10 = long

MOVE from CCR (MC68010)

15	14	13	12	11	10	9	8	7	6	5	4	3	2	1	0
0	1	0	0	0	0	1	0	1	1	Effective Address					
										Mode			Register		

NEG

15	14	13	12	11	10	9	8	7	6	5	4	3	2	1	0
0	1	0	0	0	1	0	0	Size		Effective Address					
										Mode			Register		

Size field: 00 = byte   01 = word   10 = long

MOVE to CCR

15	14	13	12	11	10	9	8	7	6	5	4	3	2	1	0
0	1	0	0	0	1	0	0	1	1	Effective Address					
										Mode			Register		

NOT

15	14	13	12	11	10	9	8	7	6	5	4	3	2	1	0
0	1	0	0	0	1	1	0	Size		Effective Address					
										Mode			Register		

Size field: 00 = byte   01 = word   10 = long

MOVE to SR

15	14	13	12	11	10	9	8	7	6	5	4	3	2	1	0
0	1	0	0	0	1	1	0	1	1	Effective Address					
										Mode			Register		

NBCD

15	14	13	12	11	10	9	8	7	6	5	4	3	2	1	0
0	1	0	0	1	0	0	0	0	0	Effective Address					

(Effective Address split into Mode [bits 5-3] and Register [bits 2-0])

LINK Long (MC68020)

15	14	13	12	11	10	9	8	7	6	5	4	3	2	1	0
0	1	0	0	1	0	0	0	0	0	0	0	1	Data Register		

High-Order Displacement
Low-Order Displacement

SWAP

15	14	13	12	11	10	9	8	7	6	5	4	3	2	1	0
0	1	0	0	1	0	0	0	0	1	0	0	0	Data Register		

BKPT (MC68010)

15	14	13	12	11	10	9	8	7	6	5	4	3	2	1	0
0	1	0	0	1	0	0	0	0	1	0	0	1	Vector		

PEA

15	14	13	12	11	10	9	8	7	6	5	4	3	2	1	0
0	1	0	0	1	0	0	0	0	1	Effective Address					

(Effective Address split into Mode [bits 5-3] and Register [bits 2-0])

EXT/EXTB (EXTB-MC68020)

15	14	13	12	11	10	9	8	7	6	5	4	3	2	1	0
0	1	0	0	1	0	0	Type			0	0	0	Data Register		

Type Field: 010 = Extend Word 011 = Extend Long 111 = Extend Byte Long - (MC68020)

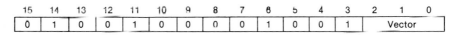

MOVEM Registers to EA

15	14	13	12	11	10	9	8	7	6	5	4	3	2	1	0
0	1	0	0	1	0	0	0	1	Sz	Effective Address					

(Effective Address split into Mode [bits 5-3] and Register [bits 2-0])

Sz field: 0 = word transfer   1 = long transfer

C

TST

15	14	13	12	11	10	9	8	7	6	5	4	3	2	1	0
										Effective Address					
0	1	0	0	1	0	1	0	Size		Mode			Register		

Size field: 00 = byte   01 = word   10 = long

TAS

15	14	13	12	11	10	9	8	7	6	5	4	3	2	1	0
										Effective Address					
0	1	0	0	1	0	1	0	1	1	Mode			Register		

ILLEGAL

15	14	13	12	11	10	9	8	7	6	5	4	3	2	1	0
0	1	0	0	1	0	1	0	1	1	1	1	1	1	0	0

MULS/MULU Long (MC68020)

15	14	13	12	11	10	9	8	7	6	5	4	3	2	1	0
										Effective Address					
0	1	0	0	1	1	0	0	0	0	Mode			Register		
0	Dl		Type	Size	0	0	0	0	0	0		Dh			

Type Field: 0 = MULU   Size Field: 0 = Longword Product
1 = MULS   1 = Quadword Product

DIVS/DIVU Long (MC68020)
DIVUL/DIVSL (MC68020)

15	14	13	12	11	10	9	8	7	6	5	4	3	2	1	0
										Effective Address					
0	1	0	0	1	1	0	0	0	1	Mode			Register		
0	Dq		Type	Size	0	0	0	0	0	0	0	Dr			

Type Field: 0 = DIVU   Size Field: 0 = Longword Dividend
1 = DIVS   1 = Quadword Dividend

MOVEM EA to Registers

15	14	13	12	11	10	9	8	7	6	5	4	3	2	1	0
										Effective Address					
0	1	0	0	1	1	0	0	1	Sz	Mode			Register		

Sz field: 0 = word transfer   1 = long transfer

TRAP

15	14	13	12	11	10	9	8	7	6	5	4	3	2	1	0
0	1	0	0	1	1	1	0	0	1	0	0	Vector			

LINK Word

15	14	13	12	11	10	9	8	7	6	5	4	3	2	1	0
0	1	0	0	1	1	1	0	0	1	0	1	0	Address Register		

UNLK

15	14	13	12	11	10	9	8	7	6	5	4	3	2	1	0
0	1	0	0	1	1	1	0	0	1	0	1	1	Address Register		

MOVE to USP

15	14	13	12	11	10	9	8	7	6	5	4	3	2	1	0
0	1	0	0	1	1	1	0	0	1	1	0	0	Address Register		

MOVE from USP

15	14	13	12	11	10	9	8	7	6	5	4	3	2	1	0
0	1	0	0	1	1	1	0	0	1	1	0	1	Address Register		

RESET

15	14	13	12	11	10	9	8	7	6	5	4	3	2	1	0
0	1	0	0	1	1	1	0	0	1	1	1	0	0	0	0

NOP

15	14	13	12	11	10	9	8	7	6	5	4	3	2	1	0
0	1	0	0	1	1	1	0	0	1	1	1	0	0	0	1

C

STOP

15	14	13	12	11	10	9	8	7	6	5	4	3	2	1	0
0	1	0	0	1	1	1	0	0	1	1	1	0	0	1	0

RTE

15	14	13	12	11	10	9	8	7	6	5	4	3	2	1	0
0	1	0	0	1	1	1	0	0	1	1	1	0	0	1	1

RTD (MC68010)

15	14	13	12	11	10	9	8	7	6	5	4	3	2	1	0
0	1	0	0	1	1	1	0	0	1	1	1	0	1	0	0

RTS

15	14	13	12	11	10	9	8	7	6	5	4	3	2	1	0
0	1	0	0	1	1	1	0	0	1	1	1	0	1	0	1

TRAPV

15	14	13	12	11	10	9	8	7	6	5	4	3	2	1	0
0	1	0	0	1	1	1	0	0	1	1	1	0	1	1	0

RTR

15	14	13	12	11	10	9	8	7	6	5	4	3	2	1	0
0	1	0	0	1	1	1	0	0	1	1	1	0	1	1	1

MOVEC (MC68010)

15	14	13	12	11	10	9	8	7	6	5	4	3	2	1	0
0	1	0	0	1	1	1	0	0	1	1	1	1	0	1	dr
A/D	Register			Control Register											

dr field: 0 = control register to general register
1 = general register to control register

Control Register field: $000 = SFC $801 = VBR
$001 = DFC $802 = CAAR   (MC68020)
$002 = CACR (MC68020) $803 = MSP   (MC68020)
$800 = USP $804 = ISP   (MC68020)

C

JSR

15	14	13	12	11	10	9	8	7	6	5	4	3	2	1	0
0	1	0	0	1	1	1	0	1	0	Effective Address					

| | | | | | | | | | | Mode | | | Register | | |

JMP

15	14	13	12	11	10	9	8	7	6	5	4	3	2	1	0
0	1	0	0	1	1	1	0	1	1	Effective Address					
										Mode			Register		

ADDQ

15	14	13	12	11	10	9	8	7	6	5	4	3	2	1	0
0	1	0	1	Data			0	Size		Effective Address					
										Mode			Register		

Data field: Three bits of immediate data, 0, 1-7 representing a range of 8, 1 to 7 respectively.
Size field: 00 = byte   01 = word   10 = long

Scc

15	14	13	12	11	10	9	8	7	6	5	4	3	2	1	0
0	1	0	1	Condition				1	1	Effective Address					
										Mode			Register		

DBcc

15	14	13	12	11	10	9	8	7	6	5	4	3	2	1	0
0	1	0	1	Condition				1	1	0	0	1	Data		
													Register		

TRAPcc (MC68020)

15	14	13	12	11	10	9	8	7	6	5	4	3	2	1	0
0	1	0	1	Condition				1	1	1	1	1	Mode		
Operand															

Mode Field: 010 = Word Operand   011 = Longword Operand   100 = No Operand

C

SUBQ

15	14	13	12	11	10	9	8	7	6	5	4	3	2	1	0
0	1	0	1	Data			1	Size		Effective Address					
										Mode			Register		

Data field: Three bits of immediate data, 0, 1-7 representing a range of 8,
1 to 7 respectively.
Size field: 00 = byte   01 = word   10 = long

Bcc

15	14	13	12	11	10	9	8	7	6	5	4	3	2	1	0
0	1	1	0	Condition				8-Bit Displacement							
16-Bit Displacement if 8-Bit Displacement = $00															
32-Bit Displacement if 8-Bit Diplacement = $FF															

BRA

15	14	13	12	11	10	9	8	7	6	5	4	3	2	1	0
0	1	1	0	0	0	0	0	8-Bit Displacement							
16-Bit Displacement if 8-Bit Displacement = $00															
32-Bit Displacement if 8-Bit Displacement = $FF															

BSR

15	14	13	12	11	10	9	8	7	6	5	4	3	2	1	0
0	1	1	0	0	0	0	1	8-Bit Displacement							
16-Bit Displacement if 8-Bit Displacement = $00															
32-Bit Displacement if 8-Bit Displacement = $FF															

MOVEQ

15	14	13	12	11	10	9	8	7	6	5	4	3	2	1	0
0	1	1	1	Data Register			0	Data							

Data field: Data is sign extended to a long operand and all 32 bits are
transferred to the data register.

OR

15	14	13	12	11	10	9	8	7	6	5	4	3	2	1	0
1	0	0	0	Data Register			Op-Mode			Effective Address					
										Mode			Register		

Op-Mode field:

Byte	Word	Long	Operation
000	001	010	$(<ea>)v(<Dn>) \rightarrow <Dn>$
100	101	110	$(<Dn>)v(<ea>) \rightarrow <ea>$

DIVU/DIVS Word

15	14	13	12	11	10	0	8	7	6	5	4	3	2	1	0
				Data						Effective Address					
1	0	0	0	Register			Type	1	1	Mode			Register		

Type field: 0 = DIVU   1 = DIVS

SBCD

15	14	13	12	11	10	9	8	7	6	5	4	3	2	1	0
				Destination									Source		
1	0	0	0	Register*			1	0	0	0	0	R/M	Register*		

R/M field: 0 = data register to data register
             1 = memory to memory
*If R/M = 0, specifies a data register
 If R/M = 1, specifies an address register for the predecrement addressing mode.

PACK (MC68020)

15	14	13	12	11	10	9	8	7	6	5	4	3	2	1	0
				Destination									Source		
1	0	0	0	Register*			1	0	1	0	0	R/M	Register*		
16-Bit Extension: Adjustment															

R/M field: 0 = data register to data register
             1 = memory to memory
*If R/M = 0, specifies a data register
 If R/M = 1, specifies an address register for the predecrement addressing mode.

UNPK (MC68020)

15	14	13	12	11	10	9	8	7	6	5	4	3	2	1	0
				Destination									Source		
1	0	0	0	Register*			1	1	0	0	0	R/M	Register*		

R/M field: 0 = data register to data register
             1 = memory to memory
*If R/M = 0, specifies a data register
 If R/M = 1, specifies an address register for the predecrement addressing mode.

SUB

15	14	13	12	11	10	9	8	7	6	5	4	3	2	1	0
				Data						Effective Address					
1	0	0	1	Register			Op-Mode			Mode			Register		

Op-Mode field:	Byte	Word	Long	Operation
	000	001	010	$(<Dn>) - (<ea>) \rightarrow <Dn>$
	100	101	110	$(<ea>) - (<Dn>) \rightarrow <ea>$

C

C-15

SUBA

15	14	13	12	11	10	9	8	7	6	5	4	3	2	1	0
1	0	0	1	Data Register			Op-Mode			Effective Address					
										Mode			Register		

Op-Mode field:

	Word	Long	Operation
	011	111	$(<An>) - (<ea>) \rightarrow <An>$

SUBX

15	14	13	12	11	10	9	8	7	6	5	4	3	2	1	0
1	0	0	1	Destination Register*			1	Size		0	0	R/M	Source Register*		

Size field: 00 = byte 01 = word 10 = long
R/M field: 0 = data register to data register 1 = memory to memory
*If R/M = 0, specifies a data register
 If R/M = 1, specifies an address register for the predecrement addressing mode.

CMP

15	14	13	12	11	10	9	8	7	6	5	4	3	2	1	0
1	0	1	1	Data Register			Op-Mode			Effective Address					
										Mode			Register		

Op-Mode field:

Byte	Word	Long	Operation
000	001	010	$(<Dn>) - (<ea>)$

CMPA

15	14	13	12	11	10	9	8	7	6	5	4	3	2	1	0
1	0	1	1	Data Register			Op-Mode			Effective Address					
										Mode			Register		

Op-Mode field:

	Word	Long	Operation
	011	111	$(<An>) - (<ea>)$

EOR

15	14	13	12	11	10	9	8	7	6	5	4	3	2	1	0
1	0	1	1	Data Register			Op-Mode			Effective Address					
										Mode			Register		

Op-Mode field:

Byte	Word	Long	Operation
100	101	110	$(<ea>) \oplus (<Dn>) \rightarrow <ea>$

C

CMPM

15	14	13	12	11	10	9	8	7	6	5	4	3	2	1	0
1	0	1	1	Destination Register			1	Size		0	0	1	Source Register		

Size field: 00 = byte   01 = word   10 = long

AND

15	14	13	12	11	10	9	8	7	6	5	4	3	2	1	0
1	1	0	0	Data Register			Op-Mode			Effective Address					
										Mode			Register		

Op-Mode field:

Byte	Word	Long	Operation
000	001	010	$(<ea>) \Lambda (<Dn>) \rightarrow <Dn>$
100	101	110	$(<Dn>) \Lambda (<ea>) \rightarrow <ea>$

MULU Word
MULS Word

15	14	13	12	11	10	9	8	7	6	5	4	3	2	1	0
1	1	0	0	Data Register			Type	1	1	Effective Address					
										Mode			Register		

Type field: 0 = MULU   1 = MULS

ABCD

15	14	13	12	11	10	9	8	7	6	5	4	3	2	1	0
1	1	0	0	Destination Register*			1	0	0	0	0	R/M	Source Register*		

R/M field: 0 = data register to data register   1 = memory to memory
* If R/M = 0, specifies a data register
  If R/M = 1, specifies an address register for the predecrement addressing mode.

EXG Data Registers

15	14	13	12	11	10	9	8	7	6	5	4	3	2	1	0
1	1	0	0	Data Register			1	0	1	0	0	0	Data Register		

EXG Address Registers

15	14	13	12	11	10	9	8	7	6	5	4	3	2	1	0
1	1	0	0	Address Register			1	0	1	0	0	1	Address Register		

C

EXG Data Register and Address Register

15	14	13	12	11	10	9	8	7	6	5	4	3	2	1	0
1	1	0	0	Data Register			1	1	0	0	0	1	Address Register		

ADD

15	14	13	12	11	10	9	8	7	6	5	4	3	2	1	0
1	1	0	1	Data Register			Op-Mode			Effective Address					
										Mode			Register		

Op-Mode field:

Byte	Word	Long	Operation
000	001	010	$(<ea>) + (<Dn>) \rightarrow <Dn>$
100	101	110	$(<Dn>) + (<ea>) \rightarrow <ea>$

ADDA

15	14	13	12	11	10	9	8	7	6	5	4	3	2	1	0
1	1	0	1	Address Register			Op-Mode			Effective Address					
										Mode			Register		

Op-Mode field:

	Word	Long	Operation
	011	111	$(<ea>) + (<An>) \rightarrow <An>$

ADDX

15	14	13	12	11	10	9	8	7	6	5	4	3	2	1	0
1	1	0	1	Destination Register*			1	Size		0	0	R/M	Source Register*		

Size field: 00 = byte   01 = word   10 = long
R/M field: 0 = data register to data register 1 = memory to memory
*If R/M = 0, specifies a data register
 If R/M = 1, specifies an address register for the predecrement addressing mode.

SHIFT/ROTATE — Register

15	14	13	12	11	10	9	8	7	6	5	4	3	2	1	0
1	1	1	0	Count/ Register			dr	Size		i/r	Type		Data Register		

Count/Register field: If i/r field = 0, specifies shift count
                        If i/r field = 1, specifies a data register that con-
                        tains the shift count
dr field: 0 = right   1 = left
Size field: 00 = byte   01 = word   10 = long
i/r field: 0 = immediate shift count   1 = register shift count
Type field: 00 = arithmetic shift   10 = rotate with extend
             01 = logical shift   11 = rotate

SHIFT/ROTATE — Memory

15	14	13	12	11	10	9	8	7	6	5	4	3	2	1	0
1	1	1	0	0	Type		dr	1	1	Effective Address					
										Mode			Register		

Type field: 00 = arithmetic shift   01 = logical shift   10 = rotate with extend   11 = rotate
dr field: 0 = right   1 = left

Bit Field (MC68020)

15	14	13	12	11	10	9	8	7	6	5	4	3	2	1	0
1	1	1	0	1	Type			1	1	Effective Addres					
										Mode			Register		
0	Register			Do	Offset					Dw	Width				

Type Field: 000 = BFTST   100 = BFCLR
001 = BFEXTU   101 = BFFFO
010 = BFCHG   110 = BFSET
011 = BFEXTS   111 = BFINS
Register Field is 000 for BFTST, BFCHG, BFCLR, and BFSET
Do field: 0 = Offset is Immediate   1 = Offset is Data Register
Dw field: 0 = Width is Immediate   1 = Width Is Data Register

COPROCESSOR INSTRUCTIONS

cpGEN (MC68020)

15	14	13	12	11	10	9	8	7	6	5	4	3	2	1	0
1	1	1	1		Cp-Id		0	0	0	Effective Address				

15	14	13	12	11	10	9	8	7	6	5	4	3	2	1	0
1	1	1	1	Cp-Id			0	0	0	Effective Address					
										Mode			Register		
Coprocessor Dependent Command Word																

cpScc (MC68020)

15	14	13	12	11	10	9	8	7	6	5	4	3	2	1	0
1	1	1	1	Cp-Id			0	0	1	Effective Address					
										Mode			Register		
0	0	0	0	0	0	0	0	0	0	Coprocessor Condition					

cpDBcc (MC68020)

15	14	13	12	11	10	9	8	7	6	5	4	3	2	1	0
1	1	1	1	Cp-Id			0	0	1	0	0	1	Register		
0	0	0	0	0	0	0	0	0	0	Coprocessor Condition					
Displacement																

cpTRAPcc (MC68020)

15	14	13	12	11	10	9	8	7	6	5	4	3	2	1	0
1	1	1	1	Cp-Id			0	0	1	1	1	1	Mode		
0	0	0	0	0	0	0	0	0	0	Coprocessor Condition					
Operand																

Mode field: 010 = Word Operand   011 = Longword Operand   100 = No Displacement

cpBcc (MC68020)

15	14	13	12	11	10	9	8	7	6	5	4	3	2	1	0
1	1	1	1	Cp-Id			0	1	Sz	Coprocessor Condition					
Displacement																

Size field: 0 = Word Displacement   1 = Longword Displacement

C

cpSAVE (MC68020)

15	14	13	12	11	10	9	8	7	6	5	4	3	2	1	0
										Effective Address					
1	1	1	1		Cp-Id		1	0	0	Mode			Register		

cpRESTORE (MC68020)

15	14	13	12	11	10	9	8	7	6	5	4	3	2	1	0
										Effective Address					
1	1	1	1		Cp-Id		1	0	1	Mode			Register		

COPROCESSOR PRIMITIVES (MC68020)

BUSY

15	14	13	12	11	10	9	8	7	6	5	4	3	2	1	0
1	PC	1	0	0	1	0	0	0	0	0	0	0	0	0	0

TRANSFER MULTIPLE COPROCESSOR REGISTERS

15	14	13	12	11	10	9	8	7	6	5	4	3	2	1	0
CA	PC	dr	0	0	0	0	1				Length				

TRANSFER STATUS REGISTER AND SCANPC

15	14	13	12	11	10	9	8	7	6	5	4	3	2	1	0
CA	PC	dr	0	0	0	1	SP	0	0	0	0	0	0	0	0

SUPERVISOR CHECK

15	14	13	12	11	10	9	8	7	6	5	4	3	2	1	0
1	PC	0	0	0	1	0	0	0	0	0	0	0	0	0	0

TAKE ADDRESS AND TRANSFER DATA

15	14	13	12	11	10	9	8	7	6	5	4	3	2	1	0
CA	PC	dr	0	0	1	0	1				Length				

TRANSFER MULTIPLE MAIN PROCESSOR REGISTERS

15	14	13	12	11	10	9	8	7	6	5	4	3	2	1	0
CA	PC	dr	0	0	1	1	0	0	0	0	0	0	0	0	0

TRANSFER OPERATION WORD

15	14	13	12	11	10	9	8	7	6	5	4	3	2	1	0
CA	PC	0	0	0	1	1	1	0	0	0	0	0	0	0	0

NULL

15	14	13	12	11	10	9	8	7	6	5	4	3	2	1	0
CA	PC	0	0	1	0	0	IA	0	0	0	0	0	0	PF	TF

EVALUATE AND TRANSFER EFFECTIVE ADDRESS

15	14	13	12	11	10	0	0	7	6	5	4	3	2	1	0
CA	PC	0	0	1	0	1	0	0	0	0	0	0	0	0	0

TRANSFER SINGLE MAIN PROCESSOR REGISTER

15	14	13	12	11	10	9	8	7	6	5	4	3	2	1	0
CA	PC	dr	0	1	1	0	0	0	0	0	0	D/A	Register		

TRANSFER MAIN PROCESSOR CONTROL REGISTER

15	14	13	12	11	10	9	8	7	6	5	4	3	2	1	0
CA	PC	dr	0	1	1	0	1	0	0	0	0	0	0	0	0

TRANSFER TO/FROM TOP OF STACK

15	14	13	12	11	10	9	8	7	6	5	4	3	2	1	0
CA	PC	DR	1	1	1	0	Length								

TRANSFER FROM INSTRUCTION STREAM

15	14	13	12	11	10	9	8	7	6	5	4	3	2	1	0
CA	PC	0	0	1	1	1	1	Length							

EVALUATE EFFECTIVE ADDRESS AND TRANSFER DATA

15	14	13	12	11	10	9	8	7	6	5	4	3	2	1	0
CA	PC	dr	1	0	Valid EA			Length							

TAKE PRE-INSTRUCTION EXCEPTION

15	14	13	12	11	10	9	8	7	6	5	4	3	2	1	0
0	PC	0	1	1	1	0	0	Vector Number							

TAKE MID-INSTRUCTION EXCEPTION

15	14	13	12	11	10	9	8	7	6	5	4	3	2	1	0
0	PC	0	1	1	1	0	1	Vector Number							

C

TAKE POST-INSTRUCTION EXCEPTION

15	14	13	12	11	10	9	8	7	6	5	4	3	2	1	0
0	PC	0	1	1	1	1	0				Vector Number				

WRITE TO PREVIOUSLY EVALUATED EFFECTIVE ADDRESS

15	14	13	12	11	10	9	8	7	6	5	4	3	2	1	0
CA	PC	1	0	0	0	0	0				Length				

APPENDIX D
ADVANCED TOPICS

This appendix provides information on the following advanced topics:
Module Support
Access Levels
Extension Words
CAS/CAS2 for Systems Programmers

D.1 MODULE SUPPORT

The MC68020 includes support for modules with the call module (CALLM) and return from module (RTM) instructions. The CALLM instruction references a module descriptor. This descriptor contains control information for entry into the called module. The CALLM instruction creates a module stack frame and stores the current module state in that frame and loads a new module state from the referenced descriptor. The RTM instruction recovers the previous module state from the stack frame and returns to the calling module.

The module interface facilitates finer resolution of access control by external hardware. Although the MC68020 does not interpret the access control information, it does communicate with external hardware when the access control is to be changed, and relies on the external hardware to verify that the changes are legal.

D.1.1 Module Descriptor

Figure D-1 illustrates the format of the module descriptor. The first long word contains control information used during the execution of the CALLM instruction. The remaining locations contain data which may be loaded into processor registers by the CALLM instruction.

The Opt field specifies how arguments are to be passed to the called module; the MC68020 recognizes only the options of 000 and 100, all others cause a format exception. The 000 option indicates that the called module expects to find arguments from the calling module on the stack just below the module stack frame. In cases where there is a change of stack pointer during the call, the MC68020 will copy the arguments from the old stack to the new stack. The 100 option indicates that the called module will access the arguments from the calling module through an indirect pointer in the stack of the calling module. Hence, the arguments are not copied, but the MC68020 puts the value of the stack pointer from the calling module in the module stack frame.

D

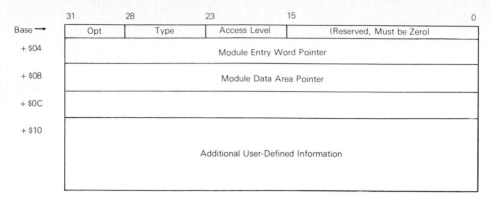

Figure D-1. Module Descriptor Format

The Type field specifies the type of the descriptor; the MC68020 only recognizes descriptors of type $00 and $01, all others cause a format exception. The $00 type descriptor defines a module for which there is no change in access rights, and the called module builds its stack frame on top of the stack used by the calling module. The $01 type descriptor defines a module for which there may be a change in access rights, such a called module may have a separate stack area from that of the calling module.

The access level field is used only with the type $01 descriptor, and is passed to external hardware to change the access control.

The module entry word pointer specifies the entry address of the called module. The first word at the entry address (see Figure D-2) specifies the register to be saved in the module stack frame and then loaded with the module descriptor data area pointer; the first instruction of the module starts with the next word. The module descriptor data area pointer field contains the address of the called module data area.

If the access change requires a change of stack pointer, the old value is saved in the module stack frame, and the new value is taken from the module descriptor stack pointer field. Any further information in the module descriptor is user defined.

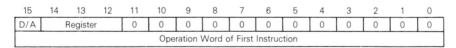

Figure D-2. Module Entry Word

All module descriptor types $10-$1F are reserved for user definition and cause a format error exception. This provides the user with a means of disabling any module by setting a single bit in its descriptor, without loss of any descriptor information.

If the called module does not wish the module data area pointer to be loaded into a register, the module entry word can select register A7, and the loaded value will be overwritten with the correct stack pointer value after the module stack frame is created and filled.

D

D.1.2 Module Stack Frame

Figure D-3 illustrates the format of the module stack frame. This frame is constructed by the CALLM instruction, and is removed by the RTM instruction. The first and second long words contain control information passed by the CALLM instruction to the RTM instruction. The module descriptor pointer contains the address of the descriptor used during the module call. All other locations contain information to be restored on return to the calling module.

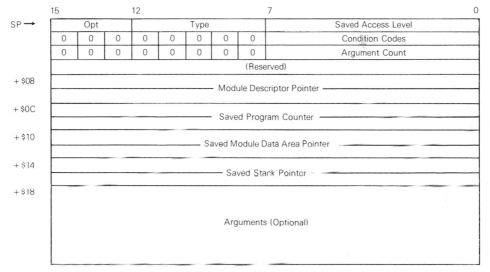

Figure D-3. Module Call Stack Frame

The program counter is the saved address of the instruction following the CALLM instruction. The Opt and Type fields specify the argument options and type of module stack frame, and are copied to the frame from the module descriptor by the CALLM instruction; the RTM instruction will cause a format error if the Opt and Type fields do not have recognizable values. The access level is the saved access control information, which is saved from external hardware by the CALLM instruction and restored by the RTM instruction. The argument count field is set by the CALLM instruction, and is used by the RTM instruction to remove arguments from the stack of the calling module. The contents of the CCR are saved by the CALLM instruction and restored by the RTM instruction. The saved stack pointer field contains the value of the stack pointer when the CALLM instruction started execution, and that value is restored by RTM. The saved module data pointer field contains the saved value of the module data area pointer register from the calling module.

D.2 ACCESS LEVELS

The MC68020 module mechanism supports a finer level of access control beyond the distinction between user and supervisor modes. The module mechanism allows a module with limited access rights to call a module with greater access rights. With the help of external hardware, the processor can verify that an increase in access rights is allowable, or can detect attempts by a module to gain access rights to which it is not entitled.

Type $01 module descriptors and module stack frames indicate a request to change access levels. While processing a type $01 descriptor or frame, the CALLM and RTM instructions communicate with external access control hardware via accesses in the CPU space. For these accesses, address bits [19:16] equal 0001. Figure D-4 shows the address map for these CPU space accesses. If the processor receives a bus error on any of these CPU space accesses during the execution of a CALLM or RTM instruction, the processor will take a format error exception.

	31	23	0
$00	CAL	(Unused, Reserved)	
$04	STATUS	(Unused, Reserved)	
$08	IAL	(Unused, Reserved)	
$0C	DAL	(Unused, Reserved)	

$40	Function Code 0 Descriptor Address
$44	Function Code 1 Descriptor Address (User Data)
$48	Function Code 2 Descriptor Address (User Program)
$4C	Function Code 3 Descriptor Address
$50	Function Code 4 Descriptor Address (Supervisor Data)
$54	Function Code 5 Descriptor Address (Supervisor Program)
$58	Function Code 6 Descriptor Address
$5C	Function Code 7 Descriptor Address (CPU Space)

Figure D-4. Access Level Control Bus Registers

The current access level register (CAL) contains the access level rights of the currently executing module. The increase access level register (IAL) is the register through which the processor requests increased access rights. The decrease access level register (DAL) is the register through which the processor requests decreased access rights. The formats of these three registers are undefined to the main processor, but the main processor assumes that information read from the module descriptor stack frame, or the current access level register can be meaningfully written to the increase access level register or the decrease access level register. The access status register allows the processor to query the external hardware as to the legality of intended access level transitions. Table D-1 lists the valid values of the access status register.

Table D-1. Access Status Register Codes

Value	Validity	Processor Action
00	Invalid	Format Error
01	Valid	No Change in Access Rights
02-03	Valid	Change Access Rights with no Change of Stack Pointer
04-07	Valid	Change Access Rights and Change Stack Pointer
Other	Undefined	Undefined (Take Format Error Exception)

The processor uses the descriptor address registers during the CALLM instruction to communicate the address of the type $01 descriptor. This allows external hardware to verify that the address is a valid address for a type $01 descriptor. This prevents a module from creating a type $01 descriptor to surreptitiously increase its access rights.

D

D.2.1 Module Call

The CALLM instruction is used to make the module call. For the type $00 module descriptor, the processor simply creates and fills the module stack frame at the top of the active system stack. The condition codes of the calling module are saved in the CCR field of the frame. If Opt is equal to 000 (arguments passed on the stack) in the module descriptor, the MC68020 does not save the stack pointer or load a new stack pointer value. The processor uses the module entry word to save and load the module data area pointer register, and then begins execution of the called module.

For the type $01 module descriptor the processor must first obtain the current access level from external hardware. It also verifies that the calling module has the right to read from the area pointed to by the current value of the stack pointer by reading from that address. It then passes the descriptor address and increase access level to external hardware for validation, and then reads the access status. If external hardware determines that the change in access rights should not be granted, the access status is zero, and the processor takes a format error exception. No visible processor registers are changed, nor should the current access level enforced by external hardware be changed. If external hardware determines that a change should be granted, the external hardware changes its access level, and the processor proceeds. If the access status register indicates that a change in the stack pointer is required, the stack pointer is saved internally, a new value is loaded from the module descriptor, and arguments are copied from the calling stack to the new stack. Finally, the module stack frame is created and filled on the top of the current stack. The condition codes of the calling module are saved in the CCR field of the frame. Execution of the called module then begins as with a type $00 descriptor.

D.2.2 Module Return

The RTM instruction is used to return from a module. For the type $00 module stack frame, the processor reloads the condition codes, the program counter, and the module data area pointer register from the frame. The frame is removed from the top of the stack, the argument count is added to the stack pointer, and execution returns to the calling module.

For the type $01 module stack frame, the processor reads the access level, condition codes, program counter, saved module data area pointer, and saved stack pointer from the module stack frame. The access level is written to the decrease access level register for validation by external hardware, the processor then reads the access status to check the validation. If the external hardware determines that the change in access rights should not be granted, the access status is zero, and the processor takes a format error exception. No visible processor registers are changed, nor should the current access level which is enforced by external hardware be changed. If the external hardware determines that the change in access rights should be granted, the external hardware changes its access level, the values read from the module stack frame are loaded into the corresponding processor registers, the argument count is added to the new stack pointer value, and execution returns to the calling module.

If the called module does not wish the saved module data pointer to be loaded into a register, the RTM instruction word can select register A7, and the loaded value will be overwritten with the correct stack pointer value after the module stack frame is deallocated.

D

D.3 EXTENSION WORDS

If it is desired to write programs that can be transported from one member of the M68000 processor Family to another, certain restrictions may have to be observed. First of all, each new member of the Family is always upward object code compatible with earlier members, with some extensions to the architecture. Thus, transporting applications code from an early machine to a new one is straightforward, since no changes are necessary. Secondly, all processors fully decode all 65,536 possible operation words and initiate exception processing if an opcode is encountered that is not implemented by a given processor. Thus, if code written for a new member of the Family is executed on an earlier machine, new instructions for the new processor will be 'trapped out' by the earlier processor and can be emulated with run-time support software on the older system. However, only the first word for an instruction is checked for legality; any extension words indicated necessary by the first word are assumed to be valid and are not checked.

The extension words are of concern when using certain addressing modes of the MC68020. Specifically, the address register memory indirect with index, and program counter relative indirect with index addressing modes are extensions of the corresponding addressing modes of the MC68000, MC68008, MC68010, and MC68012. The extension words of these effective addressing modes are shown in Figure D-5. As can be seen from this figure, the MC68020 address register indirect with index, with a scaling multiplier of one (Scale = 00) encoding, is equivalent to the MC68000, et. al., encoding so that upward compatibility is maintained. However, if any other encoding for the MC68020 is used, downward compatibility of the instruction is lost and special precautions must be taken since these extension words are not checked for validity on the older processors. The following two examples illustrate why these precautions must be observed to insure downward compatibility.

Example 1. MC68020 Address Register Indirect with Index
versus M68000 Address Register Indirect with Index

	MC68000 Program	MC68020 Program
Assembly Language Source Code	MOVE.L OFFSET(A0,D0.L),D1	MOVE.L (OFFSET,A0,D0.L*4),D1
Object Code	2230 08XX	2230 0CXX

As can be seen from the object code, only one bit (bit 10 of the extension word) is different in the two instructions, yet the source effective address values are quite different. If the MC68020 code were executed on an MC68000, the processor would interpret the code as though it were the MC68000 code and the wrong data would be fetched, but no exception would occur.

Example 2. MC68020 Address Register Indirect with Index/Indirect
versus MC68000 Address Register Indirect with Index

	MC68000 Program	MC68020 Program
Assembly Language Source Code	MOVE.L OFFSET(A0,D0.L),D1	MOVE.L ([OFFSET,A0,D0.L*4]),D1
Object Code	3230 08XX	3230 0D21 XXXX

D

A comparison of the object code in this example shows a more volatile situation that will occur if the MC68020 code is executed on an MC68000. In this case, the MC68000 will ignore bits 8-10 of the first extension word and interpret the instruction as "MOVE.L $21(A0,D0.L),D1", and then erroneously use the second extension word as the first word of the next instruction. Thus, the processor will get 'out of sync' with the intended instruction stream and unpredictable results will occur. Eventually, the processor may encounter an illegal instruction and trap to the operating system, but incorrect execution may have occurred, with no indication that the MC68020 extended addressing mode was at fault.

If it is desired to protect against the above situations, the user might precede any program that utilizes the advanced features of the MC68020 with the "TRAPF" instruction. This instruction performs no operation on the MC68020, but will cause an illegal instruction exception on the MC68000, MC68008, MC68010, or MC68012; thus preventing the program from executing on the older processors.

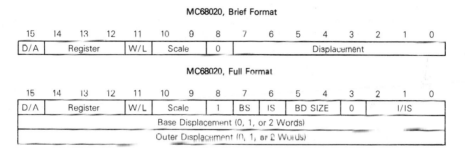

Figure D-5. Indexed/Indirect Addressing Mode Extension Words

The fields used in Figure D-5 are as follows:

Mode	Addressing Mode	Mode	Addressing Mode
Register	Index Register Number	IS	Index Suppress:
D/A	Index Register Type.		0 – Evaluate and Add Index Operand
	0 – Dn		1 – Suppress Index Operand
	1 – An	BD SIZE	Base Displacement Size:
W/L	Word/Long Word Index Size:		00 = Reserved
	0 – Sign Extended Word		01 = Null Displacement
	1 – Long Word		10 = Word Displacement
Scale	Scale Factor:		11 = Long Displacement
	00 = 1	I/IS	Index/Indirect Selection:
	01 = 2		Indirect and Indexing Operand Determined in
	10 = 4		Conjunction with Bit 6, Index Suppress
	11 = 8		
BS	Base Suppress:		
	0 = Base Register Added		
	1 = Base Register Suppressed		

D

IS	Index/Indirect	Operation
0	000	No Memory Indication
0	001	Indirect After Indexing with Null Displacement
0	010	Indirect After Indexing with Word Displacement
0	011	Indirect After Indexing with Long Displacement
0	100	Reserved
0	101	Indirect Before Indexing with Null Displacement
0	110	Indirect Before Indexing with Word Displacement
0	111	Indirect Before Indexing with Long Displacement
1	000	No Memory Indication
1	001	Memory Indirect with Null Displacement
1	010	Memory Indirect with Word Displacement
1	011	Memory Indirect with Long Displacement
1	100-111	Reserved

D.4 CAS/CAS2 FOR SYSTEMS PROGRAMMERS

The CAS instruction allows secure updating of system counters, history information, and globally shared pointers. Security is provided in single processor systems, multitasking environments, and in multiprocessor environments. In a single processor system, the non-interruptable update operation provides security in an interrupt driven environment; while in a multiprocessor environment, the indivisible bus cycle operation provides the security mechanism. For example, suppose location SYS__CNTR contains a count of the number of times a particular operation has been done, and that this operation may be done by any process or any processor in the system. Then the following sequence guarantees that SYS__CNTR is correctly incremented.

```
            MOVE.W    SYS__CNTR,D0        get the old value of the counter
INC__LOOP   MOVE.W    D0,D1               make a copy of it
            ADDQ.W    #1,D1               and increment it
            CAS.W     D0,D1,SYS__CNTR     if counter value is still the same,
                                             update it
            BNE       INC__LOOP           if not, try again
```

The CAS and CAS2 instructions together allow safe operations in manipulation of system queues. If a queue can be managed last-in-first-out, only a single location HEAD need be controlled. If the queue is empty, HEAD contains the NULL pointer (0). The following sequence illustrates the code for insertion and deletion from such a queue. Figures D-6 and D-7 illustrate the insertion and deletion, respectively.

D

```
SINSERT                                          allocate new entry, addr in A1
              MOVE.L     HEAD,D0                 move head pointer value to D0
SILOOP        MOVE.L     D0,(NEXT,A1)            establish fwd link in new entry
              MOVE.L     A1,D1                   move new entry ptr value to D1
              CAS.L      D0,D1,HEAD              if we still point to top of stack,
                                                     update the head ptr
              BNE        SILOOP                  if not, try again
```

Before Inserting an Element:

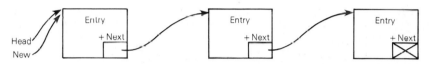

After Inserting an Element:

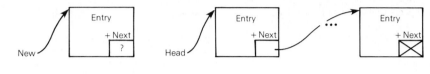

Figure D-6. Linked List Insertion

```
SDELETE
              LEA        HEAD,A0                 load addr of head ptr into A0
              MOVE.L     (A0),D0                 move value of head ptr into D0
SDLOOP        TST.L      D0                      check for null head ptr
              BEQ        SDEMPTY                 if empty, nothing to delete
              LEA        (NEXT,D0),A1            load addr of fwd link into A1
              MOVE.L     (A1),D1                 put fwd link value in D1
              CAS2.L     D0:D1,D1:D1,(A0):(A1)   if still point to entry to be deleted,
                                                     then update head and fwd ptrs
              BNE        SDLOOP                  if not, try again
SDEMPTY                                          successful deletion, addr of deleted
                                                     entry in D0 (may be null)
```

Before Deleting an Element:

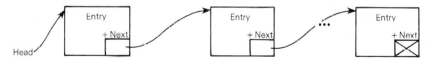

After Deleting an Element:

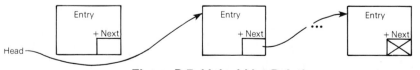

Figure D-7. Linked List Deletion

The CAS2 instruction may be used to maintain a first-in-first-out doubly linked list safely. Such a linked list needs two controlled locations, LIST__PUT and LIST__GET, which point to the last element inserted in the list and the next to be removed, respectively. If the list is empty, both pointers are NULL (0). The following sequence illustrates the insertion and deletion operations in such a linked list. Figures D-8 and D-9 illustrate the insertion and deletion from a doubly linked list.

```
DINSERT                                      (allocate new list entry, load addr
                                                into A2)
            LEA       LIST__PUT,A0           load addr of head ptr into A0
            LEA       LIST__GET,A1           load addr of tail ptr into A1
            MOVE.L    A2,D2                  load new entry ptr into D2
            MOVE.L    (A0),D0               load ptr to head entry into D0
DILOOP      TST.L     D0                     is head ptr null (0 entries in list)?
            BEQ       DIEMPTY                if so, we need only to establish ptrs
            MOVE.L    D0,(NEXT,A2)           put head ptr into fwd ptr of new entry
            CLR.L     D1                     put null ptr value in D1
            MOVE.L    D1,(LAST,A2)           put null ptr in bkwd ptr of new entry
            LEA       (LAST,D0),A1           load bkwd ptr of old head entry into A1
            CAS2.L    D0:D1,D2:D0,(A0):(A1)  if we still point to old head entry,
                                                update pointers
            BNE       DILOOP                 if not, try again
            BRA       DIDONE
DIEMPTY     MOVE.L    D0,(NEXT,A2)           put null ptr in fwd ptr of new entry
            MOVE.L    D0,(LAST,A2)           put null ptr in bkwd ptr of new entry
            CAS2.L    D0:D0,D2:D2,(A0):(A1)  if we still have no entries, set both
                                                pointers to this entry
            BNE       DILOOP                 if not, try again
DIDONE                                       successful list entry insertion
```

Before Inserting New Entry:

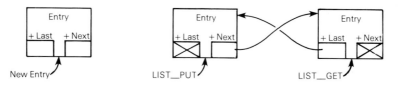

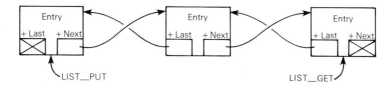

Figure D-8. Doubly Linked List Insertion

```
DDELETE
          LEA       LIST__PUT,A0              get addr of head ptr in A0
          LEA       LIST__GET,A1             get addr of tail ptr in A1
DDLOOP    MOVE.L    (A1),D1                  move tail ptr into D1
          BEQ       DDDONE                   if no list, quit
          MOVE.L    (LAST,D1),D2             put bkwd ptr in D2
          BEQ       DDEMPTY                  if only one element, update ptrs
          LEA       (NEXT,D2),A2             put addr of fwd ptr in A2
          CLR.L     D0                       put null ptr value in D0
          CAS2.L    D1:D1,D2:D0,(A1):(A2)    if both ptrs still point to this entry,
                                                update them
          BNE       DDLOOP                   if not, try again
          BRA       DDDONE
DDEMPTY   CAS2.L    D1:D1,D2:D2:(A1):(A0)    if still first entry, set head and tial
                                                ptrs to null
          BNE       DDLOOP                   if not, try again
DDDONE                                       successful entry deletion, addr of
                                                deleted entry in D1 (may be null)
```

Before Deleting Entry:

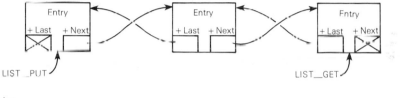

After Deleting Entry:

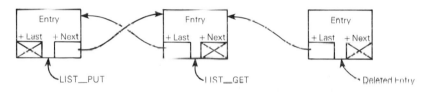

Figure D-9. Doubly Linked List Deletion

D.5 A PROGRAMMER'S VIEW OF THE MC68020 ADDRESSING MODES

Extensions to the indexed addressing modes, including indirection along with the support of full 32-bit displacements, provide the MC68020 programmer with addressing capability new to the M68000 Family.

The purpose of the following paragraphs is to indicate the new techniques available and to summarize them from a programmer's point of view. These techniques will be called "generic" addressing modes since they may or may not relate directly to a unique effective address mode as defined by the MC68020 architecture.

D.5.1 New Addressing Capabilities

The suppression of the base address register in the MC68020 indexed addressing mode allows the use of any index register to be used in place of the base register. Since any of

D

the data registers can be index registers, the new forms (Dn) and (disp,Dn) are obtained. These could be called Data Register Indirect but its probably better to think in terms of (Rn) and (disp,Rn) as just Register Indirect where any data or address register is allowed. Remember that whenever an index register appears (Xn), its size may be specified to be a sign-extended word or a long word.

Since displacements may be a full 32 bits, they may represent absolute addresses or the result of expressions which contain absolute addresses. This allows the general Register Indirect form above to become (addr,Rn), and with the base not suppressed we get (addr,An,Rn). Thus, an absolute address may be directly indexed by one or two registers.

Scaling provides for an optional shifting of an index register to the left by zero, one, two, or three bits before being used in the effective address calculation. This is equivalent to multiplying the register by one, two, four, or eight, which allows direct subscripting into an array of components of that size by an arithmetic value residing in any of the 16 indexable registers. Scaling, combined with the appropriate new modes derived above, allows new modes. Arrayed structures may be addressed absolutely and then subscripted, i.e., (addr,Rn*scale). Optionally, an address register may contain a dynamic displacement value since it may be included in the address calculation (addr,An,Rn*scale). Other variations can be generated by assuming an address register points directly to the arrayed item with (An,Rn*scale) or that an address register with displacement (i.e., a base address) points to the arrayed item (disp,An,Rn*scale).

Yet another feature of the indexing mode on the MC68020 is memory indirection. This allows a long word pointer in memory to be fetched and used to point to the data operand. Any of the modes mentioned earlier can be used to address the memory pointer. In addition, when both registers are suppressed, the displacement acts as an absolute address. Hence, absolute addressing can be used to access the memory pointer as well.

Once the memory pointer is fetched it can optionally have yet another constant displacement added to it before it is used to access the final data operand. This second displacement is called the Outer Displacement. Thus the memory pointer may itself be treated as a base address.

When memory indirection is being used, the index register may be utilized in one of three ways. It may be suppressed, used to access the memory pointer (before the indirection, or preindirect), or used to access the final data operand (after the indirection, or postindirect). This last case causes the index register to be added to the fetched pointer from memory (and optionally the Outer Displacement if present). Since index registers on the MC68020 can be scaled, subscripting also may be employed on the data operand that the fetched memory pointer accesses. However, when the index register is used to access the final data operand it is not available to address the memory pointer. That is, indexing is not allowed both before and after indirection; rather it is only allowed before **or** after indirection.

D.5.2 A General Addressing Mode Summary

Some of the generic addressing modes mentioned in the previous paragraphs do not actually exist as distinct basic MC68020 effective address modes since they either rely on a specific combination of options in the indexing mode, or may be derived from two different native MC68020 modes. For example, the generic mode called Register Indirect (Rn) would assemble to the basic mode Address Register Indirect if the register was an address register, or to the Register Indirect with Index with address register suppression if Rn was a data register. Another case is (disp,An) which depends on the size of the displacement. If the displacement fits within 16 bits, then the native Address Register Indirect with Displacement (d_{16},An) will be used, otherwise the Address Register Indirect with Index will be used since only it can support a larger displacement.

On the other hand, two or more of the modes mentioned may assemble into the very same native effective address option. For instance, an absolute address with a register index (addr,Rn) and a base address with a large displacement (disp,Rn) are both two ways of looking at the same thing — a register with a 32-bit displacement. They both assemble into the very same object code.

An assembler makes the necessary distinctions and chooses which basic addressing mode to use; always picking the more efficient one if more than one is applicable. Normally, the programmer need not be concerned about these decisions, so it is useful to summarize the addressing modes available to a programmer without regard to the native MC68020 effective addressing mode actually implemented on chip.

The 'generic' addressing modes discussed below are defined in normal programming terms which should not be directly related to any specific basic modes as provided by the MC68020 architecture, even though some will have obvious counterparts. First, some terms commonly used by programmers are defined here as to their exact meaning.

pointer — Long word value in a register or in memory which represents an address.

base — A pointer combined with a displacement to represent an address.

index — A constant or variable value which the programmer uses to add a bias into an effective address calculation. As a constant, the index ends up treated as a displacement. A variable index is always represented by a register containing the value.

disp — Displacement, a constant index.

subscript — The use of any of the data or address registers as a variable index subscript into arrays of items 1, 2, 4, or 8 bytes in size.

relative — An address based with the Program Counter. This makes the reference code position independent and the operand accessed is in Program Space. All others but psaddr (below) fall into Data Space.

addr — An absolute address.

psaddr — An absolute address in Program Space. All others but relative fall into Data Space.

D

Secondly, the generic modes are summarized as follows:

Immediate Data	— #data	The data is a constant in the instruction stream.
Register Direct	— Rn	The contents of a register is specified.
Scanning Modes	— (An)+	Address register pointer automatically incremented after use.
	− (An)	Address register pointer automatically decremented before use.
Absolute Address	— (addr)	Absolute address in data space.
	(psaddr,ZPC)	Absolute address in program space.
Register Pointer	— (Rn)	Register as a pointer.
	(disp,Rn)	Register as a pointer and constant index (or base address.)
Indexing	— (An,Rn)	Register pointer with variable index.
	(disp,An,Rn)	Register pointer with constant and variable index (or a base address with a variable index).
	(addr,Rn)	Absolute address with variable index.
	(addr,An,Rn)	Absolute address with 2 variable indexes.
Subscripting	— (An,Rn*scale)	Address register pointer subscript.
	(disp,An,Rn*scale)	Address register pointer subscript with constant displacement (or base address with subscript).
	(addr,Rn*scale)	Absolute address with subscript.
	(addr,An,Rn*scale)	Absolute address subscript with variable index.
Program Relative	— (disp,PC)	Simple relative.
	(disp,PC,Rn)	Relative with variable index.
	(disp,PC,Rn*scale)	Relative with subscript.

D

Memory Pointer	—	([*modes])	Memory pointer directly to data operand.
		([*mode],disp)	Memory pointer as base with displacement to data operand.
		([**modes],Rn)	Memory pointer with variable index.
		([**modes],disp,Rn)	Memory pointer with constant and variable index.
		([**modes],Rn*scale)	Memory pointer subscripted.
		([**modes],disp,Rn*scale)	Memory pointer subscripted with constant index.

*–allowed modes are any of the above from absolute address through program relative.
**–allowed modes are as follows:

addr	Absolute address in data space.
psaddr,ZPC	Absolute address in program space.
An	Register pointer.
disp,An	Register pointer with constant displacement (or base address).
addr,An	Absolute address with single variable index.
disp,PC	Simple program relative.

D

APPENDIX E
MC68020 EXTENSIONS TO M68000 FAMILY

This Appendix summarizes the extensions to the M68000 Family implemented by the MC68020 microprocessor.

NOTE

In the following description, the notation "MC68000" includes the MC68000 and the MC68008 together, and "MC68010" includes the MC68010 and MC68012 together, except where specifically mentioned.

Elaboration on MC68000 and MC68010 differences may be found in the **M68000 Programmer's Reference Manual**.

Data Bus Size (Bits)
    MC68020 . . . . .8, 16, 32
    MC68000/MC68010 16
    MC68008 8

Address Bus Size (Bits)
    MC68020 32
    MC68012 . . . . .30 (plus A31)
    MC68000/MC68010 24
    MC68008 20

Instruction Cache
    MC68020 . . . . .128 Words
    MC68010 . . . . .Provides Loop Mode (3 Words)

Virtual Memory/Machine
    MC68020/MC68010 . . . . .Provides Bus Error Detection, RTE Recovery

Coprocessor Interface
    MC68020 . . . . .In Microcode
    MC68000/MC68010 . . . . .Emulated in Software

Processor Signals and Pin Assignments
    Detailed in each specific data sheet.

Instruction Execution Time
    Detailed in each specific data sheet.

E

Word/Long Word Data Alignment
MC68020 . . . . Only Instructions Must be Word Aligned
MC68000/MC68010 . . . . Word/Long Word Data, Instructions, and Stack
Must be Word Aligned

Control Registers
MC68020 . . . . SFC, DFC, VBR, CACR, CAAR
MC68010 . . . . SFC, DFC, VBR
MC68000 . . . . None

Stack Pointers
MC68020 . . . . USP, SSP (MSP, ISP)
MC68000/MC68010 . . . . USP, SSP

Status Register
MC68020 . . . . T0/T1, S, M, I0/I1/I2, X/N/Z/V/C
MC68000/MC68010 . . . . T, S, I0/I1/I2, X/N/Z/V/C

Function Code/Address Space
MC68020/MC68010 . . . . FC0-FC2 = 7 is CPU Space
MC68000 . . . . FC0-FC2 = 7 is Interrupt Acknowledge, Only

Indivisible Bus Cycles
MC68020 . . . . Use $\overline{\text{RMC}}$ Signal
MC68000/MC68010 . . . . Use $\overline{\text{AS}}$ Signal (MC68012 Also Uses $\overline{\text{RMC}}$)

Exception Vectors
Detailed in each specific data sheet.

Stack Frames
MC68020 . . . . Supports Formats $0, $1, $2, $9, $A, $B
MC68010 . . . . Supports Formats $0, $8
MC68000 . . . . Supports Original Set

Addressing Modes
MC68020 extensions: memory indirect addressing modes, scaled index, and larger
displacements. Details are found in each specific data sheet.

MC68020 Instruction Set Extensions
Bcc . . . . Supports 32-Bit Displacements
BFxxxx . . . . Bit Field Instructions (BFCHG, BFCLR,
BFEXTS, BFEXTU, BFEXTS, BFFFO, BFINS,
BFSET, BFTST)
BKPT . . . . New Instruction Functionality
BRA . . . . Supports 32-Bit Displacements
BSR . . . . Supports 32-Bit Displacements
CALLM . . . . New Instruction
CAS, CAS2 . . . . New Instruction
CHK . . . . Supports 32-Bit Operands
CHK2 . . . . New Instruction

E

CMPI .... Supports Program Counter Relative Addressing
                        Modes
CMP2 .... New Instruction
cp .... Coprocessor Instructions
DIVS/DIVU .... Supports 32-Bit and 64-Bit Operands
EXTB .... Supports 8-Bit Extend to 32 Bits
LINK .... Supports 32-Bit Displacement
MOVEC .... Supports New Control Registers
MULS/MULU .... Supports 32-Bit Operands
PACK .... New Instruction
RTM .... New Instruction
TST .... Supports Program Counter Relative Addressing
                        Modes
TRAPcc .... New Instruction
UNPK .... New Instruction

A17717—1 4/85

E

NOTES

NOTES